How China Became Capitalist

D1453969

How China Became Capitalist

Ronald Coase

and

Ning Wang

First published 2013 by
PALGRAVE MACMILLAN

Palgrave Macmillan in the UK is an imprint of Macmillan Publishers Limited, registered in England, company number 785998, of Houndmills, Basingstoke, Hampshire RG21 6XS.

Palgrave Macmillan in the US is a division of St Martin's Press LLC, 175 Fifth Avenue, New York, NY 10010.

Palgrave Macmillan is the global academic imprint of the above companies and has companies and representatives throughout the world.

Palgrave® and Macmillan® are registered trademarks in the United States, the United Kingdom, Europe and other countries.

ISBN 978–1–137–01936–3 hardback
ISBN 978–1–137–35143–2 paperback

This book is printed on paper suitable for recycling and made from fully managed and sustained forest sources. Logging, pulping and manufacturing processes are expected to conform to the environmental regulations of the country of origin.

A catalogue record for this book is available from the British Library.

A catalog record for this book is available from the Library of Congress.

Contents

Maps

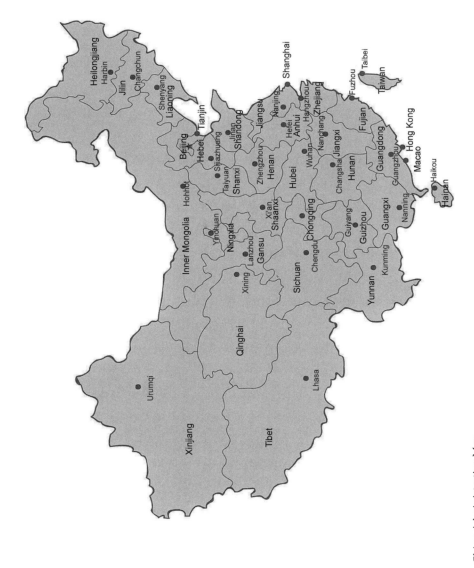

Map 1 China Administrative Map

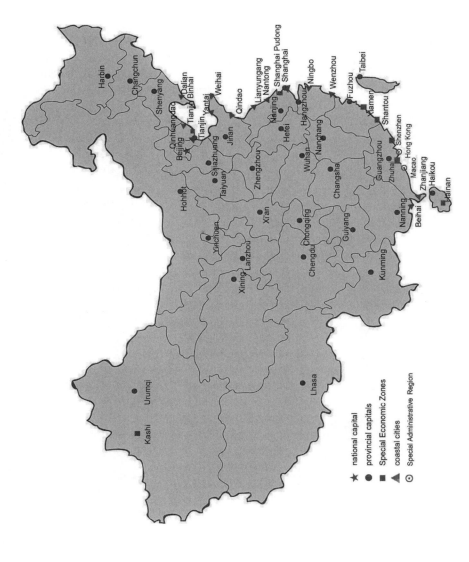

Map 2 China Administrative Map (with special economic zones)

Acknowledgments

We would first like to thank Stephen Littlechild and Philip Booth at the Institute of Economic Affairs, who have encouraged and supported this joint venture from the very beginning.

We started writing this book immediately after the 2008 Chicago Conference on China's Market Transformation, which was held on July 14th–18th. After the first draft was completed, we convened the Chicago Workshop on the Industrial Structure of Production, from July 19th to 23rd, 2010. We learnt a lot from many of the conference and workshop participants, particularly when we disagreed with them. We would also like to thank Marjorie Holme, Lennon Choi, and Joey Nahom for their excellent logistical support to make the conference and workshop possible.

Among those who read the first draft, Stephen Littlechild, Douglass North, Mary Shirley, and Chenggang Xu gave us detailed comments. We also received comments from Lee Benham, Philip Booth, and Steven Cheung on individual chapters. We'd like to thank them for their critiques and suggestions, which have resulted in many improvements. We also like to thank Hu Wei for his assistance on the maps.

The two authors were able to meet monthly over the past several years to work on this book and other related projects. We have to thank our home institutions, the University of Chicago Law School (for Ronald Coase) and the School of Global Studies and later, the School of Politics & Global Studies at Arizona State University (for Ning Wang). Former Dean Saul Levmore and current Dean Michael Schill of the University of Chicago Law School have been generous in supporting our joint work.

We also want to thank many individuals who have generously shared with us their information and views. We cannot list all their names here. But the following deserve a special mention: Alexandra and Lee Benham, Linda and Steven Cheung, Jin Lei, Liang Xiaowei, David Pickus, Richard Sandor, Guangzhen Sun, Xiao Geng, William Xiao, Xiong Jialong, Xu Liangying, Wang Tianfu, Zhang Weiying, Dingxin Zhao, Zhou Qiren, Zhou Weibing, and Zhu Xiqing.

Preface

In a paper delivered at the Chicago Conference on China's Economic Transformation held in July 2008, Steven Cheung called China's economic transition from a communist system to capitalism "the greatest program for economic reform in history."[1] Cheung's conclusion is doubtless correct, but what is equally extraordinary is that the series of events that led China to become capitalist was not programmed and that the final result was entirely unexpected. Perhaps an even more extraordinary aspect of this whole tale is that this move to capitalism was carried out under the auspices of the Chinese Communist Party. It is a striking example of what Hayek has called "the unintended consequences of human action."[2]

In 1982 the Institute of Economic Affairs in London published Cheung's pamphlet "Will China Go Capitalist?," a question he answered in the affirmative.[3] Cheung's conclusion was viewed by almost everyone with outright disbelief. Even he himself was cautious in stating his view: "The transition will not be rapid."[4] It is reasonable that he should have thought so. Communist indoctrination over the years would have given people in China an extremely unfavorable view of the workings of a capitalist system. Furthermore, as Cheung points out, a change to a capitalist system would seem likely to encounter the opposition of the army and government officials who would fear that their position would be threatened by such a change. Four years later, in 1986, when the second edition of "Will China Go Capitalist?" was published, Cheung, while acknowledging that he had "underestimated the speed of change,"[5] concluded that "economic reform in China can progress only at a considerably slower pace than in the past five years."[6] In fact, the change continued to be rapid. The effect of communist indoctrination on the views of ordinary Chinese proved to be less important and the opposition of the army and government officials weaker than Cheung had thought. China did become capitalist in a relatively short time.[7] In this book we describe the series of events that brought about this result.

Our ignorance of such an involved subject does not allow us to investigate all aspects of this astounding human drama. There is still much we do not know about China's market transformation. Moreover, many of the reported facts on the subject are actually not true. As new facts emerge, what we say will no doubt have to be modified in detail. But the broad picture sketched here is clear and is not likely to be changed.

In this joint venture, Ning Wang provided information about events in China and their interpretation. The two authors then collaborated fully in discussing their significance and relevance, correcting errors and realigning arguments. The final product is the result of close cooperation.

Our arguments are based on information we have gleaned from interviews and a vast number of Chinese and English sources, which can be found in the Notes and References at the end of the book. Our interpretation of the information may differ from how it is treated in the existing literature, as it clearly differs from the existing literature on a number of important issues. In order to keep our narrative clear, we rarely engaged the existing literature directly, which is immense and keeps growing. What follows is our account of how China became capitalist.

1
China at the Death of Mao

When Mao Zedong, founder of the People's Republic of China and Chairman of the Chinese Communist Party since 1943, died on September 9th, 1976, China was in the midst of the Cultural Revolution, which Mao had initiated a decade earlier.[1] This was meant to be the first of a series of revolutions to rejuvenate socialism, ridding it of capitalist corruption and bureaucratic rigidity.[2] The Cultural Revolution had been preceded by a series of social and political campaigns relentlessly prosecuted by Mao to push China toward the promised paradise of socialism. Mao believed that China could shrug off poverty and jump on to the "golden highway" to socialism if, and only if, the Chinese people, united in thought and action, threw all their talents and energy behind the collective cause.[3] Unselfish and property-less, the Chinese people would be reborn. Having shed the burden of history and Chinese feudalism on the one hand, and without the distraction of material interests and western capitalism on the other, the Chinese people would respond to nothing but the call of socialism. However, instead of paradise, Mao's deeply flawed ideology and ill-thought-out revolutions not only brought to the Chinese people the most lethal famine in human history, but also cut them off from their cultural roots and the progress of modern times.[4] An enterprising people were quickly reduced to lifeless cogs in the socialist machine.

It can be a hard truth to accept, but the disaster Mao inflicted on the Chinese people was matched only by his ineradicable accomplishments. "In the final reckoning," wrote *The Economist*, "Mao must be accepted as one of history's great achievers: for devising a peasant-centered revolutionary strategy which enabled China's Communist Party to seize power, against Marx's prescriptions, from bases in the countryside; for directing the transformation of China from a feudal society, wracked by war and bled by corruption, into a unified, egalitarian state where nobody starves; and for reviving national pride and confidence so that China could, in Mao's words, 'stand up' among

1

the great powers."[5] While *The Economist* was seriously mistaken about the absence of starvation in Mao's China, few could deny the inspiration and influence of Mao's revolution on both China and the rest of the world. Richard Nixon, who reopened diplomatic relations between China and the United States in 1972, called Mao "a unique man in a generation of great revolutionary leaders."[6] Pakistani Premier Zulfikar Ali Bhutto, the last foreign statesman to see him before his death, called Mao "the son of revolution, its very essence, indeed, its rhythm and romance, the supreme architect of a brilliant new order shaking the world," adding, "Men like Mao come once in a century."[7]

With this conflicting legacy, China started its post-Mao journey, with no roadmap in hand and no destination in mind. It was beyond anyone's wildest imaginings that, within three decades, the People's Republic of China would celebrate its sixtieth anniversary as a dazzling market economy. We cannot possibly understand this incredible transformation or the path that China had traveled to get there without a clear notion of where it started – China under Mao.

China's post-Mao transition to a market economy is particularly intriguing given that the post-Mao reform was by no means the first time China had tried to restructure its socialist economy. In 1958, Mao himself had instigated a bold campaign to decentralize the Chinese economic and political system.[8] But Mao's eager attempt to steer China away from Stalinism ended in the disaster of the Great Leap Forward (1958–1961). After a brief interim of retreat and recovery in the early 1960s, Mao launched the Cultural Revolution (1966–1976), during which he again attempted to decentralize the Chinese economy and political structure.[9] Both attempts failed miserably.

As far as the Chinese government was concerned, the post-Mao reform was intended to be a continuation of the great cause that Mao had started. On March 28th, 1985, in a meeting with a delegation of the Japanese Liberal Democratic Party, Deng Xiaoping for the first time introduced the latest Chinese economic reform as China's "second revolution"[10] – the first being the one led by Mao, which culminated in the founding of the People's Republic. Deng, widely acclaimed as "the architect of the Chinese economic reform," would later repeat this term on many occasions, and it became part of the official terminology used to refer to the post-Mao economic reform. In calling the economic reform a "second revolution," Deng must have believed that the first revolution fell short, despite its achievement in reunifying China after more than a hundred years of turmoil and war. But if the second revolution was meant to complete the unfinished business of the first, what exactly had Mao left undone? What prevented Mao from accomplishing it? What were the defects and limitations of the first revolution that Deng wanted to overcome?

I

In Tiananmen Square on October 1st, 1949, when Mao resolutely pronounced with his characteristic Hunan accent that the people of China had stood up, the whole nation was electrified with joy and exuberance. Hu Feng, a famous literary critic and writer who had recently returned from Hong Kong, wrote a long poem of more than 4000 lines, "Time Has Begun," to celebrate this historic moment.[11] After the lengthy, violent, and humiliating fall of the Qing Dynasty in 1911, decades of internecine fighting between warlords, a hideous eight-year war of resistance against Japan, and a bloody three-year civil war, China was at last reunified as an independent nation. Having suffered nearly a century of warfare and turmoil, the Chinese people were anxious for peace and a better life.

But their pursuit of peace and prosperity would follow a treacherous path. Like many other countries that won their independence after the Second World War, when the winds of socialism blew strong, China fell prey to this doctrine. Ideologically, the Chinese Communist Party had embraced communism since its inception in 1921 when it was founded with the help of the Communist International based in Moscow.[12] But the relationship between Moscow and the Chinese Communist Party was always a mixed blessing.[13]

In the beginning, Moscow favored the Nationalist Party of China (Chinese Kuomintang), an older, bigger, and self-proclaimed revolutionary party founded by Sun Yat-sen in 1919, and urged the Chinese Communists to join the Kuomintang, which, under the leadership of Sun, opened its doors to the Communists. But after Sun died on March 12th, 1925, his successor, Chiang Kai-shek, was far less enthusiastic in accommodating the Chinese Communist Party. Less than two years earlier, Chiang had spent three months in Moscow studying the Soviet system. He had met Leon Trotsky and other Russian leaders, and had reached the conclusion that the Soviet model was not suitable for China.[14] In 1927, while consolidating his power base in Kuomintang, Chiang turned against the Communists. A year later, he established the Nationalist government in Nanjing, which forced the Chinese Communist Party underground. Moscow then instructed the Chinese Communist Party to organize urban riots, in line with the teaching of Marxism and the Bolshevik revolution. This, however, turned out to be a suicidal strategy, as Chinese cities were heavily guarded by government military forces. The Communist movement survived only in a few "soviet bases" – areas controlled by the Chinese Communist militia – scattered in remote mountainous areas difficult for the Nationalist army to reach. In October 1934, the Communist troops lost one of their biggest and longest-surviving rural bases in Jiangxi province, where they were directed by Otto Braun (known in China as Li De), a military advisor sent by the Communist International, who assumed a commanding position in the Chinese

Communist Party.[15] Compelled to flee, the surviving Communists spent the next year on a long, treacherous journey from South to North China, passing through areas heavily guarded by the Nationalist army, other areas controlled by hostile ethnic minorities and warlords, and still others hardly visited by human beings, including snow-covered mountains and wetland. After it ended in Shaanxi in October 1935, Mao was quick to dub this journey of survival the "Long March."[16] A year later, Mao was joined by two troops of Communist soldiers. They then took Yan'an, an old dilapidated town in northern Shaanxi, as the seat of their government; Yan'an would rise as a symbol of hope for many progressive-minded young Chinese students as well as western sympathizers, and remain the center of the Chinese Communist revolution until 1948.[17] It was during the Long March that Mao rose to take command of the Party in January 1935 after the Zunyi Conference, ousting Braun over his failed military leadership. Although Mao became the undisputed leader of the Chinese Communist Party, he would never be favored by Moscow. Isolated and defiant in the caves of Yan'an, Mao was mocked by Stalin as a "cave Marxist."[18]

It was the Long March that began to remake the Chinese Communist Party as a native Chinese party and forged its independence from Moscow.[19] Mao rarely challenged Moscow directly, but the Comintern could no longer dictate the operation of the Chinese Communist Party after Mao's rise to power. Mao lost more than 90 percent of his Red Army during the Long March, but the survivors were dedicated, determined, and triumphant; they would later become the stalwart soldiers of the Chinese Communist revolution.[20] Furthermore, the Communists gained a much larger space for expansion in northern China. Unlike the remote mountainous areas in the south where they had fought before the Long March, places in northern China provided a wider platform on which to compete with Chiang Kai-shek. The Communists could now reach and recruit from a much bigger population. Close to China's northern border, they were also able to build a secure line of communication and support with the Soviets. Moreover, the strong presence of local warlords in the north meant the government military force there was not as dominant as it was in the south. Most important, Japan's invasion of China put the Nanjing government on the defensive and later on the run, giving the underground Communists a rare opportunity to grow both militarily and politically. After Japan surrendered in 1945, Chiang Kai-shek quickly found his old rival much stronger than before and far better prepared for the civil war that followed. With a corrupted government bureaucracy, a dispirited army, and a poorly managed economy, Chiang was defeated in three years and had to flee to Taiwan, losing the mainland to Mao.

The relationship between the Chinese Communist Party and Moscow did not change noticeably until the founding of the People's Republic of China in 1949. After that, Stalin could no longer ignore Mao, nor advance Soviet interests by driving a wedge between the Communists and the Kuomintang. Barely two months after the founding of the People's Republic, Mao eagerly took his first ever trip abroad, to Moscow in mid-December 1949.[21] He would meet Stalin, for the first and the last time; the man who had, in the past, preferred to work with Chiang Kai-shek, and had refused to recognize Mao's leadership in the Chinese Communist Party. With the civil war approaching its end, a devastated economy, and an inhospitable international environment, Mao was anxious to acquire a political and military ally.[22] This was the primary motive for Mao's visit, but his host was less enthusiastic. Even though Stalin began their first face-to-face meeting with a conciliatory gesture, Mao had to stay for two months to persuade Moscow to make a diplomatic alliance with Beijing. Eventually Stalin relented, and the two sides signed a comprehensive Treaty of Friendship, Alliance, and Mutual Assistance on February 14th, 1950. Mao returned in triumph, probably without realizing that in exchange for this Treaty, China would tie itself to Stalinism; the painful efforts to break away from its influence would preoccupy Mao for the rest of his life.

Nonetheless, in the first three years of the People's Republic of China (1949–1952), order was quickly restored, aided by a disciplined and dedicated governmental bureaucracy, and a strong mixed economy. China was experiencing a robust economic recovery, despite a hate-filled and violent campaign of land reform, in which the new regime aggressively provoked class divisions in rural society. But the following economic reconstruction was hampered by the doctrine of communism, a result of the vanguard role played by the Chinese Communist Party in leading the Chinese revolution, out of which the People's Republic was born. With the gradual installation of socialism, the new government experienced the full strength of centralized power in mobilizing resources and brisk growth during the first Five Year Plan (1953–1957), which was modeled after the Soviet economic central planning and aided by Moscow.[23] But collectivization chained peasants to the land and workers to work units, abruptly ending a short-lived burst of free enterprise in both rural and urban China. In the following years, the fatal defects inherent in central planning – the lack of incentives and initiatives for people at the bottom of the social pyramid, and the lack of information and accountability for those at the top – were compounded by the inevitable errors in learning and operating a new and all-inclusive social system, as well as by envy and rivalry in the pursuit of power on both the domestic and international stage.

Most tragically, the Chinese leaders' blind commitment to a foreign doctrine turned it into a fossilized dogma, which they accepted without criticism as a panacea. Even a statesman as defiant and independent as Mao fell into this trap, embracing communism as the only vehicle to take China to the land of peace and plenty. Their unconditional commitment to, and later close identification with, communism gradually turned the Chinese Communist Party from a messenger to a pawn of an ideology. At the same time, communism transformed itself from an instrument, intended to bring peace and prosperity to China, into an ultimate non-negotiable goal.[24] This self-inflicted double alienation dragged the Chinese Communist Party, and with it the Chinese people, into the dark tunnel of a closed ideology. It was only after the death of Mao that the pragmatic root of Confucianism, the practice of "seeking truth from facts," brought light to the Party, which had jettisoned all Chinese traditions with contempt in its eager conversion to Marxism.

Still, as an old Chinese idiom puts it, a starved camel is bigger than a horse. Even the disaster of the Great Leap Forward – when millions of peasants died of starvation – and the catastrophe of the Cultural Revolution could not totally wipe out the economic infrastructure laid down in Mao's time; this was the foundation on which the post-Mao reform was built.

The assessment of China's economic record during Mao's time remains a contentious issue among academic specialists.[25] Conventional accounts take Chinese economic reform as a total rejection of what went on before under Mao. One author, for example, called the post-Mao reform "the great reversal."[26] To its credit, a revisionist view has brought to light the hidden or overshadowed continuity between Mao's economy and post-Mao reform. By this process, China's economic achievements during Mao's era have been duly recognized.[27] Nonetheless, there is a massive gulf between Mao's economic record and the promises he made to Chinese peasants and workers in the name of socialism. As Mao Zedong lay on his deathbed, ruminating on power succession and the fate of the Cultural Revolution, the once sky-high morale was quashed, a once believed clear vision of socialism had become blurred, and a once vibrant social dynamism had withered from within. While the vast multitude seemed content living a life of inertia and indifference, their disappointment ran deep. If they could not articulate an alternative, they certainly had a ready ear for one. At the same time, among the most thoughtful, both within the ruling class and outside, some were asking themselves: "If this new China is not what we and our comrades-in-arms fought for, where should China head next?"

II

A striking and ironic feature of socialism – both its advantage and, if not managed well, its fatal flaw – is its inherent anti-populism. Unlike democracy, which is forced to be responsive to the average voter, socialist governments can afford to ignore and even harm the interest of the majority, often justifying these actions under some grand but empty banner. In his classic defense of the economic logic of socialism, *The Economics of Control* (1944), Abba Lerner opened with the simple statement that "the fundamental aim of socialism is not the abolition of private property but rather the extension of democracy."[28] This was not the reality of socialism in Mao's China. The largest social class in China was the peasantry, making up more than 80 percent of the population in Mao's time. Yet, it was the peasants who endured the worst consequences of collectivization. The unified procurement of agricultural products adopted in 1953 allowed the Chinese government to subsidize industrialization.[29] The 1958 introduction of the household registration system, or *hukou*, largely ruled out population mobility, in particular rural to urban migration.[30] Both these policies hit the peasants hard. The only populist policy pursued by the Chinese Communist Party was the short-lived land reform policy (1947–1952), whereby land was taken by force from rich landlords and given to poor peasants in exchange for their political support for the new regime.[31] But the government began gradually to re-collectivize land almost immediately after the end of land reform. Peasants lost their land, first to rural cooperatives and later to the communes. In 1956, Mao spoke cheerfully of "the high tide of socialism" sweeping rural China.[32] But 30 to 40 million peopled starved to death during the Great Leap Forward, a tragedy overwhelmingly concentrated in rural areas. Since then, if rural China became less chaotic under the commune system, what was unchanged was the ubiquity of hunger. As Yang Jisheng, a senior Xinhua (the state news agency) correspondent, observed, since the implementation of the unified procurement of grain, most of the Chinese peasants "no longer filled their stomachs."[33] As a result of these and other social and economic policies with a blatant anti-peasantry bias, two-thirds of peasants in 1978 had an income lower than that in the 1950s, and one-third had an income even lower than that in the 1930s before the Japanese invasion of China.[34]

Despite their colossal number, the hunger-stricken, disgruntled, but power-less peasantry did not worry the authorities too much. However, another group, which was equally, if not more, frustrated with Mao's policies, stood right at the center of Chinese politics. During Mao's various political campaigns, waves of army and party veterans were purged and lost their rank. Many were imprisoned and some lost their lives. Many of these disgraced officials were the victims of power struggles with Mao or with those close enough to Mao to be able to pursue their own agendas in his name. Some were courageous enough to voice opinions that differed from Mao's position and a few even confronted Mao directly; some of Mao's policies were so extreme that it must have been painfully difficult for any independent person not to voice their disagreement. Since tolerance was not a quality valued by Mao, or even allowed by the Dictatorship of the Proletariat, millions of "rightists" or "capitalist roaders" were created.

Liu Shaoqi, second only to Mao in the Party hierarchy in 1949 and Chairman of China at the start of the Cultural Revolution, found himself defenseless when he was labeled as the "number one capitalist roader."[35] The "number two capitalist roader" was no less than Deng Xiaoping, then General Secretary of the Central Secretariat of the Chinese Communist Party, who would re-emerge after Mao's death as China's paramount leader to welcome the market back to China.[36] Confronted with a mob of "Red Guards" eager to crush any enemy of socialism, Liu held in his hand a copy of the Constitution to defend his rights, but to no avail. Without trial or hearing of any kind, Liu lost his position and was placed under house arrest before being secretly transported out of Beijing and imprisoned. After repeated physical abuse and no access to medical treatment, Liu died unattended under a pseudonym on November 12th, 1969, in Henan province.

Zhu Rongji, the future Premier of China (1998–2003), was labeled a "rightist" and lost his job in the State Planning Commission in 1958 for criticizing the Great Leap Forward.[37] Zhu didn't return to his job until 1962, only to be purged again in 1970 during the Cultural Revolution, spending the next five years exiled to the countryside. Zhu would not be rehabilitated until 1978.

Many top party leaders lost their lives during the Cultural Revolution. Six of the ten Chinese Marshals (the highest military rank in the People's Libration Army) did not survive, including Peng Dehui, the first Defense Minister of China (1954–1959). Those purged officials who did manage to survive did not want to see Mao's policies continue. After witnessing the broken promises of Mao's ideology, they had every motive to vindicate their "rightist," capitalist, or other approaches that had been denounced and rejected by Mao. They had risked their lives to join the Chinese Communist Party in the hope of bringing peace and prosperity to the Chinese people; with the death of Mao, they now sensed that their chance was approaching. After wasting two decades in political campaigns and class warfare, it was time for China to refocus on the economy. During one of his first visits to China in the early 1980s, Steven Cheung met a group of government officials at the Central Party School of the Communist Party in Beijing. He was surprised by how strongly his audience agreed with his admonition: "You guys have messed up the country. Now, you have to fix it."[38]

III

Probably no group endured more humiliation and suffering under Mao than the intellectuals. The intelligentsia in Imperial China, a highly meritocratic but open group whose members had passed the civil service examination, was an integral part of the ruling hierarchy. The Chinese Communist Party's embrace of socialism and radical anti-traditionalism ensured that the new government would have a stormy relationship with its most educated members. And Mao's personality certainly did not help.[39] A voracious reader and gifted self-learner, with a proud and defiant mind, Mao never hid his distrust of formal learning. In his late teens, Mao once dropped out of high school for half a year and spent most of the time in the provincial library reading a large number of books, having compiled the list himself.[40] Twenty-four when he first came to Beijing, Mao worked as an assistant librarian at Peking University, checking out newspapers and magazines at a reading room for university professors. Curious and bold, he did not waste any opportunity to raise questions or simply initiate conversations with those professors whom he served. Few of them, however, showed much respect for a young man who could barely speak standard Mandarin. This dispiriting and frustrating experience with the university professors did not give Mao a positive impression of Chinese intellectuals or of the system of formal education that they represented.[41] In adulthood, Mao's power struggle for the Party's leadership against Wang Ming and others who had studied Marxism in the Soviet Union only reinforced his doubts about, and contempt for, academic learning and its embodiment, modern intellectuals.

At the birth of the People's Republic of China, many of the educated elites chose to stay on the mainland, not out of their belief in Marxism, but because of their disappointment with the corrupt and fleeing Nationalist government.[42] A number of Chinese scientists educated in the West returned to the newly founded People's Republic, including Qian Xuesen, the founding director of the Jet Propulsion Laboratory at Caltech, who would later become the father of China's rocket and space program.[43] But from the very beginning, the Communist Party was uneasy with the Chinese intelligentsia.[44]

Historically, China had been heavily influenced by Confucianism. The educated elites occupied a central and privileged social status.[45] As interpreters and messengers of Confucianism, they played a critical role in legitimizing political order and maintaining the moral compass in society. As civil servants, they directly exercised political power in the imperial court, representing an institutional counterbalance to the royal power of the emperor. In addition, they stood as the core of what was called the "gentry class," which provided local public goods and maintained social order at the sub-county level, beyond the reach of centralized imperial power. But under socialism, all these functions were appropriated by the Chinese Communist Party.[46]

Armed as he was with socialism, which was hailed as omnipotent and infallible, Mao saw only a limited role for the intellectuals in socialist China. Nonetheless, the new government initially tried to build a working rapport with them, since their potential contribution to economic reconstruction was recognized. At the same time, the intellectuals felt inferior and shameful as they celebrated the end of war and welcomed Mao and his army to Beijing.[47] Their non-participation in the liberation of the nation and the fighting of the revolutionary war made many feel impotent and guilty in the presence of their liberators, something they endeavored to offset by devoting themselves to China's post-war reconstruction. This led many to embrace the new government too eagerly and stifle their own independent judgments. Most intellectuals jumped on the bandwagon of socialism. Only a few independent minds were as courageous as Liang Shuming; the Chinese philosopher and leader in the Rural Construction Movement of the early twentieth century confronted Mao in public about China's new economic policy in 1953.[48] Chen Yinke, one of the most talented Chinese historians of the twentieth century, adhered to the principle of intellectual independence, which he had memorably put as "thoughts of freedom, spirits of independence"; a professor at Zhongshan University in Guangzhou, Chen refused to move to Beijing to head the Institute of History Study at the Chinese Academy of Science.[49] Another notable dissenter was Hu Feng, who was attacked as a "rightist" as early as 1955 for advocating writers' freedom and independence from political ideology.[50] But these few independent minds could not mount a meaningful resistance to the rising tide of socialism.

The simmering tension between the educated elites and the Communist government finally boiled over with the launch of the Anti-Rightist Movement.[51] By the end of 1956, a mixed economy had been replaced by socialism. With the elimination of private enterprise and the concentration of political power, weaknesses in the over-centralized bureaucracy soon arose. In spring 1957 Mao decided to launch a rectification movement in the Party, hoping to identify and eradicate its defects. The intellectuals were invited to voice their criticisms and recommend ways to make the Party and government work better. But Mao was not prepared to hear what he had requested. While most criticisms were meant to help the Party and new government improve their work, some directly challenged the legitimacy of the Party's monopoly of political power and questioned Mao's leadership. Offended and alarmed, Mao rounded on his critics, labeling them "rightists." A rectification campaign meant to improve the Party had quickly turned into a movement against the Party's critics, with dire consequences for both the intellectual community and the Party itself. As far as the intellectuals were concerned, the Anti-Rightist Movement officially defined their status as the class enemy of the regime. As a result, China's most educated members and the scarcest element of production were denied their right to participate in the development of socialism. For the Party, the label of "rightist" would become a powerful and convenient weapon to use against anyone who dared to criticize or deviate from the official line. Years later, Bo Yibo (1997) wrote, "For the twenty years between the start of [the] Anti-Rightist Movement and the Third Plenum of the Eleventh Central Committee (1978), what Chairman Mao called 'lively political life' was lost."[52] This is a euphemistic way of saying that Mao became the only voice in and of the Party, with no room for any other opinions.

At a critical juncture when the Chinese Communist Party transformed itself from a revolutionary to a ruling party, and began to rebuild a new China from the ashes of war, China eliminated the most educated members of its population. This movement of self-destruction severely emasculated China's access to both its cultural heritage and modern science and technology. Under the banner of an omniscient ideology, the socialist state penetrated both rural and urban society to a degree never attempted by any previous Chinese ruler. With the authority of the traditional social order and Confucian moral code discredited, there was little left as an external social force or internal moral discipline to balance the coercive power of the state. At the same time, as a victorious but young political party, the Chinese Communist Party had not had time to develop a system of institutional checks and balances. Led by a defiant and increasingly self-assured leader, it was turning into an invincible political Frankenstein.

IV

Although Mao crushed the market in ideas and monopolized the realm of thought, he was never a supporter of centralization in administration. Unlike Lenin or Stalin, who considered political and economic centralization essential for socialism, Mao throughout his life fought hard against centralized administration. Decades of guerrilla war experience had taught him that it was suicidal to put all one's eggs into one basket, no matter who looked after the basket. During its rise to power, the Chinese Communist Party had always had multiple scattered bases, each fighting independently for its own survival, with only intermittent communication with the Central Committee and even less with each other. This combination of central command and local autonomy had worked quite well.

Even after the founding of the People's Republic, Mao was rarely free of the fear of impending war. In the 1950s the danger came from US-backed Taiwan. But, after the Sino-Soviet split in the late 1950s and early 1960s, the threat from Taiwan in the south was replaced by a much more menacing threat from the north – the Soviet Union. China's relationship with the Soviet Union began to disintegrate after the "secret speech" Khrushchev gave on March 5th 1956, when he revealed the horrors committed under Stalin and openly denounced the cult of personality around Stalin. This angered China greatly since Stalin was still highly respected as a leader of the Communist movement and his portrait was displayed all over China, along with those of Marx, Engels, Lenin, and Mao. Mao and other Chinese leaders viewed Khrushchev's vilification of Stalin as a calculated attack on socialism. Later, the rivalry between Mao and Khrushchev for the leadership of the socialist world, their substantially different views on the relation between capitalism and socialism, and territorial disputes between China and the Soviet Union led to the final split between Beijing and Moscow.[53] Tensions and hostilities continued to build, escalating into the military clash of 1969 along China's northeastern border.

The fact that Mao's China rarely felt secure in its borders had a lasting impact on domestic economic policy. For Mao, the constant preparation for war perpetuated his way of thinking formed during wartime and served as a forceful deterrent against administrative centralization. This meant that, while Lenin imagined the socialist economy as one single giant firm, Mao's economy was an ocean of self-sufficient, more or less identical subunits. For Mao, the commune came close to perfection as a basic social unit in his ideal society. Each commune was inclusive in its economic and social functions, containing production teams in agriculture, commune and brigade enterprises, daycare and schools, its clinics staffed with barefoot doctors, and even its military brigade. Communes were independent of each other, with little horizontal interaction. As a result, a social economy consisting of an integrated and interdependent national economy, coordinated by the market and/or central planning, did not exist in Mao's China.

Centralization did exist once in Mao's China, but only briefly. The political and economic system installed after the socialist transition (1952–1956) was more centralized than any other in Chinese history. But it did not take long for Mao to sense serious problems with centralized administration. In his talk, "On the Ten Major Relationships," delivered in April 1956, Mao deemed "of vital importance" the balances between the state, the production units (factories in cities and production teams in the countryside), and the workers and peasants, as well as the balance between central and local authorities.[54] On the former, Mao commented:

> It's not right, I'm afraid, to place everything in the hands of the central or the provincial and municipal authorities without leaving the factories any power of their own, any room for independent action, any benefits. We don't have much experience on how to share power and returns properly among the central authorities, the provincial and municipal authorities and the factories, and we should study the subject. As a matter of principle centralization and independence form a unity of opposites, and there must be both centralization and independence.[55]

In concluding the section, Mao wrote:

> In short, consideration must be given to both sides, not to just one, whether they are the state and the factory, the state and the worker, the factory and the worker, the state and the co-operative, the state and the peasant, or the co-operative and the peasant. To give consideration to only one side, whichever it may be, is harmful to socialism and to the dictatorship of the proletariat.[56]

On the relationship between the central and local governments, Mao warned:

> Our territory is so vast, our population is so large and the conditions are so complex that it is far better to have the initiative come from both the central and the local authorities than from one source alone. We must not follow the example of the Soviet Union in concentrating everything in the hands of the central authorities, shackling the local authorities and denying them the right to independent action.[57]

And he continued:

> To build a powerful socialist country it is imperative to have a strong and unified central leadership and unified planning and discipline throughout the country; disruption of this indispensable unity is impermissible. At the same time, it is essential to bring the initiative of the local authorities into full play and let each locality enjoy the particularity suited to its local conditions.[58]

At the end, Mao recognized the problem of centralization throughout the whole spectrum of administrative hierarchy, not just confined to the central government.

> The central authorities should take care to give scope to the initiative of the provinces and municipalities, and the latter in their turn should do the same for the prefectures, counties, districts and townships; in neither case should the lower levels be put in a strait-jacket. Of course comrades at the lower levels must be informed of the matters on which centralization is necessary and they must not act as they please. In short, centralization must be enforced where it is possible and necessary, otherwise it should not be imposed at all. The provinces and municipalities, prefectures, counties, districts and townships should all enjoy their own proper independence and rights and should fight for them. To fight for such rights in the interest of the whole nation and not of the locality cannot be called localism or an undue assertion of independence.[59]

Mao's deep distrust of centralization led to his first attempt to reform the economic system, steering China away from the orthodox Stalinist model of socialism. A reform proposal was passed at the Third Plenum of the Eighth Central Committee in October 1957, to be implemented in 1958.[60] The core of this reform was a redistribution of power in favor of local authorities. As a result, local governments obtained more autonomy in economic planning, resource allocation, fiscal and tax policy, and personnel management. In addition, the administration of most state-owned enterprises was devolved to local

governments. About 88 percent of the state-owned enterprises previously affil-
iated with various ministries and departments of the central government were
transferred to the control of local authorities.[61]

As an unintended consequence of decentralization, Mao could now reach
provincial governments directly, without going through the bureaucracy of various ministries in Beijing. Local authorities in Shanghai, Sichuan, and Hubei
were particularly receptive to Mao's ideas and policies. At the same time, local
authorities now had more autonomy in running the local economy, but bore
few responsibilities for the success or failure of their decision-making. With
Mao calling for speedy economic development, local authorities were now well
positioned to begin the Great Leap Forward.

V

In retrospect, the Great Leap Forward was a man-made tragedy.[62] It did not
come out of the blue. With a handful of exceptions (such as Chen Yun), most
Chinese leaders, especially at the early stage, were just as enthusiastic about
the Great Leap Forward as Mao.[63] While Mao was the passionate initiator
and unflinching general, the Great Leap Forward enjoyed wide support and
was fortuitously aided by the decentralized administration recently installed
by Mao.

Chinese leaders – and Mao in particular – had been thrilled with the country's
economic performance since the founding of the People's Republic. To their
pleasant surprise, Mao and his comrades witnessed a swift economic recovery and smooth transition to socialism; this was in spite of the Korean War
and their total lack of experience in running a national economy. Proud of
their achievement, they were emboldened; indeed, their confidence became so
inflated that it led them to believe that further achievement was constrained
by nothing but their imaginations. On August 27th, 1958, the *People's Daily*
ran an article entitled "The land will surrender as much grain as we endeavor."
This quickly became a popular slogan, promulgated nationwide to motivate
peasants, as if the dismal law of diminishing marginal returns had ceased to
exist.[64]

At the same time, peasants were exhorted to rush into communism. After
agricultural collectivization, Chinese leaders thought the communist utopia
was just around the corner, if only peasants would simply embrace it. Rural
cooperatives gradually gave way to communes, which were seen as China's
fast track to communist success. Under the commune system, all assets were
taken away from households and managed as collective goods. A glittering
and disastrous invention that swept rural China in 1958 was the commune
canteen.[65] Originally conceived as a way to save time and facilitate coordination in farming, the commune canteen was promoted and defended as the

precursor of communism. Grain was not allotted to each household as had been the case previously, but was all left to the commune canteen. Peasants were allowed to eat as much and as often as they wished in a commune canteen. Not surprisingly, everyone ate as if there were no tomorrow. For a very short time, the commune canteen afforded Chinese peasants a glimpse of communist utopia.

The appeal and supposed economic potential of communism was greatly reinforced by exaggerated reports of agricultural production submitted to Beijing by the local governments in the fall of 1958.[66] Decentralized and without effective supervision, local governments were virtually consumed by an escalating contest of fabrication. One after another, local governments pronounced spectacular harvests of grain production. On September 18th the *People's Daily* reported that average grain productivity per mu (a mu is equal to 660 square meters) in Guangxi had reached 65,000 kilograms (a realistic estimate would be less than 500 kilograms).[67] While all local officials knew the truth, few dared not to follow the precedent. From their perspective, they were simply telling Beijing what it wanted to hear. Disappointing Beijing was the least these officials could afford to do if they wanted to stay in office, particularly in the immediate aftermath of the Anti-Rightist Movement. And that campaign had already eliminated most of those who might have stood up to speak the truth about the Great Leap Forward.

In addition, with all newspapers and media strictly controlled by the state, there was no outlet for dissenting voices, had they existed. At the same time, in a society where information was strictly controlled, whatever was transmitted through the state-controlled media was taken as authoritative and authentic. China's most famous and respected scientist, Qian Xuesen, published an article in *China Youth* on June 16th, 1958, stating that theoretically rice and wheat production could be as high as 25,000 kilograms per mu as long as the plants absorbed 30 percent of the solar energy they received.[68] With little debate, Qian's article was received by Mao as a theoretical proof of the viability of the Great Leap Forward in agriculture. With its strictly controlled media effectively silencing dissenting voices, Beijing was now a victim of its own efficacy. Naively accepting the production data submitted from local governments, the Agricultural Ministry forecasted that grain production in 1958 would increase by almost 70 percent. Mao and other leaders in Beijing were led to believe that they should start to worry about how to store and dispose of the superabundance of grain.[69] Not surprisingly, the state took much more grain from peasants in 1958 and still more in 1959. Grain exports jumped from 1.93 million tons in 1957 to 2.66 million in 1958, 4.16 million in 1959, and 2.65 million tons in 1960, before China started to import grain in 1961. In 1959 when Mao announced that grain output had reached 375 million tons in China, the actual output was probably about 170 million.[70] Nothing could be more tragic and senseless than that when millions of Chinese peasants were starving to death, China was aggressively exporting grain.

Another tragic aspect, probably the most vividly remembered initiative of the Great Leap Forward, was the push to make steel in backyard furnaces across China, which greatly reduced grain output and thereby increased the death toll from starvation. In November 1957, Mao went to Moscow for the second and last time, to attend the fortieth anniversary of the October Revolution. As the most senior and charismatic leader in the communist camp, Mao was revered by leaders of other communist countries. Even his Soviet host, Khrushchev, who was not known for his modesty, was compelled to show him respect. But Mao was embarrassed, if not ashamed, by the backward, agrarian nature of the Chinese economy. China may have stood up as a political giant, but it remained an economic dwarf. Something had to be done, and done quickly, to ensure China's economy caught up with its political status. At the time, steel production was widely regarded as a reliable index of industrialization. So when Khrushchev pronounced that the Soviet Union would overtake the United States in steel production within fifteen years, Mao was impelled in his speech to commit China to overtaking Britain – the second largest capitalist economy – in steel production within fifteen years.[71]

This overambitious plan was far beyond China's productive capacity. When it became obvious that existing steel mills could not possibly fulfill the production quotas, steel production became everyone's job. The staffs of all factories, schools, and production teams all over rural China were recruited to the race to make steel. Even during harvest, grain was left to rot in the fields, as peasants were busily engaged in making steel in their backyard furnaces. It should surprise no one that the majority of this steel was useless. But a more devastating flaw was that this improvised steel production was leading to an egregious misallocation of labor. A recent study put resource diversion from farming as the most important factor responsible for the decline of grain output between 1958 and 1961.[72]

Even after starvation was first reported in Henan province, local governments did their best to cover it up for fear of punishment. A critical but short window of opportunity to act decisively was lost. At the same time, peasants were chained to their land and banned from leaving their villages even when they were starving. Any exodus of peasants would be treated as a sign of the ineptitude of the local authority. Moreover, with private commerce effectively eliminated, no grain could be moved to where it was urgently needed. Had a free market been allowed, private enterprises would have developed to buy grain from less affected areas where prices were low and sell it in the most affected areas where prices were higher. Adam Smith, founding father of modern economics, may have had this situation in mind when he wrote that "In an extensive corn country, between all the different parts of which there is a free commerce and communication, the scarcity occasioned by the most unfavorable seasons can never be so great as to produce a famine."[73] With the movement of grain, people, and information all banned, no government could have combated such a famine. When local authorities cared more for their policies' compliance with Beijing's instruction than their actual effect on the ground, the Chinese peasants had no chance at all.

But without the breakdown of communication between central and local governments that resulted from administrative decentralization, the Great Leap Forward would not have ended so tragically. For this reason, administrative decentralization was unfortunate. The disastrous results of the Great Leap Forward and, by association, decentralization pushed the economy back to central planning. At the very least, central planning was able to restore order, and the economy was recovering by the mid-1960s. This experience led many Chinese leaders, particularly Chen Yun, who, together with Deng Xiaoping, would preside over China's economic reform from the late 1970s to the mid-1990s, to view central planning as sacred and indispensable.

But several deep structural flaws predated the administrative decentralization of 1958; without these the Great Leap Forward would probably not have happened and the death toll would not have reached millions. These flaws included an anti-market mentality, strict control of domestic migration, state monopoly of media, and radical anti-intellectualism. None of these policies had anything to do with decentralization. It is a pity that discussions of the Great Leap Forward, first within the Chinese government and later in academia, have been largely influenced by, and confined to, the original dispute between Mao and Liu Shaoqi, in which Mao claimed that the Great Leap Forward was mainly (70 percent) a natural disaster (bad weather) and to a lesser degree (30 percent) a man-made mistake, while Liu claimed the opposite.[74] Evidence available then clearly indicated that it was mainly a man-made disaster, and this view has since been borne out by later quantitative studies. This disagreement between Liu and Mao would later sow the seed for Mao's ruthless attack on Liu during the Cultural Revolution. It had the unfortunate consequence of focusing the debate too narrowly on the implied personal responsibility of decision-makers, leaving unexamined the structural flaws built into the socialist system by successive misguided policies. As a result, many of these factors, which allowed the Great Leap Forward to happen in the first place and later greatly exacerbated the ensuing disaster, were further entrenched by the restoration of administrative centralization and the revival of the Five Year Economic Plan.

Few regimes could have survived a disaster as stupendous, as tragic, and as senseless as the Great Leap Forward – Mao and the Chinese government should have been grateful that peasants did not revolt but instead allowed them a second chance to govern. In retrospect, the Great Leap Forward should have served as a wake-up call for the Chinese government to fully and thoroughly re-examine the whole political, economic, and social system to ensure that the deaths of millions of peasants had not been in vain and that no such disaster should happen in the future. Regrettably, administrative decentralization was singled out as an easy target and convenient culprit. For those who did not agree with Mao, the failure of the Great Leap Forward only served to validate administrative centralization and enshrine economic planning. In this way the Chinese government lost a vital opportunity to examine their mistakes and learn from them.

Mao's economic policy after 1949 was greatly influenced by his wartime experience. But he failed to recognize that in wartime each base area was fully responsible for the consequences of its actions. A serious mistake could easily, and often did, lead to death. Such harsh constraints did not exist for provincial and sub-provincial authorities even after decentralization. It was rare for local officials to lose their positions due to economic mismanagement. Moreover, strict centralized control of the media and communication within government made it impossible for any local government to voice a dissenting view, let alone mount any meaningful challenge to Beijing. Mao's decentralization did not allow genuine local autonomy – nor did Mao see any need for it. After China's quick transition to socialism, which contrasted with Stalin's lengthy and bloody campaign of collectivization, Mao came to believe that China had stumbled upon a blessed "golden highway" to communism. Local authorities were simply required to show their enthusiasm and willingness to obey orders. But it was the Chinese peasants who shouldered the burden when the utopian vision went sour.

The tragedy of the Great Leap Forward illustrates that the differences between a command and a market economy reflect a deep difference in mentality and attitude. A market economy can only be tolerated when no one is confident enough to claim omniscience. A point stressed by Hayek, the far-reaching implications of which have yet to be fully recognized, is that the most critical advantage of a market lies less in its allocative efficiency, and more in its free flow of information.[75] But the flow of information would not make much sense, indeed it would seem wasteful, if the problem that it helps to solve is not recognized. A market economy assumes two deep epistemic commitments: acknowledgement of ignorance and tolerance of uncertainty. It was hard for a defiant Mao and a triumphant Chinese Communist Party to accept either, even in the aftermath of the disastrous Great Leap Forward.

VI

After the Great Leap Forward, China enjoyed a return of social order and economic recovery in the early 1960s, only to see it end abruptly with Mao's launch of the Cultural Revolution in 1966. The complexity of Mao's motives for carrying out the Cultural Revolution has been scrutinized in an extensive and still growing literature.[76] It is clear that Mao's instinctive hostility toward centralization could not tolerate a return to central planning for long. A central objective of the Cultural Revolution was to eliminate government bureaucracy, which Mao considered self-serving, and to allow the people to take charge. Since he was even more hostile to market principles and never fond of the rule of law, Mao failed to recognize that an attack on central planning in a social system where local autonomy was ruled out and law did not exist would inevitably lead to chaos rather than to genuine democracy, as Mao had wished. The Chinese economy was to become trapped in a vicious circle of centralization, rigidity, decentralization, and chaos for many years to come.

Internal party politics and Mao's ideology of continuous class struggle ensured that the Cultural Revolution was even more radical in ideology than the Great Leap Forward. To preserve the purity of socialism, protecting it from capitalist encroachment on the one side and feudalist erosion on the other, Mao's Red Guards – mostly high school students and other teenagers – were urged to destroy all institutions and artifacts bequeathed from the past. These were condemned as the "four olds": old customs, old culture, old habits, and old ideas. As a result, temples, books, paintings, and other cultural relics were burned and demolished. During the second half of the 1960s, the only books available to readers in China were the collected works of Marx, Engels, Lenin, Stalin, and Mao, and a few books designated by the government to show off the triumph of socialism. All other books were banned and all libraries were closed. Teachers and professors, particularly those who returned from abroad, were subject to humiliation and abuse, resulting in many deaths and suicides. Education suffered heavily as academic learning became a target of derision and parody. "Knowledge is useless" was a popular slogan. Since most of the educated elites were denounced and many imprisoned as "rightists," knowledge itself became an often deadly political liability. At this time, all economic contact with Japan and the West was cut off and the Chinese economy was further isolated from modern technology. The brutal attack on Chinese cultural traditions, both physically and intellectually, was probably the most ironic and tragic feature of the Cultural Revolution. Its radical anti-traditionalism and extreme examples of cultural self-negation and self-destruction – which amounted to nothing less than total de-Sinification – were probably unprecedented in human history. Since the beginning of the twentieth century, when China was almost defenseless in the face of western economic, military, and cultural ascendancy, Chinese intellectuals had become increasingly critical of their own cultural heritage. But their critique of Chinese culture was always mediated by their deep emotional attachment to the very object of their attacks. Raised under socialism, most Red Guards had little respect for, and certainly no attachment to, their own cultural traditions. Juvenile rebellion was clothed in revolutionary precepts, flaring into widespread violence and becoming a deadly political weapon against the existing political system and cultural order. The political and intellectual establishments were its two major victims.

Preoccupied with the class struggle, which was deemed a constant and insidious threat to the survival of socialism, Mao let radical politics dictate economic management. Mao's subjugation of the economy to politics led to another round of economic decentralization during the Cultural Revolution, as he declared war on the central bureaucracy.[77] Economic decentralization was probably the most important, but little recognized, factor in sheltering the economy from political turmoil during the Cultural Revolution. As a result, even though China was racked by widespread political violence during the Cultural Revolution, the economy did not suffer as serious a blow as it had during the Great Leap Forward. Except for the first three years of the Cultural Revolution, when the economy was severely disrupted, production was able to grow faster than the population, even as fertility rates peaked between 1969 and 1972. With a continuing bias against consumer goods, however, the economy remained driven by state-centered investment projects and the living conditions for most Chinese remained stagnant or even deteriorated. With little improvement in welfare, a growing population, and a continuous call for class struggle, more and more people became disillusioned and began to ask themselves, "Is this the socialism we fought so hard for?"

At the same time, the Party and state apparatus suffered unprecedented damage. Unlike the Great Leap Forward when the political elites were largely sheltered from the disaster, the Party veterans were squarely at the center of the political struggle during the Cultural Revolution. The whole political structure and administrative machine was severely weakened. A rigid, centralized bureaucracy staffed with strictly disciplined but dispirited bureaucrats, which had been a defining feature of Stalinism, was certainly not among the assets Mao bequeathed to his successors. China, no doubt, remained a socialist economy – no private property or free market was allowed. But the Chinese economy had much less central planning than the name socialism might suggest.

In the West, Chinese socialism was, and probably still is, commonly perceived as more or less a copy of what was practiced in the Soviet Union. Since China was largely cut off from the rest of the world during much of Mao's time, little information was available about Mao's China. The outside world thus got to know China through the label of socialism rather than through the reality on the ground. China was seen from the angle of Stalinism and misunderstandings were bound to arise.

It is worthwhile pointing out that even though Mao was directly responsible for the decentralization of the Chinese political and economic system, other forces, more elusive but no less decisive, were also at work. The size of the Chinese continent would make life difficult for any central planner.

As an age-old Chinese axiom puts it, "Heaven is high and the emperor far away." Some local autonomy was therefore inevitable. Historically, the tension between administrative centralization (or what is called *junxian* in Chinese literature) and decentralization (or what is called *fengjian*) has been an absorbing issue for China's rulers ever since the First Emperor of Qin unified China in 221 BC.[78] Even though Imperial China is remembered for its administrative innovation, a centralized bureaucracy staffed by civilians who were selected through the civil service examination, centralization coexisted with decentralization. Centralization may be the best-known aspect of traditional Chinese politics, but the political system was kept in order by balancing the competing forces of centralization and decentralization, like the Yin and Yang in Tai Chi.

Even though China under Mao had built up, mostly from scratch, an impressive nationwide industrial base, its economic performance was an agonizing disappointment. But while Mao left behind poverty and a poorly functioning economic system, he also created much discontent among a large number of people, most of whom were desperate for change. At the end of Mao's rule, China was left with a fractured society, a fragmented economy, and a confused and disoriented politics, crawling along what was once believed the golden highway to socialism. With the end of Mao's era, China was bound to open a new chapter.

2
China in Transition

Mao's death on September 9th, 1976 pitched China into a bitter and uncertain struggle over succession.[1] On the one side was the circle around Hua Guofeng, whom Mao had picked as First Vice Chairman of the Central Committee of the Chinese Communist Party and made acting premier in February 1976 after the death of Zhou Enlai, China's long-time premier. On the other stood the Gang of Four, including Mao's widow, Jiang Qing, and her three recruits from Shanghai, who had climbed up to the top of the Chinese political hierarchy during the Cultural Revolution. In addition, Chinese politics was deeply divided along an ideological line. The above two rival groups were joined together on one side as beneficiaries and supporters of the Cultural Revolution. On the opposite side was a large and loose group of senior Party and military veterans around Marshal Ye Jianying, including Deng Xiaoping, Chen Yun, and Hu Yaobang, who were either reluctant partners in, or explicit opponents of, the Cultural Revolution. Just before his death, Mao was deeply worried that the transfer of power would be rocky and that the Cultural Revolution might be abandoned. Together with the defeat of Chiang Kai-shek and the Nationalist government, he deemed it one of his most important and lasting achievements.[2]

Two days after Mao's death, on September 11th, Hua made a bold move. He informed Li Xiannian, then Vice Premier in charge of economic affairs, of his determination to arrest the Gang of Four and asked Li to contact Marshall Ye as soon as possible. At the time, Ye was Vice Chairman of the Central Committee of the Party, Vice Chairman of the Central Military Committee, and Minister of Defense. On September 13th Li visited Ye in secret, and conveyed Hua's urgent message. Long disgruntled with the Gang of Four, Marshall Ye wholeheartedly supported Hua's decision. With Ye's active participation, a secret plan was made on September 26th to depose the Gang of Four. Ten days later, on

October 6th, the Gang of Four were arrested, without a single shot being fired. With the strong backing of Party veterans, Hua consolidated his power and seized the leadership position immediately afterwards. The People's Republic's first transfer of power turned out to be far less tumultuous than Mao had feared, if more dramatic.[3]

I

At a testing moment for the People's Republic, Hua managed to avoid a potentially devastating power struggle that could have wrecked the whole nation. To his credit, Hua was able to unite disparate forces behind him, at least for a short time, to depose the Gang of Four, and fill the power vacuum left by Mao's departure. In addition, during his brief tenure, Hua managed to turn China away from Mao's radical ideology and preoccupation with class struggle and lead the country to socialist modernization. But Hua was caught in a political dilemma. On the one hand, Hua and the Chinese government remained committed to socialism and ideologically loyal to Mao. The disappointing performance of socialism and Mao's deplorable economic record had not totally destroyed the ideological legitimacy of socialism nor broken down the cult of personality around Mao. Even after his death, Mao was still widely respected as a great leader by both the political elites and the common people. Even the arrest of the Gang of Four was legitimized by their supposed betrayal of Mao, and attributed to Mao's foresight – he had picked Hua as First Vice Chairman in 1975 rather than Wang Hongwen, a member of the Gang of Four. The legitimacy of Hua's leadership was therefore believed to depend on continued deference to Mao's teachings. On the other hand, Hua realized that he could not let some of Mao's decisions remain unchanged, in particular the ongoing Cultural Revolution and Mao's 1975 decision to depose Deng again for his reluctance to endorse the Cultural Revolution. Deng's political courage in disagreeing with Mao and his effective premiership from 1974 to 1975 helped to win the trust of many Party veterans and the support of the general public. Both groups looked up to him as a strong candidate to lead China in the post-Mao era.

Trapped by this ideological quandary, Hua allowed a new cult of personality to develop around him, hoping to firm up his legitimacy as Mao's successor. But this resort to a personality cult estranged Hua from Marshall Ye and other veterans, whose support was indispensable to Hua's leadership. As victims of Mao's purges, these veterans had deplored Mao's hubris, seeing it as a root cause of the Cultural Revolution and Mao's other disastrous policies since the Anti-Rightist Movement. With the return to power of Deng Xiaoping and Chen Yun at the end of 1978, the only two surviving members of the pre-Cultural Revolution Politburo Standing Committee, Hua stood little chance of retaining power in a political system where seniority was a critical asset. Hua gave up the Premiership in 1980 to Zhao Ziyang, and Party Chairmanship in 1981 to Hu Yaobang, the two protégés of Deng Xiaoping. Hua was criticized, and deservedly so, as being ineffective in loosening, let alone shaking free from, the stifling ideological monopolization that had suppressed free thought and human creativity during Mao's time. But this challenge Hua's successors would later find far more difficult and enduring than they had first thought.

Nonetheless, Hua acted swiftly to move China forward. The Cultural Revolution was brought to a close immediately after the arrest of the Gang of Four, even though Hua was unwilling or unable to censure what scholars would later call "Mao's last revolution."[4] Amid the political campaign of denouncing the Gang of Four as "rightists" and for practicing capitalism, Hua brought the economy to the forefront of policy, replacing ideology as the primary focus of the Chinese government. As early as December 1976, making his first public appearance as the new leader of China, Hua stressed economic development and the improvement of living conditions as the priority for the new Chinese government.[5]

At the tactical level, Hua followed an old Chinese practice: every new emperor brings his own courtiers. He quickly placed his choices in a few key positions to make sure that his new policies would be implemented. For example, Hu Yaobang was picked as the Deputy Principal of the Central Party School in March 1977 (Hua himself was the Principal), and Hu Jiwei as chief editor of the *People's Daily* in October. Both had been purged during the Cultural Revolution.[6] At the end of the year, Hu Yaobang was to lead the powerful Organization Department of the Central Committee of the Chinese Communist Party, which was in charge of the placement of Party and government officials. Upon taking the position at the Organization Department in mid-December 1977, Hu led a great and courageous campaign to rehabilitate Party and government officials as well as various "rightists," "capitalist roaders," and "anti-socialist elements" who had been persecuted during Mao's time, giving proper recognition to the dead and bringing back to work those who had survived.[7] By 1982, more than 3 million people had been rehabilitated, and many former "rightists" or "capitalist roaders" came back to government. This resulted in a huge leadership reshuffle in both central and provincial government.[8] Of the 201 members of the 11th Session of the Central Committee of the Party (August 1977), more than half were replaced in the next Session (September 1982). From 1977 to 1980, all but three provincial heads were replaced. Among the new generation of provincial leaders, two stood out: Ren Zhongyi of Guangdong and Xiang Nan of Fujian, two pioneers in pushing forward economic reform, making these two provinces among the first to experiment with a market economy in the early 1980s.

II

Concurrent with the change of personnel in 1977–1978 was a shift in ideological and political attitudes. After Mao's death China did not allow a political campaign directly repudiating him. While the Soviet Union was quick to denounce Stalin after his death, Mao still commanded enormous respect in China; his teachings were still held as the final judgment of political truth. This was partly due to the post-Mao government's strategy of keeping Mao's horrendous deeds secret, and a detailed assessment of Mao was left for later generations.[9] How to interpret Mao thus became a critical struggle for ideological control, with immediate political consequences. On one side stood Hua, who remained faithful to Mao's teachings and tried to prevent any criticism being leveled against Mao, even against the Culture Revolution. He believed that to protect Mao's reputation would assure political continuity and thus bolster his political legitimacy. The extremists on his side proclaimed that all Mao's words and policies had to be strictly followed, which, paradoxically, would have undermined and contradicted Hua's own policy changes. Opposed to this approach were the vast majority of Party veterans, who had suffered during the Cultural Revolution and were eager to repudiate it. But by and large even this group was not ready, either psychologically or politically, to completely refute Mao's legacy. Despite these attitudes, Hu Yaobang was able to use the Central Party School as a platform to promote political reform.[10] In June 1977, Hu founded a new journal, *Theoretical Trends*, which would solicit articles to question and criticize the ossified socialist doctrines and Mao's radical policies, which still had a firm grip on the minds of the people.

On May 10th, 1978, the sixtieth issue of *Theoretical Trends* published an article, "Practice is the Only Criterion for Testing Truth," that directly challenged the official Party adherence to Mao's ideology. Rejecting Maoism or Marxism, or any other ideology, as a measure of truth was mind-liberating for the Chinese people long accustomed to treating Mao's little red book as the ultimate judge of truth. Many officials and intellectuals were particularly enthusiastic; they had been attacked as "rightists" or "capitalist roaders" in Mao's time because of their criticism of Mao's policies. Since Mao himself had endorsed, and indeed popularized, the old Chinese saying, "seeking truth from facts," as a guiding principle for the Party in Yan'an, supporters of the use of social practice defended their position as a genuine development of Maoism. From their point of view, they had rescued Mao's thought from the errors of his own actions.

This debate held center stage in Chinese politics throughout 1978–1979. At the beginning, Hua's unflinching loyalty to Mao cost him political capital. Nonetheless, Hua allowed the debate to continue and ultimately altered his position, demonstrating rare qualities of political leadership and tolerance.[11] This debate, and the resounding triumph of pragmatism, watered down the ideological monopoly of radical Maoism pursued during the Cultural Revolution. Thus, without repudiating Mao or renouncing its own ideological base of legitimacy, the Chinese Communist Party opened the door for reform.

Immediately after the death of Mao, Chinese politics witnessed swift and significant changes in both personnel and ideology. Without these, the later market reforms would have been unthinkable. The conventional wisdom in the academic literature states that Chinese economic reform proceeded without political reform, and was therefore fundamentally different from the economies in the former Soviet bloc when they made their transition to capitalism. But this view does not stand up to scrutiny. While China certainly did not follow the prescription of democratization, political reform in other forms took place after Mao's death. In the late 1970s and early 1980s when Deng repeatedly mentioned political democracy as an element of Chinese political reform, he meant to allow different voices inside the Party rather than multi-party competition. During the long history of China, there has rarely been a precedent for democracy in the sense of multi-party contest for political power. Nonetheless, China's economic reforms began with a major change of personnel and political ideology, which filled leading government positions with officials who were open-minded and eager for, or at least sympathetic to, reform.[12]

III

In tandem with the political transition, there was also a rapid economic transition.[13] On December 10th, 1976, at the Second National Agricultural Conference on "Learning from Dazhai" – a socialist model village that had gained its fame for hard work and collective spirit during the Cultural Revolution – Hua underscored economic development as a prerequisite for successful socialism. This was a significant departure from the ideology of the previous decade when poverty and a hard life had been praised as glorious features of socialism. Even though politically loyal to Mao, Hua rejected Mao's policy of treating politics in general, and class struggle in particular, as a priority for the government. Hua was keenly interested in reviving the stagnant economy and intended to project himself as an economic modernizer. Compared with Deng and other veterans who had indisputable revolutionary credentials, military expertise, and strong personal networks developed over decades of revolution, Hua was almost a novice and an outsider to Beijing politics. Not surprisingly, after taking power at the end of 1976, Hua wasted no time in building up his résumé in economic statecraft, reviving the project of "four modernizations," an economic program with a history all of its own.[14]

The "four modernizations" program – the modernization of agriculture, industry, defense, and science and technology – was first proposed by Premier Zhou Enlai in December 1964 at the Third National People's Congress before the drafting of the third Five Year Economic Plan (1966–1970).[15] It was meant to serve as a long-term economic development goal, to be achieved by the end of the twentieth century. But since the degree of modernization was never clearly specified, "four modernizations" was more of a battle call than an economic program. In addition, Zhou's proposal had barely left his desk before Mao threw China into the turmoil of the Cultural Revolution. But it later gained a distinctive political significance, serving as a broad banner to counterbalance Mao's radical ideology of class struggle and continuous revolution under the Dictatorship of the Proletariat.

Hua's endeavor to revitalize the program of "four modernizations" in 1976 was preceded by a similar attempt by Deng Xiaoping.[16] In January 1975, with the Cultural Revolution still ongoing, Deng re-endorsed "four modernizations" at the Fourth National People's Congress. Though Deng would lose his position at the end of that year, he would later present his short-lived effort of economic restructuring as a harbinger of post-Mao economic reform.[17]

IV

Amid the decade-long Cultural Revolution, 1971 was a turning point when Lin Biao died in a plane crash on September 13th.[18] Lin had been designated as Mao's successor in 1969 after the purge of Liu Shaoqi. Though Mao's faithful ally since the 1930s and a Marshal, Lin rose to political power only after the Lushan Meeting in 1959 when he led the attack on Peng Dehuai, who had dared to criticize the Great Leap Forward. It is unclear whether Peng was mainly a victim of Mao's arrogance and self-conceit, as commonly portrayed, or of a power struggle beneath Mao between Liu Shaoqi, then designated successor of Mao, and other ambitious officials, such as Lin Biao himself. Peng, in the end, lost his position as Minister of Defense to Lin; this was a position Peng had held after leading the Chinese army in the Korean War. During the first few years of the Cultural Revolution, with Mao's full support, Lin managed to remove all his opponents during his rise to become Mao's designated successor. But Lin's pursuit of power ended suddenly and dramatically. After a failed attempt by his son to assassinate Mao, Lin tried to fly out of China, but the plane crashed in Mongolia, with his wife, son, and two other staff members on board.[19]

Lin's betrayal was a big blow to Mao's health, from which he never recovered.[20] Mao had picked Lin as his deputy and tasked him with executing the Cultural Revolution, against the opposition of many of his marshals and generals, only to discover that he was plotting a coup. However, Lin's death created opportunities for change in both policy and personnel. Though not ready to end it entirely, Mao now allowed the Cultural Revolution to taper off. In March 1973, the disgraced Deng Xiaoping was called back to Beijing and appointed Vice Premier. A year later, Mao promoted Deng to First Vice Premier, against the wishes of his wife, Jiang Qing.[21]

After losing his official positions at the beginning of the Cultural Revolution, Deng had spent several years as a worker in a tractor factory in rural Jiangxi province. Away from Beijing and able to reflect on the political turmoil created by the Cultural Revolution, Deng had become more and more convinced of the absurdity of ideological radicalism. Upon his return to Beijing, Deng began a full campaign of rectification, striving to rid the economy of ideological radicalism and class struggle, and re-endorsing the "four modernizations" as the goal for the Chinese government.

Deng's economic rectification of 1974–1975 had several features.[22] First and foremost, it was a brief triumph of economic pragmatism over radical ideology. During those two years, a wide range of practical policies were put into place. Education and technology were eagerly embraced as indispensable tools for economic development. The establishment of private lots and other economic practices that improved incentives were revived or, at the least, restrictions on them were relaxed; previously they had been denounced as "capitalist tails." Against the wishes of the Gang of Four, Deng supported continuing the foreign trade that had begun in 1972 with the visit of Nixon to Beijing. The second feature of Deng's rectification was his recognition of political stability as a precondition for economic development. Deng believed that the political turmoil created by the Cultural Revolution had to be brought under control. Unlike Mao, Deng did not accept class struggle and political campaigns as the best way to preserve socialism. While living in the countryside for several years, Deng had realized that starvation and poverty not capitalism were the biggest challenges that China faced. But this basic economic problem had been ignored during the Cultural Revolution. Political campaigns had to be stopped and order restored, so Deng thought, to allow the government to concentrate on economic development. Political stability was seen as a necessity without which China could not focus on, let alone resolve, its basic economic problems. Third, while Deng rejected Mao's radical political ideology of class struggle, he shared Mao's mistrust of administrative centralization and wholeheartedly embraced the solutions Mao had set out in "On the Ten Major Relationships." This article reflected what Mao had learned from the Chinese experience of moving to a socialist system. It was the theoretical foundation for Mao's attempts to decentralize the Chinese economy and government administration. But even within the Party the article was not circulated until 1975, when Deng decided to promulgate it to legitimize his economic policy. But Mao refused to let the article go public, probably due to the danger it would pose to the ongoing Cultural Revolution.[23]

V

When he revived "four modernizations" as a cornerstone of economic policy, Hua decided to let the article "On the Ten Major Relationships" go public, something Deng had tried to do in the previous year, but to no avail. On December 26th, 1976, on the eighty-third anniversary of Mao's birth, the *People's Daily* published "On the Ten Major Relationships." Hua meant the document to provide both political legitimacy and practical guidance to his economic policy.[24] While he could be criticized for the lack of originality, Hua certainly did not let the economy remain at a "standstill," as is claimed by the official assessments of his economic record.[25] In fact, his enthusiasm for "four modernizations" and desire for rapid economic development led economist and veteran official Xue Muqiao to write a letter on April 18th, 1977 to Deng Xiaoping and Li Xiannian, expressing his concern about what had started to look like another leap forward.[26] Hua's economic program would later be disparagingly referred to as "the Leap Outward." But despite the many shortcomings in his short-lived economic policy, Hua, during the two years up to the Third Plenum of 1978, did manage to lead China away from Mao's radical ideology and towards renewed economic development. Hua had neither the ambition nor the political clout to carve out his own path, and his economic program failed to deliver on its promises. But to exclude him from the account of the post-Mao Chinese economic reform not only fails to do justice to Hua, but also ignores the early fumbling attempts of the post-Mao Chinese government to stage a state-centered reform.

The "Leap Outward" was officially launched at the end of 1977, and national production increased 7.6 percent in that year. Of eighty primary industrial products, new records were set for fifty-two.[27] The state revenue also reached a record high, exceeding the planned figure by 6 percent.[28] With this strong economic recovery, and unified by a burning desire to make up for the decade lost to the Cultural Revolution, Hua and his economic team, including Deng and Li Xiannian, decided to revive and revise the Ten Year Plan (1976–1985). This was the plan for economic development that Deng had outlined in 1975, but he had not had a chance to implement it before he was purged by Mao.

A common critique of the Ten Year Plan is that it was too ambitious to be viable, just like the Great Leap Forward. But a casual inspection of the Plan suggests otherwise. For examples, take the two primary products specified in the Plan: grain and steel. Two main targets of the Plan were to produce 400 billion kilograms of grain and 60 million tons of steel annually by 1985. In reality, the grain production reached 379 billion kilograms in 1985, falling short by 5.25 percent, but two years later it surpassed the goal of 400 billion. Steel production reached 46.8 million tons in 1985, falling short by 22 percent; it took another four years to reach 61.6 million tons.[29] The goals were not conservative, but unlike those of the Great Leap Forward, they were not completely detached from reality either. The Plan's fatal flaw lay elsewhere.

The Plan prescribed some 120 brand new industrial projects, including 30 power stations, 8 coal mining fields, 10 oil and gas fields, 10 chemical fertilizer complexes, 10 iron and steel complexes, 10 petrochemical complexes, 10 nonferrous metal complexes, 6 railroad lines, and several ports, all designed to shore up the planned economy by importing modern technology. The whole reform was state directed, investment driven, and concentrated on heavy industry. It differed little from the first Five Year Plan (1953–1957), which mainly consisted of 156 Soviet-aided industrial projects. Dwight Perkins, in his contribution to the *Cambridge History of China*, called this policy a "plan of the Soviet type par excellence" – that is an apt description.[30]

In their forecasts for the Plan, Hua and his economic team dramatically overestimated China's potential export revenues from raw materials, particularly oil, and underestimated the difficulty of raising money on the global capital market, the two primary sources of funding for the Plan. As a result, the whole program quickly ran into financial difficulties. Among the twenty-two projects launched in 1978 – including one restored from the previous wave of opening up in 1972 – only nine were completed.[31] More important, the whole reform was focused almost exclusively on the hardware of industrialization, such as equipment and production facilities. Little attention was paid to the prospective management of these facilities, or to the domestic capacity to absorb all this imported technology. There was also little consideration given to the links between the new industrial facilities, their upstream suppliers and their downstream customers. As a result, even those projects successfully completed were severely underutilized. Isolated from the rest of the economy, these public projects of industrialization also failed to generate any significant technological spillover.[32] With the double pressure of financial difficulty and disappointing performance, the "Leap Outward" was called off in April 1979 at a working conference of the Central Committee, organized by Chen Yun. An adamant lifelong critic of any economic "leap," Chen had lost his position under Mao because of his opposition to the Great Leap Forward. He returned in 1978 as China's economic czar at the Third Plenum of the Eleventh Central Committee and promoted a readjustment policy, advocating a period of economic retrenchment.

A positive feature of the "Leap Outward," and one that would set a lasting precedent, was to borrow money from the West to fund the import of new technology and equipment from the capitalist world.[33] Even though this policy was not completely new, Hua and his team were credited for pushing forward the idea to an unprecedented degree, specifically in their use of foreign capital.[34] Until 1977, China had been completely hostile toward foreign capital.[35] An article in *People's Daily* on January 2nd, 1977 explicitly prohibited the use of foreign capital.[36] This policy did not change until June 1978 when Vice Premier Gu Mu made a compelling case for the selective use of foreign capital in modernizing the Chinese economy. This won the endorsement of both Hua and Deng.[37] A month later, when the State Council held a brainstorming meeting in July, the use of foreign capital became a focal issue. A novice in the game, China was only able to take out small, short-term loans. Nonetheless, China was no longer closed to the global capital market. It lasted less than a year, but this attempt to open up the Chinese economy did much to educate the technocrats and government officials involved. It opened their eyes and minds to modern technology as well as to capitalism, and gave them the hands-on experience in working with foreign capital.[38]

Even though the "Leap Outward" was the most visible economic policy pursued during Hua's short tenure, other more effective reform policies were also implemented as part of the modernization program.[39] First, "commodity production and circulation," that is, production for exchange, became legal at the end of 1976. In a document issued on December 5th, the State Council allowed private commerce to return, which had previously been denounced as "capitalist" and eradicated from the Chinese economy. "We should boldly and assuredly improve socialist commodity production and circulation," urged the document.[40] Second, monetary incentives were reintroduced. In the previous decade, pecuniary rewards were condemned as a relic of capitalism and rarely used as an instrument to motivate workers and peasants. In August 1977, salaries were raised for the majority of workers. Bonus and piece-rate payments were reinstalled in May 1978. The price mechanism gradually returned in labor management, though labor mobility was still strictly controlled. Third, after a decade of political chaos, urban factories were the first target of "readjustment." Workplace disciplines, abolished in the previous decade, were reintroduced and ordered production was restored. Under the reign of Hua, socialist modernization came to replace class struggle as the main goal of the Chinese government.

VI

A crucial aspect of socialist modernization was to open up China to modern science, culture, and technology. Hua made this goal clear in his speech at the Fifth National People's Congress on February 26th, 1978: "to accelerate the development of socialist science and culture we must stick to the policy of 'making the past serve the present' and 'making things foreign serve China'. We must conscientiously try to study the advanced science and technology of all countries and turn them to our account."[41] During the Cultural Revolution, China pursued a policy of self-isolation in diplomacy and self-sufficiency in the economy. At the same time, ideological monopolization in the name of pursuing pure socialism led to the stifling of intellectual development. Even Marxism was held to be a finished theory rather than a developing school of thought. As a result, Chinese knowledge of market principles was almost nil, and what little did exist was often erroneous. In 1980 Milton Friedman visited China and gave a week-long intensive course in price theory to the brightest Chinese bureaucrats. One day, at lunch after the lecture, a minister from the Ministry of Materials Distribution and his chief associate, who were to form part of a Chinese delegation to the United States, wanted to know who they should talk to in the United States. The first question they asked was, "Tell us, who in the United States is responsible for the distribution of materials?"[42]

This intellectual isolation and closure would soon disappear. The post-Mao government quickly put an end to Mao's foreign policy of exporting revolution, and at the same time began to cultivate relations with its Asian neighbors and the developed world. The year 1978 became "the year of foreign diplomacy" for China. Official delegations headed by vice premiers and accompanied by central government officials, top provincial level officials, and managers of big state-owned enterprises made more than twenty visits to more than fifty countries all over the world, including Japan, Thailand, Malaysia, Singapore, the United States, Canada, Yugoslavia, Romania, France, Germany, Switzerland, Denmark, and Belgium. At the same time, China also hosted approximately thirty state visits.[43]

Hong Kong and Macau were among the first capitalist economies visited by Chinese officials in 1978. Gu Mu, Vice Premier in charge of economic planning, sent a delegation of officials from the Economic Planning Council and Ministry of Foreign Trade to Hong Kong and Macau to observe how capitalism operated. The idea of setting up special trade zones was suggested to the Chinese officials by their hosts there. As China's neighbor and the most developed economy in Asia, Japan hosted several Chinese delegations in 1978. The Chinese delegations were interested in Japan's agricultural development, modern industries, management, and international trade. The two countries signed a long-term trade agreement on February 26th, 1978.[44]

As the two leading exporters of agricultural products in the world, the United States and Canada also attracted Chinese officials. On July 25th, 1978, officials from Heilongjiang, Shaanxi, Shanxi, Shandong, and Tianjin as well as the Ministry of Agriculture and Forestry visited the United States. Over the next forty days, the delegation was much impressed with how the United States used modern technology to develop agriculture. In August, officials from the Ministry of Agriculture and Forestry and several state farms made a visit to Canada. They were particularly interested in Canada's dairy and poultry farms, as well as its agricultural colleges and research institutes.[45]

As an early reformer and critic of the Soviet economic model, Yugoslavia was another nation of great interest to Chinese visitors. Several Chinese delegations visited Yugoslavia in 1978, including Hua Gofeng himself in August of that year. In April, a delegation of the Chinese Communist Party headed by Li Yimeng, Yu Guanyuan, and Qiao Shi visited Yugoslavia to learn how its economy was managed. Yugoslavia's adamant rejection of Stalinism and successful experiment with the socialism of self-management convinced the Chinese visitors that the Soviet model did not represent the full potential of socialism and that a socialist economy could take different forms.[46] Soon after the visit, the Chinese Communist Party resumed its official relations with the League of Communists of Yugoslavia, officially recognizing Yugoslavia as a variant of socialism. In 1979 and 1980, visits were also paid to Poland, Hungary, and other Eastern European socialist countries. This exposure to different socialist economies opened up the minds of the Chinese leaders, whose knowledge of socialism had hitherto been limited to Stalinism and Maoism. After these visits, a number of economists from Eastern Europe, including Wlodzimierz Brus from Poland and Ota Sik from Czechoslovakia, were invited to visit China and give lectures to Chinese government officials and economists.

Probably the most influential and certainly the most eye-opening foreign visit was the one led by Gu Mu.[47] From May 2nd to June 6th, 1978, Gu Mu led a delegation of more than twenty officials, including several ministers and provincial officials from Beijing, Guangdong, and Shandong to visit France, Germany, Switzerland, Denmark, and Belgium. This was the first visit by Chinese government officials to Western Europe since 1949. They visited twenty-five cities, and more than eighty companies including mines, ports, farms, universities, and research institutes. Deng met Gu and other members before the trip, asking them to see as much as they could and to ask questions about how the host countries managed their economies. After the trip, Gu reported to the Politburo, as well as to Deng, Hua, and other senior leaders. He was also asked to make several presentations on their visits at various meetings, including one organized by the State Council on "four modernizations."

Deng himself visited Burma and Nepal early in 1978, North Korea in September, Japan in October, Thailand, Malaysia and Singapore in November 1978, and the United States in January 1979. Deng was deeply impressed by the modern technology and efficient management he saw in Japan. After his tour at Nissan, Deng told his host, "now I understand what modernization means."[48]

There is no doubt that such intensive exposure to the outside world, particularly to the West, served as a powerful catalyst for changes in Chinese attitudes to the market, to capitalism, and to economic development. For example, when visiting Singapore in November 1978, Deng inquired in detail about the working of foreign direct investment and its contribution to the rise of Singapore's economy. To the surprise of his host, Deng openly admitted mistakes the Communist government had made and earnestly sought advice from Lee Kuan Yew,

Singapore's founding and long-serving Prime Minister, on how to improve the Chinese economy. More than a decade later, Lee still remembered his meeting with Deng.

> I had told Deng over dinner in 1978 in Singapore that we, the Singapore Chinese, were the descendants of illiterate landless peasants from Guangdong and Fujian in South China, whereas the scholars, mandarins, and literati had stayed and left their progeny in China. There was nothing that Singapore had done that China could not do, and do better. He stayed silent then. When I read that he had told the Chinese people to do better than Singapore, I knew he had taken up the challenge I quietly tossed to him that night fourteen years earlier.[49]

This exposure to the outside world was not limited to those privileged government officials who actually made the visits. Delegations would write a report after their visit, which would later be circulated within the Party and even to the general public. A good example is a report written by Deng Liquan, Ma Hong, Sun Shangqing, and Wu Jiajun.[50] In a trip organized by the Economic Committee of the State Council, a group of twenty-three visited Japan for more than a month at the end of 1978, visiting forty-three companies in several cities, as well as households and schools in urban and rural areas. In their report, two recurring themes were prominent: economic failure was admitted but confidence in socialism remained high. The following quotes are characteristic:

> In line with Marxism, distribution according to need is impossible without an extreme expansion in commodity production. This is not beyond our reach, as seen from Japan. Capitalist Japan produced commodities in much more quantities and varieties than us. We are a socialist country. It is highly likely that we can reach their level of development and move beyond. (*ibid.*, p. 4)

> We are a socialist society. Our institution is much better than capitalism. But due to the lack of experience, we made mistakes in constructing socialism. As a result, the superiority of socialism has yet to be fully realized. The recent Third Plenary Session of the Eleventh Central Committee of CPC had summed up the basic lessons of building socialism in the past three decades, and at the same time called for learning from exemplary practices from abroad. We will certainly fulfill the goal of Four Modernizations by the end of this century as long as we follow the basic roadmap pointed out by the Party, work diligently, and utilize the advanced technology and managerial know-how to serve the purpose of socialism. (*ibid.*, p. 53)

During most of Mao's time, and particularly since the mid-1950s, capitalism had been condemned as evil and decadent, forever contrasted with progressive and superior socialism and its supposedly shining future. Due to strict media control and self-isolation, the ability of the Chinese people, even its leaders, to access information about the realities of capitalism was very limited. These visits to capitalist economies exposed Chinese leaders to capitalism for the first time and, as Deng Xiaoping admitted, revealed "what modernization means." Having seen that the workers and farmers in Japan seemed to enjoy a standard of living much higher than they themselves had, Chinese visitors could not possibly return to China believing the old official propaganda against capitalism. Shocked by the creativity and energy of capitalism, the Chinese visitors were ashamed of China's economic stagnation and depressing technological backwardness. The gap was simply too wide and the contrast too great for the visitors to deny their past failures.

Moreover, these visits provided the Chinese visitors with some clues about how they could escape from poverty and catch up with the capitalist world. For example, as Deng learnt from Singapore, foreign direct investment could help China to tap into the technological expertise and managerial know-how of capitalist institutions, and push China up the ladder of industrialization. That Japan and Western Europe had been able to recover so quickly from the devastation of the Second World War convinced the Chinese visitors that China could catch up if they could open up trade with the West and import modern science and technology.

VII

As China reopened its doors to the outside world, foreign trade grew quickly. In 1977, China's foreign trade (imports plus exports) was barely 14 billion USD. By way of comparison, Taiwan's trade was then 18 billion USD, South Korea's 21 billion USD, and Japan's 141 billion USD. In 1978, China increased its trade by 50 percent. In this progress, the role of Hong Kong was of great importance. According to Richard Wong, Hong Kong has served as "an agent of China's opening to the world."[51] On August 31st, 1978 the Hong Kong businessman K. P. Chao signed a contract to open a manufacturing plant in Zhuhai county, Guangdong province.[52] It was reported in headlines in Hong Kong newspapers and was the first such instance of foreign investment in post-Mao China. Two years later, the opening of the four Special Economic Zones in Guangdong and Fujian created more opportunities for overseas Chinese and foreigners in Hong Kong, Macau, Taiwan, and elsewhere to do business in China, bringing in capital, modern technologies, and access to the world market.

Immediately after the open-door policy, many consumer products made in Hong Kong, Taiwan, Japan, and elsewhere started to flow into China and became available to Chinese consumers for the first time. Economists use two names to distinguish this phase of China's open-door policy from the one pursued under Hua a few years earlier, export promotion versus import substitution. This new approach was to form a core component of economic reform in the decades to come. It differed from the "Leap Outward" policy pursued under Hua which was to import western technology and improve China's domestic industrial capacity so that China could produce a whole range of modern capital and consumer goods. But this conventional contrast between export promotion and import substitution tends to overshadow rather than highlight a critical difference. Under the "Leap Outward" policy, imported western technology was confined to a few selected state-owned enterprises; under trade promotion, modern science and technology as embodied in imported capital and consumer goods was available to virtually the whole of society.

It was this diffusion of knowledge under a trade-promotion policy, and its absence under the "Leap Outward" policy, that determined the different outcomes of the two economic policies. That the export promotion policy also capitalized on China's comparative advantage was not in doubt. But the ultimate advantage of the export promotion policy was its long-term impact on the diffusion and accumulation of knowledge, particularly of modern science and technology, which goes beyond the rather static logic of comparative advantage.

When China opened up to the world in the late 1970s, it lagged far behind the West in technology. Once the Chinese people became free to catch up, they quickly exploited the huge gains in economic efficiency created by the technological gap between China and the West. China was bound to become capitalist, as rightly predicted by Steven Cheung.[53] But the nature of that process was not something anyone could have predicted.

VIII

Few would have predicted that a communist party would embrace the market. But it is now widely accepted that the Chinese government has masterminded China's shift to a capitalist economy. What exactly did the Chinese government do to bring about such an extraordinary transformation?

There is no better place to look for the answer than the 1978 Communiqué, which was issued on the last day of an historic five-day meeting, the Third Plenum of the Eleventh Central Committee of the Chinese Communist Party held in Beijing from December 18th to 22nd. This meeting is now widely recognized as a watershed in the history of the People's Republic of China and the beginning of China's post-Mao economic reform. This document, while evasive when it came to Mao's mistakes, was unusually explicit in admitting the past failures of the Party, and candid in stating the goals of economic reform.[54]

The Communiqué made it clear that it was imperative to "shift the emphasis of our Party's work and the attention of the people of the whole country to socialist modernization."[55] This implied a break with the doctrine of class struggle, which had been pursued by Mao for decades and resulted in the persecution of millions of Party and government officials and intellectuals. The Communiqué recognized that Maoist policy had resulted in "a series of problems left hanging for years as regards the people's livelihood in town and country."[56] Accompanying the shift in focus from class struggle to socialist modernization was the acceptance of material remuneration. Rejecting Mao's dependence on revolutionary zeal as the workers' and peasants' primary motivation, the Communiqué sanctioned and promoted material interests. "It is imperative to improve the livelihood of the people in town and country step by step on the basis of the growth of production. The bureaucratic attitude of paying no attention at all to urgent problems in the people's livelihood must be resolutely opposed."[57] If it were not for this change in attitude, Deng's famous mantra, "let some people get rich first," would have been unthinkable.

The Communiqué also stressed an underlying flaw of the existing economic system, the over-centralization of power. This echoed the central point that Mao made in "On the Ten Major Relationships." As the Communiqué put it, "The fundamental policy put forth in the report On the Ten Major Relationships which Comrade Mao Zedong made in 1956 is an objective reflection of economic law and also an important guarantee for the political stability of society."[58] Not surprisingly, the prescription given in the Communiqué also followed Mao's example. It stated that

one of the serious shortcomings in the structure of economic management in our country is the over-concentration of authority, and it is necessary boldly to shift it under guidance from the leadership to lower levels so that the local authorities and industrial and agricultural enterprises will have greater power of decision in management under the guidance of unified state planning; big efforts should be made to simplify bodies at various levels charged with economic administration and transfer most of their functions to such enterprises as specialized companies or complexes; it is necessary to act firmly in line with economic law, ... it is necessary, under the centralized leadership of the Party, to tackle conscientiously the failure to make a distinction between the Party, the government and the enterprise and to put a stop to the substitution of Party for government and the substitution of government for enterprise administration, to institute a division of responsibilities among different levels, types of work and individuals, increase the authority and responsibility of administrative bodies and managerial personnel, reduce the number of meetings and amount of paper work to raise work efficiency, and conscientiously adopt the practice of examination, reward and punishment, promotion and demotion. These measures will bring into full play the initiative, enthusiasm and creativeness of four levels, the central departments, the local authorities, the enterprises and the workers, and invigorate all branches and links of the socialist economy.[59]

The Communiqué specifically singled out agriculture as the weakest link in the chain. "The whole Party should concentrate its main energy and efforts on advancing agriculture as fast as possible because agriculture, the foundation of the national economy, has been seriously damaged in recent years and remains very weak on the whole."[60] However, the remedy it proposed was nothing more than a modification of price control:

the State Council make a decision to raise the grain purchase price by twenty percent, starting in 1979 when the summer grain is marketed, and the price of the amount purchased above the quota by an additional fifty percent, and also raise the purchase price for cotton, oil-bearing and sugar crops, animal by-products, aquatic and forestry products and other farm and side-line products step by step, depending on the concrete conditions. The factory price and the market price of farm machinery, chemical fertilizer, insecticides, plastics goods and other manufactured goods for farm use will be cut by ten to fifteen percent in 1979 and 1980 on the basis of reduced cost of production.[61]

The Chinese government expected socialist modernization to be a "new Long March" and "a profound and extensive revolution," which would call for concerted and continuous efforts. To achieve the goal, the basic approach recommended in the Communiqué was clear enough to be instructive, but left sufficient room to accommodate local initiatives.

Carrying out the four modernizations requires great growth in the productive forces, which in turn requires diverse changes in those aspects of the relations of production and the superstructure not in harmony with the growth of the productive forces, and requires changes in all methods of management, actions and thinking which stand in the way of such growth. Socialist modernization is therefore a profound and extensive revolution.[62]

It is also worthwhile to note that, according to the Communiqué, "changes in all methods of management, actions and thinking" should serve only "the growth of the productive forces."[63] In later years, the effect on "the growth in the productive forces" would be used as the primary criterion by which to judge a reform policy or practice.

While the long-term goal of reform was clearly articulated – "to make ours [China] a modern, powerful socialist country before the end of this century"[64] – there was no grand strategy or blueprint in the Communiqué. Knowing almost nothing about the markets or the market economy, the Chinese government never used the term at all in the Communiqué.[65] It has now become common practice to take the Third Plenum of the Eleventh Central Committee of the Chinese Communist Party as the starting point of Chinese market transformation. Without denying the historical significance of this meeting and the 1978 Communiqué, it is important to realize that the Chinese leaders did not even contemplate a market economy at that time. But their minds were open. They were prepared to try anything that would help "the growth of productive forces," and subject everything to the test of practice, or so they claimed.

To put the 1978 Communiqué in historical context, we must be clear that China's post-Mao economic reform was not the first effort of the Chinese Communist Party to reorganize the socialist economy. Mao's two campaigns of decentralization, the first launched in the mid-1950s and the second during the Cultural Revolution, failed to rejuvenate the socialist economy. In the aftermath of the Cultural Revolution, Mao's reliance on class conflict and continuous revolution to preserve socialism had proved quixotic and ruinous. While his solution to the embattled state of China's socialism – decentralization – might still remain ambiguous, the Chinese economy became far less centralized than other socialist economies. Moreover, Mao's diagnosis of the root problem facing the socialist Chinese economy was endorsed as one of the lasting legacies of the Communiqué.

As an economic strategy, the Communiqué did not go much beyond what Mao had proposed in "On the Ten Major Relationships." It agreed with Mao fully in his diagnosis of the most serious problem facing a socialist economy: over-centralization. In contrast to Mao's thinking, however, the Communiqué's first priority was "the growth of productive forces," or, in non-Marxian terms, economic development. But even this emphasis on economic development, or the pursuit of "four modernizations," merely revived an economic program first proposed by Zhou Enlai in 1964. Another way in which the Communiqué differed from Mao's thinking was the new solution it proposed to resolve the problem of over-centralization: devolving authority to enterprises in addition to local governments.

As a political strategy, the Communiqué was a work of genius. It began by praising Mao as "a great Marxist" and urged that the whole nation should "rally even more closely under the banner of Mao Zedong thought," only to turn the focus of the Party away from his doctrine of class struggle toward socialist modernization as the unifying mission for the whole country. Its stated goal was to make China "a great, modern, socialist power"[66] by the end of the twentieth century, which no one could possibly object to. The continuing commitment to Marxism-Leninism-Mao Zedong Thought helped to avoid ideological chaos and maintain the political stability necessary for economic reform. Given the enduring respect for Mao within the Party, the military, and the general public, a total repudiation and rejection of Mao would have undermined the legitimacy of the post-Mao government and sown the seeds for political disorder. In a calculated maneuver, the post-Mao Chinese leadership praised Mao so that they could quickly bury Mao's radical policies and move on to economic development. By re-stressing Mao's forgotten principle of "seeking truth from facts" and embracing practice as the sole criterion for testing truth, the Chinese government freed itself from the shackles of his ideology.

IX

In the two years between Mao's death and the Third Plenum, China made a decisive move away from Mao's radicalism. The death of Mao threw China into crisis, clouded by political uncertainty. With the support of Ye and other military veterans, Hua brought down the Gang of Four, ended the Cultural Revolution, and quickly restored political order. More importantly, China reopened itself to the outside world, welcoming technology, capital, and the ideas and practices of the market. At the same time, Hua gradually but decisively shifted the focus of the government away from the radical ideology of continuous revolution towards socialist modernization. This shift was further consolidated at the Third Plenum with the return of Deng Xiaoping to the Party leadership. Although the Communiqué did not contain an economic blueprint for the pursuit of socialist modernization, it manifested political wisdom in marshaling all social groups to stand beneath the banner of Mao Zedong Thought to enable China to embark on the course of socialist modernization. It was actually quite fortunate that the Communiqué did not prescribe any specific measures, with the exception of agriculture. Given how poorly informed the Chinese leaders were at the time, any prescriptions would probably have done more harm than good. But now the Chinese government was committed to a pragmatic approach, willing to subject everything to the test of practice, and eager to try anything that facilitated "the growth of productive forces." China may have been poorly equipped for a market revolution, but it was certainly mentally prepared.

3
How China's Market Reform Began

The Third Plenum of the Eleventh Central Committee of the Chinese Communist Party was a decisive event in the history of the People's Republic; it re-consolidated the power of the Party and paved the way for the reunification of a fractured society. The decisions made there would re-channel the energy, enthusiasm, and creativity of the Chinese people from the politics of class conflict to socialist modernization. At the end of 1978, China once again stood at a historic moment as it had done in 1949. This time, China would be more fortunate. Both the Chinese government and academic circles worldwide view the Third Plenum as the beginning of China's market transformation, the genesis of the extraordinary story that unfolded in the following three decades, as the world's most populous country turned from a poor, stagnant socialist economy into one of the world's most dynamic economies.[1] It is, however, tempting to read too much into this watershed event – to think that the historical significance of the Third Plenum was preordained. After all, it did not set in motion a chain of events that meticulously brought about China's great market transformation. Rather, it was the transformation itself that elevated the Third Plenum to historical prominence as the most recognizable turning point in the history of the People's Republic. Had China's economic reforms been unsuccessful, the Third Plenum would have been just another wishful attempt by the Chinese leadership to modernize the economy.

In any case, China did not wait until the end of 1978 to begin its reforms. During the two years between Mao's death in September 1976 and the Third Plenum in December 1978, China had already closed the door on Mao's radical ideology and embraced economic development as its first priority. The Cultural Revolution was ended after the arrest of the Gang of Four, and socialist modernization quickly became the primary concern of Hua and the new Chinese government. The economic program of "four modernizations" was revived in 1976; the Leap Outward was launched a year later. Under the initiatives of

Hu Yaobang, hundreds of thousands of Party officials and "rightists" purged during the Cultural Revolution were rehabilitated. Many resumed leadership positions, where they quickly became the foremost exponents of reform.

In his role as head of the Central Party School and as the editor of *Theoretical Trends*, Hu played a key role in early reform by weakening the influence of Marxist ideology on public opinion. *Theoretical Trends* served as a powerful mouthpiece for new ideas. The article "Practice is the only criterion for testing truth" ignited a far-reaching political debate. By the end of 1978 when the Third Plenum was held in Beijing, practice had prevailed, replacing Mao's little red book and Marxism. This shift in ideology was later recognized as the first "massive mind emancipation" in the history of the People's Republic.[2]

China had also begun to open up to the outside world immediately after the end of the Cultural Revolution. Chinese leaders made many trips abroad to rebuild relations ignored or damaged during the previous decade and to see for themselves the gap that had emerged between China and the modern world. The normalization of Sino-US relations on January 1st, 1979 and Deng's visit to the United States shortly afterward were powerful catalysts in China's reconciliation with the West. Ironically, after Chinese leaders were exposed to, and expressed admiration for, the economic dynamism of capitalism in Asia, Europe, and the United States, they became more committed to socialism. They believed its inherent superiority would enable China to modernize its economy even faster than the West had done, but only if China was able to appropriate the innovative strength of capitalism. These views were reinforced at the Third Plenum. With the promulgation of the 1978 Communiqué and the return of Deng Xiaoping and Chen Yun to the center of the Party, the ongoing political and economic changes gained further momentum.

Immediately after the Third Plenum, the Chinese government began a series of reforms, focused on what was perceived to be one of the weakest areas of the Chinese socialist economy, the state-owned enterprises. As the 1978 Communiqué admitted, "one of the serious shortcomings in the structure of economic management [in China] is the over-concentration of authority."[3] Consequently, more authority would be devolved to both local authorities and economic organizations so that "the local authorities and industrial and agricultural enterprises will have greater power of decision in management under the guidance of unified state planning."[4] But the idea of devolving authority directly to enterprises was totally unprecedented. After seeing Mao's previous attempts at administrative decentralization fail to revitalize the economy, Chinese leaders wanted to try a different approach. At a meeting held by the State Council in September 1978 Li Xiannian expressed his regret that earlier attempts at reforming China's economic system had devolved power to local governments, while enterprises had become still more shackled by red tape and rigidity.[5]

But the idea of enterprise autonomy was not new, at least among academics. Gu Zhun and Sun Yefang were the first Chinese economists to criticize the Soviet model of economic planning and stress the relevance of economic principles to socialism.[6] Both men argued that state-owned enterprises should become autonomous and pursue profits. As early as 1956, Gu had stressed the indispensability of the market and production for exchange under socialism. A year later, he was denounced as a "rightist" and spent most of his later life in prisons and re-education centers.[7] Gu did not survive the Cultural Revolution, dying of cancer in 1974. In Sun's view, the Achilles' heel of the Chinese socialist economy was the lack of autonomy of state-owned enterprises, and not centralization as Mao believed, nor decentralization as Mao's critics thought.[8] In 1961, Sun criticized the administrative decentralization approach favored by Mao and was promptly labeled "China's biggest revisionist"; he was imprisoned for seven years during the Cultural Revolution. After Mao's death, however, these ideas resurfaced and were to win the support of Chinese leaders.[9]

I

This change in approach from administrative decentralization to enterprise autonomy was vindicated by what the Chinese visitors had observed during their overseas trips. What impressed the Chinese delegations the most was the efficiency and dynamism within capitalist companies. In contrast to Nissan, which impressed Deng Xiaoping the most during his visit to Japan in 1978, China's firms were notoriously inefficient and mired in endless bureaucratic complexities. Not surprisingly, the Chinese leaders took enterprise reform as a key component to revitalizing the socialist economy after the Third Plenum. An editorial in the *People's Daily* on February 19th, 1979, which represented the official position of the Chinese government, stressed that "the most urgent task for the current economic reform is to expand the autonomy of big state-owned enterprises."[10] In the next few years, enterprise reform became the focal point of economic reform, and in particular the issues of devolving power to state-owned enterprises and allowing them to retain profits.[11]

For local authorities familiar with everyday economic realities, it was obvious that improving the performance of the state-owned enterprises was fundamental to the problems facing the Chinese socialist economy. Even before the Third Plenum, the reform of state-owned enterprises had begun. The first case was reported in October 1978 in Sichuan province headed by Zhao Ziyang, who was later promoted to premier in 1980 for his pioneering reforms.[12] The reform essentially curtailed the power exercised by various government departments over state-owned enterprises; this amounted to a transfer of some decision-making responsibilities to the managerial staff. For example, enterprises were now able to appoint middle-level managers (though not to lay off employees), to retain a certain amount of profits, and increase production beyond that specified in the state plan. These reforms gained more impetus after the Third Plenum. By early 1979, the number of enterprises under reform had reached a hundred in Sichuan alone.[13] In addition, fifty enterprises in neighboring Yunnan province joined.[14] Based on Sichuan's successful experience, in May 1979 the State Council selected eight large state-owned enterprises, including the flagship enterprise Capital Steel company as well as others based in Beijing, Shanghai, and Tianjin, to experiment with similar enterprise reform. By the end of 1979, more than 4200 large state-owned enterprises had been enlisted.[15] By 1981, there were more than 6600 state-owned enterprises, spread across China (with the exception of Tibet).

In addition to devolving decision-making powers to enterprises, other measures were also taken to further the reform of industry. It had become widely recognized that state-owned enterprises suffered from two crushing constraints. First, deprived of basic managerial autonomy, state-owned enterprises had become pawns of various state agents. They could not decide what and how much to produce, who to hire or lay off, how much to invest, or how to compensate managers and workers. In fact, state-owned enterprises were enterprises in name only. Accordingly, the first attempt to reform state-owned enterprises was to make them more autonomous and like real enterprises.

The second encumbrance was the fragmented industrial structure. Due to Mao's repeated attempts to make each locality (from regions to provinces to counties) as self-sufficient as possible, Chinese state-owned enterprises were small in scale but vast in number, and often completely isolated from each other. Even upstream and downstream firms in the same industry rarely interacted with each other directly, but would communicate through the government bureaucracy. State-owned enterprises in a locality thus formed a cluster under the local government.[16] To address this structural problem, in July 1980 the State Council issued a provisional stipulation calling for integration and consolidation among state-owned enterprises.[17] In machinery manufacturing (the most fragmented industry of Mao's era), the National Committee on Machinery in early 1981 encouraged the state-owned enterprises to merge. This campaign even reached the government bureaucracy. By 1982 the National Bureau of Machinery was formed, consolidating four preexisting bureaucracies into one.[18]

In addition to industrial reforms targeted at enterprises and industrial structure, the State Council also earmarked whole cities for experiment with the "National Comprehensive Economic System Reform."[19] In October 1981 Shashi, a city of 243,000 people in Hubei province, became the first of these. In March 1982, Changzhou of Jiangsu province, another city of similar size, became the second. In February 1983, Chongqing of Sichuan province became the first sizeable city to experiment with comprehensive economic reform. In May, several more large cities were added to this project. These cities – Wuhan, Shenyang, Dalian, Harbin, Guangzhou, and Xi'an – each had populations in the millions. As a pioneering city at this stage of industrial reform, the otherwise obscure Shashi left its mark on the history of Chinese economic reform. Shashi was the first city to implement reform measures such as: consolidating firms to take advantage of economies of scale and scope; allowing enterprises to decide what to produce; allowing flexibility in labor management; and introducing the managerial responsibility system. The whole episode of "comprehensive economic system reform" is scarcely documented and has received the least scholarly attention,[20] partly because of its inconspicuous performance relative to the Special Economic Zones. Nonetheless, these pilot city reforms, together with enterprise and industrial structure reforms, clearly demonstrate the concerted efforts of the Chinese government in the late 1970s and early 1980s to institute industrial reform.

In general, enterprises responded quickly and positively to the reform measures. Expanded managerial autonomy encouraged enterprises to increase production and improve efficiency. This gave rise to income growth for the workers, who had not seen any increase in their wages for many years. At the end of 1980, a managerial responsibility contract system was introduced to guarantee the autonomy of managers while detailing their specific responsibilities. At the strategic level, the most important and lasting legacy of industrial reform was to end the monopoly of state planning in coordinating industrial production. After state quotas had been fulfilled, state-owned enterprises could now decide what to produce. This provided opportunities for the socialist economy to "grow out of the plan."[21] When state-owned enterprises started producing goods outside the constraints of state planning, they became subject to the sway of market forces. This gave rise to a distinctive feature of Chinese economic reform, known as the "dual-track" system; the coexistence of central planning with the market in coordinating production in the state sector.[22] As a result, China's dominant state sector and its lack of privatization did not prevent the emergence of a fledgling market mechanism.

However, despite the progress of industrial reform, the economy as a whole had hardly improved, at least when judged by the conventional short-term macro indicators. On the contrary, since the enterprises now retained profits for investment and employee compensation, government tax revenue declined. The government slipped into deficit and the threat of inflation became very real. In 1979, the deficit reached 17 billion yuan, an alarmingly unprecedented level, and it remained high (12.8 billion) the next year. The overall price index went up 6 percent in 1980; in cities it went up more than 8 percent.[23] This level of inflation was deemed highly dangerous by the Chinese government, which viewed inflation as an evil of capitalism and had long been accustomed to price fluctuations of around 1 percent. The Chinese economy was then still recovering from the financial difficulties created by the Leap Outward, and either deficit or inflation could easily have derailed the fragile economy and threatened political stability. The Chinese government was forced to introduce an adjustment policy and put the reform agenda on hold. The first wave of the post-Third Plenum reform measures pushed by the Chinese government ended with disappointment; it had led to no real breakthrough.

II

While the state-led reforms stalled, real change was smoldering along the margins of the socialist economy. The most significant developments were to occur not at the core of the socialist economy but on its periphery, where state control was at its weakest. The real pioneers were not state-owned enterprises, the privileged actors and jewels of socialism, but the disadvantaged and marginalized. On the fringe of government bureaucracy and excluded from state planning, they had suffered the worst of the existing system. Nonetheless, it was at the margins of the Chinese economy that a concatenation of revolutions brought private actors back to the economy, paving the way for a market transformation. China became capitalist with marginal revolutions.

The most significant of these marginal revolutions erupted in agriculture, the weakest sector of the Chinese economy. In Mao's era Chinese agriculture had suffered badly, including during the catastrophe of the Great Leap Forward. Compared with industry, agriculture had been chronically underfunded. Worse, profits generated in agriculture had been diverted to subsidize industrialization, through savings forced upon the rural population and artificially depressed prices for agricultural products. As a result, starvation had been a problem for a large section of the rural population and was a looming threat for the Chinese government during Mao's time. These problems were acknowledged in the 1978 Communiqué. Accordingly, the Chinese government in 1979 significantly increased the prices paid for major agricultural products and subsidized the use of chemical fertilizers to boost agricultural production. Such measures were effective in increasing agricultural output.

But the real agricultural reforms, decollectivization and the rise of the household responsibility system, developed from the bottom upwards.

The first recorded incidence of private farming in post-Mao China occurred in Pengxi county of Sichuan province, in a village called "Nine Dragon Hill."[24] This village was one of the poorest in Qunli Commune, widely known in the region as a "village of beggars." One evening in September 1976, Deng Tianyuan, the Party secretary of the commune, summoned a small group of cadres to discuss the problem of agricultural production. After a long and heated debate, they agreed to try private farming as a solution to the managerial and incentive problems that had dogged collective farming. Aware of the political risk, they decided to allocate only marginal land to households in two production teams, while keeping collective farming intact elsewhere. That year, the output of the marginal but privately cultivated land was three times higher than that of the collectively cultivated fertile land. The next year, more land was privatized in more production teams. By 1978, before the Third Plenum was held in Beijing, private farming was practiced across the whole commune, but was kept secret from the local authorities. In 1979, at a meeting organized by the county government to discuss improvements in agriculture, Deng Tienyuan disclosed the secret of Nine Dragon Hill's success and won the endorsement of the county Party secretary. The following year, a delegation from the Ministry of Agriculture and Forestry visited Nine Dragon Hill. While he criticized private farming in principle, the head of the delegation praised Deng Tianyuan for improving agricultural production and even proposed considering the village as an experimental site for private farming.

The much better known case of Small Hill village in Anhui province, which has been documented in textbooks and the official account of agricultural reform as the pioneer of private farming, actually took place more than two years later.[25] Like Nine Dragon Hill in Sichuan, Small Hill was also known regionally as a "village of beggars." Here, it was peasants themselves rather than local cadres who initiated change. At the end of 1978, eighteen peasants in the village secretly signed an agreement to experiment with private farming, and sidestep the production teams.[26] At the time of harvest, peasants at this village collected so much more grain than their neighbors that many nearby villages were persuaded to join them in private farming the following season.

In addition to private farming, which was prohibited by government policy, there were milder forms of agricultural reform in many provinces. After the death of Mao, Chinese agricultural policy continued to be based on the fundamental principle of central planning. "In agriculture, learn from Dazhai" and "grain is the key link" were still held as guidelines for agriculture. The most damaging defect of this policy was to impose a model developed in the village of Dazhai on the whole nation.[27] This denied local governments the freedom to take into account local circumstances. For example, areas with hardly any arable land were forced to concentrate their efforts on grain production. Developing alternative streams of income, such as fishery, animal husbandry, and forestry, was criticized as capitalist and was outlawed. In the campaign to use local resources to develop the rural economy, Chi Biqing of Guizhou, Wan Li of Anhui, and Zhao Ziyang of Sichuan were the most vocal. As early as 1977, Chi, Wan, and Zhao, as provincial Party secretaries, encouraged local government officials to allow peasants the freedom to explore all opportunities available to increase their incomes. Once peasants were allowed to engage in pursuits other than grain production, it not only helped to expand their sources of income, but also increased efficiency in grain production. At the end of 1970s and early 1980s, a popular saying, "Go to Wan Li if you want rice; Go to Ziyang if you want grain," attested to the success of their efforts.[28]

After the Third Plenum, the development of fishery, forestry, animal husbandry, and craftsmanship was encouraged. Commune and brigade enterprises were also encouraged to revive the rural economy. Private farming, however, remained illegal. Two documents on agriculture that were passed at the Third Plenum singled out private farming as a criminal activity, "Decisions of the Central Committee of the Chinese Communist Party on Some Questions Concerning the Acceleration of Agricultural Development" and "Regulations on the Work in the Rural People's Communes." The ban on private farming was maintained throughout 1979. On March 15th, 1979, the *People's Daily* published a reader's letter from Henan province, along with an endorsing editorial, castigating private farming for eroding socialism in rural China.[29] It called on peasants and local government officials to stand firm against the encroachment of capitalism. The letter and editorial might have ended private farming in Anhui, if not for the staunch support of local authorities, particularly Wan Li.[30] At the Fourth Plenum held in September 1979, the government passed a document that stated that "distributing land for individual farming shall not be allowed" and "contracting output quota to each household shall not be practiced."[31] Nonetheless, private farming continued to develop in many disguised forms.

Throughout 1979, Wan Li took every opportunity he had to explain and defend private farming. A year later, leaders in Beijing began to change their position. By the late spring of 1980, Chen Yun, Hu Yaobang, and Deng Xiaoping had become convinced of the advantages of private farming. However, not all were in favor. In September, the Party reached a compromise, issuing a resolution that allowed private farming only "in those remote mountainous areas and poverty-stricken backward regions and in those production teams that have long been relying on state-resold grain for food, loans for production, and social relief," and only "if the masses have lost their confidence in the collective." In other words, decollectivization was allowed only where the collective economy had failed. The political reasons for this are not difficult to fathom. The main fear engendered by decollectivization was its potential to damage socialism, which was believed to rest upon collective ownership. But in rural areas where "the masses [had] lost their confidence in the collective," there was little socialism for private farming to damage. Thus, in poverty-stricken areas where socialism had been an abject failure, the political cost of reform was essentially negative. In its efforts to minimize the potential political fallout from agricultural reform, the Chinese government had inadvertently opened the door to revolution at the weakest part of the socialist economy, where resistance to reform was nonexistent.

Even before Beijing relaxed its ban on private farming in 1980, the practice had already been adopted in many places across rural China. It was exactly because of this challenge that the Chinese government decided to soften its policy. The case of Small Hill village, forcefully promoted by Wan Li, had played a significant political role in the defense of private farming. But even after the ban on private farming was first lifted in 1980, it took more than a year of intensive debate before the Chinese government officially recognized private farming in January 1982. The ideological resistance to private farming was so strong partly because Mao had repeatedly singled out private farming as a characteristically capitalist practice, which he believed would undermine the socialist goal of shared prosperity and economic equality. Proponents of private farming evoked its undeniable effectiveness in raising peasants' morale and increasing agricultural production. If practice really was to be the only criterion of testing truth, private farming would have to be accepted as superior to collective farming. Pragmatism eventually prevailed and private farming was promoted afterwards as a national policy.

The official account of agricultural reform sees private farming emerging clandestinely in Anhui alone and then being imposed on the rest of the country by the central government.[32] But this interpretation is misleading. Not only did private farming occur more than two years earlier in Sichuan, but, more importantly, the practice must have been under-reported before it was officially sanctioned by the Chinese government. The other known cases occurred in the provinces of Guizhou, Gansu, Inner Mogolia, and Henan.[33] But private farming must have emerged elsewhere.[34] Without broad popular support, the agricultural reform could not have proceeded as quickly and smoothly as it did.

It is easier to understand the rapid development of private farming in rural China if we realize that the practice was not new. After Mao's push for collectivization in agriculture, China witnessed at least three periods when private farming was revived.[35] The first was in 1956 right after collectivization and rural cooperatives were first launched. Supported by Deng Zihui, then Vice Premier in charge of agriculture, private farming was widely practiced in many provinces and discussed favorably in the *People's Daily*. Yongjia county in Zhejiang was the most publicized case then. But this tolerance of private farming had been reversed by 1957 and Deng Zihui was criticized harshly by Mao. The second instance was in late 1958 and early 1959, during the Great Leap Forward; many peasants resorted to private farming simply to survive. It emerged in several provinces, including Hubei, Hunan, Henan, Jiangsu, and Gansu, only to be quashed after the Lushan Meeting in July 1959. The third occurrence was in the early 1960s, after the failure of the Great Leap Forward had become clear. As a temporary solution to grain shortages, private farming was encouraged in many provinces across the country. However, even though Mao was initially supportive, private farming came under renewed political attack in mid-1962. Nonetheless, the practice survived under disguised forms in many places.[36]

It is also worth noting that private farming was not a single practice, but an umbrella name for a family of non-collective farming practices that had emerged spontaneously in rural China.[37] Collective farming was an extreme form of socialist agricultural management where farming was organized by production teams (or communes, as during the Cultural Revolution), with households treated as employees. State farms exemplified such extreme form of agricultural production. At the other extreme, farming was privately managed by each household, with the production team acting simply as a landlord. In between there was a rich variety of intermediate contractual forms, where the rights and responsibilities of the household vis-à-vis the production team were specified. All they really had in common was their departure from Mao's model of pure collective farming. When the Chinese government adopted private farming as a national policy, this diversity was lost. The household responsibility system, implemented nationwide since 1982, virtually eliminated production teams in rural China, except in a handful of places where collective farming survived in one form or another, including the famous Daqiu Village in Tianjin and Huaxi Village in Jiangsu. The household then became the only actor in farming.

III

This imposed uniformity is understandable from the perspective of policymaking and implementation. It would certainly have been far more onerous to accommodate multiple forms of farming and associated contractual arrangements. In an extreme but not unlikely scenario, some local cadres might simply have stuck to the status quo if given the choice, which would have effectively foiled the reform efforts. Imposing a uniform household responsibility system nationwide and disbanding production teams was an effective means of pushing forward agricultural reform in a top-down fashion. But once the household responsibility system was promoted as a national policy, the continuing presence of collective farming was deemed a direct challenge to the state agricultural policy. As a result, even collective farming that had performed well was under political pressure to close down.[38]

But from the perspective of institutional change, this imposed uniformity and forced breakdown of production teams was undoubtedly a setback. Before the socialist transformation in the 1950s, the family had always been the basic social unit and organizational form in rural China. Despite its disappointing performance in agriculture, Mao's socialist experiment at least ushered in an organizational revolution in rural China. For the first time in its long history, rural China saw the rise of corporate organizations not based on family ties – the production teams, brigades, and communes. Even though this organizational revolution was largely imposed by the state, it created a new organizational infrastructure beyond family, kinship, and clan ties in rural China.

In technological change, the most recent technological innovation often renders what existed beforehand outdated or even totally obsolete. The rise of personal computers with user-friendly word processing functions, for example, has made typewriters of little use today. A new generation of computer chips often supersedes and replaces the previous one. But institutional change follows a different logic. Institutions are multifaceted and too complicated to be ranked on any single scale. Institutional diversity is more conducive to innovation.

Compared with an agrarian society, a modern society is organization-intensive, depending on a wide range of formal and informal organizations coordinating with each other through rules and norms, including prices.[39] Moreover, organizations are often specialized and differ from each other in many and various ways. The constitutive rules that create organizations and specify what they can and cannot do, as well as the regulative rules that guide and police interactions among organizations, also differ. This richness and diversity in organizations, including in the ways they are formed and behave, is an important source of flexibility and resilience in social and economic life. Since production teams and communes were created in rural China by decree of the state, they did not have much organizational diversity. Nonetheless, they would have had a comparative advantage over the household for certain tasks that required collective effort, such as irrigation. Even in farming, the production team would have had to adjust and behave more efficiently to compete effectively with private farming, as shown in a few cases where production teams survived. The total disbanding of the production team in rural China amounted to the destruction of China's own scarce organizational capital.[40]

In the marginal revolution that ultimately privatized agricultural production throughout rural China, peasants and local authorities were the initiators and developers. It was a bottom-up process. Private farming re-emerged in rural China even when Beijing was still firmly opposed to the practice, as it was deemed inimical to socialism. While reform measures taken by Beijing, such as the increase in the purchasing price of grain, certainly helped the recovery of agricultural production, what ultimately brought life and character to Chinese agricultural reform came from the grassroots. The two "villages of beggars" in Sichuan and Anhui are simply two recorded examples among many where private farming re-emerged triumphantly against strong political opposition. Similar incidents of private farming with the passive acquiescence of local cadres must have occurred elsewhere and their main impact was in easing the introduction of the household responsibility system.

Nonetheless, the role of the state was still critical in sanctioning an institutional revolution that started from below. Before private farming was approved by the state, peasants had been constantly worried about the legitimacy of the practice and their own safety, and hesitant to make any long-term investment. The joint efforts of peasants, who had knowledge and experience, and the state, which was the only legitimate party with coercive power to turn a voluntary agreement into a social institution, formed an effective private–public partnership to bring about an institutional change.

Institutions that emerge spontaneously take a long time to become established, that is, to be settled in the mind of the people and incorporated as part of their habits of thought and action. Institutions developed in this way are shaped by the influence of local conditions and the spirit of the times, and this gives rise to the diversity of institutions. At the same time, institutional evolution can easily be disrupted by war, social unrest, and natural disaster. Consequently, it is a gradual but hazardous process, full of uncertainty. Political power can step in and speed up the process of institutional change without necessarily subjugating it to its authority. Once an emerging institution is endorsed by a legitimate and credible state, it can readily stand out as a common point of reference and act as a guide for relevant social actors, at least in the short run. How long a state-sponsored institution can survive depends on its perceived performance relative to expectation, as well as the strength of the state's commitment to protect it against resistance. The state faces a delicate dilemma. It can facilitate institutional change and validate it through its political support and sanction. But its helping hand can easily become an iron fist of coercion and oppression when the institution it endorses works against the will of the people. Even when the state intervenes judiciously, the coercive force of the state does not come free. Largely out of practical necessity, a collateral casualty of state enforcement is the loss of institutional diversity. This may become a serious, even fatal, liability if the performance of the institution varies significantly across regions and institutional diversity is warranted.

Fortunately, private farming worked well for most villages in rural China where the land–labor ratio was too low to allow economies of scale to prevail. After it was endorsed as a national policy, private farming did encounter some resistance, particularly in areas where collective farming had worked well and local conditions were suited to large-scale farming.[41] There were a few places where collective farming survived, but in most the national policy triumphed over local requirements.

It is important to note that decollectivization and the return of private farming in rural China were not the whole story of agricultural reform. Decollectivization freed peasants from the dictates of communes and production teams. Peasants' regained freedom to determine their own life choices was more important than decollectivization itself in bringing back commerce and private entrepreneurship to rural China. As a result, even in areas where the policy of private farming met with resistance, the economic freedom that accompanied it was wholeheartedly embraced.[42] This was another important reason for the rapid implementation of the household responsibility system, and the ultimate force underpinning the revival of China's rural economy.

IV

Along with the marginal revolution in agriculture, another revolution was taking place in rural China at almost the same time. This was rural industrialization, mainly led by the rise of township and village enterprises.[43] As the principal source of non-farming jobs to peasants, these enterprises played a pivotal role in bringing about a vibrant non-public sector across China, particularly during the first twenty years of reform. Since the official recognition of private enterprises in the mid-1990s, most township and village enterprises have now been privatized. With a few exceptions, they have all but disappeared. But their spectacular rise and quiet decline reveals much about the nature of the Chinese economic transformation.

What is most striking about township and village enterprises is that they managed to survive at all. They made a crucial contribution to China's move away from socialism to a market economy, and did so despite government hostility. Beijing had always viewed them as inferior rivals to the state-owned enterprises, and had therefore treated them with contempt and enmity. In 1987, Deng Xiaoping characterized the rise of township and village enterprises as a shocking surprise.

> In the rural reform our greatest success – and it is one we had by no means anticipated – had been the emergence of a large number of enterprises run by villages and townships ... Their annual output value has been increasing by more than 20 percent a year for the last several years. This increase in village and township enterprises, particularly industrial enterprises, has provided jobs for 50 per cent of the surplus labor in the countryside ... This result was not anything that I or any of the other comrades had foreseen; it just came out of the blue.[44]

While Deng was completely honest in admitting the astonishing performance of township and village enterprises, his speech failed to mention the policy biases and other barriers township and village enterprises had to overcome on their rise to prominence.

Township and village enterprises did not arise out of the blue. Many of them developed from the old commune and brigade enterprises; they were a legacy of Mao's attempts at rural industrialization. This heritage certainly eased the introduction of township and village enterprises. By 1978 commune and brigade enterprises employed more than 28 million peasants, and accounted for 9.5 percent of the rural labor force.[45] However, this lineage did come with strong historical baggage. Many of the commune and brigade enterprises had developed from the "backyard furnaces" of the Great Leap Forward. Of course, these facilities had been enormously wasteful, barely turning out any usable iron or steel. They also competed aggressively with state-owned steel mills for raw materials, forcing the latter to operate below capacity. At the same time, the backyard furnaces diverted the workforce from farming, which perpetuated the catastrophic famine of that time.[46] The first adjustment after the Great Leap Forward was to close down all backyard furnaces to make sure that the few big mills controlled by the central government could operate at full capacity.[47] This episode led the central government officials in charge of industrial policy to view township and village enterprises with skepticism and mistrust. Furthermore, these officials, with their close administrative relations and direct economic ties with state-owned enterprises, felt threatened by the rise of township and village enterprises. In addition, most township and village enterprises often used obsolete equipment and technology discarded by state-owned enterprises. As a result, the rise of township and village enterprises was seen as a case of inferior, backward competitors crowding out superior, more advanced operations.[48] In light of this view, Beijing crafted several policies to starve these enterprises of bank loans, raw materials, and access to the consumer markets.

In spite of these adversities, township and village enterprises managed to grow quickly. They were widely praised as "the most dynamic part of the Chinese economy"[49] and "the major engine of China's growth and industrialization at the early stages of China's reforms."[50] The number of people employed in such enterprises grew from 28 million in 1978 to a peak of 135 million in 1996. During the same time period, their share in GDP grew from 6 percent to 26 percent, at a time when the GDP itself was growing rapidly.[51] They outperformed the state-owned enterprises in both productivity and growth, even though they did not enjoy the same privileged access to raw materials, energy, credit and consumer markets, and were faced with many discriminatory policies.

Township and village enterprises have been one of the most heavily researched subjects among scholars of China's economy. In academic literature, township and village enterprises are almost unanimously viewed as communal or collective property, owned and managed by local authorities. Consequently, the spectacular performance of township and village enterprises appears to run counter to a basic tenet in modern economics, which states that private property rights are indispensable to motivate entrepreneurship and discipline market behavior.

The active role of local governments is often seen to be the key factor in the success of township and village enterprises. This is true in some regions. With the privatization of agriculture and the disbanding of production teams, township and village enterprises were the only suitable places able to employ the former officials who had administered the production teams. These officials were relatively well educated. They were also more exposed to, and had better ties with, the world outside their villages. But this alone is not a convincing explanation for the success of these enterprises.

State-owned enterprises enjoyed even better ties with, and received far more support from, the government. We have to explain why the close relationship with local governments worked in favor of township and village enterprises, while a close relationship with higher-level governments worked to the detriment of state-owned enterprises. Attributing the success of township and village enterprises to local governments offers little more than a factual description of a fortuitous feature of township and village enterprises. In running township and village enterprises, the local governments had to behave like real entrepreneurs – they had to take risks and bear full responsibility for their decisions. Unlike state-owned enterprises, township and village enterprises faced genuine budget constraints. Nothing can be more misleading than to suggest that the success of township and village enterprises vindicated the strength of the state vis-à-vis the market in directing the economy.

Also, recent studies have revealed the simple fact that a significant proportion of township and village enterprises were actually genuine private enterprises, particularly in the poor inland provinces.[52] Based on a sample survey, the *Annual Book of the Chinese Private Economy* (1994, p. 71) reported that 83 percent of township and village enterprises were private in all but name. Two years later, the 1996 *Annual Book* (p. 112) reached a similar conclusion.[53] According to the 1984 No. 4 Resolution of the State Council, which renamed the commune and brigade enterprises as township and village enterprises, they were so named because of their location; a fact recently brought to the attention of a wider audience by Yasheng Huang.[54] It certainly does not mean that they were collective enterprises run by the town and village governments.

Probably the most important advantage enjoyed by township and village enterprises was the lack of bureaucratic control from the state. Unshackled from the state industrial production plan, township and village enterprises managed their production in accord with market demand and were able to respond quickly to changing market opportunities. State-owned enterprises had to wait for approval from government agents if they wanted to deviate from the prescriptions of the plan. The flexibility enjoyed by township and village enterprises provided them with an enormous advantage. Even after the enterprise reform began, state-owned enterprises remained constrained by administrative red tape. Labor mobility between the state-owned enterprises was minimal;

worker redundancies were treated as a political decision and decided by government bureaus. While state-owned enterprises were better equipped and
financed, they never had the incentives available to the managers of township
and village enterprises. For a long time, they did not even need to worry about
how to market or sell their products – the first product advertisement made by
a state enterprise occurred on June 25th, 1979, when a machine-tool firm in
Sichuan advertised their products in the *People's Daily*. But the privilege came
with a steep price; the spirit of enterprise was lost in state-owned enterprises.[55]

As non-state entities, township and village enterprises were severely constrained in their access to all markets. However, their autonomy enabled them
to pay bribes – a "price premium" – to purchase raw materials and sell their
products. They were also free to make their own decisions about personnel
management, employment contracts, and compensation. For example, bonus
and piece-rate compensation were widely used to link rewards to contribution. In addition, township and village enterprises initially concentrated on
making goods that were in high demand as a result of economic reform but
which were ignored or underserved by the state sector. These included construction materials, residential construction, transport, light industrial products, and
household items. Compared with state-owned enterprises, township and village enterprises used labor-intensive production methods with low-technology
components. According to one estimate, the ratio of labor to fixed capital in
township and village enterprises was eight times higher than that of state-
owned enterprises.[56] In addition, between 1984 and 1988 township and village
enterprises enjoyed access to bank credits, which facilitated their growth.

It did not take long for township and village enterprises to pose a serious
challenge to the state-owned enterprises. With high compensation and other
benefits, they lured skilled workers and managers from the state sector. With
their right to retain all profits, they invested heavily in upgrading their production technology. The fierce competition unleashed by township and village
enterprises forced state-owned enterprises to respond in kind. With the rise of
township and village enterprises, Chinese industry was no longer monopolized
by state-owned enterprises, with the exception of a few sectors protected by the
state. The positive impact of township and village enterprises went far beyond
their contribution to GDP. Having introduced competition into the Chinese
economy, they acted as a powerful catalyst for economic transformation.

V

Like their rural counterparts, the marginal forces in urban China were also a
legacy of Mao's social and economic policies. A proud boast of socialism was the
lack of unemployment, at least on paper. Unemployment was viewed by socialism as an evil reality of capitalism. One of Mao's solutions to the challenge of

unemployment was to send millions of city youth "up to the hill and down to the countryside to learn from peasants."[57] Even though framed as a political campaign to re-educate the city youth, the program was enforced as it was a convenient solution to the problem of urban unemployment. At the same time, all factories, stores, hospitals, and other service providers in cities, along with governmental and educational departments, were organized into "units."[58] Since unemployment was not allowed to exist under socialism, all units in Chinese cities were tasked with absorbing as many workers as possible, even when their net product fell below their wage bill. But the problem of unemployment remained, and the practice of sending urban youth to the countryside continued from the early 1950s and reached a peak during the Cultural Revolution.

With the death of Mao and the end of the Cultural Revolution, the practice of sending city youth to the countryside was stopped, officially ending in October 1978. But long before its official termination, the young men and women had become desperate to return to the city. A phenomenon in Chinese cities at the end of the1970s and early 1980s was the sudden influx of "returned youth," estimated to be in the range of 20 million, who accounted for 10 percent of the urban population.[59] Beijing had more than 400,000 "returned youth" in 1979, accounting for 8.6 percent of the city's total population. The situation in Tianjin was worse, with 380,000, representing 11.7 percent of the total population.[60] The pressure the returned youth placed on employment was overwhelming. In addition to the government sector, the only other employers were state-owned enterprises and a small number of collective enterprises managed by street committees. These were already hard pressed and could not possibly take in such large numbers of prospective employees. Reluctant to acknowledge the specter of unemployment and admit a failing of socialism, the Chinese government coined a new term for the returning youth, "youth waiting to be employed." Creative rhetoric, however, did not change the dire situation on the ground. Protests erupted in the larger cities as few returned youth could find jobs and no solution seemed forthcoming. In early 1979, unemployed youths in more than twenty-one provinces mounted various forms of protests, including blocking railways and encircling government buildings.

Xue Muqiao, a renowned economist and economic advisor to the State Council, published a paper in the *People's Daily* on July 20th, 1979 that urged the government to permit self-employment. This strategy had been used effectively, immediately after the founding of the People's Republic of China, to tackle the problem of unemployment that many cities faced in 1949–1950.[61] As a loyal Party member, Xue was committed to socialism and the collective economy; but as an economist, Xue knew what practical measures would be effective. The mounting employment pressure and the risk of large-scale social unrest forced the Chinese government to implement Xue's suggestion.

On September 29th, 1979, at a meeting held to celebrate the thirtieth anniversary of the People's Republic, Head of the State Ye Jianying called for the recognition of the "individual economy *(geti jingji)*"; this was a euphemism for private economy.[62] Three months later, the first officially registered "individual economy" made its appearance in Wenzhou on November 30th, 1979. The floodgates were now open for a revival of private economy in urban China. What Mao had condemned as the antithesis of socialism was officially welcomed back as the "appendix to and complement of socialism."[63] Two years later, on October 17th, 1981, the Central Committee and the State Council jointly issued *Several Decisions on Opening up the Door, Enlivening the Economy, and Solving Employment Problems in Cities and Towns*, in which the "individual economy" was promoted as a "necessary complement" to the socialist collective economy.[64]

The rise of the "individual economy" ended the monopoly of the collective economy in Chinese cities and towns. Outside the state-controlled public sector, a completely new economic force came into being. Even though it was formally recognized in 1981, the individual economy did not earn equal protection until 1992, when the market economy was officially recognized as an integral part of Chinese socialism. Throughout the whole decade of the 1980s, the private sector, like township and village enterprises, was beset by policy constraints and social discrimination. For example, parents in cities would not marry their daughters to young men employed in the private sector – these jobs were deemed insecure, inferior, and quite disgraceful. Entities in the individual economy could not hire more than seven employees – any private enterprise of eight or more employees was deemed to be capitalist and was therefore illegal.[65] To get around this and other restrictions, many private firms were forced to put on "a red hat" – affiliating themselves with a township and village government and thus turning into a township and village enterprise, or with a street committee or other local governmental branches in cities and thus becoming a collective enterprise. The Chinese government still believed that the public sector was the economic foundation of socialism, and thus remained reluctant to embrace the private economy. But the challenge of mass unemployment and the accompanying potential for social unrest forced the Chinese government to give in. As a result, the policy of "Three Nos" – no promotion, no publicity, and no ban – prevailed as a compromise during the 1980s and early 1990s.

The rise of the private sector followed a marked geographic pattern, which further illustrates the marginal nature of this revolution. Wenzhou in Zhejiang was one of the poorest regions in the province during Mao's era.[66] A mountainous area with little fertile land, Wenzhou was poorly suited to farming. Being a coastal area, Wenzhou had received little state industrial investment due to the perceived risk of a war with Taiwan. Transportation in the region at the end of the 1970s remained as primitive. Nonetheless, Wenzhou quickly became the cradle of the Chinese private economy in the early 1980s. Even though the Chinese government officially recognized the private economy in 1981, their commitment to socialism led the government only reluctantly to allow it to complement the public sector, restricting its scope of operation. In the areas where the public sector was sufficiently strong, the room for private economy would be limited. With no state sector to protect, the local authority in Wenzhou was much more tolerant of the private sector than it might otherwise have been. Once the private sector began to develop, the local authority encouraged and protected it as a substitute for the collective economy; in other places with a strong state sector, the private sector was vigilantly watched. It is also important to note that pre-1949, Wenzhou had a long history of commerce and manufacture (mostly handicrafts) and this heritage, along with the lack of a public sector, allowed the private economy to thrive. In contrast, regions that had enjoyed heavy public investment during Mao's era, such as the northeast region of China, the most industrialized area in China at the eve of reform, saw only mediocre growth in the private economy.

VI

Among the marginal revolutions that started China's market transformation, one in particular played a pivotal role in opening up China to the global economy. This was the development of Shenzhen and the other Special Economic Zones. Before it became a household name in China, Shenzhen was a small poor town in Bao'an county in the southeast corner of Guangdong province. Situated across the water from Hong Kong, it would become the frontline of China's integration to the global market economy.[67]

Due to its unique location, Shenzhen had long been a favorite exit for illegal emigrants fleeing from China to Hong Kong.[68] The largest exodus during Mao's time occurred immediately after the failure of the Great Leap Forward. A journalist from the *People's Daily* by the name of Lian Yunshan was sent to investigate this incident.[69] Lian conducted investigations on both sides of the border. He spent more than a month in Hong Kong interviewing border patrol officers and residents, particularly those who had recently fled the mainland. What Lian saw and heard in Hong Kong made him acutely aware of the economic gap between the two. His investigations suggested to him that the only long-term solution was to set up a special trading zone in Shenzhen, emulating Hong Kong on the other side of the border. Lian wrote a report to his immediate boss, who thought it too radical to be publicized. Deng Xiaoping was probably the only top leader who ever saw it.

The problem of illegal emigrants arose with an unprecedented intensity in the late 1970s, mainly because of a rumor of an immigration amnesty in Hong Kong. With thousands of people rushing to cross the maritime border, many drowned and their bodies floated back to the shore of Shenzhen. Collecting and burying corpses became a regular job. In some border villages, more than half of the working population had left. Illegal emigration had escalated into a public emergency.

Deng Xiaoping visited Guangdong province in November, after his return to power in July 1977. Local officials told him of the worsening problem of illegal emigration at Shenzhen and requested more soldiers to guard the border. Deng was reported to have said, "This reflects problems in our policy. There is nothing the army can do."[70] Afraid to ask for clarification, local authorities were left puzzled. In their minds, only traitors of the motherland and enemies of socialism could possibly desert the mainland for the corrupt and backward capitalist economy on the other side of the Shenzhen River.

The Party Secretary of Guangdong province, Wu Nanshen, decided to conduct his own investigation. What he found was the tale of two Luofang villages. Many people from the village of Luofang on the Shenzhen side had fled to Hong Kong (the New Territory) and lived right across the Shenzhen River on the other side. They also named their new home Luofang. During his investigation, Wu was shocked to discover that the villagers of Luofang in Hong Kong earned almost a hundred times as much as their counterparts in Shenzhen. Now, Wu understood Deng's comments, and he reached the same conclusion.[71] Unless the economic gap was reduced, neither political nor military means could stop illegal emigration.

A year later in January 1979, Wu visited his hometown, Shantou, a coastal city in the southeast of Guangdong. In the 1930s, Shantou had been known as "little Shanghai" for its vibrant commerce and local economy, broadly comparable to Hong Kong's. Forty years later, Hong Kong had become one of the burgeoning "Asian Dragon" economies. Shantou, on the other hand, had simply decayed. How could Shantou catch up? A businessman from Singapore suggested a solution to Wu: an export processing zone, a practice that had served Taiwan and Singapore well during the take-off of their economies, might work in China as well.

A similar idea had already been tried in Shekou, another town in Bao'an county. In this case, the pioneer was not a government official trying to revamp the local economy, but a Hong Kong-based business owned by the Chinese government, China Merchants. China Merchants was originally a shipping company set up by Li Hongzhang in 1872. It managed to survive the tumultuous war years of the late nineteenth and early twentieth centuries and, after 1949, it became part of the Ministry of Transportation of the People's Republic. In June 1978, China Merchants appointed its twenty-ninth leader, Yuan Geng. Yuan was a war veteran; he had been a spy operating in south China, including Hong Kong, during the war of resistance against the Japanese. Then, after the founding of the People's Republic, he worked as a diplomat in south

Asia. He was then imprisoned for more than five years during the Cultural Revolution, but was freed in 1973 and took a high-level position in the Ministry
of Transportation. Known for his straight talking and sharp and independent
thinking, Yuan was respected by his colleagues as a capable, honest, enterprising, and open-minded individual. At the age of sixty-one, Yuan was chosen to
head the by now rather neglected China Merchants. Ambitious and energetic,
Yuan quickly formulated a plan to turn China Merchants into a competitive,
profit-making corporation, with interests in manufacturing, trade, and shipping. Since land was prohibitively expensive in Hong Kong, Yuan turned his
eyes to Shekou. In January 1979, a proposal was sent to both the Guangdong
provincial government and the Ministry of Transportation in Beijing, detailing
plans for an industrial park in Shekou. It was approved by Guangdong province
on the 6th, and the Ministry of Transportation on the 10th, and the proposal
was then sent to the State Council. On the 31st, the Deputy Prime Minister,
Li Xiannian, approved the proposal. The Shekou Industrial Park, the first such
area in China, thus became a reality. In approving Yuan's proposal, Li actually offered the whole Nantou peninsula, some 30 square kilometers at least.
But Yuan took only Shekou, at the southern tip of the peninsula. Yuan reasoned that, if the project failed in Shekou, which was barren land, it would
have little effect. Other districts on the peninsula already had some industrial
infrastructure and to incorporate them into the Park would both increase costs
and multiply the political risks.

In the meantime, Wu Nanshen discussed the setting up of an export processing zone in Shantou with other provincial leaders, particularly Xi Zhongxun
and Yang Shangkun. The leaders at Guangdong were aware of Yuan's proposal,
but developed an even more ambitious plan, aiming to turn the whole province
into a laboratory to test various practices that had brought success to Hong
Kong and Taiwan. They believed that Guangdong, which bordered Hong Kong
and Macau, should be a pioneer in the coming economic reform.

At a working conference held in Beijing in April 1979, which was attended
by all provincial heads and central government officials in charge of economic
affairs, Xi Zhongxun, the representative for Guangdong, put their proposal on
the table. He stressed that Guangdong could take advantage of its proximity
to Hong Kong and strong links to overseas Chinese to begin economic and
technological exchange with the outside world. Despite strong resistance from
some, Xi's proposal won majority support, including that of Hua Guofeng, who
was eager to open up China and strengthen economic ties to the outside world.

Gu Mu, the Vice Premier in charge of trade, reported these discussions to
Deng Xiaoping. Deng was pleased with the proposal from Guangdong and recommended the title "Special Economic Zones." In the following months, Gu
worked intensively with provincial leaders in Guangdong and also in Fujian.
On July 15th, 1979, the Central Committee and the State Council issued a

joint resolution, approving the development of special economic zones in Guangdong and Fujian. These special zones were to be more than industrial parks for export-oriented firms. They would also provide all educational, commercial, legal, and governmental services necessary to support the success of manufacturing and trade. Thus, in the special zones, an industrial park would be joined by a science and research district, a residential district, a commercial district, and a governmental district. Once completed, each special zone would be a fully equipped, self-sustaining economic entity.

Officials in Guangdong had one further concern: they wanted to write the Special Economic Zones into law, making them more credible to outside investors. The idea had been suggested to them by some businessmen from Hong Kong. On August 26th, 1980, the National People's Congress passed the Regulations for the Special Economic Zones in Guangdong Province. In the process of revising the draft of the first Special Economic Zones Regulations, the concerns of the Chinese leaders were laid bare.

First and foremost, the Special Economic Zones were intended to "appropriate capitalism for the good of socialism." After visits to Hong Kong, Macau, Singapore, Japan, the United States, and Western Europe in 1978 and 1979, Chinese officials had been shocked by the astonishing technological advancement and economic efficiency achieved by the capitalist system and the pleasant living conditions enjoyed by the middle classes. They were forced to appreciate the extraordinary strength of capitalism in innovation, technological as well as institutional, a point actually made a long time ago by Marx himself. Chinese leaders no longer doubted that China's pursuit of socialism could learn a lot from capitalism. This desire to learn from capitalism was, however, still matched by an enduring commitment to socialism. Few in the Chinese government doubted the viability of socialism. They believed that, with capital and modern technology borrowed from capitalist nations, China would catch up with the West because of the superiority of socialism. Following the steps taken by their predecessors at the end of the Qing dynasty (1861–1894), who had tried to borrow western technology to strengthen Chinese traditional culture, the Chinese communists were set to appropriate capitalism to save socialism.

The Special Economic Zones were expected to serve as a laboratory in which to experiment with capitalist principles in the advancement of socialism. The zones had autonomy and were given incentives to learn from capitalism. If still confined to the parameter defined by socialism, the Special Economic Zones would not be special at all. At the same time, they were not meant to be stepping stones for capitalism to conquer China; their ultimate goal was to serve socialism. But, as a Chinese idiom puts it, it is hard to keep a window open and let fresh air in but keep the flies out. The government's fear of encroaching capitalism would haunt the Special Economic Zones throughout the 1980s.

The first four Special Economic Zones, Shenzhen, Zhuhai, and Shantou in Guangdong and Xiamen in Fujian, were selected due to a compromise. In the first instance, all four places were located in what historians call "maritime China":[72] areas with close ties to overseas Chinese and which have a long history of maritime trade with the outside world. This geographic factor had been a disadvantage for Guangdong and Fujian during Mao's time, when Beijing invested little there in fear of a military conflict with Taiwan. But now their close proximity to Hong Kong, Macau, and Taiwan became beneficial and they were selected to spearhead China's reopening up to the West. These four cities were not the only ones that had this geographical advantage. At the time, other cities were also considered, including Dalian and Qingdao, close to South Korea and Japan, and Shanghai. These were quickly rejected on the grounds that these cities, particularly Shanghai, were so important to the Chinese economy that a failed experiment would have devastating repercussions on the socialist economy.[73] With the four places eventually chosen, the impact of failure on the rest of the economy would be minimal. This concern was clarified by a statement made by one of the vice premiers: "We [had] to put a fence around the provincial border of Guangdong so that other provinces would be sheltered from the bad influence of capitalism."[74]

Among all the Special Economic Zones, Shenzhen stands out. The pioneering role played by the Shekou Industrial Park, later incorporated into the Shenzhen Special Economic Zone, was an important factor in the unparalleled rise of Shenzhen. As a company under the Ministry of Transportation, China Merchants enjoyed many advantages not available to a local government, including direct access to various ministers in Beijing and the State Council. The Shekou Model and its motto, "Time is money; efficiency is life," shocked China in the 1980s by new ways of thinking and new practices. Shenzhen, a frontline town, now became a testing ground for market forces in China. As the first and biggest Special Economic Zone, Shenzhen attracted budding entrepreneurs and other talents from all over China, including those who were discontented with the status quo and dreamt of a better future. In the past thirty years, Shenzhen has been transformed from a fishing town of less than 30,000 people to the third largest and the fastest growing city in China with more than 14 million residents. A once perilous route of human trafficking has now become a dazzling beacon of commerce.

In 1984, after the initial success of the first four Special Economic Zones, the Chinese government decided to open fourteen other coastal cities to foreign investment. In 1988, Hainan Island, the Yangzi River Delta, Pearl River Delta, Xiamen-Zhangzhou-Quanzhou in southern Fujian, Shandong Peninsula, and Liaodong Peninsula in Liaoning were opened to foreign direct investment. In 1992, the Pudong New Area in Shanghai was created as a Special Economic Zone. After this, all provincial capital cities were gradually opened to foreign investment. The most recent ones added to the list of Special Economic Zones were Binhai New Area in Tianjin in 2006 and Kashi in Xinjiang in 2010. After three decades of reform, the Special Economic Zones have grown steadily and spread inwards from the periphery to the core of China's economy.

VII

As we have shown, Chinese economic reform gained momentum after the Third Plenum of 1978, as the Chinese government endorsed reform measures that had first begun under Hua. If there ever was an overarching principle underpinning Chinese reform at this early stage, it must be what was then called "dispel chaos and restore order." The new Chinese leadership centered around Deng Xiaoping and Chen Yun shared a fairly consensual view on the origin of the "chaos" and the foundation of political "order." To a large degree, the reforms implemented in both agriculture and industry were meant to steer China back to the economic policies designed prior to the Cultural Revolution.

In agriculture, the policy of "unified procurement and redistribution" remained intact. Even though it was adopted in the early 1950s as an emergency plan, "unified procurement and redistribution" had since become the foundation of Chinese agricultural policy. The continuity of price control stood out as the core piece in the state-led agricultural reform that was intended to fortify the role of the state. The industrial reform was largely an extension of what had begun prior to the Third Plenum, giving more autonomy to state-owned enterprises. Since the Chinese leaders still viewed them as the cornerstone of socialism, they understandably pinned their hopes of reform on state-owned enterprises.

As state-owned enterprises were given the freedom to operate beyond the state quota, they started to undergo an unplanned metamorphosis, and emerged with a dual role. On the one hand, state enterprises remained a passive robot arm of central planning, receiving various factors of production from the state quota system and producing in accord with the state plan; on the other hand, they began to operate outside the state plan for economic profits. As a result, while central planning continued its function in allocating resources, a market mechanism emerged in parallel, signaling to state-owned enterprises what and how much to produce to take advantage of changing economic opportunities. There is no doubt that the state sector benefited greatly from the dual-track mechanism. At the very least, it did not suffer a severe disruption in economic coordination and consequently avoided economic recession, which was common among other transition economies in the former Soviet bloc. The presence of this dual-track mechanism and the duality of the state-owned enterprises made it a rather complicated task to assess the relative size of the state sector in the Chinese economy. The common practice of treating the total output generated by state-owned enterprises indiscriminately as in the state sector thus led to a biased overestimation.

China would probably have stayed on the intended path to socialism were it not for the marginal revolutions that reintroduced private entrepreneurship to the economy. Initially, private farming, rural industrialization, and the return of the "individual economy" in cities were all invariably treated with open hostility and even criminalized, as in the case of private farming. These grassroots reforms helped to resolve or ameliorate urgent economic problems, such as grain production, rural poverty, and urban unemployment. At the time, they posed little threat to socialism; the Chinese government learned to grudgingly tolerate them. Only after a considerable lapse of time did the Chinese government begin to embrace them enthusiastically when economic gains generated by the private sector had been recognized as indispensable for the socialist economy.

The four marginal revolutions – enacted by actors marginalized in Mao's socialist economy – quickly gave birth to a dynamic private sector in China, freeing 800 million peasants from the state, allowing almost 20 million "returned youth" in the cities to set up their own businesses, and creating a few spots for foreign and domestic entrepreneurs to flourish and inadvertently showcase the dynamism of capitalism. Rather than the state-led efforts of Leap Outward or enterprise reform, it was these marginal revolutions that launched China onto a course of rapid economic development and transformation to a market economy. Even in the case of the Special Economic Zones where the state was deeply involved in their development, the main role of the state was to provide a relatively safe political and legal environment to allow for market competition. Instead of shoring up state-owned enterprises, the Special Economic Zones were first created in areas where socialism had failed or simply did not exist. This not only avoided the potential resistance to reform from the state sector, but kept the risk of a failed reform to the minimum.

Surprisingly, the Chinese government's remaining commitment to socialism at the beginning of reform worked to its advantage. Its loyalty to socialism was responsible for the reform strategy that preserved the core of socialism (state-owned enterprises), while allowing marginal revolutions to develop in China. It was not that the core was kept intact. But the reform measures targeted at the state-owned enterprises were to save and strengthen the state sector, instead of bringing about privatization, the common approach implemented in Russia and other transition economies. As a result, while the reformed state sector was struggling along, a non-state sector brought about by marginal revolutions was rising up strongly and swiftly outside the state-controlled economic plan. China was taken back to a mixed economy, which had benefited China before Mao rushed China into the socialist transition in the early 1950s. The contemporary shift in ideology and mentality at the political center was also crucial.

Largely due to the debate sparked by "Practice is the only criterion for testing truth," the pronouncements of Mao and Marx no longer enjoyed the divine power to dictate economic policy. As a political party brought up on strict ideology, it would take a long time for the Chinese Communist Party to fully commit to "seeking truth from facts." Hu Yaobang, first as head of the Central Party School and later as General Secretary of the Party, made a critical and lasting contribution. When most Chinese leaders took the Cultural Revolution as the beginning of the "chaos" that had consumed Mao's China, Hu went further back. Consequently, while economic reform modeled itself on "four modernizations," a program first proposed by Zhou Enlai in 1964, Hu sought to rectify the political "chaos" whose seeds were sown throughout the Party history when terror and violence were used to settle political disagreement. By recognizing the much earlier origins of the "chaos" that China had to clear up, Hu took a big step ahead of his colleagues in conceiving China's new political order.[75]

In addition, we ought to credit the political acumen and judgment of Deng. In 1992, while reminiscing on the beginnings of reform, Deng thus commented:

> On reform and opening up, there were disagreements at the very beginning...This was normal. No debate was my invention. Not engaging in debate, we thus have time to try different things. With debate, things become complicated. Time was wasted and nothing achieved. No debate, try boldly, and strike out boldly.[76]

Deng's principle of "no debate" worked surprisingly well in reorienting the Chinese Communist Party away from Communism and towards practice. Without a clear vision of where China should be heading, post-Mao Chinese leaders opened their minds. Aware of deep and wide disagreements among the Chinese leaders then, particularly between himself and Chen Yun, Deng did not believe that theoretical debates could generate political consensus or provide solutions to questions that the Chinese government was facing. It thus forced the Chinese government to resort to "practice as the only criterion of testing truth," encouraging bold experiments from below. This pragmatic shift in the political mindset of the Chinese leadership marked a distinct departure from Mao and his immediate successor, Hua. Without this, the marginal revolutions would not have been possible.

When reform started, the Chinese government first turned to industry and the state-owned enterprises. In launching a new military campaign, the general will surely send his strongest and best equipped soldiers to the battlefield. Likewise, the state will naturally rely upon its preferred and most resourceful actors to carry out economic reform. Not surprisingly, state investment and expectation were heaped upon state-owned enterprises in equal measure. The strongest elements of any society, however, are often not the best agents of change. It is not simply that the strongest actors are usually the beneficiaries of the status quo and are thus unwilling to change. Rather, the most powerful actors in society are often embedded cognitively in the existing system and can hardly think outside the box. Whatever they do is more likely to fine tune and perpetuate the system rather than transform it. It is the actors at the periphery who are able to bring to the stage different incentives, new skills, and fresh perspectives, critical ingredients for a revolution. In China, it was the peasants, the unemployed urban residents, and other marginalized actors in the socialist economy that turned out to be the vanguard of market transformation.

By 1984, when The Third Plenum of the Twelfth Central Committee was held in Beijing, the Chinese government had come to accept the goal of reform as building a "commercial economy with plan," that is, a market economy in disguise. This was a landmark event in the history of the Chinese economic reform. It consolidated the marginal revolutions that had swept China since Mao's death and officially recognized the legitimacy of the private sector under socialism. Socialist modernization – strengthening the state sector – ended its role as the leitmotif of reform. In its place, "building socialism with Chinese characteristics," first proposed by Deng in 1982, was officially embraced by Zhao Ziyang, then General Secretary of the Party, in 1987 at the Thirteenth National Congress of the Party.[77] This new unifying ideology wholeheartedly welcomed the market mechanism and, to a less degree, the private sector. The former would gradually overshadow and ultimately replace central planning; the latter would come to be treated more equally with the state sector. No one could possibly have foreseen such a sea-change in the Chinese economy as occurred in the first decade of reform.

4

A Bird in the Cage: Market Reform under Socialism

China's economic reform in the early 1980s was a tale of two economies: a stagnant state sector contrasting with a fast rising non-state economy. During the marginal revolutions, the vibrant non-state sector was born at the periphery of the socialist economy. It took very little time for ambitious entrepreneurs to find and pursue economic opportunities underexplored or unexploited. With the socialist economy's decades-long bias toward heavy industry, Chinese consumers had long been undersupplied with even the most basic consumer goods and services. All this was about to change. In the early 1980s, entrepreneurs began to address these unsatisfied demands, and doing so proved to be highly profitable. Self-employed barbers, for example, came to earn higher incomes than surgeons in state hospitals. Street vendors who sold noodles and snack foods earned more than nuclear scientists. Traders, small shop and private restaurant owners, many of them the former "youths waiting to be employed," were among the highest income groups in China during the 1980s. Not surprisingly, the number of self-employed household businesses and single proprietorships increased from 140,000 in 1978 to 310,000 in 1979, 806,000 in 1980, and reached 2.6 million in 1981.[1] City residents started to enjoy many goods and services that had not been available from state-owned establishments.

Agriculture, the economy's most troublesome sector at the time of Mao's death, witnessed remarkable growth between 1979 and1984, with output growing by 6.7 percent per annum. As a result, agricultural output jumped from 305 million tons in 1978 to 407 million tons in 1984.[2] Moreover, with the conditional sanction of private farming in 1980, Chinese peasants were gradually freed from the yoke of collective farming and, for the first time since the Land Reform, started to exercise some degree of economic freedom. June 18th, 1980 saw the first People's Commune disbanded in Sichuan province. At the end of 1982, the household responsibility system was implemented in more than 80 percent of the rural population, including at Dazhai, the national model commune during Mao's era. A year later, the rate had reached 95 percent and agriculture was effectively decollectivized.[3]

In the meantime, township and village enterprises became the fastest growing sector in the whole Chinese economy throughout the 1980s. The percentage of the total rural labor force employed by such enterprises increased from 9 percent in 1978 to above 14 percent in 1984. By the mid-1980s, output made up over half of the total rural economy, and one-quarter of China's industrial output.[4]

In contrast, the reforms intended to revitalize state enterprises – a priority of the Chinese government since 1978 – turned out to be a disappointment. Under the enterprise reform initiatives, state enterprises were given more autonomy in business decision-making, as well as the right to retain a certain amount of profit for discretionary use. This improved incentives for both managers and workers. But individual enterprises had to negotiate with their supervising authority exactly what rights they would have, as well as the proportion of profit handed to the state. In this bargaining process, political power and other non-economic considerations often overshadowed economic logic. This resulted in more profitable firms turning over a higher percentage of their profits to the state, while insolvent firms received state subsidies. Consequently, profitable firms did not necessarily grow and loss-making firms did not go bankrupt. In addition, the state-owned enterprises were still subject to multiple sources of interventions from the state. As the Chinese proverb puts it, they were under the joint supervision of many "mothers-in-law." Moreover, since these reforms were carried out within the decentralized administrative structure inherited from Mao, local governments created various trade barriers to protect firms in their jurisdiction in exchange for their influence on the operation of the firms. This grossly undermined the enterprise reforms. At the national level, local protectionism pushed the whole country towards a fiefdom economy.

I

So why were the enterprise reforms such a failure? To answer this requires a close look at China's preexisting industrial structure.[5] Due in part to Mao's repeated efforts of decentralization, the Chinese economy had rarely been run on the Soviet model. In that system, production, distribution, pricing, and investment were all strictly managed by directives from a single central planning office (or Gosplan). In China, state-owned enterprises were supervised by governments at a number of levels, from the central government (various ministries under the State Council) down to the provincial, the prefecture, and the municipal government (in cities) and the county government (in rural areas). As well as the state-owned enterprises, there existed urban collective enterprises and rural enterprises owned by the governments below the municipal and county level. Moreover, state-owned enterprises operated under two separate chains of command, the vertical chain, or "*tiaotiao*," and the horizontal chain, or "*kuangkuang*." For all industries, the vertical chain of hierarchy ran from the central government Ministry down to the local bureaus of the provincial, municipal, and county authorities. The horizontal chain in the hierarchy ran from the State Council to the provincial, municipal, and county government.

Along the vertical line of command, a state-owned steel mill, for example, fell under the jurisdiction of the Ministry of Metallurgical Industry if it was supervised by the central government and was thus classified as a central state enterprise, or the provincial (municipal, country) bureau of metallurgical industry if it was supervised by the provincial (municipal, county) government, and was thus classified as a provincial (municipal, county) state enterprise. Along the horizontal chain, a state enterprise was supervised by the central (provincial, municipal, or county) government if it was a central (provincial, municipal, or county) state enterprise. A direct chain of command ran from the central, down to the provincial, municipal, and county government. As a result, state-owned enterprises faced a grid structure of supervision.

Other factors further complicated the governance structure of state-owned enterprises. First, all the local bureaus of an industry reported to both their local governments and the higher level bureaus and, ultimately, the Ministry under the State Council. Under the Stalinist model of central planning, the horizontal line of hierarchy did not exist. In China, however, Mao's repeated attempts at decentralization gave more power to local authorities and more credence to the horizontal line of command. Second, a number of state enterprise operations were often supervised by different authorities. These included personnel (promotion, transfer, and hiring), wage control, finance, production planning, and investment planning. Personnel and wage control usually fell under the horizontal line of command, while production and investment planning were mainly supervised by the vertical line of command, though they were also influenced by the horizontal line. This partitioning of supervision and interlinking of supervising authorities made the management of state-owned enterprises overwhelmingly complex. Third, just like the Chinese Party and government officials whose salaries and privileges were (and still are) highly differentiated in accord with their ranks, the state enterprises and their managers also had different administrative rankings. Enterprises supervised by higher level authorities had higher rankings, and often enjoyed higher priorities in their access to various resources controlled by the government, such as finance and raw materials. They also shouldered higher responsibilities in fulfilling the production plan. Last, and most troublesome, the division of supervision changed from one enterprise and industry to another, and also varied over time in correspondence with the cycle of political decentralization and centralization. Thus, not only did the state-owned enterprises face a web of regulation, but that regulation was effectively different for each individual operation.

At the operational level, many practices added further variations to the constraints facing each of the state-owned enterprises. For example, governments often selectively subsidized some enterprises for a variety of temporary and contingent reasons, which consequently discriminated against others. Even when state enterprises were working outside the production targets of the state plan, which was not uncommon, they still faced the same issues. The economic plan devised by the central government did not cover all production undertaken by the state-owned enterprises. Consequently, there had always been economic transactions outside the plan which were referred to as "cooperation relations." For these transactions to take place, the involved parties had to negotiate prices, creating a problem that did not exist when meeting the targets of a production plan. Since the production plan was specified in quantities, for both inputs and outputs, prices were simply an instrument of accountancy. Due to this lack of market price information, the spot prices governing transactions outside the production plan varied greatly.

At any point in time, different enterprises faced different prices for the same raw materials or intermediate inputs, though this did not include labor – wages were fixed nationwide and, consequently, seldom reflected productivity. This is the exact opposite of what one would find in a market economy, where wages are individually negotiated, but all firms face a similar market price for other inputs. When the enterprise reforms allowed each operation to bargain individually with the government about its rights and responsibilities, it merely added to the chaos of constraints faced by each state-owned enterprise.

In a free market economy, the firm is constantly influenced by the wider market in which it operates. The product market reveals information critical to a firm's survival, such as what not to produce – when the sale price for a product will not cover the cost of its production; the factor market informs the cost of substitution between factors of production. While there is some room for price-seeking, firms cannot greatly alter the market price for their inputs. To increase its chance of survival, a firm can innovate and supply new and better products to consumers, or it can improve efficiency and produce the same goods at a lower cost than its competitors. Thus, market competition allows profitable firms to grow and causes unprofitable ones to wither, forcing them to produce something different.

At the same time, firms in a market economy adjust the wages paid to their employees in accord with their productivity; employees will lose their jobs if performance is unsatisfactory. This gives firms a powerful incentive with which to motivate their employees, whose productivity, unlike that of other factors of production, is open to the influence of the rate of compensation. This internal pressure encourages workers to make their best efforts, and whether those are good enough is judged only by consumers. The performance of the firm is decided by the ultimate test of market survival.

Prior to the enterprise reforms implemented in 1981, Chinese state industry did not really have any genuine price mechanism, or true market discipline. The price level for consumer and capital goods was largely set by the state, with little room to reflect variations in their quality. This meant that enterprises had little incentive to improve the quality of their products, let alone introduce new ones. As each state enterprise faced an idiosyncratic set of constraints imposed by a web of supervising authorities, even if a state enterprise was motivated to improve its condition it would work first on changing the constraints to its advantage rather than improving its production or innovating better products. Moreover, since workers' pay was not linked to productivity, workforce morale was understandably low. Worse still, firms could not take the decision to lay off or hire workers. In the name of socialism – secure employment and egalitarianism being foremost among these – state-owned enterprises were deprived of basic managerial methods of incentivizing workers and producing better products.

Enterprise reform gave state enterprises more autonomy in business decision-making and the right to retain profit; but they were still inclined to change external constraints rather than improve internal strength. Indeed, firms were welcome to negotiate with their supervising authorities on almost all aspects of the production process. This might include the quantity of a product the enterprise was required to produce, the quantity of raw materials it could consume, the credit it could obtain from the state, and the percentage of profit it was able to retain. It was equivalent to a firm being allowed to set its own prices for inputs and choose its rate of taxation. As the firm was able to negotiate the rules of the game, there was little pressure to improve its internal strength. In essence, this was why the enterprise reform failed. It did not subject the enterprises to market discipline, which would reward only firms whose products were favored by consumers. There was still little pressure for enterprises to innovate and improve their profitability.

II

Without a price system that would subject all firms to the same market disciplines, enterprise reform could not possibly work. Even though the reform certainly improved incentives within firms, it could not make them as efficient as Nissan, the Japanese firm that impressed Deng Xiaoping most during his first visit to Japan. One of the best-known Chinese economists and a veteran economic official, Xue Muqiao, was among the first to recognize the limitations of the enterprise reform.[6] In a document prepared for the State Council in early

1980, "Preliminary Comments on the Economic System Reform," Xue envisioned that economic reform would gradually replace central planning with market mechanisms. He believed that all government intervention would eventually be lifted from the operation of state-owned enterprises, allowing them to become fully independent profit-seeking entities.[7] Xue's report was highly praised by General Secretary Hu Yaobang after it was presented at a meeting in September 1980.[8] Its perspective on reform was echoed in Premier Zhao Ziyang's report to the People's Congress in 1981: "These reforms [enterprise and agricultural reform] are still partial and exploratory in nature and our work has suffered from certain incongruities and from lack of coordination. The task before us is to sum up our experience in these reforms and, after careful investigation and study and repeated scientific confirmation, to draw up as soon as possible an overall plan for reforming the economy and carry it out step by step." The price reform that Xue envisioned – replacing government planning with the price system as a primary mechanism of resource allocation, thus imposing market discipline on all the enterprises – would become the core of Zhao's "overall plan."

The proposal was endorsed by General Secretary Hu Yaobang and Zhao Ziyang, Premier of the State Council. However, price reform ran contrary to the accepted wisdom of socialism, which held the market antithetical to central planning and collective ownership. Throughout the 1980s Deng Xiaoping, Chen Yun, and a handful of other Party veterans remained the *eminence grise* of the Chinese Communist Party and, for this group, the old habit of thinking died hard.[9] Though age prevented them from holding official positions in the Party and government, they dictated government policy. In the debate on the relation between the market and central planning in socialism and the very nature of socialism itself, the strongest and most articulate voice was that of Chen Yun, the most economically experienced and widely respected senior Chinese leader.[10]

Chen was the architect of China's first Five Year Plan and an adamant defender of central planning. Born and raised in bustling Shanghai, Chen was also appreciative of the value of private business. His criticism of Mao's war on private enterprise in the early to mid-1950s cost him his position as the czar of the Chinese economy. Chen's economic policy, summarized as "three primaries, three supplements," was first proposed at the Eighth National Congress of the Chinese Communist Party in 1956.[11] Chen maintained that, regarding industry and commerce, the state and collective sector should be primary, supplemented by the private sector; regarding production planning, central planning should be primary, supplemented by market adjustment; regarding the whole socialist economy, the state-controlled market should be primary, supplemented by the free market. Between them, Chen's clear vision of a mixed economy and Mao's famous lecture "On the Ten Major Relationships" ensured

China's decisive ideological departure from Stalinism. However, Chen's explicit references to the private sector and market mechanism were not to Mao's liking; while Chen's view was well received at the National Congress, his views were ignored by Mao himself and had little impact on economic policy.

Chen was called back to run the economy after the disastrous Great Leap Forward, but fell out of favor again soon after. He returned to office only after the Third Plenum of the Eleventh Central Committee. His vision of socialism as "the planned economy as primary, market adjustments as auxiliary" was to serve as the guiding light of the Chinese economic reform until the mid-1980s. Chen's rationale for incorporating the market and the private sector into socialism was pragmatic: the central plan could not be designed in so complete a manner as to cover every detail of the economy. The inevitable gaps in the central plan could be filled by the private sector and the market. However, Chen believed that the macroeconomic balance of the socialist economy (investment versus saving, total government revenue versus fiscal spending, as well as the balance between the industrial, agricultural, and service sectors, and the proper speed of growth) could only be maintained through central planning. While pleased to see the return of the non-state sector and market mechanism, Chen was worried by their rapid growth and potential to undermine the economic foundations of socialism. He was not ready to accept a socialism devoid of central planning or collective ownership.

In Chen's vision, if the socialist economy was a bird, then the central planning capacity of the socialist state was represented by a cage. This bird-cage metaphor captured the core of Chen's economic thinking, and it prevailed among the Chinese government at the initial stage of economic reform. The cage in the metaphor was meant by Chen as a constraint, an interpretation widely accepted by both its opponents and critics.[12] Without the cage, the bird would flee and the economy would disintegrate; this happened during the Great Leap Forward when total decentralization allowed the economy to run out of control. Most important, the cage should continually adjust itself to the size of the bird. As the bird grows, the cage must be enlarged to allow it more space and freedom. Chen's view of the economy helped to facilitate Chinese economic reform at the early stage by easing the revival of the market and the private sector. But this representation of the state and economy was too restrictive to accommodate a genuine market economy.

This tension in the overall vision had little significance at the time, since no one in the government thought China was moving toward a market economy anyway. The goal of the reforms had always been to strengthen socialism. However, as Chen had repeatedly advocated the use of the market mechanism and private sector as a supplement to central planning and collective ownership, his view of a mixed socialist economy helped to legitimize the presence of the market and private sector in Chinese economic thinking. Not surprisingly,

Deng was content to see Chen's view prevail. He was not prepared to give up on socialism altogether, but he was eager to push forward economic reform and see the economy grow, whether it was driven by the private or state sector.

As a result, Chen's adage, "the planned economy as primary, market adjustments as auxiliary," became the government's official position in 1982. It essentially ruled out the proposal of price reform that Xue had proposed, even though the proposal had been warmly endorsed by Hu and Zhao. In his speech to the Twelfth Communist Party Congress in September 1982, Hu felt obliged to stress the primacy of the state sector and central planning in the economy. "In the past few years, we have initiated a number of reforms in the economic system . . . This orientation is correct, and its gains are apparent," as Hu reported. "However . . . cases of weakening and hampering the state's unified planning have been on the increase. . . . Hereafter, while continuing to give play to the role of market regulation, we must on no account neglect or relax unified leadership through state planning."[13] The proposal to implement wholesale price reform was shelved.

While the Chinese government had no difficulty in rejecting price reform, another genie was proving more difficult to return to its bottle: this was the rapidly expanding private sector in the Chinese economy. In the early 1980s the Chinese government was preoccupied with two dilemmas, how to keep the private sector and prevent it from squeezing out the state sector, and how to maintain the market but without sabotaging central planning. Once the market and private sectors were seen as threatening the economic foundation of socialism, the Chinese government acted resolutely. On January 11th, 1982, the Central Committee issued a notice, calling for immediate action to halt various economic crimes and preserve the socialist economic order. On 8th March the Standing Committee of the People's Congress passed the Resolution to Strike Hard against Serious Economic Crimes, and even revised certain clauses in Chinese Criminal Law to make it congruent with the Resolution. A national campaign against economic crimes was launched immediately afterward; this was intended to curb the growth of the private sector, with a particular eye on coastal areas witnessing a strong resurgence of private business. As the Resolution stated, "from now on, the struggle against the corruption from decayed bourgeois thought shall be strengthened. Emphasis is placed on preserving the purity of communism in the process of reform."[14]

III

Throughout the 1980s, the Chinese government faced an ideological dilemma. While the Chinese leaders still believed in the ultimate superiority of socialism, they were embarrassingly aware that China lagged far behind the West.

This put them in a politically vulnerable position. This sense of vulnerability, coupled with their continuous commitment to socialism, led the Chinese government to develop a paranoid fear of "peaceful evolution" – their suspicions that hostile forces outside China were constantly attempting to undermine and ultimately overthrow the Communist regime with "ideological weeds" and "cultural poisons." Ensuring that China would resist the temptations of capitalism became another preoccupation of the Chinese government. In 1983 a full-scale campaign was launched against so-called "spiritual pollution."[15] A handful of outspoken Party members was expelled from the Party for their advocacy of individual freedom. Though Deng in 1979 had marked political reform as a prerequisite for the success of economic reform, in 1983 this was still out of the question. Even discussions on market economics and liberalism were coming under attack.

In spite of this inhospitable political environment and blatant policy discrimination, China's fledgling private sector managed to survive and grow throughout the 1980s. But what enabled China's non-state sector to survive the ideological hostility of the government?

To answer that question, we have to recognize that the strengths of the rising Chinese private economy were much broader and deeper than is commonly recognized. In agriculture, for example, the implementation of the household responsibility system was instrumental to the success of agricultural reform. But other factors made a telling contribution, including a 22 percent rise in the purchase price of grain in 1979 and the increased use of fertilizers. The two pioneering villages described in the previous chapter certainly demonstrated the pure force of improved incentives. As a result, the public image of Chinese agricultural reform rests on increasing the incentives of Chinese peasants through decollectivization. However, this does not do justice to a very complex reality. When the household responsibility system was first implemented, it was no more than a performance contract between peasants and the state, which turned rural households into motivated residual claimants after the fulfillment of state quotas. Initially, it was still for the government to decide what crops to plant. But the government quickly lost its ability to enforce its directives. Gradually, the peasants came to have more and more control. The most important and long-lasting effect of decollectivization was regained economic freedom. Peasants were soon able to decide what to plant on their land, how much time to spend on farming, and what other jobs to take. The massive reallocation of time and labor from farming to non-farming activities led to greater efficiency in farming and also brought horticulture, aquaculture, commerce, handicraft, and industry back to rural China. Peasants were no longer chained to the land, and became free to make their own choices. As a result, the sources of income and employment were greatly diversified and the rural economy grew far beyond agriculture and traditional crafts.

Some critics of decollectivization had stressed what they regarded as a serious weakness of the rural reform: many local public works projects undertaken during Mao's era (particularly irrigation projects) were left to decay. Initially, this cast a long shadow on the prospect of private farming. As time went on, however, the loss of public investment in agriculture was made up by increased private investment. This saw the introduction of improved farming tools, increased use of well water (which did not require an extensive irrigation canal system), and better seeds, fertilizers, and pest controls. While private investment was not a perfect substitute for public works, private farming turned out to be out far more resilient than its critics had thought. Moreover, what was commonly regarded as local public goods, such as roads, gradually came to be provided by private interests or through the joint efforts of the private and public forces.

At the same time, since land was still owned by the state and state procurement of grain remained in place (it was not ended until 1985), agricultural reform posted little threat to either public ownership or central planning. It was therefore rarely affected by the policy debate on central planning and the campaign against economic crimes. Township and village enterprises were equally immune; under the protection of local authorities, these enterprises were officially collective rather than private concerns, even if the truth was somewhat different. Indeed, the early 1980s witnessed a proliferation of township and village enterprises all over China. At one point, the Economic Planning Committee of the State Council planned to absorb all township and village enterprises into the state production plan. The plan met strong resistance from Jiangsu and other provinces where the local governments were heavily involved in the development of township and village enterprises, and the proposal was quickly dropped.

Private business in cities was most vulnerable to accusations of "economic crime." The story of Nian Guangjiu in Wuhu of Anhui province provides an excellent example.[16] Nian, an illiterate man with no fixed job, was twice imprisoned for street peddling before economic reform began. After Mao's death and his release from prison, Nian supported himself by selling baked watermelon seeds on the street. Tasty and inexpensive, these were (and still are) a favorite snack all over China. A few years later, Nian developed his own recipe for baking watermelon seeds, with a unique flavour and delicious taste. His watermelon seeds became so popular that people often had to queue to buy them. To expand production, Nian started employing workers beyond his family. From a Marxist perspective, this was blatant exploitation. Even though in February 1979, the State Administration for Industry and Commerce allowed city residents without jobs to be self-employed for repair work, services and handicrafts, hiring workers was prohibited. Nian's wife was worried that he would be taken to prison again and asked him to give up his business. Nian's case was reported to Deng Xiaoping but, instead of denouncing Nian, Deng said, "Let's wait and see." In 1980, Nian trademarked "the Fool's Watermelon Seeds." By the end of the year, Nian had become one of the first millionaires in China. "The Fool's Watermelon Seeds" would quickly become one of the few household brand names in the food industry in China. However, Nian's business remained a political liability; Deng had to speak out again in 1984 and 1992 to defend Nian and save him from imprisonment.

Nian was probably China's luckiest private businessman. The businessmen of Wenzhou in Zhejiang province, the birthplace of the Chinese private economy, did not have the same good fortune.[17] There, and elsewhere, the campaign against economic crimes turned into a thinly disguised assault on private business. In the summer of 1982, eight private businessmen, all in different businesses, were charged with "profiteering" and arrested – though one was able to escape and remained at large for eight months. These "economic criminals" did nothing more than profit from private undertakings. By the end of 1982, more than 16,000 cases of economic crimes had been filed nationwide, and more than 30,000 people were arrested.[18] In this hostile environment many private businesses were forced to register themselves as collective or state enterprises. The owners of these businesses often paid a certain "administration fee" to a real collective or state enterprise or a supervising authority, in exchange for a nominal affiliation. This practice came to be known as putting on a "red hat"; private businesses gained the political protection needed to survive in an inhospitable political environment.

Fortunately, it did not take long for the Chinese government to realize that the most damaged part of the economy was actually the state-owned enterprises. This damage had been caused, in the main, by the lack of a proper pricing system, but state-owned enterprise was the very sector that the Chinese government had sought to protect by delaying price reform. With expanded autonomy, state-owned enterprises became more motivated. Productivity was improved and output went up. Without price reform, however, the whole pricing system was in chaos. The price signal that enterprises acted on did not reflect the true cost to the economy or genuine business opportunities. Under a convoluted price structure, enterprises with good products might not necessarily make any money, and those making large profits were often not supplying products desired by consumers. For example, because the price of coal was kept artificially low, no enterprise in the coal-mining industry was able to make any profit, despite increasing demand for coal. Moreover, state enterprises with guaranteed access to subsidized coal had no incentive to economize on their use of coal even though the real cost had gone up significantly. By holding off price reform, the Chinese government aimed to retain price control as a tool to bolster state enterprises. But without market price signals, there was no market discipline. State enterprises were thus deprived of the most effective mechanism of surviving competition.

Private enterprises and township and village enterprises, on the other hand, were in a different situation. Excluded from the state economic plan, they could buy what they needed and sell what they produced at prices more or less determined by the market. As the factor and product markets were just emerging, information cost remained high for the private firms, and sometimes prohibitively so. This period saw people in charge of purchase and sale in private firms traveling all over China, exploring new sources of inputs and new markets in which to sell their products. These salesmen also earned higher incomes. While their high wage largely reflected their contribution, it also indicated the high cost of exchange for private firms. The high transaction cost resulted in huge inefficiencies in the private economy, diverting resources away from production and innovation. But private enterprises were free of state-imposed constraints on their business decision-making and operated with hard budget constraints and genuine market discipline. Private enterprises did not always perform better than the state-owned enterprises, but those that survived the process of market selection were all but certain to do so.

Thus, the growth of China's non-state sector had as much to do with its own strength and dynamism as with the weakness of state-owned enterprises. The "non-state" sector was rarely viewed as a "private" sector in confrontation with socialist ideology. Seen as supplementary to the state sector, the non-state sector was allowed to exist outside the strict control of the state. Still, the Chinese government could have crushed it altogether if it had chosen to do so, as its campaign in the early 1980s against "economic crimes" had demonstrated, and as Mao had done previously. So why did the Chinese socialist government allow the non-state sector to grow?

IV

In its early stages, China's economic reform had a rare advantage in that the political establishment was largely free of vested interests.[19] Despite the long-standing tensions between central and local government, and the emerging conflict between the private and state sector, the political elite was united in its mission to turn China into a rich and powerful socialist country. Chen Yun's strong preference for the state sector and central planning, for example, mainly rested on his belief in the superiority of socialism over capitalism, a view that was shared, to varying degrees, among most Chinese leaders at that time.

Throughout the 1980s and early 1990s, Chinese politics was largely dominated by the veteran duo Deng Xiaoping and Chen Yun. While Deng has always been seen as the architect of economic reform, Chen is usually viewed by observers outside China as Deng's cautious, conservative foil. On the surface,

Chen and Deng could not be further apart. Deng built his career as a Party leader, with strong roots in the military, while Chen was rarely directly involved in the army or party affairs, being mainly the overseer of financial and economic affairs. Unlike Deng, Chen was deeply skeptical of fast growth, which he believed would create more economic problems than it could resolve. The failure of Mao's Great Leap Forward and Hua's "Leap Outward" only reinforced his conviction. Chen had a much stronger belief in the value of central planning and collective ownership. But unlike Mao and most other Chinese leaders, who had little knowledge of the modern economy, Chen followed an apprenticeship in Shanghai during his youth. He knew private business too well to believe in pure socialism and the total elimination of private ownership and market forces. The disagreement between Deng and Chen was so wide that in the 1980s the Politburo Standing Committee seldom convened for meetings.[20] Instead, Deng would simply call in Hu Yaobang, Zhao Ziyang, and others to his home and Deng would visit Chen only once a year. Nonetheless, the characterization of Deng as a reformer and Chen as a conservative has reinforced a simplified black-and-white view of the Chinese leaders that is a long way from the truth.

The divide between Deng and Chen was not driven by any conflict of interest or clash in ideology, even though Chen undoubtedly showed a deeper commitment to socialism. While it is generally known that this divide slowed down the speed of the Chinese reform, it is less well understood that the pair's disagreements helped to maintain a relatively tolerant political atmosphere – a stark contrast to that of Mao's era. The co-presence of Deng and Chen and their wide disagreements inadvertently turned post-Mao Chinese politics away from a "one-man show." Despite their differences and disagreements, Chen and Deng had in common a real commitment to pragmatism, a point which is seldom recognized among observers of Chinese politics. Chen's aphorism "do not rely on higher authorities, do not rely on books, but rely on facts," was an important part of the post-Mao pragmatism spearheaded by Deng.

This new feature of Chinese politics had a powerful influence on the course of economic reform. Most Chinese leaders were willing to change their views once they had been proven inconsistent with facts. Their questioning and rejection of once-unquestioned ideology created a milieu conducive to change and open to new ideas. This was not because Deng Xiaoping, Chen Yun, and other post-Mao Chinese leaders were wiser than their predecessors; the tragedy of the Great Leap Forward and calamity of the Cultural Revolution had simply dented their faith in any doctrine. If socialism could go so terribly wrong, then an omnipotent ideology must be nothing more than a fatal conceit. It was this shared conviction that brought together Chen Yun and Deng Xiaoping in their pragmatic, experimental approach to reform. Despite the commanding presence of Deng, Chen, and other veterans, in post-Mao China no political leader could simply impose his will on the Party, as Mao so frequently had done. This contributed greatly to the survival and development of a more open-minded attitude. General Secretary Hu Yaobang's liberal policies in the early 1980s clearly attested further to a profound change in attitude within the Party.[21]

The extraordinary willingness of the Chinese leaders to alter deeply ingrained views is best illustrated by the political debate on central planning and the market. In this debate, resistance to the market as a coordinating mechanism was both ideological and intellectual. Ideologically, the market was condemned as the ultimate cause of various disorders in the market economy, including unemployment, inflation, economic fluctuation, and recession. Moreover, since Marxism had hitherto been accepted unquestionably in China, and treated as the ultimate truth, there was a substantial intellectual barrier which prevented the Chinese people from appreciating the virtues of the market. Mao, for example, once proposed a return to a barter economy, which he thought would be effective in eliminating economic inequality once and for all. As a consequence, even the failure of many of Mao's radical policies was attributed to his deviation from socialism and the doctrine of central planning. For Chen Yun and many others in the Party and the government who had disagreed with Mao, Mao's failures actually validated the socialist way.

But the disappointing performance of the state-owned enterprises relative to the private sector led the Chinese leaders to soften their position. Central planning was gradually relaxed to allow both a "compulsory economic plan" and a "recommendatory economic plan"—the former continued the traditional state plan that state-owned enterprises had to follow strictly, while the latter was presented as recommendations and was not binding. As time went by, the recommendatory economic plan grew in importance. This gave the state-owned enterprises more room to exercise their economic freedom. Without any change in ownership structure, the state-owned enterprises gradually became more responsive to market forces. The part of the Chinese economy that was not subject to central planning continued to expand. It is worth pointing out that Chinese economists who had promoted a "recommendatory economic plan," including Liu Guoguang and Xue Muqiao, had a difficult time in 1982–83 during the campaign against "spiritual pollution."[22] Nonetheless, the freedoms of the recommendatory plan were not totally eliminated in the economy or in policy. In fact, in April 1984, a national conference was held to discuss and promote the recommendatory economic plan.[23]

The change of economic policy was most striking in the government's attitude toward township and village enterprises. Despite their strong contribution to economic growth, township and village enterprises were viewed by the Chinese government as an inferior rival to state-owned enterprises, and essentially disruptive to the state plan. However, in March 1984, the State Council issued what was known as the Number 4 Document.[24] This document outlined the government's support for township and village enterprises and, in particular, for the private enterprises set up by rural households. Township and village enterprises were endorsed as "an important force of the national economy and an important supplement to state-owned enterprises." Acknowledged as a key element in modernizing Chinese agriculture and industrializing rural China, township and village enterprises were now allowed to enter all industries except tobacco. They were also given tax breaks, access to bank credit, and other financial incentives. Indeed, compared with state-owned enterprises, township and village enterprises now had a lower tax burden. As one veteran scholar put it, "1984 marked a dramatic step in liberalizing the rural economy and improving the policy environment for rural enterprises, which opened the door to accelerated growth."[25]

While the Chinese government in the 1980s was certainly more pragmatic and open to the idea of reform, this did not guarantee that the new policies they adopted were necessarily better than previous ones. As the Chinese leaders then proclaimed, "reform should tolerate mistakes, but we cannot stand an absence of reform." Deng Xiaoping himself probably emphasized more than anyone else the importance of learning from mistakes in the process of reform. However, many challenges remained. Not least of these was minimizing mistakes in learning and experimenting so as to maintain the political consensus behind reform, as well as relaxing political constraints without threatening the political legitimacy of the Party.

V

Any account of the Chinese economic reform would be incomplete and misleading if the policy of opening up is not properly emphasized as a critical and integral component. China's opening up, particularly to the West, was a policy pursued by the Chinese government throughout the 1980s and beyond. Each step of China's economic reform brought it closer to the global market economy.

Five years after Deng's historic visit to the United States, Premier Zhao Ziyang visited the country in early January 1984. This was reciprocated by President Reagan's visit to China in April 1984, the first since Nixon's visit in 1972. The easing of Sino-US relations helped to open up American universities to Chinese students and American markets to Chinese goods. It also made China an attractive destination for western investment; all of this would have a long-lasting impact on the Chinese economy and society. Beyond these obvious changes, improved Sino-US relations also exerted another, subtler, but equally profound influence on the character of Chinese economic reform. The United States of America came to replace the Soviet Union as a role model for China, particularly in the minds of Chinese students. From the mid-1980s onwards, college students in China's elite universities came to view graduate training in the United States as the ultimate career opportunity. Even the sons and daughters of senior Chinese leaders began to travel to the United States to study; in the 1940s and 1950s their parents had been sent to Moscow.

No place in China was a more effective conduit to capitalism than the Special Economic Zone in Shenzhen. In January 1984, Deng Xiaoping visited Shenzhen for the first time since the founding of the Special Economic Zones. Encouraged by its rapid development, Deng praised Shenzhen as a successful model of China's "open-door" policy. Deng's visit and his affirmation sent a clear message to the West that China was committed to economic reform and opening up. As reported in the *Japan Economic Journal*, after Deng's tour, "major Japanese trading firms [were] rushing to open offices in Shenzhen."[26] Later in the year, fourteen more coastal cities were opened up, a move noticed by the *Business Week* as "China's bold new program to lure foreign investment."[27]

But the experiment at Shenzhen did not always run smoothly. No Chinese leader was more supportive and enthusiastic about Shenzhen than Deng Xiaoping. Yet, in June 1985, Deng admitted that "The Shenzhen Special Economic Zone is an experiment. We need more time to see whether it has gone well. We wish it success; if it fails, it will provide some lessons."[28] There was no shortage of disagreement among Chinese leaders on the future of China; they also kept revising their views as the reform went on. At the beginning, the leaders were united in wanting to make China "a powerful, modern, socialist country" (1978). It did not take long for them to revise their mission to put in place "socialism with Chinese characteristics" (1982) and "a commerce economy with plan" (1984), before finally embracing "a socialist market economy with Chinese characteristics" (1992). In this process, Shenzhen was caught in a constant struggle to reconcile itself with the continually shifting Party line.

As a pioneering experiment, Shenzhen never wanted for critics. Always a few steps ahead of the policies being pursued, it often found itself at odds with the prevailing ideology. This was inevitable since Shenzhen and other Special Economic Zones were created to co-opt capitalist practices to save socialism. But this strategy necessitated the adoption of a quasi-capitalist system in Shenzhen. It thus faced overwhelming ideological and practical challenges. Ideologically, China was not at all ready for a market economy, and Shenzhen was often viewed as a conduit for "spiritual pollution," suffering a wave of condemnation in 1982 and1983. Many years later, in 1992, Deng revealed his solution to such opprobrium. "It was my idea to discourage contention, so as to have more time for action. Once disputes begin, they complicate matters and waste a lot of time. As a result, nothing is accomplished. Don't argue; try bold experiments and blaze new trails."[29]

Chen Yun and Li Xiannian never visited Shenzhen, despite Li's direct role in setting up the Shekou Industrial Park. This is commonly read as indicating their disproval of the opening-up policy, and there is no doubt that Chen at the beginning was firmly opposed to the setup of the Special Economic Zones and his skepticism and reservation remained for a long time.[30] When Li died in 1992, Chen wrote an obituary, which was published in the *People's Daily* on July 21st.[31] In the article, Chen mentioned the fact that he and Li had never been to Shenzhen. He continued:

> but we have always been interested in the development of the Special Economic Zones and thought that we have to continuously accumulate lessons to make them work well. In the past few years, Shenzhen had basically changed from an importing to exporting zone, with many new high rise buildings. The development was indeed fast. Today the scale of our economy is much bigger and more complicated than ever before. Many practices that worked before had become obsolete under the current economic reform. This requires us to constantly learn new things, to explore and resolve new problems.

To many outside observers, the setting up of Shenzhen and other Special Economic Zones was interpreted as a triumph for Deng, the reformist, over Chen, the conservative. Many other episodes of the reform were also interpreted in the same fashion. However, the simple and important fact is that both Deng and Chen shared an experimental approach to reform and were both open-minded enough to learn new lessons in spite of their disagreements.[32]

The introduction of foreign capital and knowledge to China was by no means confined to Shenzhen and other Special Economic Zones. The Pearl River Delta in South Guangdong province emerged in the 1980s as the most powerful driver of China's economic growth, largely due to its ability to attract foreign investment from the overseas Chinese. Guangdong was close to Hong Kong and shared the same dialect and local culture. It quickly established itself as the first choice for investment from Hong Kong; it also gained technology, managerial know-how, and access to the international market. Many of the early joint ventures or foreign-owned companies set up in Guangdong were attracted by China's low production costs. These companies concentrated mainly in the manufacturing of clothing, shoes, and toys. They were later criticized for bringing little advanced technology to China. But in the early stage of reform, these joint ventures played a pioneering role in exposing the Chinese to the culture of private enterprise. In addition, various aspects of Hong Kong culture, including movies, music and literature, were transmitted through Guangdong to the rest of China. In the mid-1980s, Cantonese became a popular language widely learned in Shanghai and elsewhere in China. Capitalism turned out to be less threatening and corrupting than had been projected by the state-controlled media.

China's opening-up policy was not confined to attracting foreign capital and acquiring advanced technology. Expertise in management was also eagerly sought after by the Chinese government. Through the German Senior Expert Service, an organization of retired professionals in West Germany, a group of retired German engineers were invited to visit Wuhan in 1984.[33] Wuhan, the capital of Hubei province and the largest city in the middle Yangzi River, was among the top manufacturing centers in China before the economic reform. It had a high concentration of large state-owned enterprises. One of the German engineers, Willner Gehrig, stayed on and became the first foreign manager of a Chinese state-owned enterprise, the Wuhan Machine Tool Plant. During his two-year tenure, Gehrig brought in many reforms to improve workers' incentive and the firm's productivity, with a special focus on quality control. The quality of the firm's main product, diesel engines, improved substantially, and for a short time the company became the top brand in the industry in China. But Gehrig's reform measures were far ahead of their time and most did not survive after his departure in 1986: Wuhan Machine Tool Plant eventually went bankrupt. But after his success, many foreign experts were hired by China's state-owned enterprises. The impact of these foreign managers and consultants in furthering managerial knowledge in China was greatly appreciated. In 2005, two years after his death, a bronze statue of Gehrig was erected in the center of Wuhan, in remembrance of his lasting influence.

VI

The passing of the Decision on Economic System Reform at the Third Plenum of the Twelfth Central Committee in October 1984 was another landmark in Chinese economic reform. It moved China beyond Chen Yun's interpretation of socialism, which until then had served as the guiding principle for reform. The 1984 Decision stated that, in order to reform the economic system

> we first have to break down the conventional wisdom that treated the planned economy and commercial economy [a Marxian term for the market economy] as antithetical and realize that the socialist planned economy has to consciously comply with and make use of the value theory [a Marxian term for general economic theory], and is a public ownership based commercial economy with state planning. The development of a commercial economy is a necessary stage in social and economic development, a prerequisite for the realization of China's economic modernization.[34]

The Decision was praised by Deng as a "new political economy of Marxism" and it also won the endorsement of Chen Yun, who reportedly said after the meeting that the Chinese economy had grown so much that many practices of the 1950s were no longer feasible.[35]

This acceptance of both the need for and desirability of the market economy was a milestone in China's economic reform. A few years of reform had convinced the Chinese leaders that central planning, the secret weapon of socialism, could not be counted on as a panacea. Much more than an "auxiliary" to state planning, the market was recognized as an indispensable tool for regulating the economy. However, the market economy was ideologically acceptable only on the premise that it was still compatible with socialism. While central planning was no longer the sacred pillar of socialism, collective ownership was still seen as the basic economic foundation of socialism. It was still believed that only collective ownership could secure shared prosperity and prevent economic inequality. Thus, a political bias against the private sector endured beyond 1984, even though it was not as strong as before.

An immediate impact of this new interpretation of socialism was that it opened the door for price reform.[36] In the early 1980s, price reform failed to win political support because central planning was still seen as indispensible to socialism. With the changing interpretation of socialism, more policy choices became possible. The most critical difference between a market and a socialist economy is the acceptance of a market-based pricing system to coordinate the division of labor; this exists in the former and is absent in the latter. But there was no quick fix to move a socialist economy to a market economy and get all prices right immediately. Under socialism, most prices are set by government decrees. In a market economy, prices emerge from competition.[37] Policy changes may create or expand to give room for market forces to operate, but they cannot substitute for the working of the market.

In the Chinese discussion on price reform, two distinct approaches developed. The government could adjust prices through administrative fine-tuning – referred to as *"tiao"* – so that prices would gradually move toward what was deemed a proper level. Alternatively, the government could free pricing from its control and leave it to the market, an approach referred to as *"fang."*[38] After the Third Plenum of 1984, the second approach became accepted and implemented, but the first one would persist for many years to come. The co-existence of the two approaches would gradually institutionalize the dual-track pricing mechanism, one of the most recognized innovations in Chinese economic reforms.

On January 1st, 1985, the mandatory procurement program in agriculture was abolished. This system had been designed by Chen Yun to secure the food supply and was first installed in the early–mid-1950s.[39] When it was launched, it was meant to be an emergency measure because Chen recognized that its potential damage to peasants could be devastating. But it stayed in place for over thirty years and became the linchpin of Mao's agricultural policy. It thus created many serious problems. Specifically, this policy robbed peasants of their basic economic freedom. When later combined with cooperativization (the brutal imposition of agricultural cooperatives and later, communes), it enslaved all Chinese peasants and sent millions of them down the road to starvation. After the abolishing of this program, the government would purchase only a set quota of grain at a stipulated price, and any quantities exceeding the quota were purchased at prices determined by the market. Although this was not the intention, a dual-track pricing system was created across the agricultural economy. The fulfillment of state quotas at artificially low prices was simply a disguised tax on peasants. Nonetheless, peasants were no longer totally confined to the state quota system and, though still under the shadow of the state, they began to interact with China's nascent market forces. Still, urban consumers would not have to pay market price for their grain until 1992, with the government continuing to subsidize their consumption until that date. As far as rural households were concerned, the implementation of the household responsibility system in 1982 and the removal of mandatory procurement in 1985 marked the end of the era of central planning and the opening up of a new era for market and economic freedom.

Price reform in industry began on a similar course to that of agriculture, but the results were drastically different. By the end of 1984, the competitive forces vested on industry by private enterprises had ensured that the price of many consumer products was freed from state control. But the fear of inflation and other social and political concerns made the Chinese government hesitant to relinquish control over the price of raw materials. Many state-owned enterprises would have to close if they lost their access to subsidized energy and other inputs. In February 1985, the State Price Administration and Material Administration declared that state-owned enterprises could maintain two lines of material supplies, state allocation and free purchase from the market.[40] Accordingly, the prices of the goods (mainly intermediate inputs) produced in the state quota system were fixed by the state and the prices of goods produced outside the plan were left to the vagaries of the market.

Unlike agriculture, where the state bought grain from peasants at either a negotiated or market price and sold it to city residents at a fixed price, industry involved a long chain of activities and numerous enterprises before initial inputs reached consumers as finished products. Even socialism could not do away with specialization and the division of labor. This made state management and price control in industry a great deal more complex than in agriculture, and much harder to implement effectively. Since materials supplied by the state (or rather claims to such materials distributed by various authorities) could be easily sold at their (considerably higher) market price, those with personal connections to the government office or managers of state-owned enterprises had great opportunities for profiteering. As a result, China saw the rise of many "paper companies" – companies with no more than a documented presence, but whose political connections allowed them to make easy and risk-free profits selling state controlled materials on the black market. Even though such activities did help to expand the market for raw materials, they created a chaotic price environment for the whole economy. Moreover, such blatant corruption was widely resented and gave rise to a pronounced anti-reform sentiment in Chinese society.

The dual-track system was not without its merits.[41] In the non-state sector, it created more opportunities for interaction with state enterprises through the market mechanism as well as providing reliable access to raw materials strictly controlled by the state. With the dual-track system in place, private enterprises no longer depended on black market purchases for their inputs; those transactions were expensive and full of uncertainties. At a market price, the private enterprises could now openly buy inputs from state enterprises. This was an important reason for the continuous growth of the non-state sector throughout the 1980s, which, undoubtedly, speeded up the decline of state enterprises.

In state enterprises, the dual-track system created an unintended consequence. With the implementation of the system, enterprise reform became something greater than "delegating rights and sharing profits." Modeled after the household responsibility system in agriculture, a contract responsibility system had been tried among a few state enterprises as early as 1981, and this was implemented nationwide in 1984. Enterprise managers would sign a performance contract with their supervising authority, while employees signed a contract with the manager. Thus, a multi-tier contract system emerged in the state enterprises, in which rewards were tied to performance. Under the new contract responsibility system, employees of the state enterprises were given more freedom. Those who thought they possessed marketable skills and were more enterprising could now choose to produce goods and services for the market; otherwise, they could stay within the state plan and produce whatever was specified in the state plan. Thus, a proportion of state employees opted out of central planning and directed their production to the market while remaining in the state sector. Before diving into the ocean of the market, which was then called "*xiahai*," they could first dip their toes in the water. This opportunity of staying with the state enterprise but producing for the market greatly moderated their apprehension of market forces and smoothed the learning curve of embracing the market. Without privatization or any change in the ownership structure of state enterprises, some state employees were able to participate in the market; this helped to encourage risk-taking and facilitate entrepreneurship among state employees while socialism was largely kept intact.

Although full price reform would have presented a severe challenge to state-owned enterprises, the dual-track pricing system offered a more convenient and less risky approach. However, this system in industry was a formalization and an extension of practices that had emerged in many industries during the previous stage of enterprise reform, and it resulted in similar problems. It did not take long for the Chinese government to recognize the urgency of the need for full price reform.

VII

The Chinese government also took a number of measures to develop a common market across the whole economy. In a market economy, the price mechanism coordinates the flow of resources within the economy, firstly by signaling the return of competing uses of resources to all economic actors, and then by allowing resources to move to their most profitable employment. The market is able to operate in this way because all firms are constrained by a common market discipline and competition in the product market can then lead to efficient utilization of the factors of production. This system breaks down, however, when the firms' survival is not determined by their performance in the product market as judged by consumers. In China's decentralized economy, the active intervention of local authorities and a chaotic price system thwarted the operation of market forces. One of the most severe consequences was the fragmentation of the national economy, impeding the free movement of inputs and products. When the price system was suppressed, economic resources could not seek the highest returns. Enterprises could not sell products freely in the market; consumers were denied their freedom to choose. The market system was essentially paralyzed. To allow production to continue, the visible hand of the state became a necessity.

On March 23rd, 1986, the State Council issued the Decision on Several Question in Further Pushing for Horizontal Economic Integration," encouraging enterprises across different regions and under different authorities to merge.[42] Horizontal economic integration then came to be regarded as a crucial component in economic reform to overcome trade barriers created by the fragmented economy. From March 31st to May 19th, the *People's Daily* ran four editorials calling for, and giving specific guidance on, horizontal economic integration.[43] In the absence of a market system, these mergers among enterprises went some way towards promoting the efficient utilization of resources.

In support of horizontal economic integration, the Chinese government also launched reforms in labor management.[44] The "iron bowl" of socialism – lifetime employment with a single employer – began to change. Contract labor was introduced and was quickly adopted by enterprises. Many regional labor markets emerged and developed quickly. While the State Council would retain control of the total wage level for a given enterprise, in December 1986 it allowed state-owned enterprises full freedom in deciding the wages and bonuses for their employees. By introducing more flexibility to the labor market, these reform initiatives facilitated mergers among state enterprises.

At the time, the integration of enterprises had an added benefit – it helped to expand the autonomy of enterprises beyond that afforded by the contract responsibility system. A common consequence of horizontal economic integration was the creation of "share enterprises" – merged companies. In the majority of cases in China – and unlike corporate mergers in a market economy – the dominant enterprise did not purchase its junior partners outright. Instead, each negotiated for a specific amount of shares in the newly merged "mother company." Though the transfer of stock was not permitted initially, in many other ways these resembled a modern joint-stock company. Later, the joint-stock company model was widely embraced as an alternative to the contract responsibility system as a means of furthering industrial reform. In April 1984, a state owned shopping center in Beijing was allowed to sell stocks to the public to raise capital.[45] In November, Shanghai Feilo Acoustics Corporation also sold stocks to both the public and its employees; it became the first company in China to issue stocks to the public.[46] By the end of 1986, China had more than 6000 joint-stock companies.[47] With its ability to raise capital from the public and to operate in multiple sites, the joint-stock company effectively weakened the control of the local government. This represented a significant increase in the autonomy of Chinese enterprises.

VIII

At this point, the Chinese government made a serious policy blunder, with far-reaching implications. To examine this, we have to start with reforms in the banking sector.[48] Before 1978, China had one bank – the People's Bank of China, which was owned and controlled by the central government and overseen by the Ministry of Finance. Its main function was to finance the physical production plans of state-owned enterprises. With little savings in private hands and credit allocated to the state-owned enterprises through central planning, the Chinese economy did not have much need for banking. According to the World Bank's estimate, of China's total savings in 1978, household savings accounted for a mere 3.4 percent, with government savings amounting to 43.4 percent and the remaining 53.2 percent in the hands of enterprises.[49] This situation changed dramatically after the start of reform. By the 1990s, household savings had gone up remarkably, accounting for between one-quarter to one-half of the country's total savings.[50] The first step of banking reform was to install a two-tiered banking structure. The People's Bank of China became the Central Bank of China, while four state-owned banks took over the emerging conventional banking business, such as taking deposits and making loans. The Agricultural Bank of China, dealing with banking business in agriculture and rural areas, was set up in February 1979; the Bank of China, dealing with for-eign trade and investment, was founded in March. The People's Construction Bank of China, dealing with fixed capital investment, was spun off from the Minister of Finance in August 1979. The Industrial and Commercial Bank of China was set up in 1983 to deal with all commercial transactions not serviced by the other three institutions.

The new structure ended the monopoly of the People's Bank of China. The Central Bank became separated from the four specialized banks, each of which was expected to operate like a commercial bank. They competed with each other in taking deposits from enterprises and individuals, but had a protected market for loans, since each bank had a different set of customers designated by the state. The four specialized banks had little pressure to perform the basic functions of screening and monitoring; where to invest and how much contin-ued to be decided by the government. Under the decentralized administrative system, the total amount of investment specified by the central government was seen by local governments as a common pool. This led to aggressive com-petition for investment quotas and bank credit. In the face of demands from local authorities, the central government often made concessions and allocated additional loans beyond the specifications of the investment plan. In addition, the local governments could, and often did, put direct pressure on the local branches of the state banks. Consequently, "investment hunger" was a constant problem in China, as in many other socialist economies.[51]

What made China's case distinctive was that it was the local govern-ments, rather than state-owned enterprises, that worked hardest to win invest-ment. Thus, in China, "investment hunger" deepened as local governments became empowered by administrative decentralization. In addition, "invest-ment hunger" was driven by another prominent feature of the Chinese economy. Since the mid-1950s, China had sacrificed agriculture to subsidize industrialization; a common way of doing this was by depressing the price for agricultural products and other raw materials while raising the prices of manufactured goods. Once reforms began, the price gap between agricultural and industrial products began to close, but the biased price system still made industrial production much more lucrative than it would otherwise have been. As a result, industrial investment was coveted by both local governments and enterprises, particularly the non-state firms.

After the third Plenum of the Twelfth Central Committee in 1984, another round of bank reform was begun. The goal was to give more autonomy to the four specialized banks in loan-making and, by doing so, to make the banking industry more autonomous and competitive. The first step was for the Central Bank to stipulate the amount of loans each bank could make each year and then let the banks decide for themselves how to make the loans.[52] During the last quarter of 1984, the Central Bank leaked that total loans the banks would be permitted to make in 1985 would be based on the actual loans they made in 1984. Not surprisingly, all banks rushed to give out loans.

To make things worse, the Ministry of Labor was at the same time considering a wage reform policy. It proposed that the wages in 1984 would serve as a benchmark for wage increases in the following years. As a result, state-owned enterprises rushed to banks to borrow money to raise wages at a time when banks would take any opportunity to lend money. Consequently, the bank loans in December of 1984 increased almost 50 percent over those of December 1983. The bonus paid to employees of state-owned enterprises increased more than 100 percent and total wages increased by 38 percent. The money supply in the last quarter of 1984 increased by more than 160 percent. For the whole year, it increased almost 50 percent over the previous year, 45 percent higher than the figure stipulated in the economic plan.[53] Investment and consumption were both set to rise; conditions were ripe for inflation.

With this ready supply of bank credit, growth in investment accelerated over the following few years. The industrial sector expanded rapidly, particularly the township and village enterprises. In Wuxi county of Jiangsu, home to the largest concentration of township and village enterprises in China, output grew by 100 percent in each of the first two months of 1985.[54] In the meantime, inflationary pressures were building. In 1985, inflation rose to 9.3 percent, up from 2.8 percent in the previous year. It remained high in 1986 and 1987 (6.5 percent and 7.3 percent respectively), before rising to double digits in 1988. At the time, the Chinese government chose to believe that modest inflation was a necessary byproduct of economic growth; no decisive action was taken.[55]

Under the contract responsibility system, managers of the state enterprises were eager to invest in projects that were able to deliver short-term gains, leaving the long-term consequences to their successors and, ultimately, to the state. In the mid-1980s, employees of the state enterprises enjoyed steady rises in incomes, while the state had to pump increasing amounts of money into the enterprises to keep them running. In 1987, subsidies to state enterprises made up one-third of government expenditure.

At the same time, the growing pains of the enterprise reform with its dual-track pricing mechanism led the Chinese government to embrace price reform. However, the timing of this could not have been more unfortunate. In 1988, when the Chinese government announced its intention to go ahead with price reform, inflation increased rapidly. The price index jumped from 9.5 percent in January to 16.5 percent in June, 19.3 percent in July and 38.6 percent in August. This was a level unprecedented in the history of the People's Republic. February 1988 saw panic buying in many Chinese cities. It was reported that a consumer in Wuhan bought 200 kilograms of salt, and another in Nanjing bought 500 boxes of matchsticks.[56] Under such conditions, price reform came to be seen as too politically risky, and the attempt faltered. The collapse of the price reform had a wide-ranging impact. Economic reform was held back everywhere else, with reversals in certain areas. An austerity program was introduced in September and the Chinese economy entered a four-year period of "adjustment and reorganization."[57]

IX

While economic reform was halted in the mid-late 1980s, Chinese politics suffered its own misfortune.[58] Hu Yaobang, arguably the most open-minded leader the Chinese Communist Party ever had, was forced to step down in January 1987. Hu had played a critical role in the late 1970s and early 1980s in reintroducing pragmatism and common sense to Chinese politics and stressing tolerance and liberal thinking, critical for reuniting the Chinese people behind the Party. But Hu's liberal political views were many steps ahead of his fellow Party members and this put him in conflict with Party veterans, including Deng. While the Party was obsessed with the threat of "peaceful evolution" and "capitalist liberalization" throughout the 1980s, Hu stressed "feudal despotism" as the most insidious element in the Party. He believed that the Party could face up to any external challenge as long as it was able to strengthen itself from within by encouraging free airing of different views. Hu was far more willing to share political power and tolerate dissenters than allowed by the Party line. During the "Anti-Spiritual Pollution" campaign in 1983–1984, Hu was attacked for being too accommodating to intellectuals who were alleged to promote "spiritual pollution" in China, as well as being ineffective in preserving the leadership of the Party.[59] At a time when the majority of the Party leaders were preoccupied with consolidating one-party rule, Hu's persistent efforts to encourage and protect dissenting voices and to create an open and tolerant environment for political discussion was perceived as a sign of political weakness.

The explicit reason for Hu's removal was his unwillingness to use harsh measures to contain the student protests in 1985 and 1986. Throughout the mid-1980s, college students had staged occasional street protests, demanding individual freedom and political participation. Non-political concerns, such as the quality of food at school canteens, were equally important in fueling dissent on campus and motivating students to protest on the streets. In 1986, massive student demonstrations erupted in Beijing, Shanghai, and other big cities which contained concentrations of college campuses. Hu was harshly criticized by Party veterans for being too lenient in his response to students and too soft in defending the Party's monopoly of political power. At the same time, the worsening personal relations between Hu and Deng triggered Deng's withdrawal of support. Never a favorite of the Party veterans, Hu had no choice but to step down.[60] But he was widely perceived by the public (particularly college

students and intellectuals) as a defender of freedom of expression and an inno-
cent victim of party politics. A year later, his sudden death on April 15th, 1989,
triggered an outpouring of sympathy and sorrow from people in all walks of
life. Without any real avenue to express their views, college students in Beijing
took to the streets, beginning the 1989 Students Movement.

Like any political event, the 1989 Students Movement had many causes and
its development was shaped by multiple factors.[61] The particular way it began
and its tragic ending were not anticipated, but its origin and development were
clearly influenced by recognizable economic forces.

Any economic reform involves change in the rules of the game, with
inevitable distributive consequences. China's enterprise reform was no exception. Losers, in both a relative and an absolute sense, were understandably eager
to voice their discontent when the opportunity arose. The Chinese economic
reform has been applauded as a "reform without losers."[62] This cannot be true,
however, if gains are measured in relative terms. Even if everyone was made
better off during the reform, the relative position in the income ladder would
change for many members of society. In this relative sense, it was inevitable
that some would feel like losers. In addition, for those with political privileges
the enterprise reform in the 1980s created many opportunities to make easy
money. Government officials who controlled access to state-supplied materials
and managers of state enterprises were widely believed to have enriched themselves through arbitrage opportunities created by the dual-track pricing system.
The abuse of public power gave rise to widespread resentment against reform;
this explained why the 1989 Students Movement was so enthusiastically supported by the general public. Thus, reform without losers in the absolute sense
could still give rise to widespread frustration and disillusion. Moreover, mistakes in economic policy, particularly the mishandling of monetary policy since
1985, which ultimately led to double-digit inflation in 1988, created an army
of discontents ready to take to the streets.

Paradoxically, it was the sympathy and active support of the wider population that raised alarm bells in the Chinese government. Student protests in
previous years were mostly confined to college students, with little participation from others. In 1989, the Beijing municipal government was stunned
by the widespread participation of city residents in the students' street
protests. The frightened municipal leaders reported to Deng Xiaoping, char-
acterizing the peaceful, non-confrontational student demonstrations as an
"anti-revolutionary turmoil." To most Chinese people, this term evoked dark
memories of the Cultural Revolution. On April 26th, the *People's Daily* issued a
front-page editorial, "Hold the Flag Clear to Oppose Any Turmoil," charging a
few unnamed individuals – the so-called "black hands" – behind the students
with fomenting "a planned conspiracy" aiming to "plunge the whole country
into chaos and sabotage the political situation of stability and unity." The harsh

tone and outrageous charges did not scare the students into backing down, as the Chinese government had intended. On the contrary, disappointed and agitated, students became more angry and responded by conducting larger-scale demonstrations and winning more support from the non-student population.

Outside Beijing, student protests broke out in over 130 Chinese cities. Many students flocked to Beijing to show their solidarity and support, or just to tour the capital. The central government did not ask provincial governments or the Ministry of Railways to prevent their college students from traveling to Beijing. On the contrary, students were allowed to travel for free on the railway to Beijing. As Beijing was flooded with students from all over China, the situation became more disorderly. As time went by, the radical elements within the student movement prevailed. A few hundred students went on hunger strike on May 13th and gradually the protestors and the government were cornered into confrontation; neither side was willing or able to compromise. The Chinese government imposed martial law on May 20th, but could not enforce it in the face of strong resistance from students and Beijing residents. The 50,000 troops ordered to enforce martial law were stopped by Beijing residents and students on their routes to Tiananmen Square; after two days, the troops withdrew. This episode not only further antagonized the protestors, it also misled them into believing that they could beat the government if they stayed united and determined. Long accustomed to military revolutions and class struggles but with little experience in civil dialogue, the Party was unprepared to take a conciliatory stance. In addition, students who had occupied the Square since mid-May were too disorganized to be able to strike a bargain with the government. On the night of June 3rd, with the approval of Deng, armed soldiers, supported by trucks and tanks, stormed into the Square from all directions, leaving hundreds of civilians dead on the way.

The Tiananmen incident had significant repercussions for Chinese economic reform, at least in the short term. Foreign investment tumbled and international trade dropped significantly in the following years. Many reform measures were stopped and there were policy reversals in several areas. Private business witnessed its worst period since the reform began. Nonetheless, the incident did not turn into another lengthy political persecution. Nor did China close its door to the West. After a decade of reform Chinese politics had significantly changed compared to Mao's time. The political fallout of the 1989 Students Movement was quickly contained. In the long run, the Tiananmen incident did not derail economic reform. In as much as it made the Chinese people more disillusioned with politics, it may have helped to re-channel human talents into private entrepreneurship. But China had to wait for Deng's 1992 "southern tour" to rekindle the fire of market reform. The use of guns and tanks against unarmed students and other civilians clearly revealed the weakness and vulnerability of China's fragile political power, especially its total absence of institutional mechanisms to resolve public discontent and its lack of political skills to inform and engage the public peacefully and effectively.

X

Throughout the 1980s, the most stubborn resistance to market reform came neither from state sector employees worried about competition, nor from Party and government officials fearing the loss of their privileges. Instead, it originated from China's remaining commitment to socialism. Chinese politics, still largely defined by socialism, demonstrated the remarkable staying power of ideology, even as the Chinese leaders tried hard to break away from it. This is best illustrated by Chen Yun and his defense of the planned economy on the one hand and his sanctioning of the market and private entrepreneurship on the other. In this regard, the 1984 Decision on Economic System Reform marked a breakthrough in Chinese market reform because it transgressed the boundaries defined by the 1978 Communiqué. From that point on, a market economy replaced socialist modernization as the goal of China's economic reform.

Deng viewed China's economic reforms an adventure and experiment. During this trial-and-error-based learning process, the Chinese people, and particularly their leaders, had to break away from preexisting ideas and habits of thought and acquire many new ones. This was especially true of their knowledge of the market economy and the division of labor between the state and market, and between public and private ownership. In this collective learning process, self-interest is clearly the driving force behind peoples' motivation to learn. Indeed, a critical component of the Chinese economic reform was to release the power of interests, which had been condemned and brutally oppressed under Mao's radical idealism. Economic reform began with a realization that poverty was not a virtue of socialism. As Deng famously remarked, "to get rich is glorious." At the time, his endorsement of the pursuit of interests was no less than a revolution in ideas. But economic textbooks have probably oversold the insights of Adam Smith to promote, to the exclusion of all else, the role of interests in motivating human behavior. This simplified approach would have worked better were ideas fixed forever. In the real world, ideas do change and these changes have far-reaching consequences, if only because they help to redefine who we are, reset the direction of our actions, and redraw boundary lines between what is allowed and what is not. Taking an experimental approach to reform, the Chinese government believed in the preponderance of ideas over interests, and persistently stressed the importance of "the emancipation of the mind" throughout the reform period. To paraphrase Hume, interests are the slave of ideas.[63]

In general, institutional change is as much driven by interests as it is shaped by ideas. It often gets stymied due to the mishandling of conflicts of interest and clashes of ideas. The conflict of interests and its resolution through property rights and market competition has long been, and continues to be, a staple of economic analysis.[64] Clashes of ideas, however, have not received their due attention. When ideas and ideologies are recognized in institutional analysis, they are often treated as part and parcel of informal institutions, which includes norms, customs, and values that support the working of formal institutions. Less formal, and with little coercive power, informal institutions are often deemed less forceful or direct than formal institutions in their effect on human behavior. This, however, may have more to do with the way institutions have been conceptualized than with actual reality.

Broadly speaking, institutions serve two related but distinct social functions. First and foremost, institutions are man-made devices, without which human society would not be able to survive. Many institutions result from human actions but not human design; some are intentionally created, with unintended consequences that may overshadow their intended goal. A critical way institutions operate is to constitute various social organizations out of individuals, such as families, firms, political parties, and nation-states. Once created, how these corporate actors work and interact with each other to bring about the intended goals is further regulated and coordinated by other institutions. Unsurprisingly, the complicated functions institutions perform in the operation of the economy and society have of late attracted a lot of attention from a wide range of academic disciplines.[65]

Second, as institutions are deeply involved in creating and operating organizations, and the demarcation and reinforcement of social boundaries, they gradually assume an additional role. In this second function, institutions are less a tool to serve our interests than a symbol of our identity, signaling to others who we are and what we value. When we identify ourselves with an institution, instead of seeing it as a pragmatic instrument to structure our social life and advance our interests, we take it as a badge of status. A profound cognitive change takes place at the individual and societal level when an institution that we adopted for its expected pragmatic function assumes a status role, coming to define our individual and collective identity.

When Mao launched the socialist transformation in the mid-1950s, socialism was embraced as the best way to make China strong and prosperous. The Soviet Union's rapid rise from a backward agrarian economy to an industrial powerhouse convinced the Chinese leaders of the superiority of socialism; the Soviet's defeat of the German army during the Second World War lent further support to the invincibility of socialism. As a result, socialism was endorsed by the Chinese government as the blueprint from which to rebuild China. Moreover, central planning and collective ownership were believed to offer the chance to stamp out economic inequality, the perceived root of all social evils. Over time, however, the relation between socialism and China went through a process of subtle metamorphosis. Socialism was gradually transformed from a political tool to an absorbing goal, the achievement of which justified the sacrifice of the Chinese people. Under the aegis of protecting and expanding socialism the Chinese people ultimately became a mere pawn. This process of double alienation remains an irony and a puzzle: how could socialism, initially adopted as a "golden highway" to peace and prosperity be used to glorify the chaos and poverty suffered by the Chinese people? How could the Chinese people, including their defiant and grandiose leader, who prided themselves on being the masters of history, turn out to be slaves to an alien ideology?

Tragically, it took the disasters of the Great Leap Forward and the Cultural Revolution for the Chinese to rethink their identification with socialism. If the Chinese leaders had learned some lesson from their past horrendous mistakes, this was certainly the most costly human lesson ever. In any case, an important consequence of the 1978 debate on the criteria for testing truth was to challenge the sacred status of Marxism and question the rationale for China's identifying itself with socialism. When China embraced "socialist modernization" at the end of 1978, socialism was still believed to be a superior system. Nonetheless, socialism had been restored to what political ideologies should always be: a working tool rather than a non-negotiable goal. China could now subject socialism to empirical testing and judge it according to its performance. While it is hard to change one's identity, it is much easier to replace an ineffective tool.

For the Chinese, the emancipation of their collective mentality from the grip of socialism turned out to have far-reaching implications. So long as socialism had been part of their collective political identity, any doubt regarding that ideology was suicidal, any critique of socialism an act of treason. In this climate, it was simply impossible to conduct any meaningful intellectual debate. Many of Mao's political enemies, from Deng Zihui in the debate on agricultural collectivization in the early 1950s, to Peng Dehuai during the Great Leap Forward, as well as Liu Shaoqi and Deng Xiaoping during the Cultural Revolution, were victimized simply for voicing dissenting views. The lack of an institutional mechanism to resolve disputes in policy and disagreements in ideas not only cost these personalities their political careers (and even his life in the case of Liu), but also extended the life of Mao's misconceived and disastrous policies.[66]

In the aftermath of the Cultural Revolution, Chinese leaders became more patient and careful in their handling of political infighting and lenient in their treatment of parties on the losing side of debates. This was demonstrated in the trial of the Gang of Four and later in the depositions of Hua Guofeng (1981), Hu Yaobang (1987) and Zhao Ziyang (1989). The defeated party in a power struggle was not publicly denounced or humiliated, as had been the case in the past. Few on the losing side were ever executed, as had been common before the

Communists took power and during Mao's era. Throughout the 1980s, Chinese politics was conducted in a much more reasonable fashion.

This was largely due to two institutional developments. The first was the increasing participation of scholars in political life.[67] In stark contrast to Mao's time, when scholars were criticized as the "stinking ninth class," once reform began scholars were gradually recognized for their expertise. They then began to reprise their traditional role as advisors and counselors to the government. In addition to the knowledge with which they could inform policy debate, scholars were non-partisan and functioned directly in depoliticizing these deliberations.

Scholars sometimes got directly involved as members of state or quasi-state think-tanks that had emerged during the early 1980s. These included the Chinese Academy of Social Sciences (particularly its Institute of Economics), the Chinese Rural Development Research Group (established in September 1980), the Economic System Reform Office (established in 1980), the Economic Research Center (established in 1980) and the Committee on Economic System Reform (established in March 1982) under the State Council, as well as the Rural Policy Research Office (established in 1982) under the Secretariat of the Central Committee of the Party. Regardless of their status, they all worked closely with the Chinese government, informing government and conducting policy debates and formulating economic policy. The direct participation of scholars in policymaking helped to take the political heat out of policy debates and avoid direct confrontation between different Party factions. Though, in some cases, they held government positions and were trusted Party members, they were seldom contenders in power struggles. In addition, these scholars could be removed or simply ignored, with little negative impact on political stability. Debate among scholars and competition among ideas served as a proxy fight, avoiding direct clashes between rival factions at the center of political power.

In the early 1980s scholars played a significant role in framing and taming the policy debate in rural reform, enterprise reform, and price reform. A case in point was the policy debate on the "recommendatory economic plan"; this was an administrative invention to introduce market forces without abandoning central planning. While Chen Yun was firmly against it, Zhao Ziyang wanted to use it to increase policy flexibility without challenging economic planning head on. A group of economists from the Chinese Academy of Social Sciences advocated and defended the "recommendatory economic plan." When Chen confirmed his unyielding opposition, leading scholars were reprimanded for their views, sending a clear signal to Zhao. This saved a potentially damaging confrontation between Chen and Zhao.[68]

The second and more institutionalized development was the rebuilding of the Chinese legal system.[69] During the Cultural Revolution, law was essentially discarded, leaving even Liu Shaoqi, Chairman of China, unable to defend his basic rights. Since most of the Chinese leaders of Deng's era, and particularly Deng himself, had suffered personally during the Cultural Revolution, it was not surprising that they were most anxious to rebuild the Chinese legal system. Before it began work on anything else, the post-Mao Chinese government turned its energies towards the law. On March 5th, 1978, the third constitution of the People's Republic was adopted at the first meeting of the Fifth National People's Congress, restoring courts and procuratorates.

Deng Xiaoping became an advocate of what he called "legal democracy." When meeting a delegation from Japan on June 28th, 1979, Deng told the guests:

> We must strengthen both democracy and the legal system because they have been ineffective. In order to strengthen our democracy, we have to improve our legal system. Nothing can be accomplished without an extensive democracy and a sound legal system. We have suffered a great deal from disorder and turmoil. . . .

> We really have had no laws and no legal system to follow for many years now. At this session of the National People's Congress, we formulated seven laws. Some of these laws contained articles which revised the Constitution. . . . This was a necessary precondition for creating a political situation of stability, unity and liveliness. If we do not establish such a political situation, the four modernizations cannot be realized. Following this session, we shall formulate a series of laws. We lack many necessary civil laws. We also need to enact many laws governing economic development, such as those pertaining to factories. The laws that we have made are too few. We need about one hundred laws which we do not presently have. Therefore, we have much work to do and this is just the beginning. We must promote our democracy and our legal system. They are like a person's two hands; if either one is weak, the person will not be able to accomplish anything.[70]

Later, addressing government leaders on December 13th, 1979, Deng stressed the same message, admitting that "[Our] legal system needs strengthening. . . . Legal democracy needs systematizing so that the system and the laws do not change when either the leadership or its view or focus change. [In the past], people often equated the leaders' words with laws; opposing the leaders' views was deemed as against the laws. . . . When words from the leaders changed, laws surreptitiously changed as well."[71] In the next few years, a massive quantity of laws were put into place, covering criminal, civil, economic and administrative areas. This included a new constitution in 1982, which would go through four revisions – in 1988, 1993, 1999, and 2004 – and is still in use today. Between

1978 and 2008, China passed 229 national laws. Only eight pre-1978 laws are still in use.[72]

In economic areas, the progress of legal development was even more impressive. On July 1st, 1979, China passed the Law on Sino-Foreign Equity Joint Ventures, which was widely welcomed as a "landmark piece of legislation,"[73] signaling both China's determination to embrace foreign investment and its commitment to the use of law to make its policies credible internationally. The Economic Contract Law was passed on December 13th, 1981, followed by Trademark Law on August 23rd, 1982, Foreign Economic Contract Law on March 21st, 1985, Law on Wholly Foreign-Owned Enterprises and General Principles of Civil Law on April 12th, 1986, Enterprise Bankruptcy Law on December 12th, 1986, Law on Sino-Foreign Cooperation Joint Ventures and Law on Industrial Enterprises Owned by the Whole People on April 13th, 1988, and Provisional Regulations on Private Enterprises on June 25th, 1988. At the same time, other legal institutions, such as lawyers and the courts, developed in an equally impressive manner. For example, there were virtually no lawyers in 1979, but 10,000 full-time practicing lawyers in 1984, and 100,000 in 2004.[74]

What is of direct relevance to our discussions here is that China's legal development in the post-Mao era, described by William Alfred of Harvard Law School as "an event of epic historic proportions,"[75] helped to depoliticize Chinese politics and constrain the power of central government through the rule by law. Even today, the rule of law is still wanting in China, and administrative intervention in the economy and society at large is still pervasive. Nonetheless, rule by law, which China has aggressively pursued since 1978, has provided legal protection for local Chinese government officials pursuing economic development and other goals. A significant example of this is the passing of the Regulations for the Special Economic Zones in Guangdong Province by the National People's Congress on August 26th, 1980.[76] It was then unprecedented that the National Congress should pass a law drafted by a provincial legislature. The Special Economic Zone was such a bold endeavor that provincial government officials could not feel comfortable unless it was sanctioned by laws passed by the central government. This law gave the Special Economic Zones a permanent legal protection independent of local authorities and made them more credible to outside investors. However, it also provided legal protection to local authorities; with what is aptly referred to in Chinese as "the Imperial Sword," local authorities were assured of their safety in undertaking the venture.

During Mao's time, government officials were often demoted or even imprisoned when their words or deeds were deemed anti-Party, or "anti-revolutionary." Largely determined by the capricious Mao himself, the criteria for these misdemeanors were subjective and unreliable. Despite Mao's attempts at decentralization, this meant that local government officials rarely acted on their own initiative, but merely catered to Mao's changing whims. The development of China's legal system in the post-Mao era was intended to make sure that this could never happen again and, in this regard, it was largely successful.

It is also important to stress that since law enforcement was essentially in the hands of local authorities, legal development amounted to a devolution of power from the central government to local authorities. This, as we will see in the following chapter, paved the way for regional competition.

At the same time, law and order as then understood by the Chinese leaders differed fundamentally from the rule of law as commonly used in western legal and political discourse. The primary goal of legal democracy in China was to maintain political stability and continuity of policy in a one-party political system. In the aftermath of the Cultural Revolution, the Chinese government embraced the rule by law to protect the political structure from two different threats, which were believed to have pushed the Chinese political system to the verge of collapse in the past. These were reckless decisions made by political leaders and massive direct participation in politics by the masses. Neither of these had been previously subject to any legal constraint. Without proper institutional mechanisms to channel and tame popular passions, what Mao advocated as "big democracy" utterly failed its intended goal of freeing Chinese politics of bureaucratization. What Mao failed to realize was that neither democracy nor order was achievable without law. As Mao himself often acted above the law, the two sources of political chaos intertwined and paralyzed the Chinese political system during the Cultural Revolution. This was the worst nightmare for Deng and other post-Mao Chinese leaders.

As China's decentralized political structure could readily multiply the risk of whimsical decisions by local political leaders, the rule by law was urgently needed. Yet, as stated above, the rule *by* law was essentially an attempt to structure and regulate the hierarchy of power relations within the maze of Chinese politics. It meant that Beijing had to abide by legal procedures in its decision-making, and local authorities were free to act within legal boundaries. This was a significant improvement over the political system headed by Mao. But it contrasts with the rule *of* law, which primarily aims at horizontal relations among individual and corporate actors of equal political and legal status.

Moreover, since the legislative law-making power in China is concentrated in the central government, rule by law is more effective in constraining and disciplining the behavior of the central government. Its effectiveness is impressive in maintaining political stability. From 1949 to 1976, Beijing stuggled almost constantly to save itself from political chaos; in the post-Mao era, power changed hands several times with no serious threat to political order, except during the Tiananmen incident. The pursuit of the rule by law also helps to strengthen the position of local authorities vis-à-vis Beijing. Since Beijing is not willing to give up its monopoly of political power or subject itself to the rule of law, the central government is forced to exercise its power vis-à-vis local author-ities outside the legal domain, relying on non-legal administrative measures and personnel control. This has largely been accomplished through the appa-ratus of the Chinese Communist Party, particularly the powerful Organization Department.[77] Consequently, economic reform did not make the Party less rel-evant or less important. On the contrary, the Party became an integral part of a convoluted institutional framework underpinning China's economic reform. Yet, how to integrate the Party into the legal system remains an open question. As long as the Party stayed above the law, the law did not exist for those who could claim to act in the name of the Party. This inevitably undermined both the law and the leadership of the Party.

The Chinese economic reform entered the 1980s with a strong commitment to socialism and a strengthened leadership at the head of the Chinese Com-munist Party. As time went by and as the experience of reform accumulated, the grip of socialism on Chinese leaders' mentality started to weaken. This was especially true of the economic domain, where the superior performance of the private sector vis-à-vis the state sector was too obvious to be ignored. Even though the Chinese were blessed with an open and pragmatic way of thinking, old habits of thinking were difficult to do away with and practice was some-times too ambiguous to yield bases for decisions. Risks had to be taken and mistakes were impossible to avoid. Nonetheless, what Deng Xiaoping called "the great experiment" persisted.

5
Growing out of Socialism: Capitalism with Chinese Characteristics

After almost a decade of strong economic growth, China's economic reform encountered its first full-blown crisis in the late 1980s. This culminated in the 1989 Students Movement, the tragic end of which further compounded and prolonged the economic crisis. The year preceding and those that followed the 1989 Tiananmen incident are often referred to as the Tiananmen interlude (1988–1992). The Chinese term for crisis literally means danger and opportunity, and this four-year period was full of danger for the reform agenda; there was a real possibility that reform might be rejected altogether.

In September 1988, the Chinese government launched an emergency austerity program, both to curtail rising inflation (which in July was running at 19.7 percent), and to end the panic buying and bank withdrawals seen in many Chinese cities.[1] In August, the volume of retail sales jumped 38.6 percent above that of the previous year; it put further pressure on inflation.[2] The austerity program included tightening bank credit and money supply, while withholding and even reversing a selection of reform measures – particularly those pertaining to the private sector. Installed to rein in the overheated economy and control rising inflation, this program acted as a brake on an accelerating economy and effectively stalled the economic reform. Six months later, in March 1989, the *Guardian*'s headline was "Beijing's reforms grind to standstill."[3] After the crackdown on the student movement on June 4th, the outlook for the Chinese economy became even gloomier. *Newsweek* ran an article on "Deng's Great Leap Backward"[4] and *The Economist*'s analysis was entitled "How a dragon stagflates."[5] Quoting a document freshly released by the Central Intelligence Agency, the *Washington Post* reported that "China's economy is in a deep recession that shows no sign of abating and is threatening the country's social stability."[6]

The evidence on the ground corroborated this view. Local governments all over rural China had been hit hard by the austerity program and were short of credit. In the summer of 1990, local governments were forced to issue credit notes to peasants in payment for grain, which caused widespread discontent. During the students movement a year earlier, Chinese peasants had been largely absent from the demonstrations. However, as the birthplace of riots and rebellions in the past, including the Chinese Communist revolution, rural China remained politically vulnerable.

Furthermore, the number of single proprietorships (private entities with seven or fewer employees) in China declined by 15 percent in 1989. The number of private enterprises (with more than seven employees) fell by more than half from over 200,000 in 1988 to a little above 90,000 by the end of 1989. It remained at this level throughout 1990 and only rose slightly to 107,000 in 1991.[7]

Moreover, the main trends in political discourse seemed to have reversed. If Chinese economic reform had been "deadlocked" between planning and market at the end of the 1980s, as some scholars have rightly observed,[8] the political tide was now pushing the economy back to its former state. The political coalition Deng had assembled in support of reform at the end of the 1970s had begun to crack by the mid-1980s. This led to the resignation of Hu Yaobang in early 1987, and the coalition virtually collapsed after the 1989 Tiananmen crackdown. On November 23rd, 1989, Premier Li Peng of the State Council gave an exclusive interview to Manfred Schell, editor-in-chief of *Die Welt*. Asked about China's policies on economic reform and opening up, Li Peng explained that "China's reform is a self-improvement of the socialist system. Economically, to combine the planned economy with market regulation is not to lead China to capitalism."[9] Li equated the market economy, the direction of reform since 1984, explicitly with capitalism. The political consensus supportive of market reforms had been destroyed. As we discussed in the preceding chapter, the dictum "the planned economy as primary, market adjustments as auxiliary" had long been ingrained in Chinese socialism. Originally formulated by Chen Yun in 1956, it was widely embraced by Chinese leaders after 1978. Though it had served well in guiding Chinese leaders during the early stage of reform, the dichotomy represented by the planned versus the market economy, and the dogmatic defense of the plan's preeminence, led to its rejection in 1984. After that the development of a market economy replaced socialist modernization as the goal of Chinese economic reform, but from 1989, market reform lost its political support and Chen Yun's economic thinking was restored.

This reversal in the orientation of reform had an immediate impact on economic policy. When addressing the National Planning Conference on December 11th, 1989, Li assured his audience that economic reform and opening up would continue, but in a different manner.[10] His main message was to defend the austerity program and recommit the Chinese government to socialism; that is, to the preeminence of public ownership and central planning.

Specific measures were proposed to curtail the growth of the non-state sector and to reverse price deregulation. First, township and village enterprises – the most dynamic and fastest-growing economic force since the inception of reform – were to be co-opted into state planning. This had been proposed in the late 1970s but had never been considered seriously.

> Township and village authorities should earnestly organise and lead collective economic activities and service systems of various kinds; on the other hand, *collective economy should become the foundation for consolidating township and village regimes*. We should encourage development of town and township enterprises in accordance with the principle of adjusting, consolidating, reforming and improving, and should affirm the role played by town and township enterprises. These enterprises are an important form of economic activity for developing rural economy, improving production conditions in rural areas, and increasing employment opportunities in rural areas. Some unhealthy practices by township and village enterprises should be corrected, and the positive side of these enterprises should be protected and supported. *The important thing is to ensure that township and village enterprises carry out the state's industrial policies*, improve product quality, reduce material consumption and cater to market demands. Banks at all levels should provide appropriate amounts of operating funds to town and township enterprises in 1990 (italics added).[11]

Second, Li set in motion a more ambitious plan to bring the whole private sector into the orbit of the state, which, if implemented, would effectively destroy the private sector altogether.

> Individual and private economy is a beneficial and necessary complement to socialist economy. We should strengthen management of them, provide better guidance for their development, and continue to encourage them to develop within the bounds set by the state, so that they can play an active role in developing production, accommodating people's daily life and creating new employment opportunities. At the same time, we should limit those negative effects that are unfavorable to developing socialist economy.[12]

Third, in contrast to the previous policy of price liberalization, Li recommended price control as a tool to fight inflation.

> It is necessary to strengthen, in a strict manner, the management of market prices and to control the range of price rises. To reduce the inflation rate and the range of price rises year by year is a basic task to be carried out in improving the economic environment and straightening out the economic

order. The task of controlling the range of price rises in 1990 will be a very arduous one. One primary measure to control rising prices is to control continuously the total social demand. Price rises by departments and enterprises themselves must be strictly controlled. A policy to stabilize the prices of the necessities for people's basic daily life, as well as labor charges, should be adopted. Such a policy should stipulate in explicit terms that the prices of some necessities are not to increase. It is necessary to check conscientiously on various criteria for fees and to ban strictly or forbid wanton price rises and excessive charges. Efforts must be made to strengthen the controls over market prices, as well as supervision and inspection in this regard. It is particularly necessary to give full play to the role played by the masses and public opinion in controlling prices. The price-control responsibility system should be continuously implemented. Control over the range of price rises must continue to be an important gauge in evaluating the performance of governments at various levels in 1990.[13]

I

The shift in economic policy was reinforced by a wave of political campaigns against market-oriented reform, implemented throughout China in 1990. These campaigns singled out the fledgling private sector as the economic bastion of bourgeois ideology, which the Chinese government saw as the fundamental cause of the student demonstrations, culminating in the 1989 Students Movement. On February 22nd, 1990, the *People's Daily* published an article on the front page entitled "On Bourgeoisie Liberalization," in which the author suggested that the "liberalization of the bourgeoisie" – the move towards capitalism – was economically rooted in the private sector.[14] This initiated a year-long political diatribe against market reform. For orthodox Marxists and Maoists, the private sector was the hotbed of capitalism. From their standpoint, the 1989 Students Movement was a blatant attempt at "peaceful evolution," luring China into capitalism without fighting a bloody war. To preserve the socialist regime in China, the government felt compelled to nip capitalism in the bud.

The political sentiment against market reform was further exacerbated by the fall of the Soviet bloc and the domino-like bankruptcy of communist countries in late 1989–1990. These events shocked the Chinese leaders, who had just survived their own political crisis. The swift and bloodless conversion of the Soviet bloc to capitalism put the Chinese government and the Chinese Communist Party on high alert, making them ever more conscious of the rivalry between capitalism and communism. This sense of insecurity and vulnerability held by the Chinese leaders helps to account for their unusually strong antipathy towards the market in the early 1990s.

A deeply ingrained ideological prejudice against the private sector was further compounded by a plausible but mistaken economic judgment. After the economic reform began to suffer a serious setback in 1988, economists and government officials alike began to look critically at reform policies implemented before the onset of runaway inflation in 1988. Policymakers took the view that the fast growth of market forces since 1984 had been responsible for price rises and runaway inflation. After 1984, the strong growth of the non-state sector, particularly the township and village enterprises, facilitated by support from local governments, the dual-track pricing system, and easy credits from banks, helped to generate inflationary pressures. In early September of 1985, a conference was held on the Yangzi River.[15] It has since become known as the "Ba Mountain Boat Conference," after the tourist boat on which it was held. A delegation of leading Chinese economists met preeminent economists from around the world to discuss China's macroeconomic problems. The western delegation included the Hungarian economist Janos Kornai, Alexander Cairncross, and Wlodzimierz Brus from Oxford, and the Nobel laureate James Tobin from Yale. The consensus reached was that a simultaneous growth in both investment and wages was pushing the Chinese economy to the verge of hyperinflation. This warning, however, was ignored by the Chinese government in its continuing pursuit of rapid economic growth.[16] Now, in the aftermath of the 1988 hyperinflation and the 1989 Students Movement, some Chinese economists came to believe that the 1984 Decision on the Economic System Reform, which had essentially embraced the market economy, was the ultimate culprit. They found market reform guilty of causing both economic woes and political risk.

On July 5th, 1990, the Politburo of the Central Committee of the Party invited a dozen or so economists to discuss current economic affairs and policy strategy. The economists were deeply but unequally divided. The larger group believed the market reform from 1984 onward had been the catalyst for 1988's runaway inflation and the 1989 Students Movement. They argued vehemently for a retreat to the pre-1984 position, "the planned economy as primary, market adjustment as auxiliary." The voice of the few economists on the other side, defending the market-oriented reform, was totally overwhelmed. The eighty-six-year-old Xue Muqiao, a staunch supporter of market reform, was so disturbed by the attack from the other side that he was unable to speak.[17]

Throughout the whole of 1990, debates on the direction of reform and the nature of socialism occupied the center stage of Chinese politics, particularly in Beijing. South China, as we will see shortly, was in a different mood; here, market reforms had gone deeper than anywhere else. At the time, however, only one voice was heard in China; the dissenting views were silenced. The view of the Beijing government was best captured by a belligerent article in the *People's Daily* on December 7th, 1990, entitled "Social-ism Bound to Replace Capitalism."[18] It attributed all the economic difficulties and political disturbance that China had suffered since the late 1980s to mar-ket reforms undertaken in the early part of the 1980s, and it urged China to return to socialism to end the political and economic troubles. The author claimed that "the market economy is to eliminate collective property, mount-ing to the denial of the leadership of the Communist Party and denial of socialism, and to commit China to capitalism." If this view had been fully translated into economic policy, China's market reform would have been stillborn.

II

The beginning of the 1990s in China was a time of uncertainty and self-doubt. Beijing was consumed by a sustained political lambasting against capitalism; economic reform was stalled. With a mixture of luck, determination, and fore-sight, China emerged from this period of political wavering with a renewed commitment to market reform, and by the end of the 1990s a dynamic mar-ket economy was in operation all over China. China's joining the World Trade Organization in 2001 further consolidated market reform at home and expanded its role in economic globalization abroad. China by then had been irreversibly transformed into a market economy. At the end of the decade, the financial meltdown in Wall Street led to a severe economic recession and the West began to doubt the soundness of the global market order. China, how-ever, stood firmly behind the market and economic globalization: January 1st, 2010 effectively saw the beginning of a free trade agreement between China and ASEAN (the Association of South East Asian Nations). This created the world's most populated free trade zone (1.9 billion), and the third largest in volume of production after the European Economic Area and North America Free Trade Area.

We may wonder what provided the Chinese leaders with such faith in the market to carry them through the storm of uncertainty. However, this would be the wrong question to ask. During the Tiananmen interlude, the question as to whether China could grow out of socialism was wide open. It was absolutely not the case that the Chinese leaders were prescient and held a strong belief in the market, which guided them through the downturn of the Tiananmen inter-lude and ultimately led them to adopt a market economy. When China began reform in the late 1970s and early 1980s, it was as a series of marginal revolu-tions that introduced the private sector and market forces, which overshadowed the state-led reform initiatives and gave the reform a strong orientation towards the market. The market reform in the early 1990s survived in similar fashion, largely in a way unintended by the Chinese government.

China's economic reform and open-door policies were always intertwined, each supporting the other. During the Tiananmen interlude, although the Chinese government halted many of the planned reforms and reversed others, it remained committed to opening China up to the outside world. As early as June 9th, 1989, Deng Xiaoping warned the Chinese leaders that

> The important thing is that we must never turn China back into a country that keeps its doors closed. A closed-door policy would be greatly to our disadvantage; we would not even have quick access to information. People say that information is important, right? It certainly is. If an administrator has no access to information, it's as if he was purblind and hard of hearing and had a stuffed nose. And on no account must we go back to the old practice of keeping the economy under rigid control.[19]

A week later, at a meeting with new members of the Central Committee, Deng suggested

> [The State Council] should do more to facilitate reform and opening to the outside. Joint ventures involving foreign capital should be set up, and local areas should be allowed to establish development zones. If we absorb more foreign capital, it will surely benefit foreign businessmen, but we too shall benefit eventually. For example, we can collect taxes, introduce professional services for foreign-funded enterprises and establish some profitable enterprises ourselves. In this way our economy will be invigorated. Since foreigners are afraid that we shall close our doors again, we should do some things to demonstrate that our policies of reform and opening to the outside world will not change but will be further implemented.[20]

When addressing a gathering for the tenth anniversary of the Special Economic Zones in Shenzhen on November 28th, 1990, Jiang Zemin, General Secretary of the Party, clearly reiterated the socialist orientation of the reform: "Our reform is designed to improve and develop the socialist system, to eliminate various structural flaws of the past and to bring out the superiority of the socialist system."[21] Jiang also restated China's open-door policy:

> Our effort to open to the outside world is intended to actively develop foreign economic and technical co-operation and exchanges, to learn the advanced technologies, scientific management experiences and progressive cultural achievements of foreign countries, including capitalist developed countries, to resist the corrosive influence of negative and corrupt elements in capitalist society and to inherit and enhance all the fine ideological, moral and cultural traditions of the Chinese nation.[22]

It was ironic for him to acclaim the "superiority of the socialist system" in Shenzhen, an experiment set up to explore capitalism for the sake of saving socialism. Fortunately, Jiang was able to justify and celebrate the experiment on the basis that Shenzhen had served China well as a conduit for modern science, technology, and management or, in his own words, "a vanguard in conducting reform and opening to the outside world." In his speech, Jiang confirmed that "Opening to the outside world is our country's long-term, basic policy. This policy will not change."[23] At a time when market reforms were publically denounced and harshly vilified in Beijing, it was fortunate that the Shenzhen experiment and open-door policy were allowed to continue.

The separate treatments of reform and opening up worked out well at a time when reform was being questioned as a betrayal of socialism. Opening up was less politically sensitive and thus less vulnerable. Even the staunchest defenders of socialism would not question the desirability and necessity of China learning advanced science and technology from the West and accessing western capital. It is also noteworthy that Jiang reversed Mao's radical anti-Chinese tradition policy. He stressed that in "promoting the socialist material and spiritual civilizations," it was important for China "to inherit and enhance all the fine ideological, moral and cultural traditions of the Chinese nation," and "to learn the advanced technologies, scientific management experiences and progressive cultural achievements of foreign countries, including capitalist developed countries."[24] Since the 1990s China's commitment to socialism has no longer entailed enforced ignorance of the outside world, or a rejection of its own long history, as was the case during much of Mao's era, particularly during the Cultural Revolution.

The continuation of the open-door policy during the late 1980s and early 1990s protected some elements of China's economic reform from the impact of both the austerity program and the uncertain political environment. The most significant development of China's opening up in the early 1990s was the setup of the Pudong Development Zone in Shanghai in April 1990. This began the revival of Shanghai as the financial and commercial center of China.[25] Two years later in 1992, the State Council approved the establishment of the Pudong New District. Within a decade, Pudong would become the showcase of China's economic modernization. Separated from Shanghai by Huangpu River, Pudong was mainly rice fields at the beginning of the 1990s. Modeled after Shenzhen, Pudong became the central focus of China's opening-up policy in the 1990s. If Shenzhen was the symbol of China's opening up during the 1980s, Pudong became the flagship in the 1990s. Soon, the Yangzi River Delta around Shanghai would be rivaling the Pearl River Delta in South China, as a second engine of Chinese economic growth.

III

In 1990, Shanghai saw another significant development, the official opening of the Shanghai Stock Exchange on December 19th.[26] This came after more than a year of intense preparation, and in the face of an uncertain political climate. Widely regarded as a symbol of capitalism, the bond and stock trade had previously been confined to the forbidden zone of Chinese economics. In the mid-1980s, some state-owned enterprises turned themselves into joint-stock companies, in another form of enterprise reform. Bonds and non-tradable stocks were sold to their employees and the public as a new way of raising capital. The first exchange to allow a secondary market for company bonds and stocks on a trial base arose in August 1986 in Shenyang, a city in northeastern China with a strong industrial base in the pre-reform era and which had many state-owned enterprises.[27] This exchange office provided a platform for employees of state-owned enterprises to trade their bonds and stocks. Although the office was small and primitive in infrastructure, it was the very first attempt to experiment with a secondary bond and stock market and thus attracted much public attention, particularly from the foreign media. Three months later, at the end of September, another office opened in Shanghai. When John Phelan, Chairman of the New York Stock Exchange, was invited to a conference organized by the People's Bank of China in Beijing and met Deng Xiaoping in November 1986, he insisted on visiting the stock exchange office in Shanghai – a single room of merely 12 square meters.[28]

The first stock exchange to make a real economic impact was in Shenzhen.[29] Since 1986, joint-stock companies had been emerging in Shenzhen, and their number rose to more than 200 by the end of the 1980s. In June 1988, the municipal government of Shenzhen formed a Leadership Group on Stock Exchanges to explore the possibility of opening up a stock exchange market. Shenzhen's repeated applications to Beijing for permission were denied, but a stock exchange was opened anyway and was quite active, particularly after 1989. By mid-1990, Shenzhen already had more than 300 offices where people could buy or sell stocks, despite the fact that there was no official permission to trade in this way.[30]

This lag between practice and regulation was actually quite common throughout the Chinese economic reform. The phenomenon is aptly referred to in China as "get on the bus first, buy the ticket later." It may seem irresponsible or even negligent on the part of government regulators to let a new practice go ahead without first putting in place proper regulatory rules. But without the practice being tried first on the ground, how could the regulator know what and how to regulate? However, when a novel practice was first experimented with, particularly in a regulation-free environment, it was bound to go awry, giving its political opponents sufficient justification to close it down. To allow this strategy to work, the government had to be tolerant, open-minded, and learn to act quickly – either setting up a regulatory framework to allow the practice to develop or shutting it down when the experiment turned sour. The policymakers could certainly be guilty of halting promising practices too soon, as well as neglecting to end bad practices. More importantly, since the effectiveness of a practice was sensitive to the institutional environment in which it was tried, a small change in the regulatory environment could make or break it. In addition, a slight modification of the practice itself may turn it from a failure to a success. As a result, whether a new practice would be sanctioned by the government was largely determined by a race between the two sides. On the one side were its proponents, who were trying hard to make it work during the experimental stage, modifying the practice after some trial runs and adjusting the supporting institutional environment within the political perimeters. On the other side, its critics were eager to end it by pointing to the mistakes made during the experimental stage and using them as legitimate reasons to challenge their opponents. For those who wanted to push reform forward by introducing new and viable practices, the most effective method was to experiment as much as possible to find something workable within a limited time window, while recognizing the risk that more mistakes were bound to occur when more experiments were run. Indeed, this was the logic behind Deng's aphorism, "Don't argue; try bold experiments and blaze new trails."

In the case of the stock exchange market, the Chinese government headed by Jiang took a similar stance, but for different reasons. Taking office after the Tiananmen incident, Jiang did not have the political clout to overcome political hostility toward the market-oriented reform and recognize the stock exchange officially. At the same time, he was unwilling or unable to take draconian measures to suppress local experiments already under way. Thus the government officials of Shenzhen were walking a tightrope by allowing the stock exchange to continue without legal regulation or official recognition. It was not until July 3rd, 1991 that Beijing approved the opening of the Shenzhen Stock Exchange.[31]

IV

Despite a few encouraging signs of reform during 1990, the austerity program prevailed and the political atmosphere was largely hostile toward market reform. Throughout the reform era, when a political debate was conducted in China, it was rare to hear the two sides actively trading arguments. More often than not, only one voice would be heard. The voice of the opposition would be muted, seen by the prevailing political forces as incorrect or vulnerable. However, as history has shown, the opposition was merely waiting for the right moment. After a year of continuous attacks on market reform in 1990, it was time for the other side to speak out. On February 15th, 1991, the *Liberation Daily*, based in Shanghai, published an editorial under a pseudonym, entitled "To Be the Bellwether of Reform and Opening up." It was followed by three other editorials on March 2nd ("Reform and Opening up Need New Thinking"), March 22nd ("Be Stronger in the Awareness of Opening up"), and April 12th ("Reform and Opening up Need Many Cadres with Both Ability and Integrity"). Taken together, these editorials sent out an unmistakable message that market reform should be restarted.[32]

Few people knew at the time that the series of editorials were based on talks Deng had given in Shanghai where he was spending the Chinese New Year. Consequently, the editorials quickly attracted censure from other newspapers and journals, mostly those based in Beijing, directly challenging the views expressed in the four editorials point by point. On April 20th, *Current Thought*, a monthly journal based in Beijing, published a bold political tirade, "Can Reform and Opening up Disregard the Debate between Socialism and Capitalism?"[33] The article assailed the once-popular view promoted by Deng that China's economic reform should embrace any measures that helped to improve the economy, whether they were capitalist or socialist. "A disregard of the difference between socialism and capitalism," the article warned, "would inevitably mislead the reform to the road of capitalism and destroy socialism."[34]

As competing views started to engage with one another, this became another rare occasion in China when the political debate was not monopolized by one voice, similar to the 1978 debate on the criterion of testing truth. The first issue of *Social Sciences of China* in 1991 published an article by Xue Muqiao, entitled "On Several Theoretical Issues of the Socialist Economy,"[35] in which Xue criticized the entrenched and erroneous understanding of socialism as meaning economic central planning free of market forces. The Chinese economic system, as Xue argued, was a planned market economy based on the public ownership of the means of production, and planning itself must be based on market principles and economic laws. The domain of planning should be limited to the macro- balance of the economy, including the total social demand and the total social supply and the proportionate relations among various sectors of the national economy. Xue emphatically stressed that the production and circulation of all goods and services should be left to the market.

But there was no question which side dominated, especially in Beijing. The *People's Daily* ran an editorial on September 2nd, entitled "Three Questions on the Current Reform."[36] It claimed that "reform and opening to the outside must maintain a correct orientation." As the article explained,

in carrying out reform, we must uphold the four cardinal principles and must not practice bourgeois liberalization. If we privatize the economy, practice the Western multiparty political system and ideologically abandon the pluralist guide of Marxism-Leninism-Mao Zedong Thought, our party and our country will be in chaos, and all the successes achieved by the party and the people during the past 70 years will come to nought. On this issue concerning the life and death of socialism, we must have a firm and clear-cut stand, and must not have even a little bit of confusion or wavering.[37]

Another *People's Daily* editorial published on October 23rd, "Correctly Recognize Contradictions of the Socialist Society," used even more radical rhetoric, claiming that class struggle in China – the rivalry between socialism and capitalism – had never been more intense.[38]

V

China faced the real risk of being trapped again in the snare of ideology. Never before had China's economic reform faced a grimmer future. At this time, Deng, an eighty-eight-year-old man with no formal position in the Party, the army, or the government, decided to intervene. By then Deng had lost two long-serving protégés, Hu Yaobang in 1987 and Zhao Ziyang in 1989, both of whom had worked hard to push forward the reform agenda from the very beginning, without directly challenging the socialist ideology. And Deng could no longer simply call in the Party General Secretary or the Premier to give his orders.[39] With no formal means to exercise his influence in Beijing, Deng had to use indirect means. Accompanied by his family and staff, Deng left Beijing on a train on January 17th, 1992, heading south to the region where market reform had gone furthest, and resistance to Beijing's austerity program was strongest.[40]

The train arrived at its first stop, Wuchang station in Hubei, the next day. While the train halted for twenty minutes to take on water and load other supplies, Deng briefly met the Party secretary and governor of Hubei province on the station platform, spelling out his concerns.

One of our problems today is formalism. Every time you turn on the television, you see a meeting being held. We hold countless meetings, and our articles and speeches are too long and too repetitive, in both content and language. Of course, some words have to be repeated, but we should try to be concise. Formalism is a kind of bureaucratism. We should spend more time on practical matters. That means saying less and doing more. Chairman Mao never held long meetings, his essays were short and concise and his speeches succinct. When he asked me to draft the work report to be delivered by Premier Zhou Enlai at the Fourth National People's Congress, he said it should be no more than 5000 Chinese characters. I kept to 5000 characters, and they were enough. I suggest you do something about this problem.[41]

Before getting back on the train, Deng gave one last piece of advice to his visitors, who were still trying to absorb his denunciation of formalism: "Do more real work and engage in less empty talk."[42] The train made another stop at four o'clock in the afternoon, at Changsha, the capital of Hunan province, where Deng met with the provincial Party secretary. Encouraged by Hunan's economic growth reported by the secretary, Deng told his visitor to "take bolder measures to carry out the reform, and further speed up the economy."[43]

On January 19th Deng arrived at Shenzhen.[44] Eight years had elapsed since his last visit in 1984. Deng was eager to find out how his boldest experiment had fared, and particularly whether Shenzhen had succumbed to capitalism, as his critics had maintained.

In the next few days, Deng toured the city, visited factories, and met with the provincial authorities of Guangdong and the city officials of Shenzhen. In eight years Shenzhen had been transformed beyond recognition, with high-rise buildings everywhere, heavy traffic on the street, and a buoyant stock market. Deng was pleased with what he saw in Shenzhen. On the 22nd, addressing the municipal government officials, Deng urged them to be open-minded and encouraged them to continue moving forward.

> We should be bolder than before in conducting reform and opening to the outside and have the courage to experiment. We must not act like women with bound feet. Once we are sure that something should be done, we should dare to experiment and break a new path. That is the important lesson to be learned from Shenzhen. If we don't have the pioneering spirit, if we're afraid to take risks, if we have no energy and drive, we cannot break a new path, a good path, or accomplish anything new. Who dares to claim that he is 100 per cent sure of success and that he is taking no risks? No one can ever be 100 per cent sure at the outset that what he is doing is correct. I've never been that sure. Every year leaders should review what they have done, continuing those measures that have proved correct, acting promptly to change those that have proved wrong and tackling new problems as soon as they are identified.[45]

Responding to the prevailing concern that China's economic reform had introduced too much capitalism, and that China had deviated from socialism, Deng reiterated a theory he had long cherished:

> The proportion of planning to market forces is not the essential difference between socialism and capitalism. A planned economy is not equivalent to socialism, because there is planning under capitalism too; a market economy is not capitalism, because there are markets under socialism too. Planning and market forces are both means of controlling economic activity. The

essence of socialism is liberation and development of the productive forces, elimination of exploitation and polarization, and the ultimate achievement of prosperity for all. This concept must be made clear to the people. Are securities and the stock market good or bad? Do they entail any dangers? Are they peculiar to capitalism? Can socialism make use of them? We allow people to reserve their judgment, but we must try these things out. If, after one or two years of experimentation, they prove feasible, we can expand them. Otherwise, we can put a stop to them and be done with it. We can stop them all at once or gradually, totally or partially. What is there to be afraid of? So long as we keep this attitude, everything will be all right, and we shall not make any major mistakes. In short, if we want socialism to achieve superiority over capitalism, we should not hesitate to draw on the achievements of all cultures and to learn from other countries, including the developed capitalist countries, all advanced methods of operation and tech-niques of management that reflect the laws governing modern socialized production.[46]

Deng was certainly not the first to recognize common ground between cap-italism and socialism. "Market socialism" – an economy in which firms are all owned by the state but sell their products to consumers in a competitive market – had long been debated among scholars and experimented with in Eastern Europe in the 1950s and 1960s. In China, Gu Zhun, Sun Yefang, and other economists had earlier stressed that socialism as a viable economic sys-tem had to observe basic economic principles. But as a political leader, Deng went far beyond the familiar boundary of market socialism. There was no ism, no dogma of any kind to defend in Deng's view of socialism.[47] Socialism was, rather, an open system that should "draw on the achievements of all cultures and learn from other countries, including the developed capitalist countries." Socialism was no longer exclusively identified with collective ownership and central planning. Rather, "the essence of socialism" was "the ultimate achieve-ment of prosperity for all." At a time when the Chinese leadership was anxious to preserve socialism and ward off capitalism, Deng simply set aside a mean-ingless and distracting ideological debate and focused on the practicalities of moving the Chinese economy forward.

After Shenzhen, Deng continued his southern tour, reaching Zhuhai on the 23rd. This was another Special Economic Zone in Guangdong province, oppo-site Macau. Deng spent a week in Zhuhai, visiting a number of high-tech firms and meeting the local officials. He continued to press government officials for economic development.

It seems to me that, as a rule, at certain stages we should seize the opportu-nity to accelerate development for a few years, deal with problems as soon as they are recognized, and then move on. Basically, when we have enough material wealth, we shall have the initiative in handling contradictions and problems. For a big developing nation like China, it is impossible to attain faster economic growth steadily and smoothly at all times. Attention must be paid to stable and proportionate development, but stable and proportionate are relative terms, not absolute. Development is the absolute principle. We must be clear about this question. If we fail to analyze it properly and to understand it correctly, we shall become overcautious, not daring to emancipate our minds and act freely. Consequently, we shall lose opportunities. Like a boat sailing against the current, we must forge ahead or be swept downstream.[48]

Addressing the deep-rooted tension between the "Left" and "Right" tendencies within the Party, Deng emphatically warned against the danger of the "Left," deviating from the entrenched view held by Chinese Communist leaders since the birth of the Party.

At present, we are being affected by both the "Right" and "Left" tendencies. But it is the "Left" tendencies that have the deepest roots. Some theorists and politicians try to intimidate people by pinning political labels on them. That is not a "Right" tactic but a "Left" one. "Left tendencies" have a revolutionary connotation, giving the impression that the more "Left" one is, the more revolutionary one is. In the history of the Party, those tendencies have led to dire consequences. Some fine things were destroyed overnight. "Right tendencies" can destroy socialism, but so can "Left" ones. China should maintain vigilance against the "Right" but primarily against the "Left." The "Right" still exists, as can be seen from disturbances. But the "Left" is there too. Regarding reform and the open policy as means of introducing capitalism, and seeing the danger of peaceful evolution towards capitalism as coming chiefly from the economic sphere are "Left tendencies." If we keep clear heads, we shall not commit gross errors, and when problems emerge, they can be easily put right.[49]

On January 30th, Deng left Zhuhai for Shanghai, the last stop of his southern tour. The Pudong Development Zone had broken new ground less than two years earlier. Shanghai, the economic and financial center of China before 1949, clearly lagged behind Shenzhen, which, before the reform started, had been no more than a fishing village. Deng was apologetic to his hosts.

In developing the economy, we should strive to reach a higher level every few years. Of course, this should not be interpreted as encouraging unrealistic speed. We should do solid work, stressing efficiency, so as to realize steady, coordinated progress. Guangdong, for example, should try to mount several steps and catch up with the "four little dragons" of Asia in twenty years. In relatively developed areas such as Jiangsu Province, growth should be faster than the national average. Shanghai is another example. It has all the necessary conditions for faster progress. It enjoys obvious advantages in skilled people, technology and management and can have an impact over a wide area. In retrospect, one of my biggest mistakes was leaving out Shanghai when we launched the four special economic zones. If Shanghai had been included, the situation with regard to reform and opening in the Yangtze Delta, the entire Yangtze River valley and, indeed, the whole country would be quite different.[50]

When Deng was taking his southern tour, China had reached a pivotal time in the course of its economic reform. The new Chinese leadership that emerged after the 1989 Students Movement was cautious, hesitant, and drifting, distracted by domestic economic and political instability and disoriented by the fall of the Soviet bloc. Beijing's vehement criticism of the editorials in the *Liberation Daily* must have disturbed Deng deeply. It was at this juncture that Deng took it upon himself to rekindle the embers of China's market reform. In essence, Deng's main message on his southern tour was to encourage further reform to save China's second revolution. Tian Jiyun, Vice Premier between 1983 and 1993, wrote in 2004 that "Deng Xiaoping observed with cold eyes for three years [1988–1991]. He could no longer remain silent, however, seeing the reform and opening up that he advocated was in danger of collapsing. He was determined to visit the south, and make the southern tour speeches, shocking China and the outside world alike."[51]

Deng's southern tour was kept a secret at the time. The Chinese media was totally silent on the affair. More than a month after Deng returned to Beijing, the *Shenzhen Special Zone Daily* ran a long article on Deng's tour on March 26th. The Xinhua News Agency broadcast the whole paper on the 30th. The next day, the article reappeared in many national and local newspapers, and in the evening program on the same day, Chinese Central Television broadcast the whole article. Deng's southern tour and the many talks he had given quickly attracted national attention. At the time, when market reform was still under severe political attack, Deng's unequivocal endorsement of the market and unreserved call for further reform compelled Beijing to act. But as Deng no longer held any formal position, his talks had to be backed by Beijing before they could exercise any real influence on central government policy.[52] As Deng's talks were publically circulated, opposition to market reform began to decline but still persisted. On April 14th, the *People's Daily* published a long combative article entitled "Firmly, Accurately, and Comprehensively Implement the Party's Basic Line."[53] It urged China to maintain "vigilance against bourgeois liberalization" in order to avoid the fate suffered by Eastern Europe and the Soviet Union. On April 25th, 1992, Vice Premier Tian Jiyun took a lead in endorsing and elaborating on the speeches Deng had given during his southern tour.[54] In a talk at the Central Party School, Tian launched a direct attack against both leftists who openly opposed market reforms and those who "bend with the wind." They should go and live in a "special leftist zone," as Tian put it, with a purely planned economy and shortage and rationing everywhere. Tian's talk was videotaped and copies were quickly on sale on the streets of Beijing.

Clearly Deng was not Mao; China in 1992 was different from China in 1966. Three months after his return to Beijing, Deng visited the Capital Steel Corporation on May 20th. Addressing the managerial team and city officials, Deng remarked that "in regards to my talk, some people oppose it, some people take a wait-and-see attitude, and some people have been wholeheartedly working on it."[55]

In the many speeches he made on his tour, Deng was clearly preoccupied with the stagnant economic reform and urged more daring initiatives to restart it. But China faced another, more fundamental challenge: how to reconcile socialism with its policies of economic reform and opening up. The seeming contradiction between a continuing political commitment to socialism on the one hand, and market reform on the other, had confused many Chinese leaders and ordinary people, particularly those who remained loyal to orthodox Marxism. For generations of Party members who had grown up knowing nothing else but the doctrines of socialism, the market reform must have profoundly challenged their political beliefs and created some confusion. If Deng wanted to succeed in "keeping clear heads," he also had to fight a battle of ideas.

In Zhuhai, Deng warned the local leaders in plain language that what threatened Chinese socialism most was not the "Right tendencies," but the "Left tendencies." This was a radical departure from the views held dear by Chinese leaders that capitalism (or the "Right" in Chinese political terminology) was the number one enemy of socialism. As a devoted Party member, Deng never abandoned his political belief in Marxism. Yet he creatively redefined Marxism to make it not only compatible with China's market reform, but an indispensable epistemic requirement.

In studying Marxism-Leninism we must grasp the essence and learn what we need to know. Weighty tomes are for a small number of specialists; how can the masses read them? It is formalistic and impracticable to require that everyone read such works. It was from the *Communist Manifesto* and *The ABC of Communism* that I learned the rudiments of Marxism. Recently, some foreigners said that Marxism cannot be defeated. That is so not because there are so many big books, but because Marxism is the irrefutable truth. *The essence of Marxism is seeking truth from facts*. That's what we should advocate, not book worship. The reform and the open policy have been successful not because we relied on books, but because we relied on practice and sought truth from facts. It was the peasants who invented the household contract responsibility system with remuneration linked to output. Many of the good ideas in rural reform came from people at the grassroots. We processed them and raised them to the level of guidelines for the whole country. Practice is the sole criterion for testing truth. I haven't read too many books, but there is one thing I believe in: Chairman Mao's principle of seeking truth from facts. That is the principle we relied on when we were fighting wars, and we continue to rely on it in construction and reform. We have advocated Marxism all our lives. Actually, Marxism is not abstruse. It is a plain thing, a very plain truth. (italics added)[56]

Here, Deng demonstrated the pragmatism he shared with Chen Yun, making an indirect reference to Chen's adage, "do not rely on higher authorities, do not rely on books, but rely on facts." Since Chen was widely respected in the Party as a staunch defender of socialism, Deng reached out to Chen to rebuild the political coalition for reform. Even though practice was highly stressed by Marx, and he and his disciples preferred materialism to idealism, no Marxist had ever placed such a heavy emphasis on seeking truth from facts.

Mao, of course, had written an influential article in 1937 called "On Practice," which had been widely circulated and must have been carefully studied by Deng. Concluding the article, Mao wrote:

Discover the truth through practice, and again through practice verify and develop the truth. Start from perceptual knowledge and actively develop it into rational knowledge; then start from rational knowledge and actively guide revolutionary practice to change both the subjective and objective world. Practice, knowledge, again practice, and again knowledge. This form repeats itself in endless cycles, and with each cycle the content of practice and knowledge rises to a higher level. Such is the whole of the dialectical-materialist theory of knowledge, and such is the dialectical-materialist theory of the union of knowing and doing.[57]

But Mao's view on practice was tainted and severely debilitated by his class analysis. Mao believed dogmatically that the practice and knowledge of the politically progressive class, the proletariat, was superior to that of the bourgeoisie. This philosophy of class struggle had been absorbed into the blood of the Party. It gave the Party an identity as the self-claimed vanguard of the Chinese people in a revolutionary war for national independence. This self-serving rhetoric would have led the Party to isolation and self-destruction if it had not always been balanced in practice by Mao's persistent efforts to build what he called a "united front" before the Chinese Communist Party took power in 1949. Once in power, however, Mao felt no more need for the united front and the virulent ideology of class struggle was quickly instilled to penetrate every part of Chinese society. Terror and violence were sanctioned against anyone who was viewed as a class enemy. In its most ludicrous form, as seen during the Cultural Revolution, knowledge in the hands of the bourgeois class was denounced as useless and treacherous. It was thought that it was better to be an ignorant member of the proletariat than an educated petty bourgeois. In rejecting class struggle and stressing practice as the only criterion of testing, the Chinese economic reform started on a sound epistemic foundation.

In his re-embracing of pragmatism Deng tried to make his interpretation of Marxism compatible with Mao's teachings, while still downplaying the idea of class struggle. But Deng acted too generously when he attributed the principle of seeking truth from facts to Mao or Marxism. Mao clearly popularized this principle, making it the motto for the Anti-Japanese Military and Politics University in 1937, and later the Central Party School in 1947. But Mao picked up the principle of seeking truth from facts from the Yuelu Academy in Changsha – Mao was a student there between 1916 and 1919 – which also used the principle as the school motto. Around the same time, Beiyang University, the predecessor of today's Tianjin University, also adopted "seeking truth from facts" as its motto. However, this principle has deep roots in Chinese history. It first appeared in the writing of a famous Chinese historian during the Han Dynasty, Ban Gu. In the Song Dynasty, Zhu Xi, the neo-Confucian thinker, proclaimed that "investigating of things is the surest way to gain knowledge" and that "theoretical principles lie in practical affairs." If "seeking truth from facts" serves as a prescription, an even older teaching of Confucian philosophy, traced to Mencius, serves as its proscriptive counterpart: "better not to have it if we accept everything a book says." Together, these principles cultivated a strong anti-dogmatic tendency in Chinese habits of thought. To reach any decision in practical affairs, so the principles say, requires thorough investigation of the facts in the first place; this is indeed a plain truth.

Deng's reinterpretation of Marxism in line with the pragmatic spirit of Confucianism provided a solution to the ideological predicament that had constrained and confused the Chinese since the very beginning of reform: how could socialism and market reform coexist? By defining the essence of Marxism as seeking truth from facts, Deng simplified Marxism and turned it from an "abstruse" political ideology into "a plain truth."

VI

The private sector responded quickly and enthusiastically to Deng's call for further reform. Having been beset by ideological hostility since the austerity program began in 1988, the private sector bounced back strongly. By 1993, the number of private firms rebounded to 1988 levels, reaching 237,000. By 1994, that number was 432,000, and the amount of capital registered under private firms increased by almost twenty times between 1992 and 1995.[58] As the private sector enjoyed its resurgence, it attracted more and more talent from the state sector. This prompted a great reversal of social attitudes. Throughout the 1980s jobs in the private sector had been looked down on as insecure, disrespectable, and dishonorable. Even Hu Yaobang's campaign of 1983, which sought to elevate the social status of the private sector by calling it a "glorious project," failed to change public opinions. After Deng's southern tour, people began to vote with their feet, leaving the state sector for the private sector. The most eye-catching development in the wake of Deng's southern tour was the phenomenon of *"xiahai"* – government officials, managers, and employees of state-owned enterprises, and scholars at universities and research institutes, letting go of their "iron bowl" to open their own private businesses. According to the Ministry of Personnel, 120,000 government officials left their jobs in 1992 to start private businesses. In addition, there were more than 10 million government officials taking unpaid leave to start up a private business.[59] They were joined by millions of professors, engineers, and college graduates. Even the *People's Daily* published an article that year entitled "Want to Get Rich, Get Busy."[60]

As Deng's southern tour became more widely publicized and his speeches were being read all over China, the ideological opposition to reform started to fade and the political atmosphere changed once more; 1992 eventually became "the year of reform and opening up."[61] On March 20th, Premier Li announced that the austerity program had accomplished its task and the stage of readjustment was to end. This opened the door to further reforms. After three years of retraction, the pendulum of reform began to swing ever higher once it was released again.

After almost a year of preparation, the Fourteenth Congress of the Chinese Communist Party opened on October 12th, 1992. Deng's call for further economic reform was fully embraced. Jiang Zemin, in addressing the Party Congress, called for "quickening the pace of reform, opening up and modernization and striving for greater success in building socialism with Chinese characteristics."[62] Most important, the market economy was, for the first time, officially recognized as the ultimate goal of China's economic reform. After the torrent of anti-market rhetoric and policies that had swept through China in the preceding years, Jiang's endorsement of the market economy reaffirmed China's commitment to market reform. Compared with the 1984 Decision on Economic System Reform passed at the Third Plenum of the Twelfth Central Committee of the Party, which sanctioned the presence of a market economy in China's economic reform, it was accorded a much more elevated role by Jiang. However, Jiang stopped short of fully adopting Deng's pragmatic stance. In Jiang's speech, China's market economy was qualified as "socialist"; the tension between socialism and the market persisted and would occasionally erupt in the years to come. Nonetheless, sixteen years after Mao's death (1976) and thirty-six years after the socialist transformation (1956), China finally embraced (or re-embraced) the market economy.

The most serious defect of China's economic reform in the 1980s was the lack of price reform, which had resulted in chaotic pricing, massive resource misallocation, and economic disorder. Even though the Chinese government was aware of the urgency of price reform, it missed a window of opportunity in the early 1980s, and opted for a compromise strategy, the dual-track pricing system. When the government finally attempted to force through price reform in 1988 it failed mainly because of unfavorable macroeconomic conditions. Not surprisingly, the most urgent demand made of China's developing market economy was to reform the distorted price system.

In 1992 the Chinese government took a series of decisions that would ultimately abolish price control. The list of prices for raw materials, capital goods, and transportation services to be set by the central government was reduced from 737 to 89 (it would be further reduced, to 13, in 2001).[63] The market for grain was fully liberalized nationwide at the end of 1992. The National Planning Commission halved the mandatory production plan for 1993, leaving more room for market forces to operate. China also significantly reduced the import tariffs for more than 3000 items, beginning at the end of 1992. The process of price deregulation would continue throughout the coming years. In 1993, the dual-pricing practice used for steel and machinery products was ended; in 1994, dual pricing for coal and crude oil ended. By 1996, the dual-track pricing for industrial inputs became history.[64] The share of producer goods transacted at market prices increased steadily from almost zero in 1978, to 13 percent in 1985, 46 percent in 1991, and 78 percent in 1995.

The removal of price controls was greatly helped by the presence of a strong private sector which had been working for more than a decade to bring about a functioning price system. In this regard, the use of dual-track pricing was an advantage; prior to price deregulation both private and state-owned enterprises had already been more or less exposed to the market and had become familiar with the operation of market forces. By allowing economic actors to become familiar with the market, the dual-track pricing practice had reduced the cost of adjustment and learning, particularly for state-owned enterprises. The downside was a lengthened period of chaotic pricing for all, which not only brought about severe macroeconomic distortions, but also made it difficult for firms to respond to price signals. Moreover, the price discrimination suffered by non-state enterprises also led to resource misallocation. Yet it is difficult to assess how price reform would have fared without the transition period of dual-track pricing, making it almost impossible to fully evaluate the net welfare gain caused by dual-track pricing. Nonetheless, after several years of dual-track pricing, the introduction of the 1992 price reform went more smoothly than the Chinese government had expected, with few noticeably disruptive effects on society.

In the Party's embrace of the market economy, the 1992 price reform was by far the most critical step in developing a market system. Now, the price signal was able to function the way it does in any market economy, informing firms of what to produce to meet the demand of consumers and allocating resources to where they could be utilized most profitably. With a few exceptions, all firms, including both state and private enterprises, started to pay the same prices for all their materials. The black market for raw materials that had flourished under the dual-track system contracted rapidly. Private enterprises now had open access to all raw materials and intermediate inputs (with the one exception of bank loans).

But price liberalization did not automatically give birth to a functioning pricing system across all markets. Price deregulation helped to remove the distortions that had severely undermined the price system; it made possible the rise of a market-based pricing system. But when and how the system developed depended on a large number of factors. In general, a market price emerged quickly for all those goods that had been subject to dual-track pricing. When the economics textbook draws a supply curve intersecting a demand curve, the market price is magically determined at the point of intersection. But the two curves, or what Alfred Marshall called the two blades of the scissors, do not readily exist in the market economy, not in the way that business firms do once they are created. The demand and supply curves are theoretical concepts; the real movers behind them are consumers and business organizations. The conventional emphasis placed on demand and supply in the economics textbook as the moving forces in the market is thus misleading, if it is accepted literally. Rather, demand and supply forces result from the continuous process of bidding and tendering between buyers and sellers, who are constantly alert to changing opportunities. After price liberalization, it did not take long for a market price to emerge for those goods and factors with existing buyers and sellers; they had some experience of bargaining with each other under the dual-track regime. But for capital assets, which had never had a market under socialism, it was a wholly different matter. For example, how should one price an insolvent state-owned enterprise? For all goods and factors that had not previously been subject to market evaluation, it would take much learning and risk-taking on the part of buyers and sellers for prices to emerge.

VII

While freedom to set prices helped to remove many price distortions, as well as barriers among firms when they engaged in market transactions, there existed another kind of barrier standing between the state and firms in the Chinese economy. The wide use of managerial contracts in state-owned enterprises presented a prohibitive obstacle for the rise of market order during the 1980s.

The adoption of the managerial contract responsibility system in enterprise reform formalized the earlier effort of "delegating rights and sharing profits"; the goal had been to give more autonomy to the enterprises. The use of a contract between the management of a state enterprise and its supervising authority was easy to set up once the idea of the contract responsibility system became common knowledge after the implementation of the household responsibility system in rural China. This explains its wide use in enterprise reform in the 1980s.

While the household responsibility system had set Chinese peasants free, the responsibility contract failed to free Chinese state enterprises from bureaucratic red tape. With the spread of the contract responsibility system, each enterprise struck an individually negotiated contract with the state or its local agent. As a result, each enterprise ended up with a highly idiosyncratic set of constraints – what inputs to receive at what subsidized price, how much tax to pay, and so on.[65] In addition to dual-track pricing, this was another important source of price distortion in the Chinese economy. Due to their combined effects, the Chinese economy lacked a unified pricing system for all enterprises throughout the 1980s.

Under the managerial contract responsibility system, each enterprise, including those in the private sector, faced a different set of prices and tax rates. Indeed, taxes did not exist for the state-owned enterprises until 1983. The government simply collected all their profits as its main source of revenue. In 1983, the state-owned enterprises began to pay taxes instead of turning over their profits to the government. This ended a practice that had endured since the founding of the People's Republic. However, a problem remained. The amount of tax was included in the managerial responsibility contract and the tax rate varied across industries and enterprises, even after the 1983 tax reform.[66]

Moreover, the contract system was also utilized by the central government in collecting taxes from the provincial governments throughout the 1980s. This was first introduced in 1980 to give more autonomy and incentives to local governments. Despite repeated changes made throughout the 1980s, China did not have a unified tax structure and the fiscal relations between the central and provincial governments varied on a case-by-case basis until the tax reform of 1994. Some provinces paid a certain fixed amount of tax to (or received a fixed amount of subsidy from) Beijing; other provinces were taxed at a certain rate, which was often open to negotiation every few years. This inequality in the tax burden across provinces was a constant source of discontent, particularly among provinces that were at a similar level of economic development. Since a provincial government with a light tax burden would end up with less pressure to tax the firms under its jurisdiction, the tax system (or rather its absence) contributed significantly to the chaotic pricing system in the 1980s.[67]

The old tax system had another weakness, at least as seen from Beijing. Ever since the beginning of reform there had been a significant decline in government revenues. To make things worse, the proportion of government revenues collected by Beijing also went down. For example, the government's fiscal revenue represented 27 percent of GDP in 1979. It declined to 21 percent in 1986 and was down to 14.5 percent by 1992. During the same time period, the revenue going to Beijing declined from 46.8 percent of total revenue in 1979 to 38.6 percent in 1992, while the share of revenue left to local governments increased.[68] As a result, the Chinese government ran deficits during most of the years of reform.

To address both price distortions in the economy, and its declining fiscal strength, the Chinese government in 1993 decided to overhaul the old contract-based tax and fiscal regime. This came after experiments carried out in nine provinces or cities in 1992. Zhu Rongji, Vice Premier in charge of economic affairs, was directly responsible for mobilizing support from both Beijing and provincial governments, and for renegotiating a new fiscal and taxation system. In the first part of 1993, Zhu convened many meetings in Beijing to reach a consensus among all ministers and central government offices involved in taxation and fiscal policies.[69] From September 9th to November 21st, Zhu visited seventeen provincial governments to secure their support. On December 25th, the State Council announced the new tax system, to be implemented on January 1st, 1994.[70]

The comprehensive tax reform of 1994 represented another critical step towards the removal of price distortions in the Chinese economy.[71] These reforms consisted of three main components: tax simplification, tax sharing, and tax administration. The most noticeable aspect of the 1994 tax reform was the replacement of a complicated multi-tiered system of taxes on turnover by a uniform 17 percent (with a few exceptions when the rate was 13 percent) valued-added tax, applied to all manufacturing firms. A business tax was applied to services, at a rate of 3 or 5 percent of turnover depending on the nature of the business. The new tax code simplified an extremely complicated tax structure. For example, under the previous tax regime, there had been twenty-one different rates of product tax, ranging from 3 to 60 percent, and four business tax rates, ranging from 3 to 15 percent. The new tax code also eliminated the tax previously applied to foreign enterprises, which had forty rates ranging from 1.5 percent to 69 percent. As a result of these simplifications, the 1994 tax reform removed severe price distortions created by the previous tax regime, putting an end to redundant investments in sectors with lower tax rates and artificially high profit margins.

The second component of the 1994 tax reform was the establishment of a national tax administration, which greatly improved the state's capacity to collect taxes. The tax revenue collected by the government as a percentage of the GDP increased from about 10 percent in 1995 to 15 percent in 2002 and has remained between 15 and 20 percent ever since; about half of it goes to the central government.[72]

The third component of the new tax regime was to end the individually negotiated system of revenue sharing between the central government and provincial governments, and to introduce a new uniform tax-sharing scheme. Under the new tax regime, some taxes were assigned to the central government, including excise taxes, customs duty and enterprise income tax collected from financial institutions. Others were assigned to the local government, including urban land-use tax, valued-added tax on land, property tax, and business tax not covered by the value-added tax. Some were shared; these included the value-added tax (75 percent for the central and 25 percent for local government).

Even though all taxes introduce price distortion in an economy, the new tax-sharing scheme was critical in removing preexisting market distortions. The most fundamental change occasioned by the new tax system was to free Chinese firms from the direct and immediate impact of the central government's fiscal policy, separating the microeconomic environment from the government's macroeconomic policy. Under the previous tax system, the fiscal and taxation policy was an important component of the constraints that each Chinese firm faced, which was decided on individual negotiation. The 1994 tax reform greatly helped to create a competitive microeconomic environment for all Chinese firms. This was achieved in two steps.

First, recall that under the previous revenue-sharing scheme, all taxes were first collected by the provincial government, which then turned over to Beijing a certain percentage or a fixed amount in accord with an individually negotiated agreement. Since the new tax regime was to apply uniformly across China, it closed the door to favoritism and put all provinces (and enterprises under their jurisdiction) on an equal footing. Second, by eliminating the product tax, the new tax-sharing scheme weakened the incentives for local governments to pursue protectionism.[73] The product tax was paid by the enterprises to local governments based on sales irrespective of their profitability, and was introduced in the 1983–1984 tax reform. It has since become the main source of revenue for local governments. Prior to the new tax reform, local governments had strong incentives to protect their enterprises from outside competition, effectively fragmenting the national economy. As long as the enterprises were in operation, they had to pay product taxes to local governments even when they did not make any profit. After the new tax reform, the value-added tax became the main source of revenue, and enterprises had to be profitable to pay the value-added tax. As a result, the 1994 tax reform helped in reducing market distortions. This turned out to have far-reaching effects, transforming regional economic dynamics from chaotic fiefdoms into a sustainable and efficient competition. Now, local governments competed against each other to attract investment by improving their infrastructure and business environment. Regional competition has been primarily responsible for China's remarkable economic dynamics since the mid-1990s. How this came to be and the role local governments played will be our focus later in this chapter.

VIII

After Deng's southern tour and the Fourteenth Congress of the Party, the 1992 price reform and 1994 tax reform helped to reduce or eliminate many price distortions and pave the way for the rise of a single price system in the economy and a common national market. At the same time, another wave of enterprise reform was spreading all over China. With the endorsement of a market economy as the ultimate goal for China's economic reform in 1992, the proponents of enterprise reform gained a new mission: turning state-owned enterprises into independent, autonomous, and market-oriented economic entities. This pushed the Chinese enterprise reform to a new stage, beyond the basics of "delegating rights and sharing profits" and the contract based managerial responsibility system. Building a modern enterprise system freed from government intervention and disciplined by the market became the goal of the next stage of enterprise reform.

At first glance, this whole idea appeared counterintuitive. How could a state-owned enterprise be kept free of state meddling? There existed an inherent dilemma in the enterprise reform: a state-owned enterprise could not possibly free itself fully from the state. How was it possible to turn state enterprises into autonomous profit-seeking business firms while they were still owned by the state? What could be realistically hoped for was to cut down bureaucracy and red tape, streamline the relationship between the government and state enterprises and subject state enterprises to market competition. In addition, the number of state-owned enterprises had to be reduced, since the majority of them were already insolvent and had become a financial burden to the state. As we will see later, this was exactly what the Chinese government was able to achieve.

In some ways, a state-owned enterprise under socialism might look like a publicly listed company under capitalism. In both cases, the owners of the firm are faceless. A state enterprise belongs to "all the people," a public company belongs to shareholders. Management is separate from ownership in both cases. This similarity had been frequently stressed by defenders of state ownership in China. What was ignored was the fact that the operation of a publicly traded company depends on a whole set of legal and economic institutions, which in the West have developed over centuries. Still, scandals in the western corporate world frequently surface when management blatantly abuses its power and violates its fiduciary duty of care and loyalty to shareholders. The difficulties that the Chinese state-owned enterprises faced reflected more the deficiency of the state in establishing a proper regulatory framework than the defects of the enterprises themselves.

The embrace of the market economy by the Chinese government in 1992 could not, and did not, deal a quick death to the ideas of socialism that had long formed the established way of thinking for many Chinese leaders, economists, and ordinary citizens. In any case, what the Chinese government had instituted was, as they put it, "a socialist market economy." State ownership was still widely believed to be the economic foundation for the political rule of the Party. This strong and persistent political preference for state ownership made privatization the last choice for enterprise reform. In addition, this ideological bias against privatization was bolstered by an ingrained cultural prejudice. In the Chinese context, the word "public" (or *gong* in Chinese) is closely associated with public spirit and sacrifice for the common good. The word "private" (or *si* in Chinese), on the other hand, falls into the swamp of moral low ground. Throughout the 1980s and 1990s, the word "private" was almost a taboo in public discourse. Chinese private enterprises, for example, were referred to as "people's enterprises" in contrast to state enterprises. The political and cultural hostility toward privatization was strong.

On the other hand, by the mid-early 1990s, after more than a decade of enterprise reform, more and more state-owned enterprises had sunk into insolvency. They had become a growing financial burden to the Chinese government. It was reported that in 1988 about 10.9 percent of state enterprises were insolvent. The rate rose to 16 percent in 1989, 27.6 percent in 1990, over 30 percent in 1993, and 40 percent in 1995.[74] A survey of state enterprises in 16 big cities, including Shanghai, Tianjin, Shenyang, and Wuhan, jointly conducted by nine central government ministers and bureaus in 1994 revealed that 52.2 percent of state enterprises were insolvent.[75] At the same time, the share of state enterprises in industrial production plummeted from 77.6 percent in 1978 to 54.6 percent in 1990 and 34 percent in 1995.[76] In 1980, covering the losses of state enterprises accounted for 3.1 percent of government fiscal revenues; in 1994, it went up to 9.3 percent. Chinese economists and policymakers alike were compelled to ask themselves what had gone wrong with the previous rounds of enterprise reform. What prevented the state enterprises from growing with the private firms and township and village enterprises?

The most striking symptom observed among state enterprises at the beginning of reform was their lack of "vitality." The expansion of autonomy and the implementation of the managerial responsibility contract were intended to improve the incentives of workers and managers, injecting more "vitality" into the state enterprises. Under the dictates of socialism, the reform did not touch the ownership structure. State-owned enterprises, from the legal point of view, belonged to all the people. But economic resources open to everyone belong to no one, a situation which Chinese economists called "the absence of owner" in state ownership. At the time, Chinese economists drew much theoretical inspiration from a growing school of thought in modern economics, the economics of property rights, as mainly developed by Armen Alchian, Steven Cheung, Harold Demsetz, Douglass North, as well as Ronald Coase. What the Chinese economists and policymakers found particularly relevant was the idea that the delineation of rights is a precondition for a market economy.[77] If China was moving toward a market economy, it had to clearly define all property rights. This basic idea of property rights economics thus suggested a convenient way to "get property rights right" without changing the ownership structure via privatization.

While the Chinese government shied away from letting broken state enterprises close and economists debated the issue of property rights, Zhucheng, a small county-level city in Shandong, quietly privatized 272 out of its 288 state or collective enterprises. This happened between late 1992 and mid-1994.[78] Chen Guang, who became mayor of the city in 1991 and Party Secretary in 1993, oversaw this radical episode of enterprise reform. As mayor, Chen quickly found out that the majority of state enterprises were actually insolvent and had to rely upon government subsidies to survive. The local government, however, could no longer afford to subsidize the loss-making state enterprises. The first state enterprise was sold to its employees in December 1992. To stay in line with state policy, which then prohibited outright sale of state assets, the city government originally proposed to retain 51 percent of the share, selling the rest to managers and workers. This proposal, however, was rejected by the employees, who wanted outright control. In the end, the employees bought out the whole enterprise, with a contribution of 90,000 yuan from each of the nine members of the managerial team, 20,000 yuan from each of the twenty or so middle-level administrative staff, and 6000 yuan from each of the 250 or so workers. The new enterprise was registered as a "stock cooperative." It was not until after the Third Plenum of the Fourteenth Central Committee in 1993 that stock cooperatives become recognized as a tool to restructure state enterprises. After most of the state enterprises being privatized or simply closed, Chen faced little resistance in abolishing five government bureaus formerly in charge of administering state enterprises.

Around the same time, a similar scheme of restructuring state and collective enterprises was underway in several other small or medium-sized cities, including Shunde in Guangdong province, Haicheng in Liaoning province, Yibing in Sichuan province, Bing County in Heilongjiang province, Shuozhou in Shanxi province, Dongbo in Henan province, Ningde in Fujian province, and Nantong in Jiangsu province.[79] However, none of these initiatives received much media attention. For the rest of the 1990s, Chen Guang and Zhucheng remained causes of controversy at the center of national debates on enterprise reform. In a policy paper published in Beijing in early 1995, the enterprise reform conducted at Zhucheng was criticized as "privatization" and "taking the capitalist road."[80] As late as 2001, an article published in a journal based in Beijing criticized Chen for "destroying socialism."[81] In July of the same year, Zhucheng was approved in a provincial meeting on enterprise reform organized by the provincial Party Secretary and Governor. In January 1996, a delegation of twenty-three members from nine different Ministries was sent by Zhu Rongji, Premier of the State Council, to visit Zhucheng for a week.[82] Their report enthusiastically approved the Zhucheng experience of restructuring state enterprises. In March, Zhu himself led a delegation to Zhucheng, visiting many restructured enterprises. After his visit, Zhu pointed out some shortcomings in Zhucheng's enterprise reform, but praised it as a model that deserved serious consideration for other cities.

In the early 1990s Shanghai developed a different approach to reforming big state enterprises. Shanghai had long been China's economic center, including during the socialist period. The rise of Shenzhen and the Pearl River Delta in Guangdong province in the 1980s had significantly reduced the relative economic status of Shanghai. Nonetheless, Shanghai was home to many of the largest state enterprises. Moreover, the setup of Pudong as a new Special Economic Zone in 1990 and the rapid economic development in Zhejiang and Jiangsu provinces gave Shanghai a new mission. To reform their state enterprises, most of which had been the pride of China during Mao's time, officials from Shanghai visited several western European countries to study how they managed their state assets.[83] Afterward, they formulated a new plan for Shanghai.

The innovation was to set up a new government agent, the State Assets Management Committee, which would take over all state enterprises that used to be run by various government departments. The Committee established a number of state asset management companies, each becoming an investor and owner of many state enterprises. A small number of critically important state enterprises were owned singly or jointly by state asset management companies. For a bigger but still limited number of less important state enterprises, state asset management companies would hold majority control, but welcome private investors. All others – by far the largest group – were turned into limited liability corporations and joint-stock companies. Usually these had a diverse structure of owners, including other state enterprises, foreign investors, and domestic firms and individuals. Many small and medium-sized state enterprises were simply liquidated. As a result, their number was cut dramatically. Even those remaining were separated from direct government control and put in the hands of a few state asset management companies. In principle, the state asset management company would behave like a private investor, subject to certain political constraints. Moreover, all state asset companies reported directly to the State Assets Management Committee, slashing the bureaucratic red tape that had plagued state enterprises in the past.

The practices of both Zhucheng and Shanghai were incorporated into the "Decision on Issues Regarding the Establishment of a Socialist Market Economic System," which was passed at the Third Plenum of the Fourteenth Central Committee of the Party in November 1993. This meant that those practices were now part of the main approach to reforming state-owned enterprises. The strategy was then called "holding on to the big and letting go the small." Until then, the Chinese government had been firm in resisting privatization despite a rapidly growing private sector and the failure of previous enterprise reforms to revitalize state enterprises.

IX

In addition to ideological considerations, several practical reasons had been significant enough to hold back privatization. The most constraining factor was concern about massive unemployment and its dire social and political consequences. Throughout the 1980s and early 1990s, China did not have a functioning labor market to absorb or retrain laid-off workers if state enterprises should be privatized. Hence, the Chinese government forbade state-owned enterprises from laying off their workers during restructuring. At a conference held in Beijing in 1994, Vice Premier Zhu Rongji challenged a dozen or so Chinese and foreign economists in the audience to work out a strategy of enterprise reform without massive layoffs of state employees. Anyone who could come up with a solution, according to Zhu, would surely deserve a Nobel Prize.[84] Because of this concern of social stability, even though China passed its first Bankruptcy Law at the end of 1986, over the next five years, only twenty-seven enterprises declared bankruptcy.[85] Not surprisingly, a common method used to privatize small and medium-sized state enterprises was to sell them to their managers and employees, with no or limited layoffs. Essentially, this was similar to the previous round of enterprise reform of turning state enterprises into joint-stock companies. By the end of 1991, China had more than 3200 joint-stock holding companies, more than 85 percent of them with substantial employee holdings. This form of privatization avoided large layoffs and helped to mitigate the incentive problem that had long troubled state enterprises. However, it did have its limitations.

Second, the state enterprises provided an "iron bowl" to their employees, which meant lifetime employment as well as nonwage benefits, including housing, daycare and schooling for children, medical care, and pensions. The entitlement to jobs was even frequently passed from retirees to their adult children. In addition, the state enterprise was also a central anchor in an employee's social and political life. Not surprisingly, employees of state-owned enterprises, particularly the big ones, had a strong attachment to and identification with their employers. This system of the "iron bowl" essentially tied the Chinese workers to a single employer from the beginning of their career to the end of their lives. Chinese state employees literally belonged to their work units. This made it virtually impossible to separate employees from state enterprises. At the same time, however, under the managerial responsibility system, the workers had little opportunity to voice their concerns and only limited chance to "exit".

In support of its efforts to turn state-owned enterprises into modern corporations, the Chinese government took a series of measures to create a labor market so that laidoff workers from state-owned enterprises could be easily reemployed elsewhere. It also put into place a social safety net for retired workers as well as for workers who were caught between jobs. The first component of the social safety net was unemployment insurance, which was instituted in 1993.[86] This effort was made easier in 1994 by China's official recognition of "unemployment," replacing the odd phrase, "waiting to be employed."[87] By 1995, more than 70 percent of state employees were covered by unemployment insurance. At the same time, pensions for state employees were gradually separated from employers and taken over by a state pension fund. Housing reforms also began in 1994 and were basically complete by the end of 1990s; public housing was sold below the market price to current occupants to separate state employees from their employers. Employees of state enterprises could now change jobs without losing their homes.

At the Fifteenth National Congress of the Party in 1997, the role of the non-public sector was stressed as "an important component" of the socialist market economy. Joint-stock companies were officially recognized. Privatization was no longer seen as undermining socialism. Afterward, the state-owned enterprises went through a drastic process of restructuring and downsizing, resulting in massive layoffs. Like the previous rounds of enterprise reform, local initiatives played a leading role after Beijing loosened restrictions. In this round, a practice originated at Changsha, the provincial capital of Hunan, quickly attracted national attention in the new millennium.[88]

After privatization was officially approved in 1997, officials were challenged with the problem of restructuring state-owned assets – many of which had little or even negative market value – while relocating millions of state employees. What emerged at Changsha was referred to as "dual substitution," a simultaneous shift in both property rights structure and employment relations. First, the state gave up its position as the sole owner of state enterprises and became a minority shareholder by inviting outside investors and/or employees to become the majority shareholders. Second, employees of state enterprises gave up their "iron bowl" in exchange for a cash settlement, which was mainly determined by their years of service. What made the Changsha experiment work was that it successfully solved the two intertwining problems that had consistently plagued previous enterprise reforms, state ownership and unemployment.

A critical factor that allowed this scheme to succeed was that the municipal government put state assets with market value and property (which had seen significant appreciation in its value) from all state enterprises into a common pool; this meant that even insolvent state enterprises and their employees were not excluded from the benefits. The compensation received by state employees was equalized across different enterprises, which was widely perceived as fair and readily embraced by workers. To put all state assets in one common pool also helped to create a state property market, easing the transfer of assets. After its successful implementation in Changsha, the practice of "dual substitution" became the main approach to the reform of state enterprises throughout China.[89]

In the new millennium, a particular form of enterprise reform emerged and it deserves special attention: this is the use of IPOs (initial public offerings). Some state enterprises were restructured for IPOs in the domestic stock market (the Shanghai Stock Exchange and Shenzhen Stock Exchange) and also foreign stock markets, with the Hong Kong Stock Exchange being the most popular destination. This gave enterprises another means of raising capital, and it also stimulated the development of the domestic stock markets. Since its setup in 1992, the Securities Regulatory Commission had perceived the stock market as a privilege for state enterprises to enable them to raise capital directly from the public. The vast majority of listed companies were either state enterprises or those with state enterprises as the majority shareholders. The first domestic private enterprise was not listed on the stock market until 1998. Even today, after two decades of operation, the Chinese stock market remains underdeveloped; it has limited capacity as a market institution to discipline the management of listed companies, and as a result only plays a marginal role in China's fast growing capital market.[90]

After 2000, the state-owned enterprises went through another, more aggressive round of restructuring. Between 2001 and 2004, the number of state-owned enterprises dropped by almost half. In addition, in March 2003, the State

Council adopted the practice started in Shanghai more than a decade before and established a new ministerial level agent, the State Assets Supervision and Administration Commission, to manage the remaining 196 state enterprises that belonged to the central government (the number is down to 117 as of February 3rd, 2012).[91] Similar commissions at lower administrative levels were created by all provincial and municipal governments that still ran state enterprises. As a result of this restructuring, all state enterprises are now under a single supervising body, greatly simplifying the relations between the government and state enterprises, but still giving many special privileges to state enterprises over private ones, including monopoly access to several sectors. After the Third Plenum of the Sixteenth Central Committee in October 2003, enterprise reform was no longer referred to as the "central link" in China's economic reform.[92]

The last round of enterprise reform began in 1992–1993 as privatization was initiated by local governments in a desperate attempt to save local finances from disaster. It ended in 2003, with the setup of the State Assets Supervision and Administration Commission, and can be considered a measured success.[93] It consolidated the state sector and kept the remaining state enterprises financially healthy. This was due partly to cost-reduction and improvement in productivity and partly to their remaining monopoly power and political influence. During this period, the measures taken by the Chinese government to reform state enterprises were dictated by what they saw as the root problem of state ownership: the lack of incentives on the part of managers and workers in state enterprises. This focus on incentives was also reflected in the official explanation of the success of the household responsibility system in rural China; private farming was embraced by peasants and turned out to be successful because it was better aligned with their incentives. However, the failure of state-owned enterprises was more complicated.

The lack of incentive was just one reason, but at least two other factors were just as important. First and foremost, firms in a market economy face constant market selection; those which fail the market test are forced to close and release their workers and capital to the market for alternative employment. There is no secret recipe to keep firms successful. Darwinian selection is the only mechanism available to keep economic resources in good hands while liquidating firms that cannot survive market competition. What a state can help with is to facilitate the creation of new firms, which will force existing firms to become more competitive or to fail. A state can also help to facilitate the liquidation of bankrupt firms so that their remaining resources can be easily released for better employment. But China's state-owned enterprises seldom closed down once they had been set up. With no possible exit, it is no wonder that the state sector was unable to compete with township and village enterprises and other private firms, which were subject to a harsh market discipline. Moreover, since existing firms could not easily close, the setup of new firms was inevitably under strict control. A common but critical dynamics that underpins a market economy – the constant creation of new firms and annihilation of old ones – simply did not exist in China under socialism, certainly not in the state sector.

There is no doubt that poor management must take some of the blame for the inferior performance of state enterprises. However, illicit asset stripping by insiders, including managers and supervising officials, was another important factor. With no external oversight, some managers set up their own businesses to siphon money away from state enterprises. That asset stripping occurred on a large scale in state enterprises certainly had something to do with their state ownership. Their state ownership also made state enterprises unable to close. But both these factors are separate from the incentives issue.

The conventional justification for private ownership is that it solves the incentive problem. That is certainly a key advantage. After a state firm is privatized and bought by its previous manager, he becomes the private owner and residual claimant of the firm. As a result, he will now have a greater incentive in making the firm profitable. He probably will work harder and make sounder business decisions. While an improvement in incentives generally leads to higher productivity, this is not the only, or even the main, advantage of private ownership. The benefits of private ownership and privatization are more broad-based than the improvement of incentives.

First, private ownership facilitates the efficient allocation of resources and thus improves productivity. The delineation of rights makes economic resources readily transferable among economic actors, who compete to employ the resources in the most profitable way. Thus, to what degree privatization works depends on how much it helps to release economic resources to a free asset market. Without a well-functioning asset market, privatization cannot be a silver bullet for the economic problems besetting state ownership. However, this condition seldom exists in economies experiencing transition from a planned to a market economy. More often than not, privatization was pursued as a means to dismantle central planning and create such a market. But without a functioning market to reallocate resources to better reemployment, the economic benefits of privatization are limited.[94]

Second, resource allocation in a market economy is a Hayekian process of discovery. There is no magic way to place all economic resources where they can be most profitably employed; the efficient utilization of resources is not a given in any economy. Entrepreneurs have no choice but to resort to trial and error to figure out where to put their resources; in their constant search for higher profits, they unintentionally move resources to where they generate the highest returns. Thus, resource allocation in the real world is categorically different from the paradigmatic choice problem defined in textbook economics as allocating limited means to satisfy given ends. The entrepreneur is always seeking to go beyond the given ends and explore new means. In other words, resource allocation is inevitably tied to the exploitation of resource utilization in a continuously changing economy. This process often involves experimenting with new products and founding new firms, while phasing out old ones, a process called "perennial gale of creative destruction" by Joseph Schumpeter.[95]

Under socialism, factors of production are owned by the state and their distribution in the economy is carried out through economic planning, so a critical step in market transformation is the rise of a factor market to replace economic planning in resource allocation. In China's market transformation, this emerged first at the local level, giving rise to regional competition with the active participation of local governments. Steven Cheung identified competition among *xians* – county-level local governments – as the key to understanding the miraculous rise of the Chinese economy.[96] Regional competition is certainly not confined to counties. It takes place from the provincial level down to the township level. But what exactly is competed for in regional competition? Answering this question takes us a long way toward understanding the nature of the Chinese market transformation.

X

Let us start with a less controversial subject: competition between firms. In textbook economics, a perfectly competitive market implies that many firms provide identical products to consumers, forcing firms to take whatever price consumers are willing to pay to clear the market. In reality, however, probably the most important competition that firms engage in is product innovation, that is, the design and provision of novel and better products. When firms are unable to differentiate their products, they have no choice but to cut costs and thus provide goods at a lower price than their competitors. The kind of competition epitomized in economics textbooks is actually the last resort for business firms. In addition, firms also compete in the factor market to attract the best human talents and obtain other resources necessary for their operation. Unless the firm can secure its supply of inputs from a factor market, it cannot compete in the product market, even if it has great products.

It is important to highlight the critical role played by various product and factor markets in making competition between firms possible. Markets provide a platform through which firms compete for both resources and customers. How effectively firms perform these tasks depends primarily on how open the markets are, including the markets for factors and products, and how free firms can be created and compete with each other. Essentially, firms' effectiveness depends on how smoothly and quickly factors of production can change hands in response to competitive bidding, how easily factors and products can move across boundaries (physical and social) in the economy, and how readily new firms can come into being with innovative products or ideas on how to organize factors in fresh ways. The second and related operation of the markets is to provide feedback to firms, rewarding firms that do a better job in satisfying customers and punishing those whose goods and services fail to please buyers. This can be accomplished when firms that succeed in winning the patronage of customers also succeed in the factor market in securing the service of factors of production. A serious problem thus arises when an economy with an open product market does not have an equally open factor market.

Hence, in a market economy, the firm and the market work hand in hand to move resources to where they can be most profitably employed, a challenge frequently involving the introduction of new products and elimination of obsolete ones as well as the rise of new firms and demise of broken ones. While the cost of operating the market calls for the rise of the firm – otherwise all individuals would work alone and interact with each other through the pricing system – the presence of the firm does not imply the failure of the market.[97] The firm does not replace the market altogether or makes it unnecessary or less significant. Rather, the creation and operation of firms necessitate open and competitive markets, without which the firms would have no clue what to produce and how to operate their businesses. The Leninist reasoning that a national economy can be run as a giant firm without any market is an illusion, and attempts to follow this model have been disastrous. As the Chinese socialist experiment has made abundantly clear, the firm cannot perform properly without the constant support or discipline of various market forces. On the other hand, the presence of any given market cannot be taken for granted. Many modern markets require complicated rules and regulations and their operations change significantly over time. Many such rules are imposed by the state to regulate what the firms can do in hope to maintain a viable market. But like any other human endeavor, the effort of making a market more often than not ends in disappointment for various reasons. Information asymmetry between the buyers and sellers can certainly thwart the working of the market; regulations might turn out to be too restrictive or too lax to sustain market order; other factors may also limit transactions to such a low level that the cost of running the market cannot be recouped. How the firm, the market, and the state work in concert to maintain a flexible and resilient structure of production remains an intriguing issue.[98]

As we come to competition between local governments, it seems obvious that local governments compete for capital investment. When local officials hold conferences all over China and even abroad to solicit business investment, meeting with businessmen over dinner and in karaoke bars, they try to persuade potential investors to come to industrial parks in their jurisdiction.

Since 1992, various industrial parks – sometimes called high-tech economic zones, free trade zones, export processing zones, economic and technological development zones – have mushroomed all over China at various administrative levels.[99] This effort followed on from the four Special Economic Zones set up in 1980, and the opening of fourteen additional coastal cities to foreign investment in 1984, as well as the development of Pudong in 1990. In this round of opening up, the State Council approved dozens of National Economic and Technological Development Zones all over China. The Suzhou Industrial Park, jointly run by the government of Singapore and China, and the Kunshan New and Hi-Tech Industrial Development Zone, both established in 1994, are two well-known examples. As of January 2012, there are 128 National Economic and Technological Development Zones, playing a significant role in the national economy.[100] On average, the national industrial parks enjoy an economic growth rate three times as high as the national GDP growth rate. In addition to national industrial parks, there are thousands of provincial, municipal, and county-level industrial parks all over China. Indeed, many township governments even have more than one industrial park. Local governments often choose to open industrial parks on the outskirts of cities, with convenient access to the highway. To a large degree, since the 1990s industrial parks have played a role similar to that of the Special Economic Zones in the 1980s. Both created fresh opportunities for entrepreneurship outside the existing economic structure where state enterprises tended to prevail. While the Special Economic Zones are limited in number and concentrated in coastal areas, industrial parks are found all over China.

To make their industrial parks attractive to potential investors, local authorities provide civic amenities, including water, sewerage, electricity, internet and telephone infrastructure, as well as land for investors to build their own office and industrial spaces (rental spaces are also available). Once an industrial park is open, local government officials are under great pressure to solicit firms to move in. Hence, in regional competition, local governments compete head on with each other for capital investment. They often create a local infrastructure and a friendly business environment to attract investment from the business community, which is expected to create jobs, develop the local economy, and generate tax revenues. Since industrial parks at various administrative levels (national, provincial and county) are spread all over China, competition is remarkably intense. In many places, a quota-like system is used, which requires every government office (even the bureaus of education and environmental protection) to bring in a certain amount of investment to the local industrial parks.

In an industrial park, some firms are aggressively recruited; they include established industrial leaders and promising stars in high tech industries. Most firms get in through open application. A small proportion of the firms are preexisting firms that were in operation elsewhere, but the majority will be start-ups. Among these, some may be spinoffs or transplants of a preexisting firm. For example, in the 1990s many firms in coastal areas moved to inland areas to avoid increasing labor costs. With the improvement of the business environment in inland provinces and the impressive development of the transportation infrastructure in China, including highways, aviation, and railways, many firms in Guangdong, Fujian, Zhejiang, and Jiangsu provinces moved inland; these became major targets for industrial parks in inland areas. An increasing number of start-ups are newly founded ventures in high technology with venture capital backing.

The administrative system of industrial parks varies in detail from one case to another. But a broad picture is still discernable. An industrial park is generally under the supervision of two offices, but staffed with a single personnel team, a phenomenon referred to as "two signboards, one team." The first office is basically a local government branch set up exclusively for the industrial park. It provides all the governmental services needed for a business to open and operate, including registration, permits, and regulations. Instead of running from one government office to another to obtain various permits, the business in the industrial park can get everything they need in one place. The second office is non-governmental. Often called the Industrial Park Management Committee, it looks after the daily operation of the park and provides administrative services to all the resident firms. This theoretical separation between the local government and the managerial office of the industrial park has turned out to be a considerable advantage for the operation of industrial parks. Unlike the conventional government departments, the industrial park is often managed by young, enterprising, and well-educated staff members, familiar with economic affairs. The relation of the park management office and firms is like that of a service provider and its clients and bears little resemblance to the constricting bureaucratic relationship between the supervising authority and state enterprises.

At the same time, with the local government branch on its side, the industrial park management office is far from a usual business development office. Rather than passively waiting for investment, the local government reaches out to invite or solicit business. From the perspective of a businessman looking for a place to locate his firm, a key concern is the local business environment, including the efficiency of government services and access to the inputs required for his operation. In this role, the Chinese local governments act in excess of what a well-functioning local government would do in a market economy, which is no more than the provision of local public goods.

To appreciate the active role played by Chinese local governments, we first have to recognize that, in a country as big and heterogeneous as China, price deregulation and privatization do not automatically create a national market for factors of production (especially not for capital assets). The price reform of 1992 abolished price control, allowing the pricing mechanism to operate. A national market for products emerged quickly where consumer sovereignty prevailed. This was not true in the case of the factor market. Under socialism, all the means of production were owned by the state. Though privatization helped to release factors that had been controlled by the government, this did not necessarily mean that released factors could be competitively sold.

What the Chinese local governments did was essentially to provide organizational services – putting together all factors of production. This does not suggest, as we will see shortly, that local governments had better knowledge and were thus able to employ factors more profitably. The production function in textbook economics may imply that we can simply pile up factors of production and expect them to be automatically transformed into products, but this is not the case in a real economy. The transformation of factors into goods and services takes place within a structure of production in which factors are organized and coordinated by various arrangements, including the impersonal pricing mechanism, contracts, and non-contractual personal relations.[101] In this vast and still poorly understood arena, organization is critical. Organization was considered by Alfred Marshall to be a "distinct agent of production."[102] But underdeveloped economies are characteristically defined by a want of organization. Indeed, organization is often in shorter supply than capital investment. In China, this vacuum was filled up by local governments, which still have enormous power to mobilize resources.

With industrial parks cropping up all over China to win investment, local governments had to convince investors that their industrial parks had everything needed to assure the success of a business. This was no easy task, given the variety of firms moving into a park. Some simply wanted to take advantage of low labor cost, lax regulation, or other benefits – in the late 1990s, the Chinese central government gave significant tax credits and other benefits to firms that invested in China's underdeveloped western areas. Some were foreign companies or companies from coastal areas that were looking for a local partner to expand their operation. Some firms were start-ups, with promising business plans or a new technology but little capital, managerial personnel or skilled labor.

As a result, industrial parks often offered different services to different firms. For some firms, this simply meant a ready access to labor and local supplies; for others, it meant help with bank loans and senior recruitment. Thus, the local governments became heavily involved in the setup of some firms – particularly those which it was hoped would contribute significantly to local tax revenues or generate spillover effects for the park, such as enhancing its reputation and attracting other firms. The local government was eager to work with such firms to find local suppliers, hire skilled labor – sometimes even from other cities – and secure bank loans. Once the firms had moved in and started operation, the local government was happy to leave them alone.

XI

Since the mid-1990s a new kind of relationship between local government and business firms has emerged in China. In the 1980s, local governments were often an active or silent owner of state and collective enterprises, giving rise to what was called "local corporatism."[103] By the mid-1990s with more and more state-owned enterprises becoming insolvent, local governments began to withdraw equity claims on local firms. This fundamentally changed the nature of the relationship between a local government and firms in its jurisdiction. When a local government owned some firms, it would be difficult, if not impossible, for it to treat private firms fairly, particularly those competing with its own enterprises. By the mid-1990s, less than one-third of state-owned enterprises was making any profit. The financial situations of state enterprises owned by local governments (provincial and below) were much worse than those owned by the central government. At the county level, it was common that only a small percentage of state enterprises would be solvent. When state enterprises became a financial burden, local governments were eager to develop industrial parks as a new source of revenue. Not surprisingly, when the State Council called for a "transformation of government functions" in 2001, local governments responded wholeheartedly. They quickly started to promote themselves as business-friendly service providers instead of as supervisors or regulators, slashing red tape and reducing government regulation in the economy.

In the intensifying competition for investment, it did not take long for local government officials to realize that a winning strategy was to distinguish their industrial park from its peers by focusing on certain industries with a promising long-term growth, rather than accepting a group of unrelated firms. This change in strategy helped to bring out a new dimension to China's regional dynamism: the economies of localization. Even though localization of industry is a common phenomenon in the process of industrialization, regional competition in China adds a special twist to the familiar story. In the United States, for example, Silicon Valley is the preferred location for new start-ups in the computer industry. Founders of Facebook, graduates of Harvard, chose to locate their business in Silicon Valley instead of Boston. In a market economy, an entrepreneur, particularly as a new entrant to an industry, will understandably locate his firm at the established industrial center, taking advantage of various spillover benefits and in turn making his own contribution to the further growth of the center. This feedback loop reinforces the economies of localization.

In China, however, the economies of localization developed a distinctive character. The economies of localization do not necessarily imply that an industry will be concentrated in only one place. The sheer size of China encourages ambitious emerging industrial parks to challenge established industrial centers.

Seemingly duplicative investment across regions in China has been a consistent feature of the economy throughout economic reform. This phenomenon has been criticized as evidence of serious inefficiency in the Chinese economy. But reality is more complicated. We have to realize that this is not a new development. Ever since Mao's efforts at decentralization in the mid-1950s, fragmentation has been a constant character of the Chinese economy. Fragmentation was probably at its peak during the 1960s, when each region down to the county level was encouraged to set up an all inclusive and self-sufficient industrial structure. However, the repetitive investment resulting from Mao's policy of self-sufficiency differs in kind from the repetitive investment prompted by regional competition. China now has a common national market for most consumer products, thus subjecting all firms, no matter where they are located, to the same market discipline. This is in sharp contrast to Mao's policies to promote local economic self-sufficiency, where firms in each region were effectively sheltered from competition from others.

Nonetheless, the presence of duplicative investment across China seems puzzling. The fundamental economic logic of the division of labor and trade, as powerfully described by Adam Smith, states that we all specialize in supplying a single, or at most, a very limited number of products and buy most of what we consume from others. Since Ricardo, this logic of specialization has taken on a geographical twist, turning it into a law of comparative advantage. This simply states that each region will specialize in industries where it has a comparative advantage, while importing products it does not produce. Through specialization and trade, any specific industry will be concentrated in a few areas and different areas will specialize in supplying different products in accordance with their particular advantages. As a result, the fact that many regions in China make duplicative investments in the same industry is taken as unambiguous evidence of the presence of policy distortions in the economy, contradicting the economic logic of specialization and trade.

Take the automobile industry as an example. Prior to economic reform, the Chinese automobile industry was dominated by two state enterprises owned by the central government, China Number One Automotive Factory founded in 1953 in Changchun, and China Number Two Automotive Factory founded in 1966 in Shiyan; both mainly produced trucks. In the 1980s, many foreign automakers entered the Chinese market. Chrysler formed the first joint venture in 1984 with Beijing Automobile Company. Guangzhou, Nanjing, and Shanghai also emerged as important players in China's growing automobile industry. In the mid-1990s when the rate of capacity utilization for truck production was 36 percent, bus production, 30 percent, and passenger cars, 65 percent, the Shanghai government decided to enter China's already crowded auto industry, creating a brand new supply chain of automotive components for Shanghai Automotive Industry Corporation, a state enterprise controlled by the Shanghai municipal government.[104] In 2000, Changsha, the capital city of Hunan province, also entered the industry. Its aim was to attract new firms to the Changsha National Economic and Technical Development Zone, which broke ground in 1992 and was approved in 2000 as a National Economic and Technical Development Zone. Both Shanghai and Changsha were new to automotive components manufacturing; Changsha was barely recognized as a player in the industry even in the late 1990s.

The negative impact of such duplicative investment has been widely noted. As one critic put it, "as a result [of duplicative investment], regions do not specialize along the lines of their comparative advantages. Instead, they all push strongly into similar industries and product groups, resulting in a convergence of industrial production across different regions."[105] The buildup in overcapacity and ensuing low utilization rates clearly suggest some inefficiencies in resource allocation in the Chinese economy. But we have to recognize that regional competition must imply duplicative investment in one way or another. Most foreign auto makers have multiple joint ventures in different locations with different local partners across China. GM, for example, agreed in September 2011 to open its eleventh joint venture in Shanghai.[106] Without some degree of duplicative investment across regions, it would be impossible to allow regions to compete with each other head-on. If we view the development of a market economy as an open learning process, in which economic actors must figure out what to produce and how to organize the production, some "waste" in duplicative investment on the part of firms is inevitable.

Moreover, while duplicative investment has led to the underutilization of physical capital, it has at the same time helped to spread manufacturing technologies and significantly improve workers' skills all over China. The gains in human capital outweigh the losses from the underutilization of physical capital. From a different angle, the repetitive and duplicative investment across China can be seen as an effective mechanism of social learning: quickly spreading industrialization to a largely agrarian economy. When China was first opened to the outside world at the end of 1970s, Chinese factories could not produce some goods as simple as ballpoint pens, quartz watches, or mini cassette players. It is therefore an extraordinary achievement that Chinese enterprises by the end of the 1990s were able to produce a very wide range of industrial goods at internationally competitive prices. The changes in China's exports tell a similar story. In 1980, primary materials, led by petroleum products, were the largest sector of China's exports. Manufactured goods represented less than half of China's exports, of which textiles accounted for more than 50 percent. This pattern persisted until the mid-1980s when manufactured goods became the leading export category. By 2000, 90 percent of Chinese exports were manufactured goods, and the contribution of textiles to that figure had declined to 25 percent. The extraordinary speed and scale of the growth in manufacturing capacity of the Chinese economy, as embodied in physical investment, human skills, and managerial know-how, must be recognized as the driving force behind the rise of China as a global powerhouse in manufacturing.

In the conventional argument for economies of scale, the underutilization of physical capital is seen as a sign of economic inefficiency. Duplicative investment is thus singled as the reason for the failure to take full advantage of economies of scale. However, our investigation of China's industrial parks and regional competition leads to a more nuanced picture. Manufacturing requires both skilled labor and capital investment. The conventional analysis of economies of scale focuses on issues of physical and financial capital and what Alfred Marshall called the "internal economies" in the firm. What is ignored is the factor of labor and human capital and what Marshall called "external economies."[107] Duplicative investment in China, and the consequent low utilization rate of capital investment, led to widespread industrialization and an explosive growth of human capital in modern manufacturing. Many small manufacturing businesses in China, for example, were founded by former migrant workers who had been employed in a factory and gained technical skills and managerial knowledge. In this way, the loss in internal economies of scale (to capital) was compensated for by a gain in external economies of scale (to labor).

In this process the local government played a highly visible role. As we mentioned above, in the usual market economy a single firm is compelled to locate itself in an established center, reinforcing the economies of localization. Any attempt on the part of a single firm to create a center of its own would be futile and, in most cases, suicidal. A local government, on the other hand, can challenge that status quo and launch a new center, if it can convince a sufficient number of firms to move into its industrial park and quickly reach a threshold level of scale. But the local government cannot possibly succeed without the endorsement and participation of private firms. The visibility of the local governments in the operation of industrial parks all over China does not change the fact that what the local government does is essentially to "set up the stage and let firms run the show," as it is commonly put in Chinese. Moreover, intense regional competition can quickly punish those initiatives that fail to win support from the business community.

It is important to stress that the regional competition that has emerged in the course of Chinese economic reform is primarily a result of local initiatives. The 1992 price reform and 1994 tax reform have certainly helped by clearing price distortions and allowing the rise of a national common market; similarly, the privatization of state enterprises has helped to release both human talent and capital assets from state control. The privatization of local state enterprises has also made local governments an impartial service provider, creating a fair playing ground for all firms. However, the key players in regional competition are local governments and, behind them, private firms.

There is an extensive and growing literature on China's decentralized political structure and its far-reaching impact on China's market transformation.[108] As we have discussed, the legacy of Mao's repeated efforts at administrative decentralization persists. But Mao's legacy is itself rooted in China's long history, under which the so-called *junxian* system prevailed. As reflected by the well-known Chinese axiom, "the mountain is high and the emperor far away," the de facto autonomy enjoyed by the *xian* or county government has long been a distinctive feature of Chinese political structure.

But fiscal and administrative decentralization does not necessarily lead to regional competition. In Mao's time, for example, regional competition did not arise. Instead, Mao's repeated efforts at decentralization and his pursuit of local economic sufficiency was a top-down approach, seeking to turn the Chinese economy into a cellular stucture in which each region had a similar and independent economic status. Regional competition, however, is necessarily a bottom-up phenomenon. A decentralized political arrangement by itself can only provide a stage or platform for regional competition. We have to look elsewhere for the catalyst that animates the system and which, in China, generated a vibrant economic dynamism within the decentralized political structure.

This indispensable ingredient is intellectual or epistemic in nature. It can be best seen if we contrast Chinese leadership on the economy under Mao with that under Deng. Mao's overconfidence in his economic policy and unyielding determination to carry it out against all resistance was in stark contrast to Deng plainly admitting to a lack of experience in reforming a socialist economy. This self-acknowledged ignorance on the part of Chinese central leadership gave rise to an experimental approach to reform and a willingness for the central government to delegate power to local authorities. We can better appreciate the experimental approach taken by China if we compare it with other transition economies. Leszek Balcerowicz, twice Deputy Prime Minister of Poland (1989–1991 and 1997–2000), and a central figure overseeing Polish transition after the collapse of communism, was quoted as saying that "We are too poor to experiment. If the rich countries want to experiment, let them. For us, it is better to take proven models."[109] Deng Xiaoping, on the other hand, admitted frankly to being "engaged in an experiment. For us, this is something new, and we have to feel our way. Since it is something new, we are bound to make mistakes. Our method is to review our experience from time to time and correct mistakes whenever we discover them, so that minor mistakes will not grow into major ones."[110]

In addition, an economic experiment made independently by a local government is less costly and less disruptive if the experiment goes awry.[111] The logic of competitive local experiment has served the Chinese government well from the very beginning of economic reform, as was particularly noticeable in the case of agricultural reform. Once Beijing gave up its claim on a monopoly of truth in economic policy and allowed experimental policymaking, regional competition was able to take hold.

It is this profound shift in mentality on the part of the Chinese central leadership that gives life to what is called capitalism with Chinese characteristics. Still under one-party rule, economic freedom is not only tolerated but encouraged by both central and local government, although for different reasons. For Beijing, economic freedom enables local governments to take initiatives and experiment with various reforms at the local level, which has proved to be a workable approach to furthering reform. For local government officials, local economic performance is a critical criterion for promotion. All heads of Chinese local governments are appointed by the powerful Organization Department of the Party, which since the early 1990s has placed more and more stress on the growth of the local economy in its performance evaluations and promotion of local government officials.[112]

Regional competition has another important dimension that has so far eluded scholarly attention, which helps to reveal an important aspect of Chinese capitalism and sheds new light on the question raised at the beginning of this section: What exactly is competed for in regional competition? There is no doubt that investment has been the immediate target of competition between local governments. But as they compete, local governments also vie over different ideas of economic development. This subtle but critically important dimension of China's regional competition will become clear if we put it into historical context.

Under Mao, the decentralized Chinese economy inevitably opened up some room for local initiatives. But none of them lasted long before being hijacked by Mao's political campaigns. Many economic practices that were later criticized as having been responsible for Mao's economic failures first emerged as local initiatives. For example, the public canteen hall first emerged in Henan province and the People's Commune was first set up in Hebei province. The famous Dazhai model was born in Shanxi province. As a local response to local challenges, each of these local initiatives was effective. Once it was approved by Mao, however, a local invention was hailed as an economic tool that could be applied universally. All such local initiatives were promoted and imposed nationwide, regardless of local conditions. The disastrous results are apparent to all with any knowledge of this period.

Under Deng, however, the central government took a different approach to local initiatives. With the noticeable exception of private farming, Beijing became cautious in imposing a local initiative on the whole nation. More often than not, once a local initiative had won Beijing's approval, local governments from elsewhere would visit the home region where the local initiative started.

But in most cases, it was left for local governments to decide whether and how the invention could be adapted to their particular local circumstances.

As the local government of each region (from the provincial and municipal level down to the county and town level) attempted to find out how best to develop its local economy, China became a laboratory, with different economic experiments taking place all over the land. As a result, many development models emerged, each named after the city or county where it was first tried. Various experiments in institutional arrangements, different ideas in accelerating the local economy, and rival judgments on the prospect of a new industry or the future of an existing one are all put to the test simultaneously. The continental size and incredible heterogeneity of China provides space for all kinds of experiments and competition. At the same time, the unified price and tax system and common national market that have emerged since the mid-1990s impose a uniform market discipline and thus ensure that regional competition is, in general, an efficiency-improving phenomenon. Thus, the advantage that China has in space translates directly to the pace of economic development; this is key to understanding the seemingly miraculous speed of China's market transformation. Instead of "big push industrialization" engineered by a coercive central government, a development strategy that China pursued under Mao, what has emerged in China since the 1990s is thousands of industrial parks, each embodying a local vision of economic development and a local initiative in industrialization. Mao's idealistic wish of the mid-1950s, "let one hundred flowers bloom and one hundred schools of thought contend," has come into being in the economic domain.

XII

China's regional competition has another distinctive feature: the significant presence of foreign capital in China's rising market economy. Foreign investment, particularly from Fortune 500 companies, has been and remains an important target for industrial parks. Since the very beginning, the Chinese government has stressed "opening up" as a critical component in China's economic reform. As a result, China has consistently been a highly desirable destination for foreign direct investment. Even though foreign direct investment from Hong Kong and Taiwan flooded into China in the 1980s, the influx from other places only took off in the 1990s. During the 1980s, such investment averaged about 2 billion USD per year. After Deng's southern tour, it increased rapidly and has remained between 40 to 60 billion USD a year since the mid-1990s.

The "pervasive presence" of companies with foreign investment has prompted some scholars to worry about China's overdependence on foreign investment.[113] In 1994, investment from foreign companies made up about

17 percent of all fixed asset investment in China. The ratio declined to about 10 percent by 2000 and has continued to decline despite the growth of foreign direct investment in China. But the predominance of foreign capital in the Chinese economy, particularly in manufacturing, has been a constant feature since the beginning of the country's economic reform. At any point, it was common to find many industries dominated by foreign firms. In the 1980s, for example, firms from Taiwan enjoyed dominant equity positions in garments and footwear (71.8 percent), lumber and bamboo products (75.7 percent), and leather and fur products (79.6 percent). Unlike Japan and South Korea, China's growing automobile industry has been, and still is, dominated by foreign companies from all over the world, including General Motors, Ford, and Chrysler from the United States, Toyota, Honda, Nissan, Mazda, and others from Japan, Hyundai-Kia from South Korea, as well as Volkswagen, Fiat, and Peugeot-Citroën from Europe. For many years, Volkswagen commanded the largest market share in China, until overtaken by General Motors in 2007.

Foreign direct investment brings at least three economic benefits to the recipient country. First and foremost, for poor economies with inadequate domestic capital, foreign direct investment provides a ready substitute. At the beginning of China's opening up, foreign investment from Hong Kong and Taiwan to Guangdong province was critical to the rise of the Pearl River Delta. Second, foreign direct investment usually comes with advanced technology and managerial skills and thus helps the diffusion of modern technology and business management techniques to recipient countries. Third, foreign direct investment brings with it access to foreign markets. As a result of foreign direct investment, the recipient country gains a window into the home markets of foreign capital, which usually facilitates exports. In the Chinese case, special incentives are given to foreign companies if they are export-oriented. Not surprisingly, foreign companies contribute about one-third of China's total exports. In certain sectors, foreign companies are the dominant exporters. As a result, China has grown from the thirtieth largest trading economy in 1978 to the largest trading nation in 2009; it is now the world's largest exporter, and its second largest importer.

In the literature on foreign direct investment, it remains a moot question whether and to what degree foreign capital benefits the domestic economy through technological spillovers. Many econometric studies have tried to investigate to what degree the presence of foreign direct investment in an industry or a city helps to improve productivity of domestic firms in the same (or related upstream and downstream) industry. Several studies have not found any significant impact, and even those that do indicate that the impact is not as big as commonly expected. A significant amount of foreign direct investment has been attracted to China due to China's low labor cost and lax regulations. This is commonly read as further reason to doubt the contribution made by foreign direct investment to China's technological advancement.

Even when foreign capital does not embody cutting-edge technology, its wide presence in China makes it an important vehicle to transmit and spread technology. For example, the shoe-manufacturing sector in Guangdong was mainly started with investment from Taiwan in the 1980s. Despite its relative lack of high technology, such foreign direct investment has been an important transmitter of knowledge to Chinese workers. The state shoe-making enterprises in Shanghai might even have better technology than firms from Taiwan, but this cannot be taken as prima facie evidence that foreign direct investment in shoe-manufacturing does not contribute to technological growth in China. When a Taiwanese firm is opened, it hires migrant workers from rural China, who will learn the production technology. After a few years, the migrant workers may start their own businesses. If we recognize the speed with which private Chinese enterprises picked up modern technologies and improved the quality of their products as an important factor driving China's industrialization over the past three decades, the critical contribution of foreign direct investment cannot be denied.

At the same time, foreign investors have earned high returns on their investment in China. For an increasing number of western companies, the Chinese market will become even bigger than their home markets. For example, a recent *Wall Street Journal* article predicted that China's auto market would soon outpace home-market sales for several western brands, including Mercedes Benz, Audi, and several of GM's models.[114] The development of the Chinese market creates a great opportunity for the top automakers all over the world to grow. In one industry after another, China has become a showroom for global capitalism.

XIII

When Deng Xiaoping began his southern tour in early 1992, the private sector, which had enjoyed a decade of strong growth in the late 1970s and 1980s, was at its nadir; socialist ideology dominated contemporary political debate. After more than a decade of reform, the impressive growth of the non-state sector had brought much-needed vitality and dynamism to the Chinese economy, but state enterprises were still plagued by insolvency. Still committed to socialism, which was widely understood as requiring public ownership, the Chinese government in the aftermath of the 1989 Students Movement at home and the fall of the Berlin Wall abroad was deeply wary of the growing private sector and its potentially corrosive impact on the communist political regime. With the fall of socialist governments in Eastern Europe, the response in certain circles of the Party was to strengthen state ownership and contain the private sector, lest China should slide into capitalism. However, Deng thought otherwise. According to Deng, the main reason that the Chinese Communist Party had survived the 1989 Students Movement was because of the increased living standard made possible by previous economic reforms. Thus, Deng advocated further reform and opening up as an effective strategy to make China a strong and prosperous socialist country. At a critical juncture, Deng saved Chinese economic reform.

Deng's call for further reform during his southern tour effectively launched the second round of Chinese economic reform after a few years of retreat between 1988 and 1992. Three major forces dominated this second round: the development of a common national market, the privatization of state enterprises, and the rise of regional competition. These factors meant that private firms could now openly compete with each other. In turn, competition at the firm level became more intensified and effective when regional competition turned China into a giant economic laboratory. Together, they brought about capitalism with Chinese characteristics.

The remarkable economic performance China has achieved in the past three decades of market transformation has clearly boosted the Chinese leaders' and general public's confidence in the market economy, no matter whether it is called socialist or capitalist. But it is important to keep in mind that the ultimate rationale for the market is human frailty. Were the central planner as omniscient and omnipotent as is presumed in the classical model of socialism, the market would indeed be a wasteful game. A significant point, which has not been given its due in the ongoing examination of China's market transformation, is that the post-Mao Chinese leadership, particularly Deng Xiaoping, fully recognized their inexperience in building a market economy. Without a preexisting model to emulate or a blueprint to follow, they were compelled to take an experimental approach to reform. Under regional competition, the trial-and-error strategy worked well as an effective way of learning. Success breeds failure, however, when it leads people to believe that they have fortunately stumbled upon a fault-proof formula that works everywhere and forever.

6
From Capitalism to Capitalisms

In the concluding speech at the close of the 2008 Chicago Conference on China's Market Transformation on July 18th, 2008, Ronald Coase pronounced that "the struggle of China is the struggle for the world."[1] On December 10th, 2008, *Time* magazine published a commentary on China's three decades of market transformation and the heroic role played by Deng Xiaoping in this remarkable human drama. The article ended by stating "That is the great story of our time. It is our story, everyone's story – not just China's."[2]

When this narrative opened its first chapter after Mao died in 1976, the post-Mao Chinese government made a determined shift in strategy in the aftermath of the Cultural Revolution, giving up class conflict and embracing socialist modernization as an alternative approach to realizing the "superiority of social-ism." The ideological radicalism that had persisted since the mid-1950s was at last recognized as flawed and harmful, and this opened up room for common sense and pragmatism in policymaking. This shift in leadership and policy loosened the grip of socialist ideology and precipitated the ensuing Chinese economic reform. During Mao's era, waves of political campaigns to impose the dictates of socialism had failed to take China to the promised land of shared prosperity. Dismay and discontent were widespread and deeply felt, especially amongst Party veterans who had lost positions during Mao's era, intellectuals who had been attacked as "rightists," and the majority of the 800 million Chinese peasants who had been struggling to make ends meet ever since agricultural collectivization. They desperately wanted change.

Rejecting class struggle and embracing socialist modernization, China finally broke the spell of a negative sum game of political infighting and started a positive sum game of economic development. Their bitter disappointment with Mao's grandiose but disastrous socialist experiment had clearly taught the Chinese to be skeptical of any grand blueprint for reform. At the same time, having long been isolated from the outside world, the Chinese were hardly aware of any alternatives to socialism. This left their leaders with no choice but to work with whatever they could find, through improvisation and tinkering. Still rallied under the ideological banner of socialism, they tried out different ways of achieving its practical ends. However, by the end of the twentieth century, instead of celebrating itself as a "great, modern, socialist power" resting on public ownership and state planning, as intended in the 1978 Communiqué,[3] China found itself with a vibrant economy awash with private entrepreneurship and market forces. This is the most unexpected aspect of the Chinese economic transformation. China became capitalist while it was trying to modernize socialism. The story of China is the quintessence of what Adam Ferguson called "the products of human action but not human design."[4] A Chinese proverb puts it more poetically: "flowers planted on purpose do not blossom; the willows no one cared for have grown into big trees offering ample shade."

I

China's economic reform, as conceived at the beginning and thought of throughout its progress, was never intended to dismantle socialism and move to capitalism. Rather, its aim was "socialist modernization"; a second revolution, another "Long March," to carry out the economic development that Mao had failed to do, making China "a modernsocialist country before the end of the [twentieth] century," as the 1978 Communiqué put it.[5] Since communism claims to be the destined burier of capitalism, the Communist Party is widely believed to be incompatible with market reform. But we should not make the mistake of equating a political organization (the Communist Party) with its political ideology (communism). Every individual has multiple identities (a male, a professor, a husband, an economist, and an admirer of Adam Smith, for example). Likewise, political organizations also have multiple and fluid identities. Any Marxist individual or organization must be more than a Marxist.[6] While communism and capitalism as rival ideologies stand in direct opposition to each other, a communist party may allow for and experiment with anything, including capitalism, when its survival is at stake.

The failure to separate the Communist Party from communism has predisposed many to take a misleading approach to economic transition. It gave rise to a belief that market reforms were impossible in a socialist country unless the whole communist system, including both its ideology and political organization, had been wiped out first. A clear and clean break from the communist past was deemed an absolute precondition for a fresh new move toward a market economy. As a result, a piecemeal approach to reform by tinkering with the preexisting economic system was ruled out from the very beginning, giving birth to what has become known as the big bang approach to reform.[7] At the same time, many economists who served as advisors to policymakers trusted that their mastery of modern economics would enable a market economy to be constructed anew only if the traces of socialism were thoroughly erased. But the belief that a market economy could be rationally designed committed what Hayek called the "fatal conceit" of constructive rationalism.[8] Many decades earlier, Hayek warned in his Nobel lecture that "To act on the belief that we possess the knowledge and the power which enable us to shape the process of society entirely to our liking, knowledge which in fact we do not possess, is likely to make us do much harm."[9]

China was fortunate to escape from this fatal conceit only by accident. At the time when economic reform was started, China did not (and could not possibly) contemplate eradicating communism and starting afresh, and so, instead of beginning reform with a brand new blueprint, it started by adjusting the preexisting system.

But China's continuing commitment to socialism did not prevent it from recognizing the defects of socialism. Indeed, a public debate erupted after Mao's death on the nature and prospect of Chinese socialism, on what had gone wrong under Mao, and where China should be heading next. Hu Yaobang, who replaced Hua as Chairman of the Chinese Communist Party in 1981 and became General Secretary in 1982, raised a question to himself and the Party in the course of a 1984 interview with the Italian Communist daily *L'Unità*. "Since the October Revolution [of 1917], more than 60 years have passed. How is it that many socialist countries have not been able to overtake capitalist ones in terms of development? What was it [in socialism] that did not work?"[10]

Nor did their commitment to socialism prevent the Chinese leaders from re-evaluating, and even appreciating, capitalism once they were exposed to it during their trips abroad. Wang Zhen, Vice Premier in charge of industrial development at the time, visited Britain from November 6th to 17th, 1978. Wang was astonished to learn of the high level of economic and social development enjoyed by the British working class.[11] Before the visit, Wang's knowledge of British capitalism was still largely derived from Marx's writings. Wang had expected to see slums in London and poverty, destitution, and exploitation. To his surprise, Wang found that his wage was only one-sixth of that of a garbage collector in London. At the end of his trip, he reached a better and more accurate understanding of British capitalism and of China's commitment to communism.

I think Britain has done a good job. Products are abundant; the three inequalities [that between urban and rural areas, between industry and agriculture, and between mental and manual labor, the elimination of which, according to Marx, was a critical task for socialism] are almost done away with; social justice and welfare have received a lot of emphasis. Britain would simply be our model of a communist society if it were ruled by a communist party.[12]

Wang's formula of communism, which equaled Britain plus communist rule, revealed a down-to-earth, non-ideological attitude to capitalism and socialism as well as an enduring attachment to the Party. If it were not for this pragmatic mentality, China's remaining commitment to socialism would have made the ensuing market reform impossible.

The most extraordinary feature of Chinese economic reform is perhaps that the Chinese Communist Party has survived, and indeed thrived, over the three decades of market transformation. It clearly attests to the organizational flexibility and adaptability of the Party in the aftermath of a failed socialist experiment – not its own invincibility or the superiority of socialism itself.[13] But what is even more extraordinary is that a reform intended to save socialism has inadvertently turned China into a market economy. The Trojan horse in this astonishing tale is the Chinese teaching "seeking truth from facts," which Deng Xiaoping mistakenly called "the essence of Marxism." When China became a gigantic economic laboratory, the forces of competition were able to work their magic. In an experimental process of discovery, resources were directed to their most profitable utilization, institutional arrangements and organizational structures emerged to facilitate collective learning. Tinkering with Mao's legacy on the ground, China, step by step, not without side steps or retrogressive movements, found itself transformed into a market economy after thirty years of reforms which had been intended to save socialism. After the fall of the Berlin Wall socialism was abandoned in the former Soviet bloc; it was defeated on its own ground in China. Villages of starving peasants restored private farming and township and village enterprises outperformed state enterprises. In Chinese cities the introduction of self-employment and private entrepreneurship brought more vitality to the urban economy than did state-led enterprise reforms. The story of Chinese economic reform is one of obdurate private entrepreneurship, of bold but piecemeal social experiments, and of humility and perseverance in the human struggle for a better life.

II

To represent the story of Chinese reform accurately it is imperative to recognize the co-existence of two reforms in China's market transformation. First, the Chinese post-Mao government clearly attempted a state-led reform agenda. The disastrous economic record of Mao's socialism overwhelmed a once triumphant Party with disappointment, frustration, and humiliation. That sense of failure was deepened after the Chinese leaders learned of the rapid economic development achieved by their Asian neighbors and countries elsewhere. But they were also inspired and encouraged by the technological innovation and economic prosperity that they observed during their trips abroad. If only China could open itself up and learn from the developed economies, they reasoned, China could catch up. The Chinese leaders knew that there was no roadmap for the journey ahead. They probably were not even cognizant of where the journey would take them. Nonetheless, nothing deterred them from being determined reformers, eager to get the stagnant economy moving.

The state-led reform began at the end of 1976 when Hua Guofeng revived the "Four Modernizations," an inspirational economic program that was originally proposed by Premier Zhou Enlai in 1964 but was quickly shelved with Mao's launch of the "socialist education" movement and two years later, the Cultural Revolution. Under Hua, China quickly ended the self-destruction of class struggle, and embarked on socialist modernization. A year later, an ambitious economic program of opening up – which would be later called the "Leap Outward" by its critics – was launched to use foreign capital to finance two dozen or so development projects, most of which were in heavy industry and related infrastructure. But the "Leap Outward" did not last long and was ended in early 1979 partly because of its inherent defects and partly because of the shift in power after the Third Plenum of the Eleventh Central Committee in December 1978 when Deng Xiaoping and Chen Yun returned to the political center.

As Chen resumed leadership in managing the Chinese economy, the Central Committee of the Party launched in April 1979 what was then called the "Eight Character Guiding Principle" – "adjustment, reform, rectification, and improvement" [in Chinese each of the terms has two characters], which ushered in the second round of the state-led reform by the post-Mao Chinese government.[14] This new economic policy called off the "Leap Outward." Even though "reform" was included, the new policy was essentially an economic retrenchment program, with its priority squarely placed on "adjustment." What was it in the Chinese economy that cried for adjustment? The answer is easy to find: the "Leap Outward," which, in the eyes of Chen Yun, had further exacerbated China's macroeconomic problems, particularly the structural misalignment between heavy and light industry, and between industry and agriculture.

The first priority under the new economic policy was agriculture. From the government's perspective, the most serious defect of the "Leap Outward" was the continuous stress on heavy industry at the expense of agriculture, which, as admitted in the 1978 Communiqué, was in deep trouble. Food scarcity and starvation had long been a chronic and widespread problem during the Mao era. The 1978 Communiqué made several references to the bleak situation in Chinese agriculture and pledged to raise the purchasing prices for agricultural products and boost investment in rural areas. This express and urgent emphasis on agriculture would later lead the Chinese government to claim that economic reform started in agriculture. It is important to note that reform in other areas, such as the enterprise reform, proceeded at the same time. Moreover, the measures taken at the time in agriculture, raising purchasing prices for agricultural products, reducing quotas and increasing grain import to allow more food consumption for peasants, encouraging sideline productions, including the development of the commune and brigade enterprises, certainly helped to bring about a steady and significant increase in agricultural output and a reduction in inequality between rural and urban China in the next few years. But they were not the forces that set in motion what we know today as China's agricultural reform, that is, private farming under the household responsibility system, which was a grassroots innovation by starving peasants and local cadres. Private farming was conditionally accepted in 1980 after it had been widely spread underground in many provinces, and did not become a national policy until 1982.

As far as industry was concerned, the first goal of the adjustment policy was to slow down the development of heavy industry and speed up investment in light industry, to cut capital investment in production and increase spending on housing and other non-production related areas, including labor compensation. The economic rationale was to tilt the economy toward consumer spending and reduce its dependence on capital investment, particularly in heavy industry. The adjustment policy was quickly translated into a rapid improvement in living conditions in both rural and urban China.[15]

In addition, as part of the economic policy, the Chinese government also implemented a reform initiative formulated in 1978, "delegating rights and sharing profits," to decentralize the economy, giving more autonomy ("rights") and incentives ("profits") to local actors, including both local governments and enterprises in cities as well as production teams in rural areas. This government initiative was carried out mainly in three areas, state-owned enterprises, international trade, and public finance, in addition to agriculture.[16] As far as international trade was concerned, the policy effectively ended the monopoly of the Ministry of Foreign Trade, allowing trading companies to be set up by local governments and state-owned enterprises. In public finance, the policy essentially made local governments more or less autonomous in charge of local finance, independent from the Ministry of Finance.

The most critical target of this reform initiative was clearly the state-owned enterprises. Unlike the "Leap Outward," where the emphasis was placed on constructing brand new plants, the new policy aimed to improve existing state-owned enterprises. Though the enterprise reform was first tried in Sichuan under the leadership of provincial Party Secretary Zhao Ziyang, before the convening of the Third Plenum of the Eleventh Central Committee of the Party in December 1978, it became a national policy only in 1979. Its goal was to make state enterprises more autonomous, largely by shifting much of managerial decision-making from the government to enterprises, without privatization. This effort, then called "enhancing the enterprise's vitality," marked the second concerted measure after the "Leap Outward" undertaken by the Chinese government to reinvigorate the stagnant industrial sectors. Because of China's continuing commitment to socialism, the enterprise reform was severely constrained more by ideology than by economic considerations. As a result, while this reform helped to inject vitality into state enterprises and improve the incentives of managers and workers alike, it failed to free the state-owned enterprises from the state, but further confounded the convoluted relations between the two.

The overall effectiveness of the "Eight Character Guiding Principle" was rather limited, even though all measures were clearly a move in the right direction. For example, the measures taken by the Chinese government in agriculture were quite successful as far as they went; their positive effects on the living conditions of peasants were immediate and significant. But they fell far short of freeing peasants from the heavy hand of the state. Such severe limitations of the government-led agricultural reform, however, would not become clear until the upsurge of private farming, which had been explicitly ruled out by government policy. Similarly, the enterprise reform generated a quick and noticeable improvement on worker's incentives. But its shortcomings were evident, even though the most serious limitations came to light only when state-owned enterprises began to compete with non-state firms.

Besides the official track of reform directed by the Chinese government, there existed a separate track of reform. This was a combination of several spontaneous, grassroots movements, some expressly prohibited by the Chinese government (private farming before 1982, self-employment in cities before 1980), some discriminated against by government policy (self-employment in cities after 1980 and township and village enterprises), and some guarded warily by Beijing (Special Economic Zones). This made headway quietly all over China when starving peasants secretly tried private farming in defiance of government policy, when under-employed peasants turned to non-farming jobs where they could earn a higher income, when unemployed city residents were forced into self-employment and private entrepreneurship, and when thousands of illegal immigrants took the dangerous, to many fatal, path to cross the border to Hong Kong in hope of a better life. This second reform consisted of what we call "marginal revolutions."

It was this second, bottom-up reform that set in motion in the early 1980s the Chinese market transformation, bringing back to the Chinese economy a vibrant private sector and resilient market forces, while the state sector was largely kept intact. What the four "marginal revolutions" had in common was that all of them erupted outside the purview of the state. The protagonists in the four revolutions were all marginal actors under socialism. Unlike the state-owned enterprises, which were the pride of socialism and thus enjoyed the tight protection and control of the state, these marginal actors were more or less left alone, particularly when their presence was not perceived as threatening or undermining socialism. Despite many practical obstacles and blatant policy discrimination, peasants in rural China and unemployed city residents quickly translated the economic freedom they had gained into private entrepreneurship. The rising non-state sectors became the most powerful source of economic growth throughout the 1980s and beyond. On the other hand, state-led reform measures, including both the "Leap Outward" and the government initiative of "enhancing the enterprises' vitality," fell far short in turning state-owned enterprises into free, competitive enterprises.

Even the success of the Special Economic Zones, which were intentionally created by the Chinese government to experiment with capitalism, revealed the marginal and grassroots nature of the second reform. In the first place, the idea of setting up experimental zones came from the local government in Guangdong, which had been hard pressed to cope with illegal immigration along the border with Hong Kong. Inviting businessmen from Hong Kong to set up factories in Guangdong and hire local labor emerged as a viable solution. Second, the reason for carving out an industrial park or a special economic zone was to create a confined environment to try out a highly uncertain and politically risky experiment outside the socialist economy. Socialism could thus be well preserved while capitalism was allowed a chance in the periphery.

Throughout the 1980s, these marginal forces grew rapidly while the protected state enterprises were struggling to survive. As a result, the Chinese economic reform, unlike reforms in Russia and Eastern Europe, did not suffer a severe recession at the start. The overall economy had always kept growing since reform started, despite the increasing rate and scale of insolvency suffered in the state sector. When the protected and privileged state sector continued its decline, the non-state sectors were rising robustly.

III

The presence of two reforms – one state-led, one grassroots – in China's economic transformation is beyond any doubt. The failure to recognize the dual-track structure of reform has become a source of confusion in understanding the "great story of our time." As the grassroots reform was often overshadowed by, and not explicitly distinguished from, the first, the Chinese government, which clearly orchestrated the first, was also credited as the planner and instigator of the second. This misattributes a grassroots movement to the state and gives rise to a state-centered misinterpretation of Chinese market transformation. It has led some Chinese scholars to believe that the initial stages of Chinese economic reform were carried out by the Chinese government in "a top-down" fashion, and to ignore grassroots reform, which had a totally different character.[17] In his widely used and generally informative and authoritative textbook on Chinese economic reform, Professor Wu Jinglian pointed out the presence of two different reforms, one pertaining to the state sector, and the other to the non-state sectors, but writes as if both reforms were planned by the Chinese government. "When the reform of expanding enterprise autonomy in the state sector fell into plight, the Chinese leaders headed by Deng Xiaoping shifted the focus of reform from the urban state sector to the rural nonstate sectors." As the book continues, "Instead of taking major reform measures in the state sector, China focused its reform effort on nonstate sectors, aiming at establishing market-oriented enterprises so as to let them drive the growth of the economy. The new strategy was called the strategy of 'outside the system' preceding 'inside the system', or the strategy of incremental reform."[18]

Our account of marginal revolutions shows that China's market transformation in the 1980s was primarily carried out by the non-state sectors while the state-led reform failed to revitalize the state sector. But this outcome of "incremental reform" did not result from a deliberate strategy on the part of the Chinese government. It is true that the government had gradually loosened their control over farmers and also allowed unemployed city residents to seek self-employment. But it is unlikely that the authorities at the time could have hoped that non-state sectors would become a major driver of economic growth, when socialism was still believed to depend primarily on state ownership. Rather, as the state-led enterprise reform ran out of steam, the Chinese leaders were relieved to see the strong and unexpected growth of the non-state sectors. It was the emerging private firms that supplied goods and services that the state enterprises did not provide, created jobs for peasants who were no longer chained to the land, and for unemployed city residents whom the state enterprises could not absorb.

The Chinese leaders themselves were candid in admitting the presence of a second track of reform outside their control, calling private farming and township and village enterprises two "great innovations of Chinese peasants."[19] But the official account of Chinese economic reform conceals the different sources of the two reforms and portrays the Chinese government as a prescient designer, carefully and patiently overseeing the whole process of market transformation. In a meeting with Chancellor Helmut Kohl of West Germany on October 10th, 1984, Deng Xiaoping articulated this gradualist, state-centered interpretation of Chinese reform for the first time.

First we solved the problem of rural policies, instituting the contracted responsibility system for farming with remuneration linked to output, encouraging diversified production and the use of scientific advances in farming, and granting peasants the power to manage their own affairs. All these policies were so effective that, three years after their implementation, notable changes had taken place in the countryside. In 1978 we held the Third Plenary Session of the Eleventh Central Committee, and in a few days we shall convene the Third Plenary Session of the Twelfth Central Committee, which will have its own special features. The first Third Plenary Session focused on rural reform, whereas this Third Plenary Session will focus on urban reform, including the reform of industry, commerce and other sectors. We can say this will be a comprehensive reform. The basic content of both rural and urban reform is to invigorate the domestic economy and open China wider to the outside world. Although urban reform will be more complex than rural reform, since we have succeeded in the one, we are confident that we can succeed in the other.[20]

Deng's statement was a masterpiece of concealment, weaving the two reforms, one pushed by Beijing and the other resulting from grassroots movements, into a single grand narrative, in which the Chinese government was presented as the mastermind. Even though the 1978 Communiqué stated that "the whole Party should concentrate its main energy and efforts on advancing agriculture as fast as possible,"[21] it did not lift the ban on private farming. There is nothing in the 1978 Communiqué that comes close to what Deng referred to in his talk as "instituting the contracted responsibility system" or "granting peasants the power to manage their own affairs." Instead, the Communiqué stressed that "the right of ownership by the people's communes, production brigades and production teams and their power of decision must be protected effectively by the laws of the state," and "the people's communes must resolutely implement the system of three levels of ownership with the production team as the basic accounting unit, and this should remain unchanged."[22] These statements, in fact, wholeheartedly rejected private farming. Blending the second reform in agriculture spearheaded by starving peasants with the first, Deng misled his guest into believing that private farming and the ensuing changes in the Chinese countryside were brought about intentionally by the Chinese government.

In this state-centered narrative, 1978's Third Plenum of the Eleventh Central Committee launched the agricultural reform, and the Third Plenum of the Twelfth Central Committee in 1984 was responsible for starting industrial reform. Neither assertion, however, stands up to scrutiny. The first post-Mao government began economic reform and opening up in state-owned enterprises. The "Leap Outward" was aimed at heavy industry. After the "Leap Outward" was called off, the focus was shifted to "revitalize state-owned enterprises." Industrial reform was well underway by 1984.

In the official account of the Chinese economic reform, 1984 is taken as the beginning of "comprehensive urban reform,"[23] relegating all measures of industrial and urban reform made prior to 1984 to the status of "trials" or "preparations."[24] This state-centered view ignores the rise of township and village enterprises as well as the return of self-employment and private entrepreneurship in Chinese cities. Since both were non-state actors, they were simply not considered in the state-centered account of China's industrial or urban reform. But township and village enterprises and private entrepreneurs in Chinese cities were pioneers in pushing for industrial and urban reforms in the Chinese economy, creating a vibrant private sector outside the control of the state.

IV

The presence of two distinct reforms in China's market transformation was most pronounced during the late 1970s to mid-1980s. After the Fourteenth Congress of the Chinese Communist Party held in October 1992, when the socialist market economy was officially embraced as the main goal of China's economic reform, the private sector and market forces introduced to the Chinese economy, primarily by marginal revolutions, gained more political recognition. What had been marginal economic actors gradually became the backbone of the emerging socialist market economy. Ideological animosity toward the second track of reform began to dwindle soon after this. Nonetheless, the dual structure of reform remained a feature of China's market transformation in the 1990s and beyond, with one track of reform dictated by Beijing, and the other driven by local initiatives. The continuous presence of the locally initiated track of reform and its irreplaceable pioneering role in pushing forward China's market transformation were manifested in the development of stock markets in Shenzhen and Shanghai in the early 1990s, the privatization of state-owned enterprises, and the proliferation of industrial parks since the mid-1990s.

The recognition of two distinct reforms not only helps to give an accurate picture of Chinese economic reform, or at least, to avoid some factual errors that are common in the literature, but also allows us to better understand the nature of China's market transformation. In particular, it allows us to explore two of its most puzzling aspects: its extraordinary speed and the fact that the move to capitalism was carried out under the auspices of the Chinese Communist Party.

In Steven Cheung's original analysis of institutional change, the cost of institutional change arises from two sources, the information cost of discovering alternative institutional arrangements and the cost of negotiating or forcing the change itself, particularly the cost of compelling acquiescence from members of the society whose interests are expected to be hurt by the change.[25]

It was this simple but powerful analytical framework, aided by his insightful but unsystematic observation of the trend of change in China after the death of Mao, that allowed Cheung to predict that China was definitely moving toward capitalism. Its analytical clarity and logical rigor notwithstanding, this framework had a weakness. It treats society as a homogenous entity and institutional change as a single event, sweeping the whole society in one strike, in which a superior institution replaces an inferior one. Twenty years later, this still is by and large how institutional change is treated in much of the social science literature.[26] There is no process, no time in institutional change.[27]

This static view of institutional change, like the comparative static analysis in economics, is more concerned with the result or endpoint of institutional change than with the process. Institutional change in China, a country of continental dimensions and remarkable regional variations, rarely occurs as a singular event. Instead, it takes place gradually and unevenly. This compels us to treat institutional change as a process in time and space. Whether early changes encourage similar changes to follow elsewhere depends on how actors elsewhere regard the outcome of these early changes and how they assess the new constraints and opportunities they face. Thus, whether early experiments in institutional change gain momentum and ultimately prevail, or whether they encounter antipathy and are rejected, is difficult to predict. In this process of development, the state stands out as a prominent source of uncertainty, due to its regulatory role and coercive capacity to alter the costs, incentives and choices other actors face.

Benjamin Franklin observed that a great empire, like a big cake, is most easily diminished at the edges. How this logic was played out in China's marginal revolutions was heavily influenced by the dual structure of reform. The recognition of two reforms enables us to trace the interplay between them over time and the interactions of competing ideas. This allows us to examine, in a unique manner, the dynamics of change in Chinese leaders' political beliefs, specifically those related to socialism, and its relations to the market and the private sector. As we have seen, this was mainly an adaptive response to the fast changing economic reality, with the failure of state-led reform leading to a readjustment in attitudes to private-sector reform. This in turn allowed much greater scope for economic reform in both the private and state sectors.

Four marginal forces – private farming, township and village enterprises, individual entrepreneurship, and the Special Economic Zones – pioneered in transforming the Chinese economy during the 1980s. Economic experiments initiated at the grassroots level were tolerated precisely because they were conducted at the periphery of the socialist economy and so were perceived as posing little direct political challenge to the regime. Regarded as inferior and insignificant, these marginal forces of reform enjoyed some political freedom as long as their presence was no longer perceived as a threat to socialism.

Once peasants and unemployed city dwellers were allowed the freedom to pursue private entrepreneurship, it did not take long for their endeavors to out-shine the state sector and convince the pragmatic Chinese leaders to recognize these experiments as beneficial rather than inimical to socialism. When such unorthodox practices became officially recognized, they inevitably weakened the grip of socialist ideology and stretched the boundaries of political thought.

In contrast, reforms of the state sector, including the economic program launched under Hua as well as the enterprise reform started since 1978, were largely ineffective. Any reform targeting the economic core of socialism was inevitably directed and closely supervised by the state. In both cases, the Chinese leaders could not afford to take their hands off the economic sector which they deemed vital for both the wellbeing of the whole socialist economy and for political stability. The heavy-handed approach they took implies that the state-led efforts were severely constrained by socialist ideology; more often than not this resulted in disappointing outcomes. This was the price China paid for its remaining commitment to socialism.

Fortunately, with regard to private-sector reform, the government was more willing to take a hands-off approach. They were more likely to tolerate measures that appeared incompatible with socialism, partly because Chinese leaders then believed socialism could be preserved as long as they kept control of the state enterprises. Less constrained by political ideology and state bureaucracy, and strictly disciplined by competition, the marginal economic forces originating at the periphery of the socialist state were able to overtake the state sector.

As time went by, the marginal revolutions that sprang up at the periphery of the socialist economy not only won popular support and outlasted political resistance, but also served as a catalyst for changes in political ideology. They gradually moved socialism away from its traditional image as the antithesis of the market economy, and generated political tolerance for further economic reforms. As a result, the state-led reform became more open to market forces and its protagonists less hostile to the private sector. Since the Chinese government controlled many economic resources as well as the policy agenda, reform initiatives that Chinese government put into place remained critically important, even when they did not work out as intended.

For example, in Chen Yun's view of socialism, which was developed in the 1950s in the wake of Mao's radical push for socialist transition and total elimination of the market, "the planned economy as primary, market adjustments as auxiliary," served as a fundamental guiding principle in the early days of Chinese economic reform.[28] As the rapid expansion of the market and private sector helped to improve the living conditions of the Chinese people, the Chinese government became more willing to accept what was then called the "commodity economy." This Marxian term allowed the Chinese government to avoid the use of a politically sensitive name – the "market economy" – but was still able to blur the lines between socialist doctrine and the increasing dominance of the market. By October 1987, when the Thirteenth Congress of the Party was held, the Chinese economy had doubled in size since 1978. The Party was proud to announce its commitment to economic development; to recommit itself to socialism and Party rule as well as to economic reform and opening up. This policy was conveniently summarized at the time as "one center, two basic points."[29] The development of the private sector was encouraged and welcomed for its contribution to China's further economic growth. Even stock markets, a conspicuous symbol of capitalism, were allowed to open in Shanghai in 1990 and in Shenzhen one year later.

Throughout the reform, the state-led track engineered by Beijing was heavily influenced by political ideology. The policy initiatives emerging from private-sector reform were far less ideologically constrained. Successful initiatives that originated in the private sector were often accepted by Beijing and adapted to fit state-sector reform initiatives. Not by design, the dual structure of reform provided an effective and flexible institutional framework for Beijing to navigate China's move to a market economy. It first created a political buffer for Beijing, reducing the political risk of reform. When loyalty to socialism remained strong at the early stage of reform and when private entrepreneurship and market forces were still perceived as politically dangerous, Beijing could tolerate the second track of reform's experiments with capitalism without compromising its commitment to socialism. Indeed, the second track of reform was allowed to roam when Beijing was not yet emancipated from the doctrine of socialism. Moreover, economic reforms inevitably involved political risks. Political leaders could lose their positions if the economic reforms they championed went awry. The presence of the second track of reform gave Beijing more room to maneuver in reform policy without tying itself to any reform initiative undertaken by local governments. This structure helped to make the political system still controlled by one single party much more elastic, adaptable, and receptive to economic changes than it would otherwise have been.

The dual structure of reform and the decentralized political system behind it also played a critical role in facilitating collective learning throughout the market transformation. China's market reform encountered two obstacles, one ideological, the other practical. Until 1984 when Beijing first accepted the "commodity economy," the ideological hostility toward the market and private sector presented a major hurdle. In addition, the practical challenges of reforming socialism were intimidating, as attested to by the two abortive attempts at price reform in the 1980s. As ideological opposition to market reform faded and the market economy gradually gained a foothold, China's reform was hampered by a lack of understanding of the working of the market economy as a live, evolving system, with many interdependent subsystems, and by the uncertainties inherent in such a radical move. The two-track reform allowed Beijing to tap into the enthusiasm and local knowledge provincial and sub-provincial governments had gained through their own development initiatives. The local initiatives that had proved successful were carefully studied by Beijing before being adopted into national policy. This is aptly demonstrated by the case of privatization in Zhucheng and in the restructuring of state enterprises in Shanghai and Changsha. Sometimes, Beijing took a more active role, experimenting with policy initiatives first at local levels before imposing them nationwide. Examples of this include the expansion of the Special Economic Zones to include many coastal cities in 1984 and later, industrial parks all over China, as well as the 1994 tax reform.

Few would question the assumption Steven Cheung made that the move from socialism to capitalism is efficiency-improving. In China, the knowledge that such potential gains existed gave rise to a desire for change. But a desire is one thing; the actual process of change is another. For China, it involved taking actions when the information possessed by the leaders was far from complete, and the potential consequences were far from clear. The dual structure of reform helped to moderate the political risk of reform and cut down the cost of implementation which significantly eased China's move to a market economy. While Cheung's early prediction that China would go capitalist turned out to be correct, it was the two tracks of reform that actually moved China to capitalism.

IV

The unintentional presence of two parallel tracks of reform worked surprisingly well in easing the rapid return of a market economy to China while Beijing was still committed to socialism. Along the way, Beijing adopted three key reform measures in the early 1980s: extensive use of the managerial contract responsibility system, the adoption of dual-track pricing, and the use of contracts in sharing tax revenues between central and local government. To varying degrees, these were successful in moving the economy forward. However, these measures were responsible for fragmenting the national economy and creating a chaotic pricing environment for state and non-state firms in the economy. A consequence of this was to hinder market competition and undermine the emerging market economy.

In the early 1980s, the managerial contract responsibility system was introduced to formalize the autonomy gained by state enterprises vis-à-vis their supervising governmental agents. But the use of contracts in enterprise reform opened a Pandora's box. Each state enterprise created its own idiosyncratic constraints through individual bargaining with its government agent, including prices and quantities for inputs as well as their tax burden. In collaboration with the government regulatory agents, each state enterprise wrote its own rules.

At the same time, the Chinese government expanded dual-track pricing – as a substitute for price reform. Dual-track pricing emerged as early as in the late 1970s when the Chinese government allowed state oil companies to sell their product in the market for a higher price after fulfilling the state quotas. As a result, state enterprises were exposed to and disciplined by market signals without privatization. At the same time, dual-track pricing allowed non-state firms to access materials controlled by the state, and opened the door for them to compete head on with state enterprises. They often paid a much higher price for their inputs, but had much greater freedom in running their businesses, including labor relations; they also faced a stricter market discipline. As a result, by the early 1990s, township and village enterprises were contributing 40 percent of China's industrial growth and 40 percent of China's exports.[30] But the widescale adoption of dual-track pricing led to chaos in the Chinese economy. The gap between the government price and the market price, which could be many times higher, was a gray area where the spot price would have fallen. Because of the wide variations in the prices paid by different firms for their inputs, it became impossible to compare their productivity and economic efficiency even when they competed in the product market. In addition, dual-track pricing also engendered lucrative arbitrage activities, which not only became a source of resource misallocation, but also created social resentment and popular opposition to economic reform.

In addition to price distortions at the enterprise level, the enterprises also faced distortions at the macro level; both these factors worked together to create a chaotic pricing environment, particularly by undermining market discipline for state enterprises. Throughout the 1980s, the Chinese central government used a contract system to collect taxes from the provinces. This was introduced in 1980 to impose fiscal discipline and to give incentives to local governments. Under the contract-based tax regime, the tax burden of each province was negotiated individually with Beijing. As a result, each region had a different tax burden, further compounding the chaotic pricing environment created by the managerial contract responsibility system and dual-track pricing.

The most fundamental difference between capitalism and socialism is the operation of a market pricing mechanism in the former and its replacement by state planning in the latter. Textbook economics treats the market – the adjustment of demand and supply through price changes – as an efficient mechanism of resource allocation. But the market is also essentially a mechanism of collective learning. It provides all economic actors with scope for trial-and-error-based learning, allowing them to explore existing opportunities and create new ones.

To make this process of collective learning effective, one condition must be met. All economic actors must be free to act and be held responsible for their actions. Probably for this reason, the market economy used to be more commonly called "the free enterprise economy," as opposed to a command economy. This implies that, in a market economy, all actors are equally disciplined by a common set of constraints – buying from a competitive factor market and selling in a competitive product market – so that competent or fortunate learners are rewarded with access to more resources and are thus able to expand and serve more consumers, and poor or unlucky learners are punished, forcing them to withdraw from their current pursuit and start something new.

In the Chinese market transformation, two factors effectively bring this process to a complete halt even after private firms are allowed to operate. First, when the national economy is so fragmented that each local economy is essentially sheltered from the outside world, competition will lose its disciplinary force on firms; in turn, the firms lose a feedback mechanism critical to their operations. In such an extreme situation, there is little direct competition among firms in different locations. Inefficient firms face no pressure to improve or close, giving rise to static inefficiency in resource misallocation. Moreover, good business practices – the ones that allow economic actors to serve their consumers better and improve their market performance – cannot be quickly recognized and imitated widely, leading to dynamic inefficiency in collective learning. The more integrated and bigger the national economy is, the more firms and human talents will be brought into the game of collective learning, and the faster will they learn. As a result, it improves firms' static efficiency and dynamic efficiency. When a common national market exists, all firms, no matter where they are located in the economy, are part of the collective process of experimental learning.

Second, the process of market competition and experimental learning can be severely undermined if firms in the economy are not equally constrained by common market discipline even when they compete with each other. In a market economy, firms are disciplined because competition winnows poorly performing firms from good ones. The experiments firms engage in, such as what products to bring to consumers and at what price, involve many uncertainties – resulting from the lack of information about consumer preferences, other firms' plans and the price of inputs, as well as relevant government regulations. Market discipline works when firms can survive only by providing products consumers are willing to buy and, with receipts from consumers, firms can secure the services of more factors of production. The system breaks down when firms can survive on other grounds, such as political favors.

The most damaging effect of chaotic pricing was not attributable to the presence of multiple prices for industrial inputs per se. Despite the law of one price, different firms often purchased the same materials at different spot prices due to various information problems and other differential costs of using the market mechanism. Nor was repetitive and duplicative investment across regions the main problem; rather, the lack of a common national market severely weakened market discipline, a critical feedback mechanism that is indispensable if market competition is to function. This created a problem beyond the soft budget constraint, a chronic defect of state enterprises under socialism when the government was willing to subsidize them on political grounds.[31] In addition to the budget, many other constraints that state enterprises faced were not only soft but worse, idiosyncratic and open to ad hoc negotiation. There was hardly any disciplinary mechanism in place to discriminate between firms with diverging performance records. As a result, the real economic performance of state enterprises became almost unknowable to outsiders. Moreover, it created a distorted incentive structure for state enterprises – managers could gain more by striking an advantageous contract with the government agent than by improving enterprise productivity or winning the patronage of consumers. Consequently, massive inefficiency in resource allocation was inevitable. Just as destructive was the massive redistribution effect when arbitrage opportunities created by the chaotic pricing system were exploited by government officials and managers of state enterprises.

After Deng's southern tour in 1992, China took a series of steps to consolidate the market economy. The 1992 price reform and 1994 tax reform greatly removed price distortions and facilitated the rise of a common national market. Dual-track pricing was gradually phased out by the mid-1990s. As a result, the market became a meaningful and significant disciplinary mechanism in the economy. Firms were compelled to improve their products to attract consumers, rather than cultivate *guanxi* or relationships with its supervising government. A clear indicator of increasing market competition in the Chinese economy is the rapidly growing ratio of the total amount of losses to the total amount of profits made by state enterprises. It was on average 5 percent in the period 1981–1985 and 28.2 percent in the period 1986–1990, and jumped to 74.6 percent in 1990–1995, reaching almost 200 percent in 1996.[32]

Another related development was the privatization of state enterprises. After more than a decade of enterprise reform, the Chinese government finally came to the conclusion that delegating rights and sharing profits had failed to make state enterprises independent and autonomous. As more and more state enterprises fell into insolvency and became a financial burden for local governments, economic logic started to prevail over ideology. Local governments started to drop their ideological commitment to public ownership; the way to privatization was clear. At the same time, the recovery of the private sector after 1992 and its further consolidation started to attract employees from the public sector. The development of the urban housing market, pension reform, and health insurance began to free state sector employees from their employers. All this helped to ease the process of privatization and make it politically acceptable.

With the privatization of state enterprises, most local governments at the county level let go of all their state enterprises. The number of state enterprises owned and managed by the central, provincial and municipal governments was also significantly reduced. Since only a few monopoly industries were in the hands of state enterprises, local governments could no longer rely upon state enterprises as the backbone of the local economy or the main source of tax revenue. Instead, government officials had to provide local public goods and cultivate a business-friendly environment to attract investment, setting up a new stage for regional competition.

V

Regional competition was rejuvenated in the 1990s after the rise of a common national market and the privatization of state enterprises. In the previous decade, local protectionism and various barriers to internal trade effectively fragmented the national economy. The Chinese economy was decentralized; but competition among regions was restrained. As more and more state enterprises became a financial burden to local governments in the 1990s, local governments began to take a non-ideological approach to the private sector, which quickly became recognized as the foundation of the local economy. From the perspective of local public finance, after the 1994 tax reform, value added taxes and land rent became the main sources of revenue for local governments. Both were positively linked to the growth of the local economy. At the same time, the development of a common national market implied that regional competition was now subject to strict market discipline. As a result, regional competition in the 1990s and beyond arose as the most powerful driving force behind China's economic transformation.

Much attention has been paid to the strong connection between China's decentralized political structure and intense regional competition in the economy.[33] Since local government officials are ultimately appointed by Beijing based on the performance of the local economy, Chinese local governments run their jurisdiction – the province, city, county, town, and village – much like a business corporation.[34] The active role played by the Chinese government is similar to that of the leadership of a corporate entity. In addition, the Chinese government still controls many important economic resources, particularly bank loans as well as access to sectors under state monopoly. It is no surprise that the Chinese government has been duly emphasized as a critical force in the transformation of the Chinese economy.

The continuous preponderance of the state in the rising Chinese market economy is a result of the unique nature of China's economic reform. As detailed in earlier chapters, this reform did not follow a blueprint but was carried forward by a combination of grassroots initiatives and state-led policy experiments. The rise of the Chinese market economy did not follow the path suggested by some property rights economists. However, it is not the case that the Chinese experience of market transformation challenges secure and well-defined property rights as a legal foundation in the working of a market economy. The success of township and village enterprises did not negate the critical importance of private property rights because many of them were indeed private. Even those township and village enterprises owned by local governments had a better defined structure of property rights relative to state-owned enterprises. But what really mattered was that township and village enterprises were subject to market discipline while state-owned enterprises were not. The focus on the ownership structure of township and village enterprises was rather misplaced.

It was peculiar, though, that China did not first delineate property rights, specify other relevant institutional rules and then allow market forces to allocate rights to the highest bidder. Instead, what rights economic actors were allowed to have, such as the discretionary rights peasants had over farmland or residual rights held by managers of state-owned enterprises, and what institutional constraints they faced in exercising their rights were delineated when the state released the rights of control to private economic actors. The delineation and transfer of rights took place in one step. During the first two decades of reform, as China remained committed to socialism and against outright privatization of state assets, what rights private actors obtained from the state were subject to individual negotiation. A major advantage of combining rights delineation, and rights transaction or reallocation into one step was to speed up the introduction of market forces into the economy. If all had to wait until rights were delineated by the state before initiating any business dealing, it would have subjected the state to a test of wisdom – getting the rights right before their economic values were revealed in competition between entrepreneurs – and private entrepreneurs to a test of patience – waiting for the state to delineate all the rights. The first test would require the state to make a correct first-time decision on rights delineation with little information on the market value of the rights. This challenge was so demanding by itself that it could readily delay, if not derail, China's economic reform.

This approach to reform conflicts with the conventional portrayal of the state in economics. As commonly assumed in economics, a primary economic function of the state is to delineate property rights and then withdraw itself from the economy to make room for free bargaining among private actors. Unless conflicting claims to rights arise and call for resolution, the state stays at arm's length from the economy.[35] In the Chinese case, since rights delineation and transaction were combined in one step, decisions on what rights were significant and thus worth delineating was part of the negotiation between economic actors and the state. Most of the rights delegated by the state were not initially transferrable. For example, the household responsibility contract did not allow peasants to transfer land use rights, nor were managers of state-owned enterprises able to transfer their rights. As a result, the state was called back to the bargaining table every time rights changed hands. Moreover, as economic conditions changed over time, certain rights which were excluded in the original bargaining became economically significant. Even the rights that were included in the original contract may have changed so much in significance that a revision was warranted. The state was thus frequently called in to revise and redefine the structure of rights. In addition, as the original contracts were up for renewal – some contracts would last as long as seventy-five years, as in the case of many land contracts; many more lasted five to ten years, as in the case of performance contracts between managers of state enterprises and the supervising agents, as well as between firms and industrial parks – the state was called forth to re-open the contractual negotiation, which inevitably involved re-specification of rights. Not surprisingly, the Chinese state remained an important actor in the economy.[36]

But it is misleading to suggest that Chinese economic reform represents the triumph of state interference over market forces. It is true that Chinese local governments are heavily involved in the operation of the local economy. In most cases, local governments compete with each other in mobilizing factors of production to figure out the best economic development model for local conditions. This service is essentially what Alfred Marshall called organization, the fourth independent agent of production. When local governments open up a new industrial park and solicit potential investors, what they do is to clear the ground and set the stage, and to facilitate the inception and growth of private firms. The local government may get involved in the conception of the plots and selection of actors, but the show is run by business firms. And the fate of an industrial park – whether firms located there can survive and grow – is not dictated by the government but determined by market competition.

The most crucial contribution made by the local governments in regional competition is to capitalize on China's physical size and internal diversity. Their actions translate the advantage China has in space to superior speed of industrialization. When each of the local Chinese governments, including 32 provincial level governments, 282 city governments, 2862 county governments, 19,522 town and 14,677 village governments, tests out its way of developing the local economy, numerous different experiments are conducted simultaneously, each in competition with the other. The time of collective learning based on trial and error is cut significantly. The diffusion of successful practices is made fast and easy. Regions compete not only in factor markets – capital and labor have become increasingly mobile since the mid-1990s – and product markets, but also in the provision of local public goods, the structuring of business–government relations, and the local organization of production. Repetitive and duplicative investment is inevitable, and indeed, an essential part of the process. This has resulted in an erosion of economies of scale to capital due to its under-utilization, but has greatly accelerated and diffused industrialization, turning China into a formidable workshop of the world in less than thirty years. The loss in what Alfred Marshall called "internal economies" is more than compensated for by what he called "external economies." This is the key to understanding the extraordinary speed of market transformation in China during the 1990s and beyond.

VI

Today, the Chinese Communist Party remains the only political party in China. In the past three decades or so, many observers and commentators have hoped that China would eventually drift towards a western model of capitalism. In this process, the Chinese Communist Party would either become less relevant, with the progress of market reform, or even obsolete, along with communism, or embrace democratization, following in the steps of Taiwan and South Korea. Today, there is little sign that the Chinese Communist Party is ready to reform the system of one-party rule. With more than 80 million members (at the end of 2011), from every profession, including a rising percentage of private entrepreneurs and college graduates, the Party appears as strong as it has ever been. With the endurance of the Chinese Communist Party, the Chinese model of capitalism is increasingly seen by some as an alien, belligerent force, with the potential to confront, if not overthrow, western capitalism.

The persistence of the Communist Party in China, which certainly is one of the most striking features of the Chinese economic reform, has led many to focus on the seemingly unfailing role of the Chinese party-state during the whole process of reform. Unlike other transition economies, in the former Soviet bloc for example, where the former ruling communist parties have collapsed one after another to make room for market-oriented reforms, China stands out as an unique instance where the Communist Party and market economy seem to be able to thrive together. This perplexing partnership between economic liberalization and the continuity of communist rule is widely perceived as a key to understanding the extraordinary record of China's market transformation. In a simplified and widely circulated version of events, the enviable performance of the Chinese market reform is mainly attributed to an all-powerful Chinese party-state. The Chinese economic model is commonly referred to as "authoritarian capitalism,"[37] or "state-guided capitalism,"[38] highlighting the role played by the Chinese government and the Party. Even the pervasive and corrupt intervention of the state and special interest groups in the Chinese economy, what critics call "crony capitalism"[39] or "*quan-gui*" capitalism[40] in Chinese, are seen to vindicate a state-centered view of the Chinese economic reform.

Readers who have followed our account of how China became capitalist have good reasons to dismiss such a statist interpretation of China's economic reform as self-serving propaganda of the Chinese Communist Party. Even the Chinese leaders, particularly during the 1980s, have described the reform as "crossing the river by groping for stones." Time and again, the Chinese government was taken by surprise – when the starving peasants proved the superiority of private farming and township and village enterprises; when the formerly unemployed city residents earned higher incomes than state employees with "an iron bowl"; when Shenzen was quickly transformed from a fishing village to an urban center in South China and a hub of capitalism. The Chinese leaders were also disappointed and embarrassed when their repeated efforts to revive state-owned enterprises failed to save them and they were forced to allow millions of workers to become unemployed. China's transformation into a rising economic power certainly did not come about through the deliberate and patient designs of an omniscient government.

The continuity of the Chinese Communist Party and its monopoly of political power have concealed two important changes. First, the role of the Chinese state in the economy has become progressively less significant, no matter what measurement is used. Before the economic reforms, the Chinese people had little economic freedom and the state controlled every aspect of the economy, from production, to retail, and even consumption. Today, private entrepreneurship is the primary driving force of the Chinese economy. The size of the state sector in the economy has fallen significantly relative to the non-state sector. Many international comparative studies have characterized the Chinese economy as state-led capitalism, due to the still considerable size of the state sector. But the undeniable fact is that the Chinese state has steadily withdrawn itself from the economy over the past few decades of reform. If the state is seen as contributing to the rise of the Chinese economy, it must be the gradual withdrawal of government from the economy, rather than the strength or omnipresence of the political leadership, that explains the success of Chinese market transformation.

Second, the Chinese Communist Party today no longer identifies itself as a revolutionary vanguard. The "mandate of heaven" has replaced communism; the party-state rests its legitimacy on effective governance and the improvement of living standards for the people.[41] At the 2002 APEC (Asia-Pacific Economic Cooperation) meeting held in Los Cabos, Mexico, the then President Jiang Zemin made the following statement:

Despite the host of problems facing the international community and more that will still crop up unexpectedly in the future, the tide of history in favor of peace and development cannot be reversed, nor will the people of all lands change their yearning for a better life. Wherever they live, people want lasting peace and stability in the world, a world that enjoys universal prosperity and sustainable development. If world peace and common development are to be secured, it is necessary for statesmen of all countries to display the vision and courage needed to move history forward in response to the will of the people.

The key to our success lies in our ability to respect diversity in light of the varied interests and concerns of the members, seeking common grounds while shelving differences. Our world is a diverse and colorful place. Even more so is the Asia-Pacific region. Respecting the historical and cultural diversity in the members and their different paths or models of development is the important foundation for us to achieve common development and prosperity. The mingling and mutual influencing of different cultures throughout history have provided the engine for the development of human civilization. We should follow the law of history, conduct intercultural exchanges more vigorously and draw upon each other's strength more consciously so as to ensure common progress of all human societies.[42]

Hu Jintao, the current President of China, at the Opening Ceremony of the Boao Forum for Asia Annual Conference held on April 12th, 2008 in Hainan, was equally emphatic on economic development.

If a country or a nation is to develop itself in this increasingly competitive world, it must advance with the times, carry out reform and opening up, boost development, put people first and promote harmony. This is the conclusion we have drawn in the great cause of reform and opening up.

There is no ready or unchanging path and model of development that suits all countries in the world. We must explore and improve our development path and model in keeping with China's national conditions. In so doing, we must adapt to new trends both at home and abroad and meet the people's growing expectation for a better life. We must make Chinese society more vibrant. And we must truly keep up with the trend of the times and share the same destiny with the people.[43]

Few, if any, of the new Party members are attracted to, or even familiar with, communism. When Professor Richard Madsen of the University of California at San Diego spent the year 2007–2008 visiting Fudan University he found a top student in his class who was joining the Party but had barely heard of the *Communist Manifesto*.[44] When a communist party has put aside class struggle between the proletariat and capitalists as well as rivalry between socialism and capitalism, and has committed itself to seeking truth from facts, it is no longer a communist party as we understand the term in the West. In this sense it is misleading to continue to treat China as a communist regime.

To what degree China was a communist regime even before the start of economic reform is an open question. At the very least, Mao's China was much more than communism. The history of Marxism in China is fleetingly short, even if we take the founding of the Chinese Communist Party in 1921 as the start, as long as we bear in mind the long and continuous history of Chinese civilization and the continuing predominance of Confucianism. Since Marxism was sanctioned as the official ideology under Mao, it has had a more significant influence on China's economy and society than its short lifespan might suggest. But, if we look at Chinese political thought as an accumulation of ideas over thousands of years, Marxism is no more than surface decoration.

Moreover, Marxism was rarely, if ever, seriously studied or understood by Mao and his comrades.[45] Those who had studied Marxism more systematically either died at the hands of the Nationalist government before 1949 or lost out to Mao in the Party's repetitive power struggles. Since Mao's rise to power, the Chinese Communist Party has always been more Chinese than communist. Mao's vision of communism, for example, was based more on his immersion in the Chinese classics than in his reading of Marx or Lenin, which was quite limited.[46] Despite his repeated efforts to uproot China from its traditions, Chinese socialism remained profoundly influenced by China's long social and political history. China under socialism remained Chinese.

For example, even though socialism was believed to rest on public ownership and central planning, those two pillars were not regarded equally in China. While the sacred status of public ownership meant that private property rights were under constant attack in Mao's China, central planning was enforced for only a few years during the first Five Year Plan. This patent disjunction between public ownership and central planning in Chinese socialism has deep historical roots. The idea of an ideal society founded on public ownership has a long intellectual history in China; this can be traced back to the time of Confucius. Traditional Chinese legal-political thinking has an entrenched bias against the "private." This contrast between the public and private was forcefully reformulated in the late nineteenth and early twentieth century by Kang Youwei, who popularized the Confucian terms, the society of Datong, as a utopia, in contrast to Xiaokang. In Kang's vision, public ownership stood as the foundation for the ideal Datong society. This view had a lasting impact on Mao and other Chinese communists.[47] However, decentralization had, historically, also been a prominent feature of Chinese politics. The commanding emperor, an embodiment of Chinese political authoritarianism, could not micromanage a landmass as big and diverse as China.

Since communism was born in the western intellectual tradition, it was not surprising that the West chose to view Mao's China through the lens of communism. That Mao was eager to rebuild China in accordance with the teachings of communism and was aggressive in ridding China of its cultural heritage also facilitated such a reading. Moreover, since the Soviet Union was the first socialist country, the West found it convenient to think of China as being similar to the Soviet Union. This was understandable, as while Mao's China was closed to the outside world, the Soviet Union was more accessible. But even during the high tide of socialism, China was strikingly different from the Soviet Union, in ideology as well as organization. China under Mao was certainly not another Soviet Union.

Whether we call China communist or capitalist, we have to recognize the legacy of Chinese history in order to develop a better understanding of China's rapid economic transformation and its future prospects. China is no stranger to capitalism, and certainly not to free commerce and private entrepreneurship.[48] It is widely known among students of Chinese history that the operation of long-distance trade, the common use of paper money, and flourishing market activities were ubiquitous in China's past. This is particularly true of the late Tang and Song dynasties as well as during Ming and Qing times. When Marco Polo traveled to China during the thirteenth century, he was deeply impressed by the burgeoning commerce and sophisticated industry in China. He was particularly intrigued by the use of paper money, which did not emerge in the West until the seventeeth century.[49] However, such early buds of commerce did not give rise to a full-scale modern industrial revolution; a world-leading civilization began to stagnate exactly when the West began its rise. Nonetheless, China's historical precedents of capitalism bear direct and significant relevance to the current revival of a market economy in China.

Even though this account of how China became capitalist in the past three decades does not allow us to do justice to China's long and involved history, it is worth stressing that Chinese civilization has always been remarkably open. Before Qin unified China in 221 BC, a wide variety of schools of thought emerged and engaged with each other, giving birth to the Chinese axiom "let a hundred schools of thought contend." From the Han to the Tang dynasties, the Silk Road served as the highway of commerce linking China to the rest of the world, allowing China to absorb many ideas from India, central Asia, and beyond. The perceived continuity of Chinese civilization leads many people to forget that Chinese culture went through a long and significant transformation after its encounter with Buddhism in the third century. It took several centuries for Confucianism to absorb Buddhism, giving rise to Neo-Confucianism in the Song dynasty.[50] As of today, China has barely started its interaction with the West on equal terms. China holds the promise of developing a different form of capitalism, one that builds upon its own rich and diverse cultural traditions while engaging openly with the West as well as the rest of the world. Any society or civilization thrives on cross-fertilization and hybridization in an open, tolerant, and politically stable environment, and dies when subjected to close-mindedness and political chaos. As we free ourselves from a locality-centered point of view and look at human history from a global perspective, China did not rule the world in the past, nor does the West dominate the world today. Only an open and tolerant civilization could and will prevail, and all other familiar identifiers, including its geographic origin or ethnic face, are accidental and contingent.

Under the visible and powerful hand of the Chinese Communist Party, the emerging Chinese market economy is often treated as a distinct species, not simply different from, but even inimical to, a liberal market order. It is true that the Chinese market economy is different from the British, the American, or any other preexisting model of capitalism. This is partly due to historical influences, along with many other distinctive features that China has, such as its sheer size in both population and geography and the role of the Chinese Communist Party. It is also partly due to the fact that China is one of the latest members of the global market economy and is able to learn from different models of capitalism. There was an enormous gap between China and the developed world in technology and production possibility frontier. Once the Chinese people were freed from the shackle of ideology, they were able to catch up quickly. At the same time, the huge potential of the Chinese market made China a favorite destination of foreign direct investment from all over the world. From the 1990s for example, Shanghai became a showcase of global capitalism.

But the charge that the Chinese economy poses a threat to the global market order is based more on fear and misapprehension than on reason. On the contrary, the post-Mao economic reform marked the beginning of the fall of communism. China's re-embracement of market forces since the death of Mao dealt a deadly blow to the socialist experiment that began in the Soviet Union at the beginning of the twentieth century. China's market-oriented reforms, including the setup of the Special Economic Zones and the inflow of foreign direct investment, quickly pulled millions out of poverty and raised the living standards for a quarter of humanity. These remarkable outcomes have convinced other countries, including India and Vietnam, of the benevolence of the market and the folly of state planning.

Moreover, the Chinese market transformation has opened up new horizons for global capitalism. As a rising economic power, China is now contributing to the development of many countries in Central and Southeast Asia, Latin America, and Africa, whose economies have been increasingly integrated with the Chinese market. China's great economic transformation has already become a pillar of the emerging global market economy. More important, the operation of a vibrant and distinctive market economy in China makes a compelling case that capitalism can take root and flourish in an ostensibly non-western society. Capitalism with Chinese characteristics arises as an example for other developing countries whose cultures and histories are also different from those in the West to embrace the market. By breaking the West's monopoly on capitalism, China helps to globalize capitalism and fortifies the global market order by broadening the cultural milieu of and adding cultural diversity to capitalism. A global liberal economic order will be far more resilient and sustainable if capitalism grows beyond the West and blooms in varying cultural backgrounds and political systems.

VII

In January 2010 *Foreign Policy* published a bold forecast by Professor Robert Fogel, who predicted that the Chinese economy in 2040 will make up 40 percent of global GDP, while the United States will be a distant second (14 percent).[51] Fogel's prediction was challenged by a rebuttal that appeared in the same issue, which criticized Fogel for "entirely overestimating the Chinese government's omniscience."[52] It is important to reiterate a point that has been consistently stressed throughout this book that the remarkable growth record that China has achieved recently cannot be attributed to "the Chinese government's omniscience." Were that the case, our confidence in the future of China's market economy would be much weaker. This account of how China became capitalist cites on a number of occasions the crucial part played by Deng Xiaoping and other Chinese leaders. But Deng, unlike Mao, was never what Adam Smith called "a man of system."[53] While Mao prided himself on forming a utopian blueprint and imposing it on the Chinese people, Deng was too down to earth to hold dear any theory in defiance of facts. What Deng did was to hold politics and ideology at bay and keep the Chinese government cool-headed. Few people would doubt that the course and outcome of the Chinese economic reform would be quite different had it not been for Deng's unfailing pragmatism and shrewd political skills. But the root cause of the miraculous rise of the Chinese economy is the Chinese people, full of optimism, energy, creativity, and determination.

We share the optimism that Professor Fogel held about China's future. But the framework of analysis presented here does not provide a model of economic growth that is able to predict the quantitative trajectory of the Chinese economy. Many have criticized Fogel for his overestimation. But even if we cut his prediction by half it would not change the broader picture.

The most critical advantage China has is its vast population of 1.3 billion enterprising, hard-working, and persevering people. Despite the birth control policy implemented since the late 1970s, China still is the most populous country in the world. After decades of rapid urbanization, half the country's population today continues to live in rural areas. There is a core among the rural population that is eager to move to cities for a better job and better life, and there remains room for continuous urbanization and industrialization, which will be critical to the continuous growth of the Chinese economy in years to come. But China has a population which is ageing at an alarming rate. When many countries in the developed world subsidize childbirth, the Chinese government should feel fortunate that many Chinese still desire a big family. When each individual is educated and inventive, not someone waiting in the line to be employed as was the case under socialism, government-imposed birth control seems a wrong-headed policy. The one-child policy was meant to be a temporary emergency policy; if it persists too long its detrimental impact on the Chinese economy and society will be lasting and severe.[54]

Even a highly educated and capable labor force will not realize its potential unless it is eager and free to discover economic opportunities anywhere in the country, free to set up business organizations to pursue the opportunities, and free to compete against any other actors. Since the beginning of reform, China has made great progress in facilitating labor mobility and encouraging private entrepreneurship. The migration of millions of rural workers to cities and the privatization of state enterprises, which allowed the transfer of human capital to the private sector, have been two major channels of labor movement. The gradual development of a national labor market has not only greatly improved labor productivity but also brought real economic benefits to peasants. But considerable barriers still exist today in the labor market, particularly the household registration (or *hukou* in Chinese) system and various institutional hurdles faced by migrant workers. Their gradual removal will provide a strong source of gain in labor productivity in years to come.

Private entrepreneurship has clearly enjoyed a great leap forward in China. Prior to reform, private entrepreneurship was illegal; today, it has been recognized as a primary driver of the economy. Nonetheless, private entrepreneurs still face many prejudices and adversities. The most menacing force they have to deal with is state monopoly. While most state enterprises have been restructured or privatized since the mid-1990s, the remaining ones have retreated into a few monopolized sectors, including banking, energy, and communication. Such state enterprises in monopolized industries have become a powerful interest group in the Chinese economy. The inflationary monetary policy implemented since 2008 has further pumped up the state sector. Most of the bank credits created by the 4-trillion yuan (about 586 billion USD) stimulus package were channeled into state-owned enterprises and local governments. The state sector has grown on cheap credit at the expense of the private sector. In 2009, an unprecedented total of thirty-four Chinese firms (not including three from Hong Kong) were listed in the Fortune Global 500. Only one, however, was a private enterprise.[55] In 2010, forty-two Chinese firms (not including four based in Hong Kong) made it to the Fortune Global 500, two of them being private.[56]

What is disturbing is not state ownership per se, but the prima facie assumption that state enterprises better serve public interests than private firms. This has been used to justify state monopoly and restrict entry for private firms to many industries which the government deem "strategically important." In reality, state monopoly enables many state enterprises to work as tax collectors and take in enormous profits, allowing the government revenue to grow almost twice as fast as the growth of GDP in the new millennium.[57] The easy profits enjoyed by state enterprises shelter them from market discipline and hide their weaknesses. With access to monopoly profits, state enterprises are freed from the constant pressure of innovating to satisfy consumers, and are thus inadvertently deprived of the learning mechanism that is indispensable if any firm is to survive market competition. In addition, the artificially high profit margins are readily translated into a widening gap in wages between monopolized and competitive sectors. For example, while the sectors monopolized by the state employ 8 percent of China's non-farming workforce, the state workforce takes away 55 percent of wages.[58] Moreover, the monopoly profits enjoyed by state enterprises give them advantages even in sectors open to private firms. State enterprises also use their political connections and monopoly profits to force or buy out private firms, undermining market competition. In addition, the presence of state enterprises also undermines the development of China's capital market. For example, banks prefer to lend money to state enterprises because of their protected profit margins, not to mention the political preferences that state banks have shown for state-owned enterprises. Private firms, particularly start-ups, are often denied access to bank credit, partly because they face high uncertainties and are more likely to fail. As a result, state banks, with a ready and safe group of clients, can afford not to do business with private firms, denying themselves the opportunities to learn how to effectively screen and monitor the debtors. This makes them even more reluctant to extend credit to private firms.

The entrenched socialist view, which is still commonly invoked by the Chinese government, that public ownership always serves public interests and guarantees shared prosperity is clearly no more than wishful thinking. On this issue, the ancient Chinese statesmen and philosophers actually knew better. It is relevant to quote at length a Chinese classic, the *Book of Lord Shang* (Lord Shang twice helped the emperor of Qin to reform his state, which ultimately unified China in 221 BC).

> Law is the authoritative principle of the people and is the basis of government; it is what shapes the people. Trying to govern while eliminating the law is like a desire not to be hungry while eliminating food, or a desire not

to be cold while eliminating clothes, or a desire to go east while one moves west. It is clear enough that there is no hope of realizing it.

That a hundred men will chase after a single hare that runs away, is not for the sake of the hare, for when they are sold everywhere on the market, even a thief does not dare to take one away, because their legal title is definite. Thus if the legal title is not definite, then even men like Yao, Shun, Yu, or Tang would all rush to chase after it. Now if laws and mandates are not clear, nor their titles definite, the men of empires have opportunities for contention; in their contentions people will differ and there will be no definiteness. The ruler may make laws from above, the inferior people will quarrel and contend, the law will not be definite and the inferiors will prevail. This may be called a condition where rights and duties are indefinite. When rights and duties are indefinite, even men like Yao and Shun will become crooked and commit acts of wickedness, how much more then the mass of the people! This is the way in which wickedness and wrong-doing will be greatly stimulated, the ruler of men will be despoiled of his authority and power, will ruin his country and bring disaster upon the land and its people.[59]

A similar stress on the delineation of rights can be found in the work of a still earlier Chinese philosopher, the *Book of Master Shen*: "[When] a rabbit crosses a street; one hundred people will run after it. Even though those who chase after the rabbit are greedy, no one blames them because to whom the rabbit belongs is unsettled. The meat market is full of rabbits. People walk by but barely look at them. This is not because people do not want the rabbits. But after the rights are settled, even greedy people do not quarrel any more."[60]

The strong presence of state enterprises would be less troubling if the state subjects itself to the rule of law, as recommended by Lord Shang. But few socialist economies, with a heavy presence of state ownership, have ever been ruled by a government under the rule of law. When a government stays above the law, but possesses enormous assets, it inevitably leaves many rights unspecified and open in the public domain. This corrupts politics, invites plunder and engenders injustice, planting the seeds of social unrest and political disorder. When state enterprises operate above the rule of law and make themselves immune to market competition they not only threaten the operation of private firms, but also, as Master Shen and Lord Shang have made clear, put the economic and political foundation of the whole society at risk.

VIII

A market economy does not operate in an institutional vacuum. When the price system is investigated in isolation from the broad institutional setting under which it works, all non-market institutions, including the state, the law, social norms, and moral codes, are deemed external to and separated from the working of the market. Nothing can be further from the truth. Economists have increasingly been trained to forget that most economic phenomena are what sociologists call "*social* facts," distinct from natural or physical facts on the one hand, and psychological data on the other.[61] Contract, money, and property rights are social constructions. A distinctive feature of social versus natural or psychological phenomena is, as Hayek reminded us many decades ago, that "[they] are what people think they are."[62] What is known as a social fact in one society at one time – the belief that business partners are treated honestly, for example, or that business contracts are usually honored – may not be so in another place or at a different time.

In this regard, our confidence in the long-term prospects for the Chinese market economy is further strengthened by another development in China, less visible than China's growth record and the rise of market institutions but of no less significance to the future of market economy in China. In 2004, a new Chinese edition of the *Wealth of Nations* was published.[63] The first was translated by Yan Fu (1854–1921), and published in 1902; the second came out in 1930 (with a revised edition in 1972). In the preface to this new Chinese edition, the translators explained why a new translation was necessary. "China has now returned to the market economy. A market economy calls for a corresponding economic theory. And Smith's *Wealth of Nations* is the theoretical foundation of the market economy."[64] Since China's re-embracement of the market economy, it has become an imperative for the ordinary Chinese to have access to the *Wealth of Nations*, but the language used in the first two translations is too outdated and scholarly for current readers.

It is of great interest to note that the recent translators of the *Wealth of Nations* bemoan the under-appreciation of the *Theory of Moral Sentiments* by contemporary economists.[65] This has resulted in an unbalanced understanding of Smith, and worse, a much impoverished economics. In China, Smith is read and respected as the author of both the *Wealth of Nations* and the *Theory of Moral Sentiments*.

In an interview with Lionel Barber, editor of the *Financial Times* on February 2nd, 2009, Wen Jiabao, China's Premier, stated that "The society that we desire is one of equity and justice, is one in which people can achieve all round development in a free and equal environment. That is also why I like Adam Smith's *Theory of Moral Sentiments* very much."[66] When asked about the future of China's political and economic reform, Wen had the following to say.

In 1776, Adam Smith wrote the *Wealth of the Nations*. And in the same historical period, he wrote the *Theory of Moral Sentiments*. Adam Smith made excellent arguments in his *Theory of Moral Sentiments*. He said in the book to the effect that if fruits of a society's economic development cannot be shared by all, it is morally unsound and risky, as it is bound to jeopardize social stability. If the wealth of a society is concentrated in the hands of a small number of people, then this is against the popular will, and the society is bound to be unstable.[67]

In an earlier interview with *Newsweek*'s Fareed Zakaria on September 23rd, 2008, Wen made a similar comment: "I very much value morality, and I do believe that entrepreneurs, economists and statesmen alike should pay much more attention to morality and ethics. In my mind, the highest standard to measure the ethics and morality is justice."[68] On February 28th, 2009, when Wen shared with Chinese readers via the internet his understanding of Smith, he stressed that Smith actually emphasized two "invisible hands" in the working of a commercial society, one being the market, the other morality.[69]

Wen was absolutely right in recognizing the crucial importance of the laws of justice and rules of morality that Smith placed in the working of society. Justice, according to Smith, is

the main pillar that upholds the whole edifice. If it is removed, the great, the immense fabric of human society, that fabric which to raise and support seems in this world, if I may say so, to have been the peculiar and darling care of Nature, must in a moment crumble into atoms. In order to enforce the observation of justice, therefore, Nature has implanted in the human breast that consciousness of ill-desert, those terrors of merited punishment which attend upon its violation, as the great safe-guards of the association of mankind, to protect the weak, to curb the violent, and to chastise the guilty. Men, though naturally sympathetic, feel so little for another, with whom they have no particular connexion, in comparison of what they feel for themselves; the misery of one, who is merely their fellow-creature, is of so little importance to them in comparison even of a small conveniency of their own; they have it so much in their power to hurt him, and may have so many temptations to do so, that if this principle did not stand up within them in his defence, and overawe them into a respect for his innocence, they would, like wild beasts, be at all times ready to fly upon him; and a man would enter an assembly of men as he enters a den of lions.[70]

Comparing justice and morality, Smith believed that "the rules of justice are the only rules of morality which are precise and accurate; that those of all the other virtues are loose, vague, and indeterminate; that the first may be compared to the rules of grammar; the others to those which critics lay down for the attainment of what is sublime and elegant in composition, and which present us rather with a general idea of the perfection we ought to aim at, than afford us any certain and infallible directions for acquiring it."[71] Nonetheless, as Smith also pointed out, the hard and definite laws of justice cannot work unless supported by loose but pervasive principles of morality.

Wen's reading of Smith on inequality is clearly influenced by China's rising economic inequality, which has of late become a serious social problem.[72] In *The Theory of Moral Sentiments*, the term "justice" appears ninety-three times and "injustice" fifty-two times. In comparison, "equality" appears four times and "inequality" twice. When Smith talked about equality, he was more concerned with equality of treatment by the sovereign power to all subjects, the violation of which is an act of flagrant injustice. Smith did not intent this to refer to the equal distribution of all of produce from labor. Indeed, as Smith recognized, economic inequality as so currently understood is inevitable.

> Wherever there is great property there is great inequality. For one very rich man there must be at least five hundred poor, and the affluence of the few supposes the indigence of the many. The affluence of the rich excites the indignation of the poor, who are often both driven by want, and prompted by envy, to invade his possessions. It is only under the shelter of the civil magistrate that the owner of that valuable property, which is acquired by the labour of many years, or perhaps of many successive generations, can sleep a single night in security. He is at all times surrounded by unknown enemies, whom, though he never provoked, he can never appease, and from whose injustice he can be protected only by the powerful arm of the civil magistrate continually held up to chastise it. The acquisition of valuable and extensive property, therefore, necessarily requires the establishment of civil government.[73]

Because economic inequality is inevitable, the laws of justice become critical to sustain social order. Smith was fully aware that "No society can surely be flourishing and happy, of which the far greater part of the members are poor and miserable."[74] If not for other reasons, flagrantly polarized distribution of wealth could flare up resentment against the rich, which could run so deeply and widely that even the most powerful and ruthless state cannot control it through coercion alone, leaving the rich always unsecure and even in fear. If just for the sake of the rich, the acquisition of wealth must conform to the laws of justice. When it is believed that justice is observed and opportunities are open to all, even the least fortunate class of society by and large respect existing social institutions – whatever their faults – and accept their social positions. They would work hard to provide better conditions for their children, instead of challenging or overthrowing the prevailing social system through revolution.

Thirty years ago it would have been inconceivable for a leader of a socialist country to read, let alone praise, Adam Smith, the intellectual forefather of modern capitalism. It is striking that Smith has emerged as a guiding figure in China thirty-two years after the death of Mao. It is even more extraordinary that a Premier of China admires Smith as the author of the *Wealth of Nations* and the *Theory of Moral Sentiments*. How many western political leaders have read the *Theory of Moral Sentiments*? On many different occasions Wen has recommended *The Theory of Moral Sentiments* to Chinese businessmen, writers, college students, and the general public. On the popular Chinese online bookstore, dangdang.com, there are more than a dozen Chinese editions of *The Theory of Moral Sentiments*, from different translators and publishers. On the cover page of several, it is printed in big red characters, "A Classic by a Master, Highly Recommended Five Times by Premier Wen." After thirty years of market transformation, China has not only endorsed capitalism as an economic system which facilitates the creation of wealth, but also its moral character and ethical foundation, without which capitalism itself cannot be sustained.

In one respect, however, we should not be surprised that Smith is appreciated in China as a moral philosopher and the founder of modern economics. Confucianism stresses the importance of personal ethics as the foundation for social harmony. Confucius stressed that law could not be the only or primary source of social order.[75] Instead, he took benevolence as the ultimate virtue and the foundation of social harmony. Clearly, morality itself is not sufficient to make a modern society well governed; Smith makes this point himself. It is equally clear, however, that no society could possibly be well governed without a strong moral code, a point rarely considered in modern economics. A market economy would be severely crippled if all businessmen behave opportunistically, cheating partners whenever they think they can or reneging on contracts for short-term gains.

A traditional Chinese moral precept, "do not give up a good deed because it is trivial; do not commit a misconduct because it is trivial," ostensibly contradicts the basic tenet of modern economics. The economic principle of maximization would command one to commit misconduct as long as the personal gain overwhelms the cost. This is clearly expressed in the economic approach to crime. Doing a good deed, on the other hand, would be mocked for its violation of self-interest. This Chinese teaching focuses on an aspect of human nature that is largely ignored in modern economics; that our character is formed gradually and almost imperceptibly by what we do. Since the economy is essentially about people making a living, the national character of an economy inevitably reflects the character of its people. Frank Knight made a valuable point in stressing that a society should be judged more by "the wants it generates, the type of character it forms in its people, than by its efficiency in satisfying wants as they exist at the time."[76] Modern economics takes as a given the wants that the choice of resource allocation intends to satisfy and disregards the long-term cumulative impact that choice inevitably has on shaping the wants – it takes a snapshot view of a continuous process. But the economy both satisfies wants and simultaneously sows the seeds of new wants, which in turn drives the next round of economic production and consumption. Any action that promises short-term gains but has a corrupting effect on the moral character of the people dims the long-term future of the market economy.

IX

How China became capitalist is an extraordinary tale. Steven Cheung, who thirty years ago correctly predicted that China would turn capitalist, did not expect that the Chinese market transformation would happen so rapidly.[77] The Chinese leaders as well as economists both within and outside China were caught by surprise when the marginal revolutions brought market forces back to China so speedily. The economic forces that tilted China towards capitalism in the late 1970s have grown stronger over the past three decades of reform. Despite rising economic inequality, economic gains are widely shared in China. Economic freedom and private entrepreneurship, even though still constrained by remaining state monopolies, are flourishing across the country. China will carry on experimenting with the market economy in the foreseeable future. Drawing upon its rich and long traditions in commerce and private entrepreneurship, capitalism with Chinese characteristics will continue to strike out on its own way.

But what exactly is capitalism with Chinese characteristics? In other words, what kind of capitalism has China ended up with after its extraordinary market transformation? Most commentators have focused on the visible hand of the Chinese government and the remaining monopoly power of the Chinese Communist Party as the defining features. While these are undeniably important, they do not hold the key to understanding capitalism in China.

According to the World Bank, the GDP of the United States, amid a devastating recession, stands at 14.58 trillion USD (2010 data).[78] In comparison, the Chinese GDP is 5.88 trillion USD. Since China has a population four times as large as that of the United States (1.34 billion versus 312 million), China still lags far behind the United States in terms of GDP per capita (4260 USD versus 47,140 USD) and labor productivity.[79] Even if China becomes the world's largest economy in the middle of the twenty-first century, as many have so predicted, it will still be ranked as a mediocre performer in terms of productivity unless it significantly improves its innovation capacity. This will set an unprecedented example in modern human history: the largest economy in the world will not be the most productive one.

The same structural flaw in the Chinese economy manifests itself in another manner, more visible to outside observers. Today, "Made in China" can be readily found in Wal-Mart as well as high-end American retail and department stores. From shoes, clothing, to furniture and electronic products, China's manufacturing sector now produces almost all types of consumer goods. The rapid increase in quantity of Chinese exports has notably benefited global consumers with the advantage of a wide range of consumer products at the "China price." Nonetheless, most American consumers would be hard pressed to name any Chinese brands, even though their houses are full of products made in China.

This weakness of the Chinese economy becomes readily perceptible if we take a historical perspective. When Britain was the leading economy in the nineteenth century and when the United States became the economic superpower in the twentieth century, they not only invented a wide range of new products but also created new industries. It was their lead in innovation and productivity that defined their economic power. When the Great Exhibition was held in 1851 at the Crystal Palace in London, the English exhibits "held the lead in almost every field where strength, durability, utility and quality were concerned, whether in iron and steel, machinery or textiles."[80] The twentieth century saw the rise of American giants Rockefeller, Carnegie, Ford, GM, GE, Boeing, IBM, Coco-Cola, P&G and, more recently, HP, Apple, Intel, Motorola, and Microsoft. And the list goes on and on. When Japan became the second largest economy in the late 1960s, it became home to Sony, Fuji, Toyota, Honda, Nissan, Mazda, Canon, Toshiba, Panasonic, JVC, and Sharp. South Korea, whose economy is one-sixth of China's (and has only 48 million people), can boast of Samsung, LG, Hyundai, Kia, and Daewoo.

By contrast, even the best-known Chinese firms, such as Lenovo, Huawei, Tsingtao, Haier, and Geely, are not household names in the West. The top ten Chinese firms listed by Fortune are Sinopec, China National Petroleum, State Grid Corporation, Industrial and Commercial Bank of China, China Mobil Limited, China Life Insurance, Bank of China, China Construction Bank, China Southern Power Grid, and China Telecom. These are all state-owned and concentrated in energy and services (banking, communication, and insurance); they are not open to global competition. While Chinese manufacturing firms are globally competitive, most of them can only compete on price in the global market due to the advantage gained by low production costs; they are still struggling to provide new and better products. Short on innovation and lacking their own distinctive products, many Chinese firms depend on ordered manufacturing – taking orders from overseas markets and selling them under foreign brand names. This situation – best described as "production without products" – does not bode well for an economy aiming to top the world. As late as 2009, the United States still manufactured more goods (1.7 trillion USD in manufacturing value added) than China (1.3 trillion USD).[81] After a decades-long decline in employment (fewer than 12 million workers at the second quarter of 2010), the US manufacturing sector still enjoys a significant lead over China, where manufacturing employs over 100 million Chinese workers. Moreover, given the large presence of foreign firms and joint ventures in China, the growth of domestic capacity in manufacturing in China is far less impressive than the name, the "workshop of the world," might suggest.

X

The economic reforms that have freed most Chinese firms, forcing them to face market competition, have not had the same liberating effect on Chinese universities. Most Chinese universities and the educational system in general still remain under state control. It is here that the most serious deficiency of China's market reform reveals itself. This deficiency stands at the root of the troubling symptoms we have indentified above, as well as other shortcomings in the Chinese economy.

Ironically, the post-Mao educational reform started in 1977 with the resumption of the college entrance examination, predating the 1978 Third Plenum. At the time Deng Xiaoping proposed that the Party should serve as the "logistics department" for Chinese scientists and scholars, enabling them to pursue scientific research independently and freely. Deng and other Chinese leaders predicted that, unless China became a nation of scientific discovery and technological innovation, it could not possibly accomplish "socialist modernization."[82] Unfortunately, Deng's pledge did not stop the government from dictating how Chinese universities and research institutions operated. Most Chinese universities are run as an administrative bureaucracy under pervasive ideological control rather than as institutions of learning. As a result, while the Chinese market transformation has spawned a booming market for goods and services and allowed China to become a leading global player in manufacturing, it has not yet created an active market for ideas. Indeed, the whole process of creating, spreading, and consuming ideas, from the education system to the media, has remained under tight ideological control and state surveillance.

The most significant change in Chinese universities in the past few decades of rapid market reform has been the commercialization and expansion of higher education. Under socialism, higher education was fully funded by the state and available only to a tiny percentage of the population, if it was provided at all (during much of the Cultural Revolution, Chinese universities were shut down entirely). At the end of the 1980s, Chinese universities started to enroll fee-paying students who otherwise would not have been able to attend college because of their poor performance at the national college entrance examination. As a result, the state ceased to be the only funder of higher education. The pace of commercialization and expansion of the higher education sector picked up greatly in the 1990s, giving rise to what is widely referred to as "China's great leap in higher education." In 1995, only 5 percent of age group 18–22 had access to higher education; by 2007, that had increased to 23 percent.[83] China is now the world largest producer of Ph.D.s. Yet Qian Xuesen, a most respected Chinese scientist, asked a sobering question before his death in 2009: "Why have Chinese universities not produced a single world-class original thinker or innovative scientist since 1949?"[84]

The education system makes it all too clear that growth in quantity will not compensate for a lack of progress in quality. No wonder the question raised by Qian, widely referred to in China as the "Qian puzzle," has attracted extensive media coverage. The fatal organizational flaw of Chinese universities is their lack of autonomy. The majority of Chinese universities remain primarily funded by the state and under the strict control of the Ministry of Education. The Ministry appoints Party secretaries and presidents of major Chinese universities. Within a university, the Party secretary enjoys a higher administrative ranking than the president, and often has more say in running the university. All the degree programs that the universities offer must first be approved by the Ministry. Through its direct control of finance, personnel, and degree programs, the Ministry of Education exercises a pervasive influence over Chinese universities, a level of control the Chinese government only exercised over state-owned enterprises in the pre-reform era. During the period of reform when the Chinese state-owned enterprises were gaining autonomy from government agents and opening up to competition, China's universities moved in the opposite direction. The most noticeable competition faced by the universities comes from abroad. Tens of thousands of China's brightest students leave China every year for universities in Japan, Australia, Canada, the United States, and Europe. Their decision attests to their disappointment with the offerings of their own universities.

Under rigid governmental control, Chinese universities have become more skilled in currying favor with the Ministry of Education than in offering innovative research and educational programs; this situation is not so different from state-owned enterprises before reform. In addition, hard pressed for financial resources, Chinese universities compete in their enrollment figures and focus on other avenues of money-making. Consequently, higher education in China may have been commercialized and have expanded, but the education reform has not brought about a free market in ideas. On the contrary, as the state pours money into its designated projects in the hope of creating world-class universities, the Ministry of Education has come to wield even more power over Chinese universities. This means that they are more responsive to administrative directives than to the emerging challenges in higher education.

In 1995 and 1998, the Chinese government launched Project 221 and Project 985, with the aim of building up a few world-class universities and critical academic disciplines.[85] The Ministry of Education introduced the piece rate compensation system to Chinese universities, an incentive scheme that had served well in manufacturing firms. University professors are evaluated and rewarded according to their publications. The total compensation of a professor typically consists of a basic salary, which is tied to his or her academic rank, and a performance-based reward, which is mainly dependent on publications. In most cases, the basic salary is set so low that all professors have to publish to earn a decent living. Not surprisingly, this scheme, which is now widely applied, has turned Chinese professors into publication machines. On the positive side, China has become a significant producer of academic articles worldwide. But this growth has come with a steep price tag, which is best demonstrated by the "Qian puzzle."

In almost all human endeavor, the gap in achievement between the average and the very best is often enormous. In all science, the subject has historically been carried forward by a few giants. Human ingenuity works best and science has a higher chance to advance when self-selected and motivated scholars are given the freedom and support to pursue their own research. A performance-based reward system can force scholars to publish, but nothing works more effectively to suffocate creativity and originality than this overt link to material interests.

Given the pervasive administrative meddling of the state, it is not difficult to understand the mediocre performance of Chinese universities. As Milton Friedman remarked, the surest way to destroy an industry is to protect it with state monopoly. The state monopoly in China has severely curtailed the production of ideas. Administrative interference is so severe that even in areas such as physical and biological sciences and technology, where the impact of political ideology is limited, a free market for ideas hardly exists. As a result, the Chinese traditional proverb "to let one hundred flowers bloom and let one hundred schools of thought contend" remains a pipedream.

As far as Chinese universities are concerned, the government essentially controls both inputs (finance and personnel) and outputs (degree programs), leaving them very little autonomy. Recently, the delayed opening of the South University of Science and Technology provided a frustrating but illustrative example of this situation.[86] This new university is a local initiative, fully supported by the Shenzhen municipal government. Even though it is not a private university, the South University of Science and Technology will operate independently from the Ministry of Education as well as the local government. It is modeled on the Hong Kong University of Science and Technology and aims to be a first-rate research institution in South China, providing a much needed hub of scientific research and technological innovation for the fast-growing regional economy. The new university planned to open in the fall of 2010. But after more than three years of preparation, the Ministry of Education refused to approve and accredit its degree programs, thus making it hard for the university to attract students.

In addition to education, Chinese law and politics have also suffered severely from the lack of an active market for ideas. Although Chinese economic performance has surpassed the wildest expectations, progress in political reform has been disappointing. Many problems explicitly acknowledged in the 1978 Communiqué are still present and many of its objectives remain unfulfilled. "The bureaucratic attitude of paying no attention at all to urgent problems in the people's livelihood" is still pervasive. China is in no way near the point where "the constitutional rights of citizens must be resolutely protected and no one has the right to infringe upon them."[87] After more than three decades, the Chinese legal system is still far away from where it can "guarantee the equality of all people before the people's laws and deny anyone the privilege of being above the law."[88]

The government's monopoly on ideas has given rise to the dire situation that Deng had deplored at the beginning of reform, that is, "opposing the leaders' views is deemed as against the law."[89] Without a forum to express their concerns or articulate their views, dissidents are forced into conflict with the government. People of critical thinking and independent thought, the most valuable human assets in any society, often find themselves labeled political dissidents. In turn, political dissidents often find themselves deemed to be "anti-Party," or "anti-socialism," a charge that can end their career, if not their life.

From the economy to education, from law to politics, the absence of an active market for ideas has left its imprint throughout Chinese society. On the surface, the Chinese economy has achieved remarkable growth since the inception of reform, even without a free market for ideas. Enriched and empowered by a free market for goods and services, the political leadership, which bases its legitimacy on continuous economic growth, might think that the market for goods and services is all that is needed.[90]

But nothing could be further from the truth. The lack of a market for ideas is directly responsible for the lack of innovation in science and technology, the Achilles' heel in China's growing manufacturing sector. The dearth of innovation and remaining state monopolies gravely reduces the range of investment opportunities that Chinese entrepreneurs find profitable. Taking manufacturing orders from others rather than inventing their own product becomes the dominant strategy for Chinese entrepreneurs. Without a free and open market for ideas, China cannot sustain its economic growth or advance itself into a global center of technological innovation or scientific discovery. At the beginning of reform, China quickly began to close the enormous gap in science, technology, and know-how between itself and the West almost as soon as the ideological blockades had been removed. But to sustain a similar growth rate in the future, China has to become more innovative, providing new products to global consumers with less and cleaner energy. While it has been transformed in a short period of three decades from a poor agrarian socialist economy into a leading dynamic manufacturing powerhouse of the global economy, China still has a long way to go to become a powerhouse in the production of ideas.

Moreover, the lack of a market for ideas also undermines China's effort to build a harmonious society and renovate itself culturally. Harmony, as well expressed in its Chinese meaning, requires the presence of different voices. Harmony arises only as a result of interactions of different voices through a market for ideas. The fate of any government must turn on its capacity to create and defend material abundance. But it also depends on its capacity to cultivate and sustain a universe of ideas. This universe of ideas resembles what Karl Popper called the "World 3,"[91] including products of human mind resulting from our attempt to understand who we are and how the natural and social world works. These two tasks, often called the development of "material and spiritual civilization" in China, are intrinsically intertwined. The world of material abundance will be boring and brittle if it is not enlivened by a rich universe of ideas; the universe of ideas will be illusory and short-lived if not rested firmly on a world of abundance. In our contemporary world, as the economy becomes more and more knowledge-intensive, the long-term health of the market for goods depends on a vibrant market for ideas through which knowledge is discovered, shared, and accumulated. The pace at which new enterprises are established, new products are invented, and new industries are created is critically dependent on an active market for ideas. Moreover, the market for ideas drives the market for goods and services in a fundamental way. As the market for goods operates under the assumption of consumer sovereignty, it is the market for ideas that directly shapes consumer wants, crucially determines what kind of consumers (as well as entrepreneurs, politicians, and lawyers) we find in the economy, their characters and values, and thus ultimately decides what the market for goods is and how effectively it works.

With a competitive market for goods and services, China has long been a favored destination for foreign capital, attracting investment from many of the global Fortune 500 companies. Without an active market for ideas, however, China's own human talents are fleeing the country. The mounting surplus China has accumulated in financial capital is only matched by a tremendous deficit in human capital. This glaring imbalance reveals a profound flaw in the market economy with Chinese characteristics as it exists today.

XI

State intervention is not the only force in China preventing the rise of the market for ideas. As a historical fact, modern Chinese politics, under both the Kuomintang and the Communist Party, has rarely been receptive to the market for ideas. At the turn of the twentieth century, when China was struggling for its survival, facing western powers from without and infighting among warlords from within, the modern political parties that first emerged in China were overwhelmingly preoccupied with national survival.[92] Both the Kuomintang and the Chinese Communist Party were born as secret revolutionary organizations, and they quickly turned into quasi-military affairs. Heavily influenced by the Russian Revolution, both quickly resorted to terror and violence, and valued discipline and control. The Communist International was directly involved in the setup of the Chinese Communist Party and the reorganization of the Kuomintang during the 1920s. This legacy has had a lasting and formative impact on the development of modern political parties in China. Moreover, the hostilities between them led each to inflict terror and violence on the other, reinforcing their authoritarian inclination to use force and coercion. Under such circumstances, Mao's statement that "the power of government comes out of the barrel of a gun" encapsulated the reality of Chinese politics. A market for ideas was preserved only beyond the reach of both parties in places like the Shanghai International Settlement and in Hong Kong.

Probably influenced by the Japanese translation of the word "party," both the Kuomintang and the Chinese Communist Party referred to themselves as *dang* in Chinese. This is a term with strong negative connotations in Chinese political thought. Party politics had been persistently regarded as a secretive, insidious force, promoting narrow group interests detrimental to good governance and public interests. This is suggested by the Chinese axiom *"jie tang ying shi,"* which literally means "form parties to pursue private interests." This is in direct contrast to the spirit of traditional Chinese political thinking, *"tian xia wei gong,"* or "the world is for the public."[93] The experience of party politics throughout the twentieth century in China has not negated the validity of this axiom, but this historical legacy does not bode well for multiparty competition as a way to bring about a free market for ideas in China.

In China, the government's monopolization of the production and transmission of ideas is largely driven by fear of sedition. The first Qin Emperor buried alive hundreds of Confucian scholars and burned books to suppress ideas that he deemed a source of danger to his rule. But, as a Tang poem put it, "Even before the ashes in the burning pit became cold, riots had begun in Shandong; it turned out that Liu and Xiang [two riot leaders] did not read books." Mao knew this poem by heart,[94] but its historical warning still failed to stop him from instituting his Anti-Rightist Movement in 1957. The Anti-Rightist Movement

led to the persecution of millions, but perhaps the most damaging consequence of this oppression of the market in ideas was to undermine the regime's
capability to govern.

A salient weakness of government bureaucracy, or any big organization for
that matter, is that decision-makers at the top are often at the mercy of information controlled by those below.[95] As a result, hierarchical organizations,
including government bureaucracy, often find themselves trapped in a double asymmetry of power and information. Decision-makers at the top are given
enormous discretionary power but fed with narrowly selected and often biased
information; gatekeepers at the lower levels of the power pyramid are better
informed, but with little power to act. An active market for ideas, independent
of political power, provides an indispensable institutional safeguard to ensure
that decision-makers are reasonably well informed. As Wang Fu, a Confucian
philosopher in the Han dynasty, put it, "[the Emperor] is enlightened because
he listens to different views; he becomes benighted when he heeds only one
side." After the Anti-Rightist Movement was launched in 1957, a government
bureaucracy that once was disciplined, responsive, and efficient quickly became
demoralized and degenerated into a blind, self-destructive political machine,
bringing about in peacetime the worst man-made famine in history.

That some "rightists" were seditious does not justify the closing down of
the market for ideas. An ideal society is not one entirely free from the risk
of sedition. Given the cost of controlling sedition, a society is better off not
eliminating it. After a certain point, the cost of further reducing the risk of
sedition simply outweighs any possible additional gains. Moreover, since a well-
intended but misinformed political machine can inflict a catastrophe on its
own people, as shown in the Great Leap Forward, a market for ideas, as imper-
fect and vulnerable as it is, offers an effective remedy to the double asymmetry
problem that government bureaucracy can fall victim to.

While a market for ideas can be readily suppressed and fatally undermined by
political censorship, an oppressive state is not the only predator. A less alarming, but equally dangerous, enemy of an open market for ideas comes from a
different source. In China, Marxism has been, and still is, taught to students
from primary school as a "scientific" theory and the final truth on human history and social evolution. Even when Marxism has been challenged and largely
discredited in the past thirty years of reform, the dogmatic teaching of Marxism
has cultivated a certain habit of thought, which has survived Marxism itself: the
mentality to take truth as final, complete, permanent, and authoritative. But
all empirical knowledge is exactly the opposite; it is provisional, incomplete,
and conjectural. For an open market in ideas to operate, participants have to
recognize that an unimpeachable truth does not exist. Truth emerges only in
an endless struggle against ignorance and bigotry, and it rarely wins by a single, decisive, once-and-for-all battle. No authority qualifies as the final judge

of truth. It is exactly due to human fallibility and irreducible ignorance in the process of seeking knowledge that an open market for ideas is the best possible tool to get as close to truth as possible. Otherwise, the market for ideas would be unnecessary and wasteful, or worse, subversive and treacherous. A critically minded public, willing to challenge authority, but tolerant and open-minded, offers circumstances conducive to a free market for ideas.[96]

XII

Steven Cheung's prediction that China would become capitalist was essentially based on the analysis that economic gains of adapting the market (for goods and services) would be so substantial as to overwhelm any resistance after China had opened itself up to the outside world. Today, a stronger argument can be made regarding the prospect of the market for ideas in China.

The market for ideas has a root as deep as, and probably more respectable than, the market for goods in China. Confucius is celebrated today in China first and foremost as an educator. It was Confucius who started the first private school in China more than 2000 years ago, ending education as a privilege of the powerful. Ever since then, education – the creation and transmission of knowledge – was largely left in private hands, even after the rise of the civil service examination. Despite much opposition and adversity, an active market for ideas was a persistent feature of Chinese history, generating intriguing technological innovations as well as splendid art and literature that we still enjoy today. In traditional China only a small percentage of the population could afford to devote themselves to study. Today, with the spread of higher education and modern communications, China in the twenty-first century may well witness a blossoming market for ideas.

The primary creators of ideas in traditional Chinese society, the literati class or *shi*, had a unique social, political, and cultural status that cannot be found in many other historical civilizations. This literati class essentially ruled China during much of its history, from the Qin unification of China in 221 BC to the fall of the Qing dynasty in 1911. In addition to staffing the state bureaucracy as mandarins, *shi* also served as the moral compass of Confucian society.[97] For the great man (*da zhang fu*), the embodiment of *shi*, in the memorable words of Mencius, "wealth and fame never mean much to him, poverty and obscurity never sway him, and imposing forces never awe him." Today's China is no longer a *shi*-centered society. Under the current political system, the intellectuals, the modern successors to *shi*, are not as dominant in politics or as active and influential in civil affairs as the literati class once was. But the ideal of *shi* and its moral calling still strike a strong chord with many educated Chinese. Trained in humanities, social sciences, and modern science and technology, Chinese intellectuals today have a much better and more sophisticated understanding of how nature and human society work than their predecessors. With an active market for ideas, there is no reason why China cannot witness another cultural renaissance that rivals past glories achieved in the Tang and Song dynasties.

Without a free market for ideas, the Chinese political system is often a cause of pessimism. But pessimists tend to forget that the same facts also support cautious optimism. China has achieved an astonishing growth record over the past three decades in spite of many serious political problems. Hence, the rise of a market for ideas and changes in the Chinese political system for the better would help to release further creativity and entrepreneurship among the Chinese people and cut down the institutional cost of running the market system, thus providing a strong source of economic growth. The potential marginal benefits from adopting an active market for ideas are even higher than the expected gains that led Cheung in the early 1980s to predict China's move to capitalism.

Moreover, the market for ideas points to a gradual but direct, and more viable, avenue for political reform in China. The absence of political democracy and the market for ideas in China should not lead us to conflate the two. Adam Smith, for example, did not have the right to vote, a political entitlement we take for granted today in any democracy. But Smith enjoyed freedom of speech and expression, enabling his work to enrich the market for ideas forever. It is possible to have a flourishing market in ideas without a government being elected within a multi-party democracy even though the affinity between the market for ideas and democracy is undeniable. It is true that the market for ideas flourishes in most democratic countries but is harshly suppressed in most non-democracies. At the same time, however, the tyranny of the majority is inimical to the working of the market for ideas. In a multi-party environment, when political leaders vie to win a majority vote, which is regarded as the ultimate source of political legitimacy, few in the political system can afford to indulge in genuine and meaningful political debates. Even in a democracy, when the political system depends on votes for its survival, whether it facilitates a free market for ideas can become secondary.[98]

While democratization (or its lack thereof) has attracted much attention in today's political debate, an open market for ideas is a key institution fundamental to the working of the political system, be it a democracy or not. There are democracies where there is little genuine intellectual debate and, at the same time, throughout history, there have been societies that have been melting pots for new ideas that have not been democracies. A significant advantage of the free market for ideas is its compatibility with diverse cultural and political systems. A market for ideas clearly flourished in China during the Warring States period when many schools of thought, including Confucianism, Taoism, and Legalism, emerged; it also flourished during the Tang dynasty when Chang'an, the capital city, attracted scholars from Korea,

Japan, Vietnam, India, and Persia. A market for ideas flouished in the city-states of ancient Greece; it also prospered at Baghdad between the ninth and thirteenth centuries when the city was the center of learning for the Abbasid Empire, where many of the tales in *One Thousand and One Nights* were set. Without imposing a single uniform political system, the market for ideas, instead, fosters tolerance, cultivates diversity, facilitates experiment and innovation, and enhances social resilience. A market for ideas is not always synonymous with democracy.[99]

As remarkable as the Chinese market transformation is, capitalism with Chinese characteristics is impoverished by the lack of a free market for ideas; this deficiency has become the most restrictive bottleneck in China's economic and social development. Ever since the start of economic reform, the Chinese government has been persistently calling for the "emancipation of the mind," but nothing is more effective than an active market for ideas in freeing people's minds.[100] Indeed, without this, any "emancipation of the mind" is doomed. The creative minds of the Chinese people and their inventive power have been underexploited. This is unfortunate since capitalism with Chinese characteristics could definitely be more innovative and more driven by quality rather than quantity. As the largest producer of Ph.D.s in the world, China could have contributed much more to the growth of human knowledge. In today's world, new products and industries, novel ideas and practices, flexible and innovative organizations and institutions urgently need to tackle global challenges, from poverty and disease to war, from energy conservation and water shortage to environmental protection. We simply cannot afford to set aside the human potential of one-fifth of humanity.

XII

The post-Mao Chinese economic reform in the past few decades has profoundly transformed the Chinese economy and society. At Mao's death in 1976, China was one of the poorest countries in the world, with a GDP per capita below 200 USD. By 2010, China was the world's second largest economy, with a GDP per capita at more than 4000 USD. During the same time span, China's share of the global economy rose from below 2 percent to about 9 percent. Private entrepreneurship was strictly forbidden during Mao's era; it now thrives throughout the country and stands firmly as the backbone of the Chinese economy. With the world's largest population of internet and cell phone users and the largest car market in the world, Chinese society is open, energetic, mobile, and well informed, full of dynamism and aspiration. Even Chinese universities have recently shown signs of improvement, realizing academic freedom as a precondition for excellence. There is still tremendous room for growth in the Chinese economy.

No one would have believed it if the tale of Chinese market transformation had been told beforehand. Probably the only economist who had predicted its coming, Steven Cheung repeatedly underestimated its speed. Those few who believed in Cheung's analysis and prediction thought it would take a hundred years, not twenty or thirty.

It is also extraordinary for another reason. The reform efforts undertaken by the post-Mao leadership were meant to be a "socialist revolution," turning China from a backward country to "a great, modern, socialist power." China did not abandon socialism when it began its reform. Throughout reform the Chinese government remained committed to socialism. Only under the crushing pressure of famine and unemployment was private entrepreneurship allowed some breathing room in rural and urban China. But once the floodgate of private entrepreneurship was opened, a series of marginal revolutions, rather than state-led reform initiatives, quickly brought market forces back to the Chinese economy. While socialism was simply banished from Moscow, Warsaw, and Prague, it was defeated on its own terms in Sichuan, Anhui, Zhejiang, and Guangdong.

This is also a tale with distinctive Chinese characteristics. The political debates that have emerged and shaped the course of reform, particularly those on the nature of socialism, did not take place elsewhere. The policy choices regarding centralization and decentralization were rooted in and informed by the political history of imperial China. The philosophical discussions on the criteria of testing truth with facts could only have the significance and resonance that they had through the influence of traditional Chinese culture. In the coming decades, capitalist China will inevitably remain Chinese, as socialist China has unfailingly been, despite the terrible violence inflicted upon Chinese traditions in the course of the twentieth century.

As it stands now, the emerging market economy in China may appear too coarse to many observers in the West, where capitalism has evolved over centuries. Capitalism with Chinese characteristics is very much like traffic in Chinese cities, chaotic and intimidating for many western tourists. Yet Chinese roads deliver more goods and transport more passengers than those in any other country. In a similarly intriguing fashion, the Chinese market economy works in its own way. Because of its unique cultural traditions and political institutions, the Chinese market economy will retain some, and develop more, peculiar Chinese features. It is neither possible nor desirable for the Chinese style of capitalism to rid itself of its individual character. This is by no means a blanket endorsement of capitalism as currently practiced in China, the defects and shortcomings of which are too obvious to hide. But at the same time we should resist our human instinct to embrace what is like us and banish what appears unfamiliar. An open society thrives on diversity and tolerance. Self-imposed uniformity and rigidity have brought a once powerful and seemingly unstoppable train of socialism to a halt. If there is one lesson to be learnt from the failure of socialism, it is that diversity is a cause for celebration not for caution or suspicion.

Historically, China has always been a land of commerce and private entrepreneurship. Confucius, when asked how to govern the state, recommended "(first) to populate the state, (then) to enrich the people, and (last) to educate the people." Lao Tzu, who founded Taoism, stated that "So long as I [the ruler] do not attend to anything, the people will of themselves get prosperous." "The Dao of governing a state," as told by Sima Qian, the grand historian of China, "starts with enriching the people." That Deng Xiaoping's slogan, "getting rich is glorious," served as a battlecry of reform throughout the 1980s reveals how far China had disconnected itself from its traditional teachings in commerce and statecraft. In its attempt to build a market economy with Chinese characteristics at the end of the twentieth century, China, after one century and half of self-doubt and self-denial, has come full circle to embrace its own cultural roots by way of capitalism. On January 11th, 2011, a 9.5 meter high bronze statue of Confucius was quietly erected in Tiananmen Square.[101]

China's long history and its modern manifestations have critically and formatively shaped capitalism in China. As the market economy with Chinese characteristics continues to develop, in ways that we cannot imagine today, layers of Chinese history stand as a firm foundation.

In this regard, a lesson from Mao's era is of great relevance. Immediately after the founding of the People's Republic of China, Mao arranged a meeting with Liang Shuming, whom a sinologist would later call the "last Confucian,"[102] to seek his advice on how to build a new China.[103] Liang was a well-known expert on Chinese philosophy (particularly Confucianism and Buddhism), a scholar of great integrity, pragmatic and active in social affairs. Born in the same year (1893), Liang and Mao had known each other since the late 1910s when Liang was a professor and Mao an assistant librarian at Peking University. Liang was convinced that "building a new China" and "knowing the old China" must go hand in hand. Without a thorough understanding of the old China, both its strengths and weaknesses, the new China would be disoriented and crippled. Mao, however, thought otherwise. In Mao's view, and that of most Chinese leaders at the time, socialism provided a reliable roadmap to prosperity and any legacy of the past was nothing but a hindrance to China's march toward socialism. China knows better now, but only after thirty years of a failed socialist experiment and another thirty years of market transformation. As China is fast moving forward in the twenty-first century, developing a market economy of its own kind and further aligning itself with the global division of labor, it is also going back to its cultural traditions. Bringing the past into the future while openly engaging with the outside world, China stands a favorable chance for another renaissance. An open, tolerant, confident, and innovative China will surprise the world even more in the years to come.

This account of how China became capitalist is not the final word on China's market transformation. There is still much to be learnt about this extraordinary tale. What we have attempted is mainly a historical narrative of the chain of actions that brought it about. But there is no way to present a coherent narrative of how China became capitalist without certain theoretical perspectives. Facts have to be selected and their significance assessed. Neither can be accomplished without proper guidance from theory. "Progress in understanding the working of the economic system," in our view, "will come from an interplay between theory and empirical work. The theory suggests what empirical work might be fruitful, the subsequent empirical work suggests what modification in the theory or rethinking is needed, which in turn leads to new empirical work. If rightly done, scientific research is a never-ending process, but one that leads to greater understanding at each stage."[104] It will take us decades, if not centuries, to fully explain why China became capitalist the way it did, resolving all intriguing puzzles. But we must first establish a solid understanding of how China became capitalist and ascertain exactly what we have to explain before we can possibly venture any causal explanation.

As we come to the end of this book, it is evident that the tale we have told is not the end, but the very beginning of Chinese capitalism. The Chinese market economy will continue to develop with its own characteristics, integrating its rich traditions and the diversity of the modern world. After all, capitalism is not an end state, but an open-ended evolutionary process of collective learning and self-transformation.

What had happened in China since the death of Mao is certainly breathtaking. China today would hardly be recognized by Mao if he walked out of his mausoleum. He would be astounded to find out that private entrepreneurship and free markets could actually realize his broken dream, one shared by the Chinese people for more than a century, of remaking China a rich and powerful nation. With the rise of an open market for ideas, the growth of the Chinese economy will be even stronger and more sustainable. Professor Robert Fogel's estimate that the Chinese economy in 2040 would be as large as two-fifths of the world total may be too high,[105] but it may well be too low. Production per capita in China (4393 USD, 2010 data) is still very low compared with that of the United States (47,184 USD), Britain (36,100 USD), France (39,460 USD), Germany (40,509 USD), or even with that of its Asian neighbors, such as Japan (43,137 USD), South Korea (20,757 USD), and Hong Kong (31,758 USD). There remains ample room for rapid growth in China's economic productivity.

Lack of access to high-quality human talent has been a restrictive constraint on the development of Chinese firms. Today, Beijing and Shanghai have become new lands of opportunity for American graduates, not mentioning the growing number of returned Chinese students who have been educated in the West. Chinese firms have also opened up R&D offices from California to New York, from Illinois to Arizona. With increasing access to the global pool of human talents, the Chinese economy stands a great chance to climb up the technological ladder and become more innovative and productive.

Economic productivity in any society is fundamentally determined by the makeup and quality of its human talent and the performance of its human capital market, which determines how effectively human talent is cultivated and exercised. No one would deny the critical importance of commodity exchanges, stock markets, banks, courts, and governments in the working of a modern economy. But all these institutions are regulated and operated by people. No institution is foolproof, nor set in stone. How institutions function and how they adapt to changing circumstances inevitably reflect the character of its regulators and operators.

No factor exerts more influence on the quality and performance of the human capital market than the market for ideas. The "Qian puzzle" makes it clear that a vibrant market for ideas is both a precondition for scholarly excellence and an indispensable moral and epistemic foundation for an open society and free economy, without which the great diversity of human talent would wither. During the past decades of reform and opening up, the introduction of the market for goods has brought prosperity back to China and fortuitously led the country back to its own cultural roots. The development of a market for ideas will make the growth of the Chinese economy more knowledge-driven and innovative. More important, it will enable China to revive its rich traditions through transformative integration with the diversity of the modern world. China will then stand not only as a manufacturing center of the world, but also as a lively source of creativity and innovation.

Epilogue

In 1955, Qian Xuesen, a rising star scientist at Caltech, who later would become the father of China's space program, was deported by the United States on the charge of being a Communist. Before boarding the *President Cleveland* for Hong Kong, Qian told a crowd of reporters at the Los Angeles harbor, "I plan to do my best to help the Chinese people build up the nation to where they can live with dignity and happiness." In 1991, when receiving his friend and former Caltech colleague, Frank Marble, in Beijing, Qian said quietly, bewilderingly and apologetically to his visitor, "You know, Frank, we've done a lot for China. People have enough food. They are working and progress is being made. But Frank, they are not happy."[1]

In a public gathering held on February 12th, 2010 to celebrate Chinese New Year, Premier Wen Jiaobao proclaimed that the all the Chinese government has done and will do is "to make the Chinese people live with more happiness and dignity," renewing the same lofty dream Qian held more than half a century ago.[2] At the annual National People's Congress in March 2010, the pledge to ensure the Chinese people lead a better life, with happiness and dignity, was reiterated in Wen's 2010 Government Report and stressed as an overarching task for the government in the decades to come. A year later, when Premier Wen presided over the National People's Congress for the last time, he reiterated the government's commitment to building a "happy China." On March 19th, 2011, *The Economist* reported on its cover page, "China pursues happiness, not growth."[3]

This shift in the government's mission from socialist modernization, a goal that had been driving the Chinese economic reform since its inception, to a better life with happiness and dignity for the Chinese people reflects the sea change in values and attitudes that have occurred during China's transformation to a market economy. Wen is fully aware that economic development, let alone a growing GDP, does not necessarily increase happiness. He also knows well that economic development cannot be sustained, nor does it mean much, unless it increases the happiness and the quality of life in general for the people.

Moreover, the Chinese government in modern times, under both Nationalist and the Communist rule, has always perceived itself as a vanguard in modernizing China. Its mission has always been project-centered, be it "Socialist Transformation," "Four Modernizations," and more recently, "Economic Reform and Opening up." The pursuit of happiness, on the other hand, is humanist in orientation and can hardly be materialized by political campaigns in a top-down fashion. As Adam Smith told us in *The Theory of Moral Sentiments*, one of Wen's favorite books, the pursuit of happiness rests upon a tranquil and modest mind in a free society where justice prevails.

The great source of both the misery and disorders of human life, seems to arise from over-rating the difference between one permanent situation and another. Avarice over-rates the difference between poverty and riches: ambition, that between a private and a public station: vain-glory, that between obscurity and extensive reputation. The person under the influence of any of those extravagant passions, is not only miserable in his actual situation, but is often disposed to disturb the peace of society, in order to arrive at that which he so foolishly admires. The slightest observation, however, might satisfy him, that, in all the ordinary situations of human life, a well-disposed mind may be equally calm, equally cheerful, and equally contented. Some of those situations may, no doubt, deserve to be preferred to others: but none of them can deserve to be pursued with that passionate ardour which drives us to violate the rules either of prudence or of justice; or to corrupt the future tranquillity of our minds, either by shame from the remembrance of our own folly, or by remorse from the horror of our own injustice. Wherever prudence does not direct, wherever justice does not permit, the attempt to change our situation, the man who does attempt it, plays at the most unequal of all games of hazard, and stakes every thing against scarce any thing. [...] In the most glittering and exalted situation that our idle fancy can hold out to us, the pleasures from which we propose to derive our real happiness, are almost always the same with those which, in our actual, though humble station, we have at all times at hand, and in our power. Except the frivolous pleasures of vanity and superiority, we may find, in the most humble station, where there is only personal liberty, every other which the most exalted can afford; and the pleasures of vanity and superiority are seldom consistent with perfect tranquillity, the principle and foundation of all real and satisfactory enjoyment. Neither is it always certain that, in the splendid situation which we aim at, those real and satisfactory pleasures can be enjoyed with the same security as in the humble one which we are so very eager to abandon. examine the records of history, recollect what has happened within the circle of your own experience, consider with attention what has been the conduct of almost all the greatly unfortunate, either in private or public life, whom you may have either read of, or heard of, or remember; and you will find that the misfortunes of by far the greater part of them have arisen from their not knowing when they were well, when it was proper for them to sit still and to be contented. The inscription upon the tomb-stone of the man who had endeavoured to mend a tolerable constitution by taking physic – "I was well, I wished to be better; here I am" – may generally be applied with great justness to the distress of disappointed avarice and ambition.[4]

Modern economists, who are used to reducing consumer behavior to utility-maximization, may be bewildered to read that Adam Smith penned this paragraph. The moral spirit captured in this long paragraph is so different in character from the "economic man" that populates modern economic theories. The stupendous loss in the depth and richness of human nature is a noticeable part of the price we have paid in transforming economics from a moral science of man creating wealth to a cold logic of choice in resource allocation. No longer a study of man as he is, modern economics has lost its anchor and drifted away from economic reality. As a result, economists are hard pressed to say much that is coherent and insightful, although their counsel is badly needed in this time of crisis and uncertainty.

In the meantime, it is probably more than a coincidence that Smith's tone and message resonates strongly with ancient Chinese wisdom. "Isn't it a joy to study and regularly practice? What's more, isn't it a joy to receive friends from afar?" These are the opening sentences of the *Analects* of Confucius. The subject of study that Confucius refers to is not limited to book learning. It also includes character building, cultivating social relationships, learning how to run a family and govern a country, and ultimately, bringing harmony to the whole world. Learning about humanity and gradually perfecting it in our daily life, especially in the company of kindred spirits, fills us with joy and serenity. Remembering his most favorite student, Yan Hui, who devoted himself to learning but died an early death, Confucius applauded, "Eating out of a bamboo container, drinking out of a gourd ladle, and living in a narrow shack – others would be utterly dejected, Hui always remained happy." At a time when most people were struggling to eke out a meager existence, learning was inevitably a luxury pursuit affordable by only a few. "Make people rich first; then educate them," goes the pragmatic teaching of Confucius.

In the pursuit of wealth, the division of labor and the market for goods have long been appreciated as essential institutions. Together, they are responsible not only for the improvement of economic productivity but also for the development of new products, allowing the market economy to constantly evolve and never be short of novelty. Enabling us to think independently and critically and to explore the world in our own way, the market for ideas nudges us to get into closer contact with reality in nature and our human society. The life experience of each of us might be a small drop in the ocean. But our distinctive individuality and rich diversity together make human society resourceful and resilient. When the market for goods and the market for ideas are together in full swing, each supporting, augmenting, and strengthening the other, human creativity and happiness stand the best chance to prevail, the material and spiritual civilizations march on firm ground, side by side. In the everlasting pursuit of human happiness and dignity, the story of how China became capitalist, as extraordinary and transformative as it is, is but a small leap forward.

Notes

Preface

1. Cheung (2008), p. 2. It is now available in both Chinese and English as Cheung (2009).
2. Hayek (1967), ch. 6.
3. Cheung (1982).
4. *Ibid.*, p. 19.
5. Cheung (1986), p. 66.
6. *Ibid.*, p. 79.
7. Our book is so titled because it is intended as a sequel to Cheung's (1982, 1986) pamphlets. Terms like "capitalist" and "capitalism" are bound to invite controversy. China today remains committed to socialism, calling itself "a socialist market economy with Chinese characteristics." Some readers in China may protest against our wording of the title. That China is still ruled by the Chinese Communist Party will probably lead many western readers to challenge us on our choice of title as well. Nonetheless, China has transformed over the past three decades from a broken economy where the market and entrepreneurship were banned to a vibrant one where market forces prevail and private enterprises blossom. Our book explains how this happened.

1 China at the Death of Mao

1. The Cultural Revolution was Mao's last and most horrendous effort to mold China into socialism. Like other policy disasters, it remains a politically sensitive topic in China and the relevant government archive data are still classified and inaccessible to most scholars. For the relevant literature, see, for example, Nianyi Wang (1989); Esherick, Kickowicz, and Walder (2006); MacFarquhar and Schoenhals (2006); and Guo, Wang, and Han (2009), Vol. 3. A shortcoming of most historical accounts is that the voice of the victims – a conservative estimate put the human toll at 1,070,000, see Yung-fa Chen (2001), p. 846 – can hardly be heard. The courageous efforts of Dr Youqin Wang (2004), who has collected the tragic stories of 659 victims, have helped to fill the lacuna. For an early attempt along the same lines, see Jicai Feng (1990). Walder (2009) offers a fresh perspective on the most violent and cruel period (1966–1968) of the Cultural Revolution.
2. It remains an open question why Mao instigated the Cultural Revolution right after China had barely recovered from the catastrophe of the Great Leap Forward. Power struggles were clearly a factor, particularly Mao's increasing discontent with Liu Shaoqi, who became the President of China in 1959. Nonetheless, it was the official justification to preserve socialism that gave the Cultural Revolution its distinctive ideological fever, making it an unprecedented political campaign in Chinese history. In addition, the fact that Mao at the end of his life still highly regarded the Cultural Revolution was a compelling reason against power struggles being his primary motivation.
3. The term "golden highway" was made popular by Ran Hao; he used it as the title for his four-volume novel that eulogized the socialist transformation in rural China.
4. For the most recent accounts of Mao's great famine, see Jisheng Yang (2008) and Dikötter (2010). During the Cultural Revolution, the political campaign of

anti-traditionalism and anti-intellectualism reached its peak; Chinese universities were closed, most books were banned or burned. For the early origin of anti-traditionalism in modern China, see Yu-sheng Lin (1979).

5. "Mao is Dead," *The Economist* (September 11th, 1976).

6. *New York Times* (September 10th, 1976), section 1, p. 17.

7. *World News Digest* (September 11th, 1976), accessed from LexisNexis.

8. Jinglian Wu (2005), pp. 46–49; Angang Hu (2008), pp. 244–253.

9. Angang Hu (2008), pp. 512–515.

10. "Reform is China's Second Revolution," *Selected Works of Deng Xiaoping*, Vol. 3. This characterization is found in a book title by Harding (1987).

11. The first section of this long poem, "Ode to Joy" (*Huanle Song*), was published in the *People's Daily* (November 20th, 1949).

12. For the early history of the Chinese Communist Party, including the influence of the Communist International (or Comintern), see Bianco (1971); Dirlik (1989); Pantsov (2000); and Steve Smith (2000). See also the multiple volumes edited by the First Department of the Research Office of the History of the Chinese Communist Party (1997) and Chen Yung-fa (2001). For documentary accounts of the Party history, see Saich (1996) and the Research Office of the History of the Chinese Communist Party (2001).

13. The Chinese Communist Party in its early years financially depended on the Comintern; but it was uneasy with the latter's attempt to dictate its action. Their relationship was further complicated by the presence of the Kuomintang. For the triangular relationship among Moscow, the Chinese Communist Party and the Kuomintang, see Garver (1988); Heinzig (2004); Kuisong Yang (1999).

14. Chiang's three-month visit to the Soviet Union in 1923 was a critical event in his rise to power in the Kuomintang, even though he failed to accomplish the main mission, which was to seek direct military assistance from Moscow. At the time, Chiang's attitude toward Soviet practice was ambivalent. But compared with Sun, Chiang was clearly far less sanguine about the cooperation with the Chinese Communists and the Soviet Union. For the recent literature on Chiang's visit, see Wang and Li (2004), pp. 92–94; Tianshi Yang (2008), pp. 95–145; Pakula (2009), pp. 122–124; Taylor (2009), pp. 41–45; and Heming Xing (2009), pp. 12–25. In his own retrospective account, Chiang (1956) portrayed himself as a more adamant critic of communism than he probably was.

15. Braun (1982) provided his account of the extraordinary experience he had in China as a Comintern agent.

16. Mao Zedong, "On tactics against Japanese imperialism" (a speech delivered on December 27th 1935), in *Selected Works of Mao Tse-tung*, Vol. 1, p. 179.

17. The account best known to western readers was Edgar Snow (1937), which has over the years gone through several revisions, with more chapters added.

18. The complicated relationship between Stalin and Mao, particularly Stalin's early disdain toward Mao, has been well documented. See, for example, Radchenko (2009), p. 5. See also Kuisong Yang (1999).

19. For a recent account of the "Long March," see Shuyun Sun (2006).

20. For an authoritative account of Mao's consolidation of leadership during the Yan'an period, see Hua Gao (2000). For early treatments of the rise of the "Yan'an Way" and its transformative impact on the Chinese Communist Party, see Selden (1971, 1995) and Yung-fa Chen (1990).

21. On Mao's first visit to Moscow and meeting with Stalin, see Radchenko (2009), pp. 3–9. For the Chinese source, see Pang and Jin (2003), pp. 28–58.

22. It is still hard to gauge why Mao, a grand strategist with a defiant mind, would bind China to a foreign policy that he called "leaning toward one side." It was this misstep

that gradually set Mao's China down a disastrous path (e.g., a military conflict with the United States on the Korean peninsula, economic and political isolation from the West, and a rush to socialism).

23. The major component of China's first Five Year Plan was the so-called "156 projects" – 156 industrial projects supported by Soviet technology and loans, which became the "cornerstone" of China's industrial development. See, for example, Dong and Wu (2004).

24. It is not entirely clear when and how communism ceased to be a tool and became embraced as an ultimate goal. For Mao's decision to take China to Stalinism, see Hua-yu Li (2006).

25. The literature on Mao's China is overwhelming and grows fast, partly due to the increasing recognition that China after Mao cannot be severed from Mao's China. A convenient starting point is the last two volumes of *The Cambridge History of China* edited by MacFarquhar and Fairbank (1987, 1991). Meisner (1999) and Gray (1990, 2006) provide some of the best accounts offered by historians. Bramall (2009) provides an account of the Chinese political economy since 1949, with equal coverage of Mao and post-Mao eras. Naughton's (2007) work has a fair amount of coverage of Mao's China, even though its focus is on the reform period. For an earlier account, see Riskin (1987). For the Chinese literature, the three-volume series on Mao's China (1949–1976) – Lin, Fan and Zhang (1989); Jin Cong (1989); and Nianyi Wang (1989) – is a useful starting point. For a comprehensive coverage, see the ten-volume series on the history of the People's Republic (1949–1981), published by the Chinese University of Hong Kong. In addition, the first three volumes of the five-volume series, *Zhonggua Renmin Gongheguo Zhuanti Shi Gao* [The Thematic History of the People's Republic of China], published by Sichuan People's Press (2004), provide a fairly balanced and focused coverage of major events during Mao's era. For historical accounts of Mao's economy, see Jian Sun (1992); Li Wu (1999); Shaozhi Su (2002); and Angang Hu (2008). The most comprehensive account available is the five-volume series edited by Dexin Zhao (1988–1999). See also Ning Wang (2008) for a critical assessment of Mao's economy.

26. Hinton (1990).

27. See, for example, Meisner (1999); Angang Hu (2008); Bramall (2009).

28. Lerner (1944), p. 1.

29. For origins of the policy, see Walker (1984); Yibo Bo (1997), pp. 180–199; and Yunhui Lin (2009), pp. 90–116.

30. China's household registration system is one of the few institutions that have so far survived the three decades of reform. See Tiejun Cheng and Selden (1994) and Fei-ling Wang (2005).

31. Even though it was and continues to be hailed as a success, land reform set a vicious example of employing brutal force and fanning hatred dressed in the rhetoric of class struggle in policy implementation. Pinghan Luo (2005), pp. 173–221 reveals that many arbitrary and inhumane measures adopted during land reform against the landlords and rich peasants would foreshadow the terror of the Cultural Revolution. The Chinese communists' "preoccupation with hatred coupled with an enthusiasm for singling out enemies" was identified by the late political scientist Lucian Pye (1992, p. 67) as the dominant theme in Mao's politics. According to Pye, "No other political culture places as much stress upon the emotion of hate as does the Chinese" (*ibid.*).

32. For a recent reflection on Mao's agricultural policy, see Kueh (2006).

33. Jisheng Yang (1998), p. 17.

34. Jisheng Yang (2004), p. 40.

35. For the death of Liu Shaoqi, see Zheng Huang (2004), pp. 155–176.

36. Vogel (2010) provides a meticulously documented biography of Deng, with a focus on his last two decades.
37. For Zhu Rongji's dramatic rise to power, see Hancheng Zhou (2003).
38. For Steven Cheung's visit to Beijing and his encounter with Chinese officials in the early 1980s, see Cheung (2009), p. 101.
39. For Mao's life, including his rise to power, see Spence (1999); Short (1999); and Mao's official biography, edited by Chongji Jin (1996) and by Pang and Jin (2003). Cheng-tung Wei (1999) attempts an account of Mao's life from the perspective of modern psychology. A well-known episode that best reveals Mao's intolerant and vengeful personality was his dealing with Zhang Shenfu, one of the early founders of the Chinese Communist Party and his boss at Peking University; for Zhang's life, see Schwarcz (1992). See also Rui Li (1999); Hua Gao (2000); and Ruoshui Wang (2001).
40. For Mao's adventurous and rebellious student life in Changsha, see Spence (1999), pp. 16–30; Short (1999), pp. 39–81; and Chongji Jin (1996), pp. 15–39.
41. To describe his humiliating experience at Peking University, Mao, many years later, reminisced that "[M]y office was so low that people avoided me. One of my tasks was to register the names of people who came to read newspapers, but to most of them I did not exist as a human being. Among those who came to read, I recognized the names of famous leaders of the [Chinese] 'renaissance' movement, men … in whom I was intensely interested. I tried to begin conversations with them on political and cultural subjects, but they were very busy men. They had no time to listen to an assistant librarian speaking a southern dialect." Quoted in Short (1999), p. 83. One of these busy men that Mao mentioned resentfully was Fu Ssu-nien (Fu Shi Nian), who would visit Mao in Yan'an right before the outbreak of the civil war and later flee to Taiwan to rebuild the National Taiwan University. After 1949, Fu was denounced as a war criminal and the tombs of his ancestors were destroyed. See Fan-Sen Wang (2000) for an account of Fu's colorful personality and extraordinary life.
42. Chinese intellectuals at the founding of the People's Republic in 1949 were bitterly divided in their attitude toward the communist regime (e.g., Fu (2010)). Some left for Hong Kong or Taiwan as they feared that the Communists, emboldened by socialism, would not tolerate the Chinese traditional culture or leave any room for intellectual freedom. Many stayed to embrace wholeheartedly the new China, but quickly found themselves the target of Mao's "thought reform" and political campaigns, e.g., Ningkun Wu (1993) and Junyi Wei (1998).
43. For the life story of Qian Xuesen, see Iris Chang (1995).
44. Immediately after the founding of the People's Republic, a political campaign was launched to "re-educate" the intellectuals and instill in them the doctrine of Marxism. This marked the beginning of the closing of a free market for ideas in the People's Republic of China. For many chilling accounts, see Ningkun Wu (1994); Junyi Wei (1998); Yiliang Zhou (1998); Zuguang Wu (2004); Kedi Liu (2005); and Rongzu Wang (2005).
45. Balazs (1964), p. 6, for example, called "the uninterrupted continuity of a ruling class of scholar-officials" in Imperial China "one enduring feature of Chinese society." Qian Mu coined a new term, "scholars-run-government" (*Shi Ren Zheng Fu*), to refer to the traditional Chinese political system. See Mu Qian (2001), p. 15 and Ying-shih Yu (2004).
46. The Communist Party and Confucian scholar-officials represent two contrasting types of organizations. The former exemplifies a hierarchically structured organization where order is imposed from above, while the latter comes close to what Polanyi (1966) called a "society of explorers" where authority emerges out of the common pursuit of knowledge.
47. Liang Shuming provided a good example. See Shuming Liang (2004), p. 139.

48. For Liang's confrontation with Mao, see Shuming Liang (2004), pp. 146–155. See also Alitto (1979); Kedi Liu (2005); and Liang and Alitto (2009).
49. See Jiandong Lu (1995) for Chen's two decades of life struggle for intellectual independence. See also Rongzu Wang (2005).
50. For the tragedy of Hu Feng, see Hui Li (2003).
51. The Anti-Rightist Movement violently ended a fragile market for ideas in the People's Republic, imprisoning many who had followed Mao's call to criticize the government and Party policy. For its origins and consequences, see the relevant chapters in Guo, Wang and Han (2004), Vol. 2; Zheng Zhu (1998); and Zhihua Shen (2008). For a personal account, see Yangxiang Shao (2007). The chain of events that led to the Anti-Rightist Movement is widely known. A remaining point of debate is whether Mao changed his mind in the middle of the "Double Hundred Movement" and turned against the critics of the Party, a position held by the Chinese government, or whether Mao intentionally designed the "Double Hundred Movement" as a "strategic plot" to snare non-Party members whom Mao deemed a potential challenge to the one-party rule. Nonetheless, both sides agree that the Anti-Rightist Movement registered a critical turning point in the history of the People's Republic. After the collectivization of the private sector and the oppression of the market for ideas, China was set on its tragic path to self-destruction.
52. Yibo Bo (1997), pp. 438–439.
53. For the rivalry between Mao and Khrushchev, see Luthi (2008) and Radchenko (2009).
54. Mao (1977), "On the Ten Major Relationships," pp. 284–307, in *Selected Works of Mao Tse-tung*. Vol. 5.
55. *Ibid.*, p. 290.
56. *Ibid.*, p. 291.
57. *Ibid.*, p. 292.
58. *Ibid.*, p. 294.
59. *Ibid.*
60. Jinglian Wu (2005), pp. 43–57; Yibo Bo (1997), pp. 548–565.
61. Angang Hu (2008), p. 250.
62. The Great Leap Forward was widely recognized as the first policy disaster under Mao. It has recently attracted a lot of attention. *China Economic Review* (1998) published a special issue, 9(2), on China's great famine during the Great Leap Forward. For a full historical account, see Jisheng Yang (2008) and Dikotter (2010). For a popular account, see Becker (1998). For a recent investigation of the Great Leap Forward in a Henan village, see Thaxton (2008).
63. Yibo Bo (1997), pp. 478–510.
64. *People's Daily* (August 27th, 1958).
65. Pinghan Luo (2001).
66. *Ibid.*, pp. 61–65.
67. *People's Daily* (September 18th, 1958).
68. Qian Xuesen, *China Youth Daily* (June 16th, 1958).
69. Jian Sun (1992), p. 244.
70. *Ibid.*
71. Yibo Bo (1997), pp. 466–489; Yunhui Lin (2008), p. 12.
72. Wei Li and Dennis Tao Yang (2005).
73. Adam Smith (1976 [1776]), Book IV, p. 33.
74. At what was commonly referred to as "the Seven-Thousand-Attendee Meeting" (from January 11th to February 7th, 1962), Liu expressed in public his different diagnosis of the cause of the great famine during the Great Leap Forward. This disagreement with, and implied criticism against, Mao made Liu a major target in Mao's launch

of the Cultural Revolution. See, for example, Jin Cong (1989), p. 299; Shuhua Zhang (2006), pp. 277–288.
75. Hayek (1937).
76. See, for example, references given in note 1.
77. Li Wu (1999), pp. 650–658.
78. For the tension between *junxian* and *fengjian* as two competing political systems in Chinese history, see Mu Qian (2005), pp. 1–37, 38–56; Schrecker (2004), chs. 1 and 2. For the origin and development of *fengjian*, see Tianyu Feng (2006).

2   China in Transition

1. For the power struggle between Hua and the Gang of Four as well as the ideological divide between them and Deng and his associates, see Chuntao Xie (2008); Cheng, Wang, and Li (2008); Liu and Xu (2009); Donglian Xiao (2008); and Jisheng Yang (1998), ch. 2.
2. Spence (1999), p. 178.
3. For the arrest of the Gang of Four and the critical role played by Hua, see Xichen Ji (2000); Gensheng Zhang (2004); and Dongling Chen (2004), pp. 567–592; Shi and Li (2008), pp. 668–707; Gang Han (2011).
4. MacFarquhar and Schoenhals (2006).
5. After taking office, Hua repeatedly emphasized the development of "productive force" as the first priority. See, for example, Cheng, Wang, and Li (2008), pp. 72–75.
6. For Hua's appointment of Hu Yaobang and Hu Jiwei, see respectively, Mei Man (2005), pp. 212–213 and Jiwei Hu (1997), pp. 29–30.
7. e.g., Huang Dai (1998).
8. Jisheng Yang (1998), pp. 164–165.
9. The passage in 1981 of the "Resolution on Certain Questions in the History of Our Party since the Founding of the People's Republic of China" was meant to "confirm the historical role of Comrade Mao Zedong and explain the necessity to uphold and develop Mao Zedong Thought," as Deng Xiaoping (1981) put it. See *Selected Works of Deng Xiaoping*, Vol. 2. A comprehensive and truthful evaluation of Mao was not even attempted because the priority then was to "unite the Party" and "look to the future."
10. For Hu's leading role in political reform during the early 1980s, see Baoxiang Shen (1997) and Cheng, Wang, and Li (2008), pp. 85–121.
11. That Hu's efforts were supported, or at least, tolerated by Hua was an important factor for their success. See Gang Han (2004), pp. 29–47. Jiwei Hu (1997), pp. 84–85 also recognizes Hua as an "open-minded and democratic" leader.
12. This approach to reform was consistent with traditional Chinese practice, in which change in personnel was as important as institutional change in enacting political reform. See, for example, Mu Qian (2001), pp. 1–2 for a brief exposition of these two strategies of political reform.
13. Li Wu (1999), pp. 756–807; Dali Sun (2004).
14. Harding (1987), pp. 53–57; Jisheng Yang (1998), pp. 108–110; Meisner (1999), p. 429.
15. For the origin and rise of "four modernizations" as an economic policy, see Yaguang Han (2006), pp. 65–70.
16. For Deng's revitalization of "four modernizations" in 1975, see Hua Zhang (2004).
17. See "We regard reform as a revolution," a talk Deng gave on October 10th, 1984, in his meeting with Chancellor Helmut Kohl of the Federal Republic of Germany. It is available in *Selected Works of Deng Xiaoping*, Vol. 3.
18. e.g., Shi and Li (2008).

19. Yu and Wang (2004). But the whole incidence remains murky. As acknowledged by the authors at the very beginning, the Lin Biao incidence is "one of the strangest" events in the history of the People's Republic (p. 302).
20. Congji Jin (1996), p. 1610.
21. Jisheng Yang (1998), pp. 55–63; Jieshe An (2004).
22. Hua Zhang (2004); Angang Hu (2008), pp. 477–485; Peng and Chen (2008), pp. 125–128; Shi and Li (2008), pp. 527–558.
23. Shi and Li (2008), p. 583.
24. *People's Daily* (December 26th, 1976).
25. As pointed out by Li Wu (1999), for example, "In fact, national economic construction in 1977 and 1978 had achieved a relatively steady and fast development" (p. 763).
26. Muqiao Xue (1996), p. 7.
27. Jinhua Chen (2005), p. 95.
28. Cheng, Wang, and Li (2008), p. 161.
29. The calculation is based on statistics data provided in Li Wu (1999).
30. Perkins (1991), p. 496.
31. Jinhua Chen (2005), p. 98.
32. *Ibid.*, pp 105–106.
33. This open door policy was preceded by two previous attempts. During the first Five Year Plan (1953–1957), China, with loans from the Soviet Union, imported a significant amount of equipment from the Soviet bloc. In 1972, China bought from Japan and Western Europe equipment in steel, chemical, and fertilizer production lines and power generators to modernize its industrial structure. This was the first time in the history of the People's Republic that China opened its door to western capitalist economies. See Jinhua Chen (2005), pp. 10–14. It is noteworthy that Hua was a co-author of a 1972 proposal submitted to the State Economic Council to import chemical and fertilizer production equipment. See Yan Li (2008), p. 150.
34. Li Wu (1999), p. 776.
35. But China had started trading with the West since the early 1970s. An article in *People's Daily* (September 19th, 1978) reported that the Beijing Second Sweater Plant borrowed 1.3 million USD from a bank to buy weaving machines from abroad in May 1975. In 1976, the plant earned 4 million USD from exports.
36. *People's Daily* (January 2nd, 1977).
37. Yan Li (2008), p. 134.
38. Jisheng Yang (1998), pp. 110–111; Li Wu (1999), pp. 776–777; Jinhua Chen (2005), pp. 145–151.
39. Cheng, Wang, and Li (2008), pp. 59–84.
40. Li Wu (1999), p. 758.
41. Hua (1978), "Unite and Strive to Build a Modern Powerful Socialist Country: Report to the Fifth National People's Congress," *Peking Review*, no. 10 (March 10th), p. 39.
42. Milton Friedman (1984), p. 26.
43. Cheng, Wang, and Li (2008), pp. 122–132; Yan Li (2008), pp. 68–96; Yang and Chen (2009), pp. 153–179.
44. Yan Li (2008), p. 69.
45. *Ibid.*, pp. 76–80.
46. Guangyuan Yu (2008), p. 55.
47. Yang and Chen (2009), pp. 153–167.
48. *Ibid.*, pp. 168–179.
49. Lee (2000), p. 645.
50. Deng , Ma, Sun, and Wu (1979).
51. Richard Wong (2008), p. 4.

52. Mingming Tu (2008).
53. Cheung (1982, 1986).
54. The 1978 Communiqué is widely available online in both Chinese and English. It was collected in Harold Hinton (1982), pp 457–462.
55. *Ibid.*, p. 459.
56. *Ibid.*
57. *Ibid.*, p. 460.
58. *Ibid.*, p. 459.
59. *Ibid.*, pp. 459–460.
60. *Ibid.*, p. 460.
61. *Ibid.*
62. *Ibid.*, p. 459.
63. *Ibid.*
64. *Ibid.*
65. In the official English translation, "market" appeared twice in "market price," which should rather be "sale price" in contrast to "factory price."
66. *The 1978 Communiqué*, in Hinton (1982), p. 462.

3   How China's Market Reform Began

1. It is striking that almost all writings on China's economic reform agree that the reform had a clear and clean start. For most, China's "post-Mao reform" and "post-1978 reform" are inter-exchangeable. We find this consensus puzzling and misleading in many ways.
2. Baoxiang Shen (2004), p. 71; Licheng Ma (2008), pp. 6–15.
3. *The 1978 Communiqué*, in Hinton (1982), p. 459.
4. *Ibid.*
5. Donglian Xiao (2004), p. 189.
6. Jianguo Gao (2000), pp. 377–392.
7. *Ibid.*, pp. 411–427.
8. Jinglian Wu (2003), p. 52.
9. *Ibid.*, p. 138; Peng and Chen (2008), p. 89.
10. *People's Daily* (February 19th, 1979). See also Donglian Xiao (2008), pp. 507–544. It is noteworthy that this section of Xiao's book is simply titled "The Reform of the Economic System Began as Delegating Rights and Sharing Profits." As Xiao put it, "At least during 1978–1980, the focus of reform was always placed on the expansion of enterprises' autonomy" (p. 522).
11. Li Wu (1999), pp. 841–846; Jinglian Wu (2003), pp. 138–144; Donglian Xiao (2004), p. 191.
12. Jisheng Yang (1998), p. 358; Li Wu (1999), p. 842.
13. Li Wu (1999), p. 842.
14. Shirk (1993), p. 200.
15. Jinglian Wu (2005), p. 145.
16. This is what is called M-form (multi-divisional) industrial structure in the research literature (e.g., Qian and Xu (1993); Maskin, Qian, and Xu (2000); and Qian, Roland, and Xu (2006)), in contrast to the U-form structure that characterized the former Soviet economy.
17. Donglian Xiao (2004), p. 204.
18. Kuang and Gai (2004), pp. 311–312.
19. Han Zong (2007), pp. 30–41; Peng and Chen (2008), pp. 125–128.
20. For example, it is not discussed in Jinglian Wu (2003, 2010) or Naughton (2007).

21. Naughton (1995). As Naughton (p. 8) points out, the term may mean two distinctive approaches. First, it refers to a conscious strategy of reform pursued by the Chinese government; it is to keep central planning fixed and allow market forces to grow so that over time "the plan would becomes proportionately less and less important until the economy gradually grew out of the plan" (*ibid*). Second, it could mean that the Chinese economy evolved in ways that the policymakers did not anticipate and "the economy and its reform both developed 'out of plan'" (p. 23). The first interpretation seems to be what Naughton endorses and it has gained much acceptance in the literature (p. 8), even though Naughton admits that the phrase he coined "may be understood" in the second fashion (pp. 22–23). Now we believe that the first approach may capture part of the reform dictated by the Chinese government – such as enterprise reform – but the overall process of reform is better described by the second approach.

22. Jinglian Wu (2005), pp. 68–71. The best known economic analysis which endorses the practice is provided by Lau, Qian, and Roland (2000). For an early rather critical assessment, see Wu and Zhao (1987).

23. The data can be found in Muqiao Xue (1996), pp. 281–282.

24. This case of private farming can be found in *Gan Wei Tian Xia Xiang* [Bold to Be the First in the World] (edited by the Provincial Propaganda Department of the Party in Sichuan, Provincial Academy of Social Sciences in Sichuan, and Sichuan Daily, 2008), a collection of economic experiments that first emerged in Sichuan province.

25. The story of Xiaogang village in Anhui province is widely documented, in both Chinese and English. For detailed coverage of agricultural reform in Anhui, see *Anhui Nongcun Gaige Zi Lu* [The Road of Agricultural Reform in Anhui] (2006) and *Anhui Nongcun Gaige Kou Shu Shi* [The Oral History of Agricultural Reform in Anhui] (2006), both edited by the Research Office of the Party History of the Anhui Provincial Party Committee.

26. The agreement reads: "We distribute land to households, to which the head of each household has agreed by signing his signature or affixing his seal. If this works, each household pledges to pay its share of the required agricultural tax in grain to the State and not to ask for money or grain from the State any more. If this does not work, we cadres are willing to be condemned to prison or even death, and commune members collectively pledge to raise our children to the age of 18." It can be found in Jinglian Wu (2005), p. 111.

27. See Lianshen Song (2005) for an account of the rise and fall of Dazhai.

28. Unlike Wan and Zhao, both of them were later promoted to Beijing, Chi and his pioneering role in reform in Guizhou was rarely known even in China. But see Runshen Du (1998), pp. 268–298.

29. *People's Daily* (March 15th, 1979).

30. For a detailed account of the critical role Wan Li played in promoting private farming, see Zhang and Ding (2006), pp. 154–231. See also Niansun Qian (2008).

31. See Zhengfu Shi (2008) for a version of the official account. According to Wu Xiang, a journalist at the *People's Daily*, the case of private farming was far from confined to the Xiaogang village, but widespread in China. Chi Biqing, the Party chief at Guizhou province from 1978 to 1985, stated that by May 1978, more than 10 percent of production teams in his province had already embraced some form of private farming. Both can be found in Runshen Du (1998), pp. 214 and 269, respectively. As one of the poorest provinces in China, Guizhou under the leadership of Chi was probably the earliest to embrace province-wide private farming.

32. For example, see Yougui Zheng (2009), p. 233 .

33. Jinglian Wu (2005), p. 112.

34. Runshen Du (1998), p. 214.

35. Xiaochun Fan (2009). See also Runshen Du (1998), pp. 16–79; Angang Hu (2008), pp. 341–345.
36. Xiaochun Fan (2009), pp. 382–384.
37. Tsou (1986), pp. 198–211; Zweig (1997), pp. 55–56.
38. In a detailed case study of a village in Jiangsu province, Huaiyin Li (2009) showed that decollectivization was "primarily a top-down process planned and imposed by the state" (p. 268).
39. For a classical empirical investigation of the importance of organizations in economic life, see Banfield (1967). For an early emphasis on business enterprise in the rise of capitalism, see Weber (1981). For modern treatments of the subject, see Arrow (1974); Williamson (1985); and Coleman (1990).
40. The production team as organizational capital may survive in different manners. See Ning Wang (2005), ch. 5, for an example.
41. See Chung (2000) for a comparative study of provincial differences in the implementation of the household responsibility system.
42. Huaiyin Li (2009) provides an illustrative example. Even the household responsibility system was met with resistance from the villagers, Li concludes by stating that "The most significant achievement of the rural reform after 1980,..., was not the remarkable increase in agricultural production, as the reform designers originally intended, but the unexpected emancipation of the rural labor force and the consequent diversification of income sources of the rural population" (p. 290).
43. The literature on township and village enterprises is massive. See Xu and Zhang (2008) for a recent review.
44. Deng Xiaoping, "We Shall Speed up Reform," Talk with Stefan Korosec, member of the Presidium of the Central Committee of the League of Communists of Yugoslavia, June 12th, 1987. Available from *Selected Works of Deng Xiaoping*, Vol. 3.
45. Li Wu (1999), p. 792.
46. e.g., Wei Li and Dennis Tao Yang (2005).
47. e.g., Muqiao Xue (2008), p. 19.
48. e.g., Lanqing Li (2008), pp. 28–29.
49. Naughton (2007), p. 274.
50. Xu and Zhang (2008). For a general discussion of the township and village enterprises, see Findlay, Watson, and Wu (1994).
51. Naughton (2007), pp. 274–275.
52. Yasheng Huang (2008), p. 10.
53. Quoted from Jisheng Yang (2009), p. 297.
54. Yasheng Huang (2008), p. 77.
55. At a 1985 conference held in Japan, a Japanese scholar proclaimed that modern enterprise did not exist in China. This comment resonated strongly with Chinese economists in the audience and quickly attracted a lot of attention in China. Quoted from Jinglian Wu (2003), p. 135.
56. Findlay, Watson, and Xu (1994), p. 19.
57. For a detailed historical account of the event, see Yizhuang Ding (2008) and Xiaomeng Liu (2008).
58. For an insightful account of Chinese danwei, see Walder (1986). For a more updated account, see Lu and Perry (1997). For an early but still useful reference, see Schurmann (1968).
59. Licheng Ma (2005), p. 147.
60. Donglian Xiao (2008), p. 621.
61. Muqiao Xue (1996), pp. 268–272.
62. Licheng Ma (2005), p. 150.
63. *Ibid.*

64. *Ibid.*, p. 151.
65. A Chinese economist by the name of Lin Zili, based on an example given in Marx's *Das Capital*, concluded that an employer, when hiring eight workers or above, would engage in capitalistic exploration and therefore should be prohibited. Quoted in Licheng Ma (2005), p. 178.
66. For the tale of Wenzhen, see Jinglong Ma (2008) and Xingzhong Qian (2008).
67. What follows is primarily based on Hong Chen (2006); Mingtian Xu (2008); and Qiao Tu (2008). See also Donglian Xiao (2008), pp. 757–778.
68. Hong Kong benefited greatly from the exodus of human talents and capital from the mainland before and after 1949. At a time when entrepreneurship was attacked in the mainland, Hong Kong provided a safe shelter. Later it was from Hong Kong that human and financial capital first returned when China reopened its arms to capitalism, see Richard Wong (2008).
69. See Hong Chen (2006), pp. 24–27.
70. *Ibid.*, p. 7; Mingtian Xu (2008), pp. 5–6.
71. Hong Chen (2006), p. 8.
72. For example, Gang Deng (1997).
73. Another rationale attributed to Chen Yun to exclude Shanghai was that the whole Yangzi Delta region "was famous for its opportunists who would, with their consummate skills, emerge from their cages if given the slightest chance" (Ziyang Zhao (2009), p. 102) . Zhao's observation adds another testimony to Chen's complicated role in China's reform.
74. Hong Chen (2006), p. 12.
75. Hu's early revolutionary experiences had a formative impact on him. Hu was a victim during the Anti-Bolshevik League incident (1930–1931) when he was still a teenager (Mei Man (2000), pp. 50–51). Hu was saved at the last minute when a large number of Red Army officers were executed after being accused of belonging to the Kuomintang intelligence agency "Anti-Bolshevik League." Later, Hu was involved in the Yan'an "Rectification Movement" (1941–1945) (Yung-fa Chen (1990), pp. xx; Hua Gao (2000), p. 517; see also Mei Man (2000), p. 63), when many intellectuals who had been attracted to Yan'an and Party members were imprisoned as suspected spies of the Kuomintang. These early incidents and his suffering during the Cultural Revolution must have convinced Hu that the Party's use of terror and political control of thought had only damaged the long-term cause of the Party (e.g., Li, Hu, Xie, et al. (2009)). This conviction placed Hu apart from other Chinese leaders.
76. Deng Xiaoping, "Excerpts from Talks Given in Wuchang, Shenzhen, Zhuhai, and Shanghai," in *Selected Works of Deng Xiaoping*, Vol. 3.
77. Ziyang Zhao (2009), pp. 203–206 proposed that China was at the "initial stage of socialism" so that it could free itself from the constraints of orthodox socialist doctrines, legitimizing many reform experiments that were inconsistent with socialism.

4   A Bird in the Cage: Market Reform under Socialism

1. Licheng Ma (2005), pp. 150–152.
2. Li Wu (1999), p. 886.
3. Chung (2000); Zhengfu Shi (2008).
4. Xu and Zhang (2008).
5. For a succinct description of the major problems China's state-owned enterprises faced, see Granick (1990), pp. 25–31.
6. Muqiao Xue (1996), pp. 272–277.

7. *Ibid.*, pp. 273–274.
8. *Ibid.*, p. 277.
9. For Chinese politics during this time period, see, for example, Shirk (1993); Fewsmith (1994); and Jisheng Yang (2004).
10. For Chen's economic thinking and the critical role he played under Mao and Deng, see Lardy and Lieberthal (1983); Liu and Xu (2009). As admitted by Ziyang Zhao (2009) in his biography, "Chen Yun was enormously influential within the Communist Party and in economic policy" (p. 122).
11. Donglian Xiao et al. (1999), pp. 93–95.
12. An alternative view would see the cage as a shelter for the economy. This reinterpretation would make Chen's view broadly compatible with the working of the market economy, where the role of the state is to protect and facilitate the market, rather than restrict market forces.
13. Hu Yaobang, "Report to the 12th Party Congress," *People's Daily* (September 8th, 1982).
14. Quoted from Ziyang Zhao (2009), p. 103. See also Li Wu (1999), p. 852.
15. Jisheng Yang (2004), pp. 275–285; Ziyang Zhao (2009), pp. 162–168.
16. Licheng Ma (2005), pp. 162–166; Yasheng Huang (2008), pp. 50–51.
17. Licheng Ma, pp. 175–177; see also Jinglong Ma (2008) and Xingzhong Qian (2008).
18. Peng and Chen (2008), p. 138.
19. Yao (2008) called the Chinese government in the reform era a "disinterested government." This description fits the early period of reform better.
20. Jisheng Yang (2004), pp. 341–342.
21. But Chinese politics remained institutionally unstable, as later demonstrated by the nonprocedural removal from office of both Hu and his successor, Zhao Ziyang.
22. Jisheng Yang (2004), pp. 188–189 and 196–199.
23. Muqiao Xue (1996), pp. 297–298.
24. Peng and Chen (2008), p. 180; Yasheng Huang (2008), p. 97.
25. Wong (1988), p. 11.
26. *Japan Economic Journal* (May 29th, 1984).
27. *Business Week* (October 15th, 1984).
28. Deng Xiaoping, "Reform and Opening to the Outside World Are a Great Experiment," *Selected Works of Deng Xiaoping*, Vol. 3.
29. Deng Xiaoping, "Excerpts from Talks Given in Wuchang, Shenzhen, Zhuhai, and Shanghai, January 18th, February 21st, 1992," *Selected Works of Deng Xiaoping*, Vol. 3.
30. See, for example, Ziyang Zhao (2009), p. 101.
31. *People's Daily* (July 21st, 1992).
32. Another similarity shared by them was rather unfortunate. Deng was as keen to hold on to political power as Chen was to economic centralization. Nonetheless, the differences between Deng and Chen were many and significant. For example, they held almost opposite views on the speed of reform and foreign capital – for the latter, see Ziyang Zhao (2009), p. 102.
33. Peng and Chen (2008), pp. 189–192.
34. 1984 Decision on the Economic System Reform, its Chinese version available at http://cpc.people.com.cn/GB/64162/134902/8092122.html.
35. Muqiao Xue (1996), p. 310.
36. Li Wu (1999), pp. 908–912; Peng and Chen (2008), pp. 214–218. For a diagnosis of China's pricing system prior to price reform, see Furen Dong (1986) .
37. Before price reform, the Chinese government thought prices could be 'scientifically" calculated if a powerful computing machine was available. The State Council appointed Xue Muqiao in 1981 to lead a team of more than 50 economists to use input–output data and the most advanced computers bought abroad to calculate theoretical prices. See Weiying Zhang (2010), p. 200.

38. For the debate between proponents of the two approaches, see Weiying Zhang (2008) and Jun Zhang (2010), pp. 3–30.
39. Peng and Chen (2008), p. 209.
40. Jinglian Wu (2003), p. 65.
41. e.g., Lau, Qian, and Roland (2000).
42. Peng and Chen (2008), p. 240.
43. *Ibid.*, pp. 240–241.
44. *Ibid.*, pp. 243–244.
45. *Ibid.*, p. 196.
46. *Ibid.*, pp. 196–197.
47. *Ibid.*, p. 198.
48. For changes in China's financial system, see Riedel, Jin, and Gao (2007) as well as Allen, Qian, and Qian (2008). For a concise view of China's banking system up to the mid-1980s, see Zhou and Zhu (1987).
49. Quoted in Jinglian Wu (2005), pp. 190–191.
50. Kraay (2000). Wu Jinglian's estimate (2005), p. 191 puts the household saving as high as 83 percent during the 1990s, which is probably too high an estimate. But the steady increase of household saving since the late 1970s, in both absolute terms and relative to enterprise and government saving, is well documented.
51. For a classic formulation and analysis of the problem, see Kornai (1979, 1980, 1986). For a systematic analysis of the role of Chinese local governments in investment, see Yasheng Huang (1996). For a more updated account, see Shih (2007).
52. The following is based on Muqiao Xue (1996), pp. 312–319; Li Wu (1999), p. 948; Jinglian Wu (2010), pp. 339–342.
53. Muqiao Xue (1996), p. 313.
54. *Ibid.*, p. 316–317.
55. *Ibid.*, p. 324.
56. Jisheng Yang (1998), p. 394; Peng and Chen (2008), p. 319.
57. Peng and Chen (2008) p. 321. For its political ramification, see Ziyang Zhao (2009), pp. 223–234.
58. The following is based on Jisheng Yang (2004); Ruoshui Wang (1997); and Jiwei Hu (1997). See also Fewsmith (1994).
59. See also Ziyang Zhao (2009), pp. 161–166.
60. But the decision to remove Hu was made by a few Party veterans, including Deng and Chen, rather than the official Party organ, blatantly violating the constitution of the Party. This incident began a series of actions in the following years that would critically undermine the political legitimacy of the Party and gradually turn the Party into a powerful interest group. No longer united by a common political belief, the Party would resort to material interests to hold on to power. While this transformation would depoliticize the Party and weaken its ideological commitment, it would also delay political reform and open the economy to the infiltration of political forces.
61. For a book-length sociological account of the 1989 Students Movement, see Dingxin Zhao (2001).
62. Lau, Qian, and Roland (2000).
63. David Hume, as quoted by Hirschman (1977), wrote "reason is, and ought only to be the slave of the passions" (p. 24).
64. See, for example, Coase (1959, 1961); Alchian (1961); Alchian and Demsetz (1973); and Barzel (1997). For the impact of property rights economics on Chinese economic reform, see, for example, Geng Xiao (1997); Cheung (2009); and Qiren Zhou (2008). See also Jun Zhang (1991).

65. See, for example, Schotter (1981); Coase (1984, 1988); Williamson (1985); Bromley (1989); North (1990); Ostrom (1990); Powell and DiMaggio (1991); Brinton and Nee (1998); Menard and Shirley (2005); and Mahoney and Thelen (2010).

66. In the past, disagreement with the Party line was regarded as the highest treason. This practice essentially ruled out any meaningful debate between Party lines. This imposed uniformity might have helped to bring the Party to power, but it became a deadly liability for a ruling party.

67. For a discussion of the role of economists in policymaking under Mao and the early years of reform, see a doctoral dissertation by Halpern (1985). See also Donglian Xiao (2008), pp. 458–465 and 511–516. For changes up to the 1990s, see Naughton (2002). For a most recent study of China's various think tanks and their influences on government policy, see Xuefeng Zhu (2009).

68. Jisheng Yang (1998), pp. 324–325; (2004), pp. 195–199.

69. For legal reforms in China, see Lubman (2000); Peerenboom (2002); Ruoying Chen (2008); and Potter (2008). For "restricted" reform in Chinese courts, see Liebman (2007).

70. Deng Xiaoping, "Neither Democracy nor the Legal System Should Be Weakened," *Selected Works of Deng Xiaoping*, Vol. 2.

71. Quoted in Raphael Shen (2000), p. ix.

72. Gilboy and Read (2008), p. 155.

73. Clark, Murrell, and Whiting (2008), p. 381.

74. For this and other indicators of legal development, see Jingwen Zhu (2007).

75. Alfred (1999), p. 193.

76. Hong Chen (2006), pp. 19–23; Donglian Xiao (2008), pp. 766–768.

77. For China's cadre management system and Beijing's use of personnel appointments to control local governments, see Manion (1985) and Chan (2004). Chenggang Xu (2009) coined a new term, a "regionally decentralized authoritarian system," to refer to Beijing's tight personnel control and economic decentralization.

5   Growing out of Socialism: Capitalism with Chinese Characteristics

1. Peng and Chen (2008), pp. 321–323.

2. Li Wu (1999), p. 980.

3. *The Guardian* (March 21st, 1989).

4. *Newsweek* (June 19th, 1989).

5. *The Economist* (October 28th, 1989).

6. *Washington Post* (June 29th, 1990).

7. Licheng Ma (2008), p. 149.

8. e.g., Shirk (1993); Gordon White (1993).

9. Li Peng, "Interview with Western German Newspaper Reported," BBC Summary of World Broadcasts, November 25th, 1989, accessed at LexisNexis.

10. "Premier Li Peng Addresses the National Planning Conference," BBC Summary of World Broadcasts, December 29th, 1989. All three quotations can be found in the text, accessed at LexisNexis.

11. *Ibid.*

12. *Ibid.*

13. *Ibid.*

14. *People's Daily* (February 22nd, 1990).

15. This conference is well documented in Chinese. See, for example, Jun Zhang (2010), pp. 41–65.

16. Muqiao Xue (1996), pp. 319–326.

17. Xiaobo Wu (2010), pp. 147–148; Muqiao Xue (1996), p. 336.

18. *People's Daily* (December 7th, 1990).
19. Deng Xiaoping (June 9th, 1989), *Selected Works of Deng Xiaoping*, Vol. 3.
20. Deng Xiaoping (June 16th, 1989), in *Selected Works of Deng Xiaoping*, Vol.3.
21. "Jiang Zemin on Anniversary of Shenzhen Special Economic Zone," BBC Summary of World Broadcast, November 28th, 1990, accessed at LexisNexis.
22. *Ibid.*
23. *Ibid.*
24. *Ibid.*
25. Peng and Chen (2008), pp. 353–356.
26. *Ibid.*, pp. 360–364.
27. *Ibid.*, pp. 254–259.
28. *Ibid.*, pp. 256–258. See also "Chinese Get Wall Street Guide to Capitalist Road," *New York Times* (November 12th, 1986).
29. Peng and Chen (2008), pp. 364–368.
30. *Ibid.*, p. 366.
31. *Ibid.*, p. 368.
32. Jisheng Yang (1998), pp. 509–510.
33. Peng and Chen (2008), p. 375.
34. *Ibid.*
35. See Muqiao Xue (1996), p. 356.
36. *People's Daily* (September 2nd, 1991).
37. *Ibid.*
38. *People's Daily* (October 23rd, 1991).
39. As revealed in Vogel's (2010) recent account, Deng was still able to summon Jiang Zemin and Li Peng – at least twice in 1990 (March 3rd and December 24th), but his words "had little effect" (p. 667).
40. For the first report in China of Deng's southern tour, see "Spring Wind Blows East – Deng Xiaoping in Shenzhen," which first appeared in the *Shenzhen Special Zone Daily* (March 26th, 1992). For a fuller account, particularly Deng's talks at Wuchang and Changsha, see Wu and Yu (2008). Deng's talks appear as "Excepts from Talks Given in Wuchang, Shenzhen, Zhuhai, and Shanghai," in *Selected Works of Deng Xiaoping*, Vol. 3. See also Wong and Zheng (2001).
41. Deng Xiaoping (1992), "Excerpts from Talks Given in Wuchang, Shenzhen, Zhuhai, and Shanghai," in *Selected Works of Deng Xiaoping*, Vol. 3.
42. "Unknown Stories during Deng Xiaoping's Southern Tour," provided by Xinhua, accessed at http://news.xinhuanet.com/misc/2008-09/27/content_10119788.htm.
43. *Ibid.*
44. Deng Xiaoping (1992), "Excerpts from Talks Given in Wuchang, Shenzhen, Zhuhai, and Shanghai," in *Selected Works of Deng Xiaoping*, Vol. 3.
45. *Ibid.*
46. *Ibid.*
47. Deng had long held this pragmatic view of socialism. When hosting a political leader from Africa in the early 1980s, Deng told his visitor, "I would recommend that you do not practice socialism, but rather concentrate on economic development. Once the economy is developed, the people's living conditions improved, and they are satisfied, you can call it whatever ism you like." These words were deemed too radical to be included in the *Selected Works of Deng Xiaoping*. See Daozheng Du (2008).
48. Deng Xiaoping (1992), "Excerpts from Talks Given in Wuchang, Shenzhen, Zhuhai, and Shanghai," in *Selected Works of Deng Xiaoping*, Vol. 3.
49. *Ibid.*
50. *Ibid.*

51. Jiyun Tian (2004). For a collection of Tian's articles on reform, see Tian (2009).
52. For internal political debates in early 1992 after Deng's southern tour, see Jisheng Yang (2004), pp. 476–517; Fewsmith (2008), pp. 68–72.
53. *People's Daily* (April 14th, 1992).
54. Licheng Ma (2008), pp. 158–159.
55. *Ibid.*, p. 156.
56. Deng Xiaoping (1992), "Excerpts from Talks Given in Wuchang, Shenzhen, Zhuhai, and Shanghai," in *Selected Works of Deng Xiaoping*, Vol. 3.
57. Mao Zedong (1967), in *Selected Works of Mao Tse-tung*, Vol. I, p. 380.
58. Licheng Ma (2005), p. 194.
59. *Ibid.*, p. 201.
60. *Ibid.*, p. 199.
61. Peng and Chen (2008), pp. 400–403.
62. This is the title of Jiang's speech at the Party Congress. For a full text of the speech, see http://www.bjreview.com.cn/document/txt/2011-03/29/content_363504.htm
63. Peng and Chen (2008), p. 409.
64. *Ibid.*
65. Jisheng Yang (1998), pp. 356–361.
66. See Shanda Xu (2008), pp. 525–537. Originally, the Minister of Finance only allowed the income tax to be subject to negotiation under the managerial responsibility system – the turnover tax was still controlled directly by the Minister. But when the managerial responsibility system was implemented, the State Council was not diligent in enforcing the rules. For example, the contract signed by Beijing Capital Steel Corporation, approved by the State Council, included clauses on both income tax and turnover tax.
67. For a detailed analysis of China's tax system before and after the 1994 reform, see Jiwei Lou (1998).
68. Jisheng Yang (1998), p. 426.
69. Peng and Chen (2008), pp. 441–445.
70. *Ibid.*, pp. 445–450.
71. Jinglian Wu (2005), pp. 269–274; (2010), ch. 7.
72. Jiwei Lou (2008), p. 334.
73. We thank Weibing Zhou for pointing us to the information on product tax; Zhou worked at a county tax bureau in the early 1990s. We are responsible for the interpretation.
74. Zhang and Yuan (2008), p. 79; Peng and Chen (2008), p. 515.
75. Zhang and Yuan (2008), p. 81.
76. The calculation was made based on data provided by Li Wu (1999), p. 1525.
77. This idea first appeared in Coase (1959). This was the version of Coase Theorem that Steven Cheung stressed and introduced to the Chinese readers. See Cheung (2009).
78. The story of Chen Guang was widely known in China. See, for example, Licheng Ma (2005), pp. 203–208.
79. Wenkui Zhang and Dongming Yuan (2008), p. 113.
80. Licheng Ma (2008), p. 175.
81. *Ibid.*
82. *Ibid.*, p. 176.
83. We thank Professor Chenggang Xu of the University of Hong Kong for this information; Xu was then at London School of Economics and was directly involved in arranging for Shanghai officials to visit several Western European countries to learn their practice of state assets management.
84. This episode was revealed to us by Professor Chenggang Xu in his comments (April 7th, 2010) on an early version of the book.

85. Peng and Chen (2008), p. 460.
86. *Ibid.*
87. *Ibid.*, p. 463.
88. We thank Professor Xiqing Zhu of Changsha University of Science and Technology and Mr. Xiaoming Liu, who was Vice Mayor of Changsha for the information. Both Zhu and Liu attended the 2008 Chicago Conference on China's Economic Transformation. See Xiaoming Liu (2008).
89. Zhang and Yuan (2008), pp. 132–138.
90. See Riedel, Jin, and Gao (2007) for a systematic analysis of China's financial system in the course of Chinese market transformation. An important reason for the underdevelopment of China's stock market is the rise of state assets exchange centers. In 2009, the total value of assets that were transacted at such centers reached 500 billion yuan; this was way higher than the combined amount of capital raised at Shanghai and Shenzhen Stock Exchange. For an updated account of the development of the state assets exchange market in China, see Heping Cao (2009).
91. The homepage of the State Assets Supervision and Administration Commission provides updated information about the agent itself, relevant policies, and state enterprises under its jurisdiction: http://www.sasac.gov.cn.
92. Jiantang Ma (2008), p. 356.
93. A challenging task of the Commission today is to oversee the state assets exchange market. Given the tremendous and still growing size of state assets – by the end of 2010, the total assets of 120 enterprises controlled by the central government reached 24 trillion yuan, representing a 16 percent growth over the previous year – how efficiently this market operates has a critical impact on the overall performance of the economy. The data were retrieved from the website of the Commission on December 20th, 2011.
94. This is confirmed by a detailed empirical study (Gan, Guo, and Xu (2010)) based on a nationwide firm survey on China's privatization in the period of 2002 to 2006. The study shows that privatized enterprises that later went through restructuring, such as changing core management teams, adopting international accounting standards and professional independent auditing, and establishing boards of directors, had significantly improved corporate performance, while privatized firms that did not undertake restructuring measures performed poorly.
95. Schumpeter (1942), p. 84. For a recent biography of Schumpeter and his lasting contribution to economics, see McCraw (2007).
96. Cheung (2009).
97. Coase (1937).
98. For a preliminary effort, see Coase and Wang (2011).
99. The following descriptions of industrial parks are mainly based on Ning Wang's fieldwork in Zhejiang, Shanghai, Anhui, Guangdong, Fujian, Hubei, Jiangsu, Hunan, Sichuan, and Beijing. See Douglas Zeng (2011) for a recent review of the critical part played by industrial parks in China's market transformation.
100. The updated full list of China Economic and Technological Development Zones can be found at the website of the Minister of Commerce, accessed on February 3rd, 2012, at http://www.mofcom.gov.cn/xglj/kaifaqu.shtml.
101. e.g., Coase and Wang (2011).
102. Marshall (1920), p. 115.
103. Oi (1992); Lin (1995).
104. See Thun (2006) for the rise of Shanghai in China's auto industry.
105. Yasheng Huang (2003), p. 261.
106. Tang (2009).
107. Marshall (1920), p. 221.

108. The best known article in the literature is probably Montinola, Qian, and Weingast (1995); see also Jin, Qian, and Weingast (2005) for an update. For various critiques, see Cai and Treisman (2005, 2006) and Tao and Yang (2008). See Chenggang Xu (2009) for an updated and more sophisticated reformulation of the decentralization argument.
109. Sachs (1994), p. 6.
110. Deng Xiaoping, Interview with Mike Wallace (September 2nd, 1986), *Selected Works of Deng Xiaoping*, Vol. 3.
111. This logic is stressed by Qian and Xu (1993).
112. For a detailed and insightful analysis of this political system, see Chenggang Xu (2009).
113. e.g., Yasheng Huang (2003), p. 20.
114. "China's Auto Sales Run Hot," *Wall Street Journal* (October 23rd, 2010).

6 From Capitalism to Capitalisms

1. Coase (2008), Concluding speech at the 2008 Chicago Conference on China's Economic Transformation.
2. Elliott (2008).
3. In Hinton (1982), p. 462.
4. Ferguson (1980 [1767]), p. 122. Ferguson's original formulation is "the result of human action, but not the execution of any human design." It was Hayek (1967), ch. 6 who popularized the phrase, "the result of human action but not of human design."
5. In Hinton (1982), p. 459.
6. In his recent book on the rise and fall of communism, Brown (2009) concurs: "how little it revealed about a particular person to be told that the individual was a Communist" (p. 1). For a general exposition of the fluidity and complexity of identity, see Sen (2006).
7. See, for example, Murphy, Shleifer, and Vishny (1992) and Sachs (1992). For a review of the relevant literature on gradualism versus shock therapy, see Roland (2002). Gradualism proposes optimal sequencing in contrast with the big bang approach. Both sides take economic transition as a technical problem and fail to recognize transition as essentially a Hayekian economic problem (Hayek 1945).
8. Hayek (1988). What makes socialism a "fatal conceit" is the belief that scientific socialism calls for a thorough eradication of traditions on the one hand and a complete redesign of social institutions on the other, thus enabling a rationalistic reconstruction of human society from scratch. Similar intellectual hubris was discernible in the dominant economic thinking on transition in the 1990s.
9. Hayek (1974). "The Pretense of Knowledge," the Nobel Prize Lecture.
10. Hu Yaobang interview with *L'Unità* (September 30th, 1984), Foreign Broadcast Information Service (FBIS), No. 194 (October 10th, 1984).
11. The following is based on Ri Yu (2002) , which has attracted a lot of attention in China, partly because Wang Zhen later became a dogged opponent of Hu Yaobang and his liberal policy.
12. *Ibid.*
13. For recent discussions on the resilience of the Party and the Chinese state, see Dali Yang (2004) and Shambaugh (2008). For a critical assessment, see Pei (2006).
14. Xuewei Chen (2004).
15. e.g., Li Wu (1999), pp. 828–830 and Donglian Xiao (2008), pp. 541–544.
16. Xuewei Chen (2004).

17. Donglian Xiao (2004) began his entry, an otherwise solid and carefully researched article, by stating that "China's reform was launched through a top-down fashion" (p. 185). Naughton (2008) also called the initial approach of reform "top down" (p. 100).
18. Jinglian Wu (2005), p. 64.
19. E.g., Jiang Zemin's Report at the Fourteenth Party Congress (1992). Available at http://www.bjreview.com.cn/document/txt/2011-03/29/content_363504.htm.
20. Deng Xiaoping, "We Regard Reform as a Revolution," talk on October 10th, 1984, with Chancellor Helmut Kohl of the Federal Republic of Germany, in *Selected Works of Deng Xiaoping*, Vol. 3.
21. In Hinton (1982), p. 460.
22. *Ibid.*
23. Deng Xiaoping, "We Regard Reform as a Revolution," talk on October 10th, 1984, with Chancellor Helmut Kohl of the Federal Republic of Germany, in Selected Works of Deng Xiaoping, Vol. 3.
24. Zhao Ziyang's report on government work, Xinhua General News Service, May 31st, 1984.
25. Cheung (1982).
26. The consistent efforts of North (1981, 1990, and 2005) stand out as one of the few exceptions. But we are still far away from a dynamic theory of institutional change. See also Greif (2006); North, Wallis, and Weingast (2009); Kuran (2010); Acemoglu and Robinson (2012)
27. The literature on path dependence is a noticeable exception, e.g., Arthur (1994); Mahoney (2000); David (2001); and Pierson (2004). For a recent critical review of the literature, see Vergne and Durand (2010). Desjardins (2011) offers a critique from the perspective of evolutionary biology.
28. See, for example, Ziyang Zhao (2009), pp. 119–124.
29. Peng and Chen (2008), p. 280.
30. Lin and Yao (2001).
31. Kornai (1979, 1980, 1986) first introduced the concept of "soft budget constraint." For more recent reviews, see Maskin (1996, 1999) as well as Maskin and Xu (2001).
32. Zhang and Yuan (2008), p. 89.
33. For a recent review of the literature, see Chenggang Xu (2009); see also Cheung (2009) and Sheng (2010).
34. Oi (1992); Walder (1995). See also Nee (1992).
35. For a classic defense of the minimum state, see Nozick (1974).
36. The continuous presence of the state in defining and redefining property rights has raised a serious challenge. The discretionary power that the Chinese state still holds undermines the credibility of China's emerging private property rights. Since the power can be and has been abused by government officials, it remains a big hurdle for the Chinese government to protect private property rights that has been recognized by the new constitution since 2004.
37. See, for example, a book review by Levinston (2010), that is simply titled "China's Authoritarian Capitalism Undermines Western Values" *Washington Post* (May 30th), accessed at http://www.washingtonpost.com/wp-dyn/content/article/2010/05/28/AR2010052801859.html. The three books reviewed are Halper (2010); Bremmer (2010); and Kampfner (2010).
38. Baumol, Litan, and Shramm (2007). But the authors are quite skeptical of the common claim that China is a "quintessential state-guided economy" (p. 145).
39. Yasheng Huang (2008), p. 236.
40. The Chinese economist Wu Jinglian first coined the term in 1998, which is meant to criticize the economic privilege of political power. See Xiaobo Wu (2010), p. 196.

41. Dingxin Zhao (2009).
42. See http://www.mfa.gov.cn/eng/wjb/zzjg/gjs/gjzzyhy/2604/2606/t15288.htm.
43. See http://news.xinhuanet.com/english/2008-04/12/content_7966431.htm.
44. Madsen, talk given at a panel held at the University of California at San Diego on October 1st, 2009, to celebrate the 60th anniversary of the People's Republic of China. Available at http://www.youtube.com/watch?v=BgckHmsghmc.
45. See, for example, Short (1999), pp. 101–105.
46. As Short (1999) put it, for Mao, "Chinese culture was still the foundation on which everything else had to be built – and would remain so for the rest of his life" (p. 103).
47. As Mao admitted later, "I read and re-read them [Kang Youwei and Liang Qichao] by heart. I worshiped Kang Youwei and Liang Qichao." Quoted from Spence (1999), p. 9.
48. As Kang Chao (1986) stated, China had a specific form of "market economy for more than two millennia before the 1950's," which he called the "atomistic market economy" (p. 5). Hill Gates (1996) referred to it as "a thousand years of petty capitalism." For the history of capitalist development in China since the late Ming period, see the three volumes edited by Xu and Wu (2007).
49. *The Travels of Marco Polo* (translated by Henry Yule 1923).
50. For a readily accessible introduction to Confucianism, including its development over time, see Yao (2000). For an early assessment of the fate of Confucianism in modern China, see Levenson (1968).
51. Fogel (2010). For a more elaborated argument, see Fogel (2006). For a recent and sophisticated prediction, see Subramanian (2011).
52. Nicholas Consonery (January 7th, 2010), "A 123 Trillion China? Not Likely," appeared on the online edition of *Foreign Policy*.
53. Adam Smith (1969 [1759]), pp. 380–381.
54. The late Chicago economist, D. Gale Johnson (1994, 1999) had persistently criticized the economic reasoning behind China's one-child policy.
55. See http://money.cnn.com/magazines/fortune/global500/2009/countries/China.html.
56. See http://finance.eastday.com/m/20100525/u1a5224725.html.
57. For a critical analysis of the role of state-owned enterprises in the Chinese economy, see a recent working paper done by the Unirule Institute of Economics (2011).
58. Xiaolu Wang (2007); see also a study conducted by the Unirule Institute of Economics (2011), particularly ch. 4.
59. Yang Shang (1928), pp. 331–333.
60. Master Shen (Shen Zi), "Yi Wen." See Qiu Hanping (or Henry H. P. Chiu), "Shenzi de Falu Shixiang" [The Legal Thoughts of Master Shen], originally appeared in *Faxue Jikan [Law Quarterly]* 3 (1927), reproduced in He and Li (2003), pp. 343–344.
61. E.g., Durkheim (1982), pp. 50–59. See also Berger and Luckmann (1966). Searle refers to them as "institutional facts" in contrast to "brute facts" (1969), pp. 50–52.
62. Hayek (1948), p. 60.
63. There are as many as eight different Chinese translations available. This edition was translated by Tang Risong (2004).
64. *Ibid.*, "Translator's introduction," p. 8.
65. *Ibid.*, "Translator's introduction," pp. 4–5.
66. Interview with Wen Jiabao by *Financial Times* (February 2nd, 2009), available at http://www.ft.com/cms/s/0/795d2bca-f0fe-11dd-8790-0000779fd2ac.html#axzz1 CqDI0Ten.
67. *Ibid.*
68. Interview with Wen Jiaobao by Fareed Zakaria, available at http://www.newsweek.com/2008/09/28/we-should-join-hands.html.

69. Wen's comments on Adam Smith were widely discussed on the internet, e.g., http://book.163.com/special/009242BF/guanyuan.html.
70. Adam Smith (1969 [1759]), pp. 167–168.
71. *Ibid.*, p. 517.
72. e.g., Zhiping Liang (2010). For a different assessment, see Whyte (2010).
73. Adam Smith (1976 [1776]), Book V, p. 232.
74. Adam Smith (1976 [1776]), Book I, p. 88.
75. e.g., Ren (1997); Xiaohong Ma (1997, 2004).
76. Knight (1976), p. 43.
77. Cheung (1982, 1986).
78. See http://siteresources.worldbank.org/DATASTATISTICS/Resources/GDP.pdf.
79. http://siteresources.worldbank.org/DATASTATISTICS/Resources/GNIPC.pdf
80. Ffrench (1950), p. 203.
81. See http://moneywatch.bnet.com/economic-news/blog/macro-view/manufacturing-surprise-the-us-still-leads-in-making-things/2134/.
82. See, for example, Deng Xiaoping's speech at the opening ceremony of the National Conference of Science on March 18th, 1978. It is available in *Selected Works of Deng Xiaoping*, Vol. 2.
83. "China's Great Leap Forward in Higher Education," *Asia Times* (July 3rd, 2002).
84. A Google search of "Qian Xuesen zhi Wen" (Qian Xuesen Puzzle)" generated 542,000 responses (February 2nd, 2011).
85. See Ryan (2010) for a discussion of recent development in China's higher education.
86. "Nan Keda Did Not Receive Approval after Three and Half Years of Preparation," *People's Daily* (October 20th, 2010).
87. The Communiqué, in Hinton (1982), p. 461.
88. *Ibid.*
89. This quote is from Deng's talk given on December 13th, 1979, to government leaders. Quoted from Raphael Shen (2000), p. ix.
90. Deng Xiaoping's conviction that "development is the hard truth" remains the core foundation of the political legitimacy of the Party. For scholarly treatment on China's performance-based political legitimacy, see Lynn White (2005); Dingxin Zhao (2009).
91. Popper (1978).
92. For an account of the rise of political associations in the late nineteenth and early twentieth century, see Yu-fa Chang (1982, 2004).
93. This old political credo is attributed to Confucius; it exhorts the ruler to take an impartial stand and serve the public welfare. It is unfortunate that it has been misunderstood as a call for public ownership. As stressed by Shang Yang and Master Shen (see pp. 182–83) as well as modern property rights economics, it is not public ownership but clearly delineated property rights that offer the best chance to secure and advance the interests of the general public.
94. Mao once wrote the poem to Fu Ssu-nian in 1945 upon the latter's request for his calligraphy. Fu and Mao had knew each other since their days at Peking University when Fu was a prominent student leader and Mao, a library assistant; but Mao "had always been denied inclusion in discussion groups with Fu" Fan-sen Wang (2000), p. 170.
95. For a classic account of the problems of bureaucracy, see Simon (1997 [1947]).
96. For an insightful exposition and powerful defense of the market for ideas and the free pursuit of knowledge, see Polanyi (1951, 1958). See also Coase (1974).
97. Mu Qian, one of the best known Chinese historians in the twentieth century, called traditional China a "shi-run government" (2001), p. 15 or "shi-centered society" (2010), p. 80. Balazs (1964) agreed with Qian on facts regarding the role

of *shi* in Chinese history, but offered a more critical interpretation. The scholar-officials' state, according to Balazs, "was so strong that the merchant class never dared to fight it openly in order to extract from it liberties, laws, and autonomy for themselves" (p. 23). See also note 33.

98. Hayek (1973), p. 2 went even further to warn us that "the predominant model of liberal democratic institutions, ... *necessarily* leads to a gradual transformation of the spontaneous order of a free society into a totalitarian system conducted in the service of some coalition of organized interests" (italic added).

99. John Dunn (2005) provides an illuminating account of the rise of democracy from "parochial eccentricity and protracted ignominy" (p.18) to become "a single worldwide name for the legitimate basis of political authority (p. 15). Rather than election or multi-party competition, democracy is identified by Dunn as "the name for political authority exercised solely through the persuasion of the greater number" (p. 132). But a free market for ideas is indispensable for any genuine persuasion.

100. For an insightful exposition of the logic of liberty, see Polanyi (1951) and Hayek (1960).

101. However, about one hundred days later the statue was removed, with little explanation given by the authority. This incident reveals certain hesitation and even resistance to China's return to its own cultural roots. Tradition, as T. S. Eliot (1932) put it well, "cannot be inherited, and if you want it you must obtain it by great labor" (p. 14). In renewing its own cultural traditions, China has to overcome layers of intellectual barriers and ideological apprehensions left by radical anti-traditionalism and revolutionary ideology that had dominated the Chinese minds since the dawn of the twentieth century. For an elaborate discussion of the critical role of tradition in human society, see Shils (1981).

102. Alitto (1979).

103. See Shuming Liang (2004), pp. 126–130; Liang and Alitto (2009), pp. 87–99.

104. Coase (2006), p. 276.

105. Fogel (2010).

Epilogue

1. All the quotes can be found in a carefully researched biography of Qian by Iris Chang (1995).

2. Wen Jiabao, "Let People Live with More Dignity," accessed at http://news.163.com/10/0212/18/5VBEJINR000120GU.html.

3. *The Economist* (March 19th, 2011). The story "Don't worry, be happy; China" appeared on p. 49.

4. *Theory of Moral Sentiments* (1979), III.I.73, The full text is available online at http://www.econlib.org/library/Smith/smMS.html

References

Acemoglu, Daron and James Robinson. 2012. *Why Nations Fail: The Origins of Power, Prosperity, and Poverty*. New York: Crown.

Alchian, Armen. 1965. "Some Economics of Property Rights," *Il Politico* 30: 916–929. Reprinted in *Economic Forces at Work* (1977). Indianapolis, IN: Liberty Fund.

Alchian, Armen and Harold Demsetz. 1973. "The Property Rights Paradigm," *Journal of Economic History* 33: 16–27.

Alfred, William. 1999. "A Second Great Wall? China's Post Cultural Revolution Project of Legal Construction," *Cultural Dynamics* 11: 193–213.

Alitto, Guy. 1979. *The Last Confucian: Liang Shu-min and the Chinese Dilemma of Modernity*. Berkeley, CA: University of California Press.

Allen, Franklin, Jun Qian and Meijun Qian. 2008. "China's Financial System: Past, Present, and Future," ch. 14 in *China's Great Economic Transformation*, ed. Loren Brandt and Thomas Rawski, pp. 506–568. New York: Cambridge University Press.

An, Jieshe. 2004. "Deng Xiaoping Zaidu Fuchu" [Deng Xiaoping's Return to Power], in *The Thematic History of the People's Republic of China*, ed. Dehong Guo, Haiguang Wang and Gang Han, Vol. 3, pp. 369–88. Chengdu: Sichuan People's Press.

Anhui Provincial Party Committee (ed.), 2006. *Anhui Nongcun Gaige zi Lu* [The Road of Agricultural Reform in Anhui]. Beijing: Chinese Communist Party History Press.

—— 2006. *Anhui Nongcun Gaige Kou Shu Shi* [The Oral History of Agricultural Reform in Anhui]. Beijing: Chinese Communist Party History Press.

Arrow, Kenneth. 1974. *The Limits of Organization*. New York: Norton.

Arthur, W. Brian. 1994. *Increasing Returns and Path Dependence in the Economy*. Ann Arbor: University of Michigan Press.

Balazs, Etienne. 1964. *Chinese Civilization and Bureaucracy*. New Haven, CT: Yale University Press.

Banfield, Edward. 1967. *The Moral Basis of a Backward Society*. New York: Free Press.

Barzel, Yoram. 1997. *Economic Analysis of Property Rights*, second edition. New York: Cambridge University Press.

Baumol, William, Robert Litan, and Carl Shramm. 2007. *Good Capitalism, Bad Capitalism, and Economics of Growth and Prosperity*. New Haven, CT: Yale University Press.

Berger, Peter and Thomas Luckmann. 1966. *The Social Construction of Reality: A Treatise in the Sociology of Knowledge*. New York: Doubleday.

Becker, Jasper. 1998, *Hungry Ghosts: Mao's Secret Famine*. New York: Holt.

Bianco, Lucien. 1971. *Origins of the Chinese Revolution, 1915–1949*. Stanford, CA: Stanford University Press.

Bo, Yibo. 1997. *Ruogan Zhongda Jueche yu Shijian de Huigu* [Recollections of Several Important Decisions and Events], revised edition. Beijing: Chinese Communist Party History Press.

Bramall, Chris. 2009. *Chinese Economic Development*. London: Routledge.

Braun, Otto. 1982. *A Comintern Agent in China 1932–1939*, trans. Jeanne Moore, with an introduction by Dick Wilson (first published in German in 1975). Stanford, CA: Stanford University Press.

Bremmer, Ian. 2010. *The End of The Free Market: Who Wins the War between States and Corporations*. New York: Portfolio Hardcover.

Brinton, Mary and Victor Nee (eds.), 1998. *The New Institutionalism in Sociology*. New York: Russell Sage Foundation.

Bromley, Daniel W. 1989. *Economic Interests and Institutions*. New York: Blackwell.

Brown, Archie. 2009. *The Rise and Fall of Communism*. New York: HarperCollins.

Cai, Hongbin and Daniel Treisman. 2005. "Does Competition for Capital Discipline Governments? Decentralization, Globalization, and Public Policy," *American Economic Review* 95: 817–830.

—— 2006. "Did Government Decentralization Cause China's Economic Miracle?" *World Politics* 58: 505–35.

Cao, Heping (ed.). 2009. *Zhongguo Chanquan Shichang Fazhan Baogao 2009–2010* [Progress Report of China's Assets Exchange Market: 2009–2010]. Beijing: Social Sciences Academic Press.

Chan, Hon S. 2004. "Cadre Personnel Management in China: The *Nomenklatura* System, 1990–1998," *The China Quarterly* 179: 703–734.

Chang, Chung-Li. 1955. *The Chinese Gentry: Studies on Their Role in Nineteenth Century Chinese Society*. Seattle, WA: University of Washington Press.

Chang, Iris. 1995. *Thread of the Silkworm*. New York: Perseus Books Group.

Chang, Yu-fa. 1982. *Qing Ji de Geming Tuanti* [Revolutionaries of the Late Chin Period]. Taiwan: Taiwan: Institute of Modern History, Academia Sinica.

—— 2004. *Minguo Chunian de Zhengdang* [Political Parties in the Early Republic Era] (first published in Taiwan in 1985). Changsha: Yuelu Academy Press.

Chao, Kang. 1986. *Man and Land in Chinese History: An Economic Analysis*. Stanford, CA: Stanford University Press.

Chen, Dongling. 2004. "Fensui 'Sirenbang' He 'Wenhua Dagenming' De Zhongjie" [The Arrest of the 'Gang of Four' and the Close of the Cultural Revolution], in *The Thematic History of the People's Republic of China*, ed. Dehong Guo, Haiguang Wang, and Gang Han. Vol. 3, pp. 567–592. Chengdu: Sichuan People's Press.

Chen, Hong. 2006. *1979–2000 Shenzhen Zhongda Jueche he Shijian Minjian Guancha* [Private Observation of Critical Decisions and Events in Shenzhen during 1979–2000]. Wuhan: Changjiang Wenyi Press.

Chen, Jinhua. 2005. *Guo Shi YiShu* [Remembering National Affairs]. Beijing: Chinese Communist Party History Press.

Chen, Ruoying. 2008. "The Information Challenge to China's Legal System under the Economic Transition," Paper presented at the 2008 Chicago Conference on China's Market Transformation.

Chen, Xuewei. 2004. "Qishi Niandai Mo Bashi Niandai Chu Guomin Jingjie de Tiaozhen" [Economic Adjustment in the late 1970s and early 1980s], in *The Thematic History of the People's Republic of China*, ed. Dehong Guo, Haiguang Wang, and Gang Han. Vol. 4, pp. 163–184. Chengdu: Sichuan People's Press.

Chen, Yung-fa. 1990. *Yan'an de Yinying* [In the Shadow of Yan'an]. Taiwan: Institute of Modern History, Academia Sinica.

—— 2001. *Zhongguo Gongchan Geming Qishi Nian* [Seventy Years of the Chinese Communist Revolution]. Taipei: Nianjing Press.

Cheng, Tiejun and Mark Selden. 1994, "The Origins and Consequences of China's Hukou System," *The China Quarterly* 139:644–668.

Cheng, Zhongyuan, Wang Yuxiang, and Li Zhenghua (2008). *Zhuanzhe Niandai – 1976–1981* [Transition Era: China during 1976–1981]. Beijing: Central Compilation & Translation Press.

Cheung, Steven N. S., 1982. *Will China Go "Capitalist"? An Economic Analysis of Property Rights and Institutional Change*. The second and revised edition was published in 1986. London: Institute of Economic Affairs.

—— 2008. "The Economic System of China," Paper presented at the 2008 Chicago Conference on China's Economic Transformation.

—— 2009. *The Economic System of China*. Beijing: China CITIC Press.

Chiang, Kai-shek. 1956. *Su E zhai Zhongguo* [Soviet Russia in China]. Taipei: Zhongyan Wenwu Gongyingshe.

Chung, Jae Ho. 2000. *Central Control and Local Discretion in China: Leadership and Implementation during Post-Mao Decollectivization*. New York: Oxford University Press.

Church, George. 1986. "Deng Xiaoping," *Times* (January 6).

Clark, Donald, Peter Murrell, and Susan Whiting. 2008. "The Role of Law in China's Economic Development," in *China's Great Economic Transformation*, ed. Loren Brandt and Thomas Rawski, pp. 375–428. New York: Cambridge University Press.

Coase, Ronald. 1937. "The Nature of the Firm," *Economica* 4: 386–405.

—— 1959. "The Federal Communication Commission," *Journal of Law and Economics* 2: 1–40.

—— 1961. "The Problem of Social Cost," *Journal of Law and Economics* 3: 1–44.

—— 1974. "The market for goods and the market for ideas," *American Economic Review* 64 (2): 384–91.

—— 1984. "The New Institutional Economics," *Journal of Institutional and Theoretical Economics* 140: 229–231.

—— 1988. *The Firm, the Market, and the Law*. Chicago: University of Chicago Press.

—— 2006. "The Conduct of Economics: The Example of Fisher Body and General Motors," *Journal of Economics & Management Strategy* 15: 255–278.

—— 2008. Concluding Speech at the 2008 Chicago Conference on China's Market Transformation.

—— and Ning Wang. 2011. "The Industrial Structure of Production," *Entrepreneurship Research Journal* 1(2): Article 1.

Coleman, James. 1990. *Foundations of Social Theory*. Cambridge, MA: Harvard University Press.

Cong, Jin. 1989. *Qu Zhe Fa Zhan de Sui Yue* [Years of Tortuous Development]. Zhengzhou: Henan People's Press.

Dai, Huang. 1998. *Hu Yaobang Yu Pingfan Yuanjia Zuo'an* [Hu Yaobang and the Rehabilitation]. Beijing: Xinhua Press.

David, Paul. 2001. "Path Dependence, its Critics and the Quest for 'Historical Economics'" in *Evolution and Path Dependence in Economic Ideas: Past and Present*, ed. Pierre Garrouste and Stavros Ioannides. Cheltenham: Edward Elgar.

Deng, Gang. 1997. *Chinese Maritime Activities and Socioeconomic Development*. Westport, CT: Greenwood Press.

Deng, Liqun, Ma Hong, Sun Shangqing, and Wu Jiaju. 1979. *Fang Ri Gui Lai de Shi Shuo* [Reflections on the Return of a Visit to Japan]. Beijing: China Social Sciences Press.

Deng, Xiaoping. 1975–1992. *The Selected Works of Deng Xiaoping*, Vol. 1–3, People's Daily Online, http://web.peopledaily.com.cn/english/dengxp/.

Deng, Zihui. 2007. *Deng Zihui Zishu* [Recollections of Deng Zihui]. Beijing: People's Press.

Desjardins, Eric. 2011. "Reflections on Path Dependence and Irreversibility," *Philosophy of Science* 78: 724–738.

Dikötter, Frank. 2010. *Mao's Great Famine*. New York: Walker & Co.

Ding, Yizhuang. 2008. *Zhongguo Zhiqing Shi: Chu Chao* (1953–1968) [History of China's Educated Youth]. Beijing: Contemporary China Press.

Dirlik, Arif. 1989. *The Origins of Chinese Communism*. New York: Oxford University Press.

Dong, Furen. 1986. "China's Price Reform," *Cambridge Journal of Economics* 10: 291–300.

Dong, Zhikai and Wu Jiang. 2004. *Xin Zhongguo Gongye de Dianjishi – 156 Xian Jianshe Yanjou* [The Foundation of New China's Industry – A Study of the 156 Project]. Guangzhou: Guangdong Economic Press.

Du, Daozheng. 2008. "How Do We Treat Deng Xiaoping Today," interview with Caijing, see http://www.caijing.com.cn/2008-12-08/110036057.html.

Du, Mingming. 2008. "Canyu Gaige Kaifan de Diyi Gang Shang" [The First Hong Kong Businessman to Partake Economic Reform and Opening up]. *Yan Huang Chun Qiu* (Issue 9, September).

Du, Runshen (ed)., 1998. *Zhongguo Nongcun Gaige Jueche Jishi* [The Chronicle of Decision-making during the Chinese Rural Reform]. Beijing: Zhongyang Wenxian Press.

Dunn, John. 2005. *Democracy: A History*. New York: Atlantic Monthly Press.

Durkheim, Emile. 1982. *The Rules of Methodological Method*, ed. Steven Lukes and trans. W. D. Halls. New York: Free Press.

Eliot, T.S. 1932. *Selected Essays*. London: Faber and Faber.

Elliott, Michael. 2008. "Thirty Years after Deng: The Man Who Changed China," *Time Magazine* (December 10th), available at http://www.time.com/time/world/article/0,8599,1865539,00.html.

Esherick, Joseph, Paul Kickowicz and Andrew Walder (eds). 2006. *The Chinese Cultural Revolution as History*. Stanford, CA: Stanford University Press.

Fan, Xiaochun. 2009. *Gaige Kaifang Qian de Baochan Daohu* [Private Farming before Reform and Opening up]. Beijing: Chinese Communist Party History Press.

Fenby, Jonathan. 2003. *Generalissimo Chiang Kai-Shek and the China He Lost*. New York: Free Press.

Feng, Jicai. 1990. *One Hundred People's Ten Years*, Beijing: Foreign Language Press.

Feng, Tianyu. 20006. *Fengjian Kaolun* [On Fengjian]. Wuhan: Wuhan University Press.

Ferguson, Adam. 1980 [1767]. *An Essay on the History of Civil Society*. New Brunswick, NJ: Transaction.

Fewsmith, Joseph. 1994. *Dilemmas of Reform in China*. Armonk, NY: M. E. Sharpe.

—— 2008. *China since Tiananmen*, second edition, New York: Cambridge University Press.

Ffrench, Yvonne. 1950. *The Great Exhibition: 1851*. London: Harvill Press.

Findlay, Christopher, Andrew Watson, and Harry Wu. 1994. *Rural Enterprises in China*. New York: St. Martin's Press.

Fogel, Robert. 2006. "Why China is Likely to Achieve its Growth Objectives," NBER Working Paper 12122.

—— 2010. "123,000,000,000,000." *Foreign Policy* (Jan/Feb) 177: 70–75.

Friedman, Milton. 1984. "Market or Plan: An Exposition of the Case for the Market," The Center for Research into Communist Economies, London (previously given as the 1981 Warren Nutter Memorial Lecture).

Fu, Guoyong. 2010. *1949 Nian: Zhongguo Zhishi Fengzhi de Shiren Jilu* [1949: Private Record of the Chinese Intellectuals]. Taiwan: Baqi Culture Press.

Gan, Jie, Yan Guo, and Chenggang Xu. 2010. "Privatization and the Chance of Control: The Case of China," Working paper.

Gao, Hua. 2000. *Hongtaiyang Shi Zenyang Shengqi de* [How Did the Sun Rise over Yan'an? A History of the Rectification Movement]. Hong Kong: Chinese University of Hong Kong Press.

Gao, Jianguo. 2000. *Gu Zhun Quan Chuan* [The Biography of Gu Zhun]. Shanghai: Shanghai Wenyi Press.

Garver, John. 1988. *Chinese-Soviet Relations, 1937–1945*. New York: Oxford University Press.

Gates, Hill. 1996. *China's Motor: A Thousand Years of Petty Capitalism*. Ithaca, NY: Cornell University Press.

Gilboy, George, and Benjamin Read. 2008. "Political and Social Reform in China: Alive and Walking," *The Washington Quarterly* 31: 143–164.

Granick, David. 1990. *Chinese State Enterprises: A Regional Property Rights Analysis*. Chicago: University of Chicago Press.

Gray, Jack. 1990. *Rebellions and Revolutions: China from the 1800s to the 1980s*. New York: Oxford University Press.

—— 2006. "Mao in Perspective," *China Quarterly* 187: 659–79.

Greif, Avner. 2006.. *Institutions and the Path to the Modern Economy: Lessons from Medieval Trade* New York: Cambridge University Press.

Guo, Dehong, Haiguang Wang, and Gang Han (eds.), 2009. *Zhonghua Renmin Gonghe Guo Zhuanti Shi Gao* [The Thematic History of the People's Republic of China], revised edition, Vol. 1: *Kaiguo Chuangye 1949–1956* [The Exploit of a Founding Nation]; Vol. 2: *Quzhe Tansuo 1956–1966* [Tortuous Search]; Vol. 3: *Shinian Fengyu 1966–1976* [Ten Years of Wind and Rain]; Vol. 4: *Gaige Fengyun 1976–1990* [The Experience of Reform]; Vol. 5: *Shiji Xinpian 1990–2009* [A New Chapter in the Century]. Chengdu: Sichuan People's Press.

Halper, Stefan. 2010. *The Beijing Consensus: How China's Authoritarian Model Will Dominate the Twenty-First Century*. New York: Basic Books.

Halpern, Nina. 1985. "Economic Specialists and the Making of Chinese Economic Policy, 1955–1983." University of Michigan PhD dissertation.

Han, Gang. 2004. "Liangge Fanshi de Youlai Jiqi Zhongjie" [The Beginning and End of the Two Whatevers], in *The Thematic History of the People's Republic of China*, ed. Dehong Guo, Haiguang Wang, and Gang Han, Vol. 4, pp. 29–47. Chengdu: Sichuan People's Press.

—— 2011. "Guanyu Hua Guofeng de Ruogan Shishi" [On Several Historical Facts of Hua Guofeng]. *Yan Huang Chun Qiu* (Issue 2, February).

Han, Yaguang. 2006. "Zhou Enlai Yu Sige Xiandaihua de Tichu" [Zhou Enlai and the Proposal of the Four Modernizations]. *Dandai Zhongguo Shi Yanjiu* [Study of Contemporary Chinese History] 13: 65–70.

Hao, Ran. 1972. *Jin Guang Da Dao* [Golden Highway], Vol. 1. Beijing: People's Literature Press.

Harding, Harry. 1987. *China's Second Revolution: Reform After Mao*. Washington, DC: Brookings Institution Press.

Hayek, F. A. 1937. "Economics and Knowledge," first published in *Economica* 4: 33–54. Reprinted in *Individualism and Economic Order*, Chicago: University of Chicago Press.

—— 1945. "The Use of Knowledge in Society," *American Economic Review* 35(4): 519–530.

—— 1948. *Individualism and Economic Order*. Chicago: University of Chicago Press.

—— 1960. *The Constitution of Liberty*. Chicago: University of Chicago Press.

—— 1967. *Studies in Philosophy, Politics, and Economics*. Chicago: University of Chicago Press.

—— 1973. *Law, Legislation and Liberty*, Vol. 1. Chicago: University of Chicago Press.

—— 1974. "The Pretense of Knowledge," Nobel Prize Lecture.

—— 1988. *The Fatal Conceit: The Errors of Socialism*. Chicago: University of Chicago Press.

He, Qinhua and Xiuqing Li (eds.), 2003. *Minguo Faxue Lunwen Jingcui* [Collections of Research Articles on Law in the Republic Era], Vol. 1, *Jichu Falu Pian* [Basic Law], pp. 337–50. Beijing: Falu Press.

Heinzig, Dieter. 2004. *The Soviet Union and Communist China 1945–1950: The Arduous Road to the Alliance* (it was first published in German in 1998; the Chinese translation was published by Xinhua Press in 2001). Armonk, NY: M.E. Sharpe.

Hinton, Harold (ed.). 1982. *Government & Politics in Revolutionary China: Selected Documents, 1949–1979*. Wilmington, DE: Scholarly Resources Inc.

Hinton, William. 1990. *The Great Reversal: The Privatization of China, 1978–1989*. New York: Monthly Review Press.

Hirschman, Albert O. 1977. *The Passions and the Interests*. Princeton, NJ: Princeton University Press.

Hu, Angang. 2008. *Zhongguo Zhengzhi Jingji Shilun* [On the History of Chinese Political Economy]. Beijing: Tshinghua University Press.

Hu, Feng. 1949. *Shijian Kaishi le* [Time Has Begun]. *People's Daily* (November 20th).

Hu, Jiwei. 1997. *Cong Hua Guofeng Xiatai do Hu Yaobang Xiatai* [From the Fall of Hua Guofeng to the Fall of Hu Yaobang]. Hong Kong: Mirror Press.

Huang, Yasheng. 1996. *Inflation and Investment Controls in China*. New York: Cambridge University Press.

—— 2003. *Selling China: Foreign Direct Investment during the Reform Era*. New York: Cambridge University Press.

—— 2008. *Capitalism with Chinese Characteristics*. New York: Cambridge University Press.

Huang, Zheng. 2004. "Liu Shaoqi Yuan'an Shimo" [The Beginning and End of the Liu Shaoqi Case], in *The Thematic History of the People's Republic of China*, ed. Dehong Guo, Haiguang Wang, and Gang Han. Vol. 3, pp. 155–176. Chengdu: Sichuan People's Press.

Ji, Xichen. 2000. "Fensui 'Sirenbang' Quanjing Xiezhen" [Panoramic View of the Arrest of the Gang of Four]. *Yan Huang Chun Qiu* (Issue 5 and 11, May and November).

Jin, Chongji (ed.), 1996. *Mao Zedong Zhuan 1893–1949* [The Biography of Ma Zedong 1949–1976]. Beijing: Zhongyang Wenxian Press.

Jin, Hehui, Yingyi Qian, and Barry Weingast. 2005. "Regional Decentralization and Fiscal Incentives: Federalism, Chinese Style," *Journal of Public Economics* 89: 1719–1742.

Johnson, D. Gale. 1994. "The Effects of Institutions and Policies on Rural Population Growth with Application to China," *Population and Development Review* 20: 503–531.

—— 1999. "Population and Economic Development," *China Economic Review* 10: 1–16.

Kampfner, John. 2010. *Freedom For Sale: Why the World Is Trading Democracy for Security*. New York: Basic Books.

Keynes, John M. 1936. *The General Theory of Employment, Interest and Money*. London: Macmillan.

Knight, Frank. 1976. *The Ethics of Competition*. Chicago: University of Chicago Press.

Kornai, Janos. 1979. "Resource-Constrained Versus Demand-Constrained Systems," *Econometrica* 47, pp. 801–819.

—— 1980. *Economics of Shortage*. Armsterdam: North Holland Publisher.

—— 1986. "The Soft Budget Constraint," *Kyklos* 39: 3–30.

Kraay, Aart. 2000. "Household Saving in China," *World Bank Economic Review* 14: 545–570.

Kuang, Jiazai and Jun Gai (2004). "Bashi Niandai de Chengshi Jingji Tizhi Gaige" [Reform of the Urban Economic System during the 1980s], in *The Thematic History of the People's Republic of China*, ed. Dehong Guo, Haiguang Wang, and Gang Han. Vol. 4, pp. 304–322. Chengdu: Sichuan People's Press.

Kueh, Y. Y. 2006. "Mao and Agriculture in China's Industrialization: Three Antitheses in a 50-Year Perspective," *China Quarterly* 187: 700–723.

Kuran, Timur. 2010. *The Long Divergence: How Islamic Law Held Back the Middle East*. Princeton, NJ: Princeton University Press.

Lau, Lawrence, Yingyi Qian, and Gérard Roland. 2000. "Reform without Losers: An Interpretation of China's Dual-Track Approach," *Journal of Political Economy* 108: 120–143.

Lardy, Nicholas and Kenneth Lieberthal (eds.), 1983. *Chen Yün's Strategy for China's Development: A Non-Maoist Alternative.* Armonk, NY: M. E. Sharpe.

Lee, Kuan Yew. 2000. *From Third World to First: The Singapore Story 1965–2000.* New York: HarperCollins.

Lerner, Abba. 1944. *The Economics of Control.* London: Macmillan.

Levenson, Joseph. 1968. *Confucian China and its Modern Fate.* Berkeley, CA: University of California Press.

Levinston, Steve. "China's Authoritarian Capitalism Undermines Western Values, argue three new books" (*Washington Post*, May 30th, 2010, available at http://www.washingtonpost.com/wp-dyn/content/article/2010/05/28/AR2010052801859.html.

Li, Hua-yu. 2006. *Mao and the Economic Stalinization of China, 1948–1953.* New York: Rowman & Littlefield Publishers.

Li, Huaiyin. 2009. *Village China under Socialism and Reform: A Micro-History, 1948–2008.* Stanford, CA: Stanford University Press.

Li, Hui. 2003. *HuFeng Jituan Yuan'an Shimo* [History of the HuFeng Clique]. Wuhan: Hubei People's Press.

Li, Lanqing. 2008. *Tuwei: Guomen Chukai de Suiyue* [Breakthrough: The Initial Era of Opening China's Door]. Beijing: Central Compilation & Translation Press.

Li, Rui. 1999. *Mao Zedong de Wannian Beiju* [The Tragedy of Mao's Later Life]. *Haikou: Southern Press.*

Li, Rui, Jiwei Hu, Tao Xie et al. 2009. *Hu Yaobang yu Zhongguo Zhengzhi Gaige* [Hu Yaobang and China's Political Reform]. Hong Kong: Morning Bell Press.

Li, Wei and Dennis Tao Yang. 2005. "The Great Leap Forward: Anatomy of a Central Planning Disaster," *Journal of Political Economy* 113:840–877.

Li, Yan. 2008. *Duiwai Kaifan de Yunniang yu Qibu* (1976–1978) [Preparation and Beginning of Opening-up 1976–1978]. Beijing: Social Sciences Academic Press.

Liang, Shuming. 2004. *Liang Shuming Zi Shu* [Autobiographical Notes of Liang Shuming]. Zhengzhou: Henan People's Press.

Liang, Shuming and Guy Alitto. 2009. *Has Man a Future? Dialogue with the Last Confucian.* Beijing: Foreign Language Teaching and Research Press.

Liang, Zhiping (ed.). 2010. *Zhuang Xing Qi de Shehui Gongzheng* [Social Justice during the Time of Transition]. Beijing: SDX Joint Press.

Liebman, Benjamin. 2007. "China's Courts: Restricted Reform," *China Quarterly* 191: 620–638.

Lin, Justin and Yang Yao. 2001. "Chinese rural industrialization in the context of the East Asian miracle," in Joseph Stiglitz and Shahid Yusuf (eds.), *Rethinking the East Asian Miracle,* Washington, DC: The World Bank and Oxford University Press.

Lin, Nan. 1995. "Local Market Socialism: Local Corporatism in Action in Rural China," *Theory and Society* 24: 301–354.

Lin, Yunhui. 2008. *The Utopian Movement: The Great Leap Forward and the Great Famine* (1958–1961) (in Chinese), *The History of the People's Republic of China,* Vol. 4. Hong Kong: Chinese University of Hong Kong Press.

—— 2009. *Moving Toward Socialist: The Transformation of China's Economy and Society (1953–1955)* (in Chinese), *The History of the People's Republic of China,* Vol. 2. Hong Kong: Chinese University of Hong Kong Press.

Lin, Yunhui, Shouxin Fan, and Gong Zhang. 1989. *Kai Ge Xing Jin de Shi Qi* [Times of Triumphant Progress]. Zhengzhou: Henan People's Press.

Lin, Yu-sheng. 1979. The *Crisis of Chinese Consciousness: Radical Antitraditionalism in the May Fourth Era*. Madison, WI: University of Wisconsin Press.

Liu, Jie and Lushan Xu. 2009. *Deng Xiaoping He Chen Yun Zai Shiyijie Sanzhang Quanhui Qianhou* [Deng Xiaoping and Chen Yun around the Third Plenum of the Eleventh Central Committee]. Beijing: Central Compilation & Translation Press.

Liu, Kedi. 2005. *Liang Shumin de Zuihou 39 Nian* [The Last 39 Years of Liang Shuming]. Beijing: China Wenshi Press.

Liu, Xiaomeng. 2008. *Zhongguo Zhiqing Shi: Da Chao (1966–1980)* [History of China's Educated Youth]. Beijing: Contemporary China Press.

Liu, Xiaoming. 2008. "Learning through Local Experiments: The Path to Knowledge in Chinese Economic Reform," Paper presented at the 2008 Chicago Conference on China's Market Transformation.

Lou, Jiwei, 1998. *Macroeconomic Reform in China: Laying the Foundation for a Socialist Market Economy*. Washington, DC: World Bank.

—— 2008. "Zhongguo Sanshinian Caishui Gaige de Hugu yu Zhanwang" [Thirty Years of Financial and Tax Reform in China: Retrospect and Prospect], in *Zhongguo Jingji wushi Ren kan Sanshi Nian: Huigu yu Fenxi* [Thirty Years of Reform: Retrospect and Analysis], ed. Jinglian Wu et al., pp. 323–346. Beijing: China Economic Press.

Lu, Jiandong. 1995. *Chen Yinke de Zuihou Ershi Nian* [The Last Twenty Years of Chen Yinke]. Beijng: SDX Joint Press.

Lu, Xiaobo and Elizabeth Perry (eds.), 1997. *Danwei: the Changing Chinese Workplace in Historical and Comparative Perspective*. Armonk,NY: M. E. Sharpe.

Lubman, Stanley. 2000. *Bird in a Cage: Legal Reform in China after Mao*. Stanford, CA: Stanford University Press.

Luo, Pinghan. 2001. *Daguofan: Gonggong Shitang Shimo* [The Big Pot: The History of the Public Dinning Hall]. Nanning: Guangxi People's Press.

—— 2005. *Tudi Gaige Yundong Shi* [History of Land Reform]. Fuzhou: Fujian People's Press.

Luthi, Lorenz. 2008. *The Sino-Soviet Split: Cold War in the Communist World*. Princeton, NJ: Princeton University Press.

Ma, Jiantang. 2008. "Sanshi Nian Jubian: Guoyou Qiye Gaige Jincheng Jianyao Huigu yu Pingshu" [Great Change in Thirty Years: A Review and Analysis of the Process of State-owned enterprise Reform], in *Zhongguo Jingji Wushi Ren Kan Sanshi Nian* [Thirty Years of the Chinese Economy: From the Eyes of Fifty Economists], ed. Jinglian Wu et al., pp. 347–358. Beijing: China Economic Press.

Ma, Jinglong. 2008. "Standing Tall at Thirty: The Dream and Glory of Privatization in Wenzhou," Paper presented at 2008 Chicago Conference on China's Market Transformation.

Ma, Licheng. 2005. *Da Tupo: Xin Zhongguo Siying Jingji Fengyun Lu* [Breakthrough: Development of Private Business in New China]. Beijing: China Industry and Commerce United Press.

—— 2008. *Jiaofeng Sanshi Nian* [Thirty Years of Confrontation]. Nanjing: Jiangsu People's Press.

Ma, Xiaohong. 1997. *Zhongguo GuDai Shehui de FaLu Guan* [Law in Ancient Chinese Society]. Zhengzhou: Daxiang Press.

—— 2004. *Zhong Guo Gu Dai Falu Shixiang Shi* [History of Legal Thought in Ancient China]. Beijing: Falu Press.

McCraw, Thomas. 2007. *Prophet of Innovation: Joseph Schumpeter and Creative Destruction*. Cambridge, MA: Harvard University Press.

MacFarquhar, Roderick and John K. Fairbank (eds.), 1987. *The Cambridge History of China*, Vol. 14, *The Emergence of Revolutionary China, 1949–1965*. New York: Cambridge University Press.

—— 1991. *The Cambridge History of China*, Vol. 15: *Revolutions within the Chinese Revolution, 1965–1982*. New York: Cambridge University Press.

MacFarquhar, Roderick and Michael Schoenhals. 2006. *Mao's Last Revolution*, Cambridge, MA: Harvard University Press.

Mahoney, James. 2000. "Path Dependence in Historical Sociology," *Theory and Society* 29: 507–548.

Mahoney, James and Kathleen Thelen (eds.). 2010. *Explaining Institutional Change: Ambiguity, Agency, and Power*. New York: Cambridge University Press.

Man, Mei. 2005. *Shinian Yiran Wujing* [Endless Missing]. Beijing: Beijing Press.

Manion, Melanie. 1985. "The Cadre Management System, Post-Mao: The Appointment, Promotion, Transfer and Removal of Party and State Leaders," *The China Quarterly* 102: 203–233.

Mao, Zedong. 1967–1977. *Selected Works of Mao Tse-tung*, Vols. 1–5, Beijing: Foreign Language Press.

Marshall, Alfred. 1920. *Principles of Economics*, eighth edition. London: Macmillan.

Maskin, Eric S. 1996. "Theories of the Soft Budget-Constraint," *Japan & the World Economy* 8: 125–133.

—— 1999. "Recent Theoretical Work on the Soft Budget Constraint," *American Economic Review* 89: 421–425.

—— and Chenggang Xu. 2001. "Soft Budget Constraint Theories: From Centralization to the Market," *Economics of Transition* 9: 1–27.

——, Yingyi Qian, and Chenggang Xu. 2000. "Incentives, Information, and Organizational Forms," *Review of Economic Studies* 67: 359–378.

Meisner, Maurice. 1999. *Mao's China and After*, third edition. New York: Free Press.

Menard, Claude and Mary Shirley (eds.), 2005. *Handbook of New Institutional Economics*. Berlin: Springer.

Montinola, Gabriella, Yingyi Qian, and Barry Weingast. 1995. "Federalism, Chinese Style: The Political Basis for Economic Success in China," *World Politics* 48: 50–81.

Murphy, Kevin, Andrea Shleifer, and Robert Vishny. 1992. "The Transition to a Market Economy: Pitfalls of Partial Reform," *Quarterly Journal of Economics* 107: 889–906.

Naughton, Barry. 1995. *Growing out of the Plan: Chinese Economic Reform 1978–1993*. New York: Cambridge University Press.

—— 2002. "China's Economic Think Tanks: Their Changing Role in the 1990s," *China Quarterly* 171: 625–35.

—— 2007. *The Chinese Economy: Transition s and Growth*. Cambridge, MA: MIT Press.

—— 2008. "A Political Economy of China's Economic Transition," in *China's Great Economic Transformation*, ed. Loren Brandt and Thomas Rawski, pp. 91–135. New York: Cambridge University Press.

Nee, Victor. 1992. "Organizational Dynamics of Market Transition: Hybrid Property Forms and Mixed Economy in China," *Administrative Science Quarterly* 37: 1–27.

North, Douglass. 1981. *Structure and Change in Economic History*. New York: Norton.

—— 1990. *Institutions, Institutional Change and Economic Performance*. New York: Cambridge University Press.

—— 2005. *Understanding the Process of Economic Change*. Princeton, NJ: Princeton University Press.

——, John Wallis, and Barry Weingast. 2009. *Violence and Social Order: A Conceptual Framework for Interpreting Recorded Human History*. New York: Cambridge University Press.

Nozick, Robert. 1974. *Anarchy, State, and Utopia*. New York: Basic Books.

Oi, Jean. 1992. "Fiscal Reform and the Economic Foundation of Local State Corporatism," *World Politics* 45: 99–126.

Ostrom, Elinor. 1990. *Governing the Commons: The Evolution of Institutions for Collective Actions*. New York: Cambridge University Press.

Pakula, Hannah. 2009. *The Last Empress: Madame Chiang Kai-Shek and the Birth of Modern China*. New York: Simon & Schuster.

Pang, Xianzhi and Chongji Jin (eds.), 2003. *Mao Zedong Zhuan 1949–1976* [The Biography of Mao Zedong 1949–1976]. Beijing: Zhongyang Wenxian Press.

Pantsov, Alexander. 2000. *The Bolsheviks and the Chinese Revolution 1919–1927*. Honolulu, HI: University of Hawaii Press.

Peerenboom, Randall. 2002. *China's Long March toward Rule of Law*. New York: Cambridge University Press.

Pei, Minxin. 2006. *China's Trapped Transition: The Limits of Developmental Autocracy*. Cambridge, MA: Harvard University Press.

Peng, Shen and Li Chen. 2008. *Zhongguo Jingji Tizhi Gaige Zhongda Shijian* [Major Events during China's Economic System Reform]. Beijing: People's University Press.

Perkins, Dwight. 1991. "China's Economic Policy and Performance," in *Cambridge History of China*, ed. Roderick MacFarquhar and John Fairbank, Vol. 15, Part 2, pp. 475–539. New York: Cambridge University Press.

Pierson, Paul. 2004. *Politics in Time: History, Institutions, and Social Analysis*. Princeton, NJ: Princeton University Press.

Polanyi, Michael. 1951. *The Logic of Liberty*. Chicago: University of Chicago Press.

—— 1958. *Personal Knowledge*. Chicago: University of Chicago Press.

—— 1966. *The Tacit Dimension*. Chicago: University of Chicago Press.

Polo, Marco. 1923. *The Travels*, translated by Henry Yule. Mineola, NY: Dover.

Popper, Karl. 1978. "Three Worlds," Tanner Lecture, delivered at the University of Michigan, on April 7th, available at http://www.tannerlectures.utah.edu/lectures/documents/popper80.pdf

Potter, Pitman. 2008. "The Chinese Legal Regime: Adapted to Authoritarian Rule," Paper Presented at the 2008 Chicago Conference on China's Market Transformation.

Powell, Walter and Paul DiMaggio (eds.), 1991. *The New Institutionalism in Organizational Analysis*. Chicago: University of Chicago Press.

Provincial Propaganda Department of the Chinese Communist Party in Sichuan, Provincial Academy of Social Sciences in Sichuan, and Sichuan Daily (eds.). 2008. *Gan Wei Tian Xia Xiang* [Bold to Be the First in the World]. Chengdu: Sichuan People's Press.

Pye, Lucian. 1992. *The Spirit of Chinese Politics*, second edition. Cambridge, MA: Harvard University Press.

Qian, Mu. 2001. *Zhongguo Lidai Zhengzhi Deshi* [Merits and Flaws in Chinese Political History]. Beijing: SDX Joint Press.

—— 2005. *Guo Shi Xin Lun* [New Lectures on Chinese History]. Beijing: SDX Joint Press.

—— 2010. *Zhongguo Sixiang Shi Niu Jiang Zhongguo Xueshu Sixiang Shi Ba Jiang* [Six Lectures on Chinese Thoughts and Eighteen Lectures on Chinese Academic Thoughts]. Beijing: Jiu Zhou Press.

Qian, Niansun. 2008. *Long Taitou: 'Da Baogan' de QianQian Houhou* [History of Private Farming]. Nanjing: Jiangsu Wenyi Press.

Qian, Xingzhong. 2008. "Functional Orientation of Local Governments: The Practice of Reform in Wenzhou," Paper presented at the 2008 Chicago Conference on China's Market Transformation.

Qian, Yingyi and Chenggang Xu. 1993. "Why China's Economic Reforms Differ: The M-Form Hierarchy and Entry/Expansion of the Non-State Sector," *Economics of Transition* 1(2): 135–170.

Qian, Yingyi, Gerald Roland, and Chenggang Xu. 2006. "Coordination and Experimentation in M-Form and U-Form Organizations," *Journal of Political Economy* 114: 366–402.

Radchenko, Sergey. 2009. *Two Suns in the Heaven: the Sino-Soviet Struggle for Supremacy, 1962–1967*. Stanford, CA: Stanford University Press.

Ren, Xin. 1997. *Tradition of the Law and Law of the Tradition: Law, State, and Social Control in China*. Westport, CT: Greenwood Press.

Research Office of the History of the Chinese Communist Party (ed.). 2001. *Zhongguo Gongchandang Lishi* [The History of the Chinese Communist Party], Vol. 1, 1921–1949. Beijing: Chinese Communist Party History Press.

—— 2011. *Zhongguo Gongchandang Lishi* [The History of the Chinese Communist Party], Volume 2, 1949–1978. Beijing: Chinese Communist Party History Press.

Research Office of the History of the Chinese Communist Party (the First Department) (translated and edited). 1997. *Liangong, Gongchan Guoji, he Zhongguo Guomin Geming Yundong* [The Soviet Party, Comintern, and the Chinese Revolution]. Beijing: Beijing Library Press.

Research Office on the Party History of the Anhui Provincial Party Committee (ed.). 2006. *Anhui Nongcun Gaige zi Lu* [The Road of Agricultural Reform in Anhui]. Beijing: Chinese Communist Party History Press.

—— *Anhui Nongcun Gaige Kou Shu Shi* [The Oral History of Agricultural Reform in Anhui]. Beijing: Chinese Communist Party History Press.

Riedel, James, Jing Jin, and Jiang Gao. 2007. *How China Grows: Investment, Finance, and Reform*. Princeton, NJ: Princeton University Press.

Riskin, Karl. 1987. *China's Political Economy: The Quest for Development since 1949*. New York: Oxford University Press.

Roland, Gérard. 2002. "The Political Economy of Transition," *Journal of Economic Perspectives* 16: 29–50.

Ryan, Janette. 2010. *China's Higher Education Reform and Internationalisation*. London: Routledge.

Sachs, Jeffrey. 1992. "Privatization in Russia: Some Lessons from Eastern Europe," *American Economic Review* 82: 43–48.

—— 1994. "Shock Therapy in Poland: Perspectives of Five Years," Tanner Lecture delivered at University of Utah, April 6 and 7, 1994. Available at http://www.tannerlectures.utah.edu/lectures/documents/sachs95.pdf

Saich, Anthony. 1996. *The Rise to Power of the Chinese Communist Party: Documents and Analysis*. Armonk,NY: M. E. Sharpe.

Schotter, Andrew. 1981. *The Economic Theory of Social Institutions*. New York: Cambridge University Press.

Schrecker, John. 2004. *The Chinese Revolution in Historical Perspective*. Westport, CT: Praeger.

Schumpeter, Joseph. 1942. *Capitalism, Socialism, and Democracy*. New York: Harper and Brothers.

Schurmann, Franz. 1968. *Ideology and Organization in Communist China*. Berkeley, CA: University of California Press.

Schwarcz, Vera. 1992. *Time for Telling Truth is Running Out: Conversations with Zhang Shenfu*. New Haven, CT: Yale University Press.

Searle, John. 1969. *Speech Acts*. New York: Cambridge University Press.

Selden, Mark. 1971. *The Yanan Way in Revolutionary China*. Camrbridge, MA: Harvard University Press.

—— 1995. *China in Revolution: The Yanan Way Revisited*. Armonk,NY: M.E. Sharpe.

Sen, Amartya. 2006. *Identity and Conflict: The Illusion of Destiny*. New York: Norton.

Shambaugh, David. 2008. *China's Communist Party: Atrophy and Adaptation*. Washington, DC: Woodrow Wilson Center Press.

Shang, Yang. 1928. *The Book of Lord Shang*. Translated by J. J. L. Duyvendak. London: Arthur Probsthain.

Shao, Yanxiang. 2007. *Bie Le, Mao Zedong* [Farewell to Mao Zedong]. New York: Oxford University Press.

Shen, Baoxiang. 1997. *Zhenli Biaozhun Wenti Taolun Shimo* [The History of the Debate on the Criterion of Testing Truth]. Beijing: China Youth Press.

—— 2004. "*Zhenli Biaozhun Wenti Da Taolun* [Debate on the Criterion of Testing Truth], in *The Thematic History of the People's Republic of China*, ed. Dehong Guo, Haiguang Wang, and Gang Han. Vol. 4, pp. 48–71. Chengdu: Sichuan People's Press.

Shen, Raphael. 2000. *China's Economic Reform: An Experiment in Pragmatic Socialism*. Westport, CT: Praeger.

Shen, Zhihua. 2008. *Reflections and Choices: The Consciousness of the Chinese Intellectuals and the Anti-Rightist Campaign (1956–1957)* (in Chinese), The History of the People's Republic of China, Vol. 3. Hong Kong: The Chinese University of Hong Kong Press.

Sheng, Yumin. 2010. *Economic Openness and Territorial Politics in China*. New York: Cambridge University Press.

Shi, Yun and Danhui Li. 2008. *When The "Continuous Revolution" Goes Awry: From the Anti-Lin Biao Campaign to the Anti-Deng Xiaoping Campaign 1972–1976* (in Chinese), The History of the People's Republic of China, Vol. 8. Hong Kong: Chinese University of Hong Kong Press.

Shi, Zhengfu. 2008. "Rationality and Path Dependence in Agricultural Reform: The Origin of China's Model of Reform Governance," Paper presented at the 2008 Chicago Conference on China's Market Transformation.

Shih, Victor. 2007. *Factions and Finance in China: Elite Conflict and Inflation*. New York: Cambridge University Press.

Shils, Edward. 1981. *Tradition*. Chicago: University of Chicago Press.

Shirk, Susan. 1993. *The Political Logic of Economic Reform in China*. Berkeley, CA: University of California Press.

Short, Philip. 1999. *Mao: A Life*. New York: Henry Holt and Comany.

Sichuan Provincial Propaganda Department of the Party, Sichuan Provincial Academy of Social Sciences, and Sichuan Daily (eds.), 2008. *Gan Wei Tian Xia Xiang* [Bold to Be the First in the World]. Chengdu: Sichuan People's Press.

Simon, Herbert. 1997 [1947]. *Administrative Behavior*, fourth edition. New York: Free Press.

Smith, Adam. 1969 [1759]. *The Theory of Moral Sentiments*. Indianapolis, IN: Liberty Classics.

—— 1976 [1776]. *The Wealth of Nations*. Chicago: University of Chicago Press.

Smith, Steve. 2000. *A Road in Made: Communism in Shanghai, 1920–1927*. Honolulu, HI: University of Hawaii Press.

Snow, Edgar. 1937. *Red Start over China*. London: Left Book Club (it was published in 1938 by Random House in New York, with slight changes; the most recent version was published in 1994 by Grove Press in New York).

Song, Lianshen. 2005. *Nongye Xue Dazhai Shimo* [The Beginning and End of Learning from Daizhai]. Wuhan: Hubei People's Press.

Spence, Jonathan. 1999. *Mao Zedong: A Penguin Life*. New York: Viking.

Su, Shaozhi. 2002. *Zhongguo Jingji Tongshi 10 Juan Shang* [The General Economic History of China, Vol. 10 (I)], ed. Zhao Dexin. Changsha: Hunan People's Press.

Sun, Dali. 2004. "Wenge Hou Guomin Jingjie de Huifu He Xin Maojin de Chuxian" [Economic Recovery after the Cultural Revolution and the Rise of New Leap], in *The Thematic History of the People's Republic of China*, ed. Dehong Guo, Haiguang Wang, and Gang Han. Vol. 4, pp. 16–28. Chengdu: Sichuan People's Press.

Sun, Jian. 1992. *Zhonghua Renmin Gongheguo Jingji Shi: 1949–1990 Niandai Chu* [Economic History of the People's Republic of China: 1949-the Early 1990s]. Beijing: People's University Press.

Sun, Shuyun. 2006. *The Long March*. London: Harper Collins.

Subramanian, Arvind. 2011. *Eclipse: Living in the Shadow of China's Economic Dominance*. Washington, DC: Peterson Institute for International Economics.

Tang, Rachel. 2009. "The Rise of China's Auto Industry and its Impact on the U.S. Motor Vehicle Industry," Congressional Research Service, November 16th, 2009.

Tao, Ran and Dali Yang. 2008. "The Revenue Imperative and Local Government in China's Transition and Growth," Paper Presented at 2008 Chicago Conference on China's Economic Transformation.

Taylor, Jay. 2009. *The Generalissimo: Chiang Kai-shek and the struggle for Modern China*. Cambridge, MA: Harvard University Press.

Thaxton, Ralph A., Jr. 2008. *Catastrophe and Contention in Rural China: Mao's Great Leap Forward Famine and the Origins of Righteous Resistance in Da Fo Village*. New York: Cambridge University Press.

Thun, Eric. 2006. *Changing Lanes in China: Foreign Direct Investment, Local Governments, and Auto Sector Development*. New York: Cambridge University Press.

Tian, Jiyun. 2004. "Huainian Xiaoping Dongzhi" [Remembering Comrade Deng Xiaoping]. *Yan Huang Chun Qiu* (Issue 8, August 2004).

—— 2009. *The Great Practice of Reform and Opening Up* [Gaige Kaifang De Weida Shijian). Beijing: Xinhua Press.

Tsou, Tang. 1986. *The Cultural Revolution and Post-Mao Reform: A Historical Perspective*. Chicago: University of Chicago Press.

Tu, Mingming. 2008. "The First Hong Kong Businessman to Join Economic Reform and Opening Up," *Yan Huang Chun Qiu* (Issue 9, September).

Tu, Qiao. 2008. *Yuan Geng Zhuan: 1978–1984 Gaige Xianchang* [The Biography of Yuan Geng: 1978–1984 Reform in Action]. Beijing: Zhuojia Press.

Unirule Institute of Economics. 2010. "The Nature, Performance, and Reform of the State-owned enterprises," Working Paper (July 12th).

Vergne, Jean-Philippe and Rodolphe Durand. 2010. "The Missing Link Between the Theory and Empirics of Path Dependence," *Journal of Management Studies* 47:736–759.

Vogel, Ezra. 2010. *Deng Xiaoping and the Transformation of China*. Cambridge, MA: Harvard University Press.

Walder, Andrew. 1986. *Communist Neo-Traditionalism: Work and Authority in Chinese Industry*. Berkeley, CA: University of California Press.

—— 1995. "Local Governments as Industrial Firms," *American Journal of Sociology* 101: 263–301.

—— 2009. *Fractured Rebellion: The Beijing Red Guard Movement*. Cambridge, MA: Harvard University Press.

Walker, Kenneth. 1984. *Food Grain Procurement and Consumption in China*. New York: Cambridge University Press.

Wang, Fan-Sen. 2000. *Fu Ssu-nien: A Life in Chinese History and Politics*. New York: Cambridge University Press.

Wang, Fei-ling. 2005. *Organizing through Division and Exclusion: China's Hukou System*. Stanford, CA: Stanford University Press.

Wang, Nianyi. 1989. *Da Dong Luan de Nian Dai* [The Decade of a Great Turmoil]. Zhengzhou: Henan People's Press.

Wang, Ning. 2005. *Making a Market Economy: The Institutional Transformation of a Freshwater Fishery in a Chinese Community*. London: Routledge.

—— 2008. "The Chinese Economic System under Mao," Paper presented at the 2008 Chicago Conference on China's Economic Transformation.

Wang, Rongzhu. 2005. *Shijia Chen Yingke* [Chen Yingke: A Historian]. Beijing: Peking University Press.

Wang, Rongzhu and Ao Li. 2004. *Jiang Jieshi Pingzhuang* [A Biography of Jiang Kai-shek]. Beijing: Chinese Friendship Press.

Wang, Ruoshui. 1997. *Hu Yaobang Xiatai de Beijing* [The Background of Hu Yaobang's Fall]. Hong Kong: Mirror Books.

—— 2001. *Xin Faxian de Mao Zedong* [Newly Discovered Mao Zedong]. Hong Kong: Mingpao Press.

Wang, Xiaolu. 2007. "Guomin Shouru Fenpei Zhuangkuang [National Income Distribution and Grey Income]" Caijing (May 31st).

Wang, Youqin. 2004. *Wenge Shounan Zhe* [Victims of the Cultural Revolution]. Hong Kong: Kaifang Magazine Press.

Weber, Max. 1981. *General Economic History*, translated by Frank Knight. New Brunswick, NJ: Transaction.

Wei, Cheng-tung. 1999. *Infinite View from the Perilous Mountain: Mao Zedong's Character and Fate*. Taiwan: New Century Press.

Wei, Junyi, 1998. *Si tong Lu* [Reflections on Sufferings]. Beijing: October Wenyi Press.

White, Gordon. 1993. *Riding the Tiger: The Politics of Economic Reform in Post-Mao China*. Stanford, CA: Stanford University Press.

White, Lynn (ed.), 2005. *Legitimacy: Ambiguities of Political Success or Failure in East and Southeast Asia*. Singapore: World Scientific Publishing Company.

Whyte, Martin. 2010. *The Myth of Social Volcano: Perceptions in Inequality and Distributive Justice in Contemporary China*. Stanford, CA: Stanford University Press.

Williamson, Oliver. 1985. *The Economic Institutions of Capitalism*. New York: Free Press.

Wong, Christine. 1988. "Interpreting Industrial Growth in Post-Mao China," *Modern China* 14: 3–30.

Wong, John and Yongnian Zheng (eds.), 2001. *The Nanxun Legacy and China's Development in the Post-Deng Era*. Singapore: Singapore University Press.

Wong, Richard. 2008. "The Role of Hong Kong in China's Transformation," Paper presented at the 2008 Chicago Conference on China's Market Transformation.

Wu, Jinglian. 2003. *Dandai Zhongguo Jingji Gaige* [China Economic Reform]. Shanghai: Shanghai Far East Press.

—— 2005. *Understanding and Interpreting Chinese Economic Reform*. Mason, OH: Thomson Higher Education.

—— 2010. *Dandai Zhongguo Jingji Gaige Jiaocheng* [Tutorials on Chinese Economic Reform]. Shanghai: Shanghai Far East Press.

Wu, Jinglian and Renwei Zhao. 1987. "The Dual Pricing System in China's Industry," *Journal of Comparative Economics* 11: 309–318.

Wu, Li. 1999. *Zhonghua Renmin Gongheguo Jingji Shi* [Economic History of the People's Republic of China]. Beijing: China Economic Press.

Wu, Ningkun. 1993. *A Single Tear: A Family's Persecution, Love, and Endurance in Communist China*. Boston, MA: Back Bay Books.

Wu, Xiaobo. 2010. *Wu Jinglian Chuan: Yige Zhongguo Jingjixue Jia de Xiaoxiang* [The Biography of Wu Jinglian: A Portrait of a Chinese Economist]. Beijing: China CITIC Press.

Wu, Zhifei and Ling Yu. 2008. *Deng Xiaoping de Zuihou Ershi Nian* [The Last Twenty Years of Deng Xiaoping]. Beijing: Xinhua Press.

Wu, Zuguang. 2004. Yi Beizi: *Wu Zuguang Huiyilu* [*My Life: A Memoir*]. Beijing: China Wennian Press.

Xiao, Donglian. 2004. "1978–1984 Nian Zhongguo Jingji Tizhi Gaige Shilu de Yanjing" [Evolution of the Thinking on the Reform of China's Economic System during 1978–1984], in *The Thematic History of the People's Republic of China*, ed. Dehong Guo, Haiguang Wang, and Gang Han. Vol. 4, pp. 185–213. Chengdu: Sichuan People's Press.

—— 2008. *Turning Point in History: Re-examination of the Cultural Revolution and the Policy of Reform and Opening (1979–1981)* (in Chinese). The *History of the People's Republic of China*, Vol. 10. Hong Kong: Chinese University of Hong Kong Press.

Xiao, Donglian et al. 1999. *Qiusuo Zhongguo: Wenge Qian Shinian Shi* [China in Struggle: The Decade before the Cultural Revolution]. Beijing: Hongqi Press.

Xiao, Geng. 1997. *Chanquan yu Zhongguo de Jingji Gaige* [Property Rights and Chinese Economic Reform]. Beijing: Chinese Social Science Press.

Xie, Chuntao (ed.), 2008. *Zhuanzhe Zhongguo, 1976–1982* [China in Transition, 1976–1982]. Beijing: People's Press.

Xing, Heming. 2009. *Jiang Jieshi Yu Mosike de Enen Yuanyuan* [The Hate and Love Relationship between Chiang Kai-shek and Moscow]. Beijing: People's Press.

Xu, Chenggang. 2009."The Institutional Foundations of China's Reforms and Development." Manuscript.

Xu, Chenggang and Xiaobo Zhang. 2008."The Evolution of Chinese Entrepreneurial Firms: The Township and Village Enterprises Revisited," Paper presented at the 2008 Chicago Conference on China's Market Transformation.

Xu, Dixin and Chengmin Wu (eds.), 2007. *Zhong Guo Zi Ben Zhu Yi Fa Zhan Shi* [History of Capitalist Development in China]. Vols. 1–3. Beijing: Social Science Academic Press.

Xu, Mingtian. 2008. *Chuntian de Gushi: Shenzhen Chuanye Shi* [The History of the Rise of Shenzhen]. Beijing: China CITIC Press.

Xu, Shanda. 2008. "Wo suo Jingli de Caisui Gaige de Huiyi Pianduan" [Memories of My Experience with the Reform of Fiscal Revenue and Taxation], in *Zhongguo Jingji Wushi Ren Kan Sanshi Nian* [Thirty Years of the Chinese Economy: From the Eyes of Fifty Economists], ed. Jinglian Wu et al., pp. 523–37. Beijing: China Economic Press.

Xue, Muqiao. 1996. *Xue Muqiao Huiyi Lu* [Memoirs of Xue Muqiao]. Tianjin: Tianjin People's Press.

—— 2008. *Xue Muqiao Gaige Lunji* [A Collection of Xue Muqiao's Works on Economic Reform]. Beijing: China Fazhan Press.

Yang, Dali. 2004. *Remaking the Chinese Leviathan: Market Transition and the Politics of Governance in China*. Stanford, CA: Stanford University Press.

Yang, Jisheng. 1998. *Deng Xiaoping Niandai: Zhongguo Gaige Kaifang Jishi* [The Era of Deng Xiaoping: Documentary of China's Reform and Opening-up]. Beijing: Central Compilation & Translation Press.

—— 2004. *Zhongguo Gaige Niandai de Zhengzhi Douzheng* [Political Conflicts during China's Reform]. Hong Kong: Excellent Culture Press.

—— 2008. *MuBei: Zhongguo Liushi Niandai Jihuang Jishi* [Tombstone: Documentary of Hunger in China during the 1960s]. Hong Kong: Tiandi Tushu Press.

—— 2009. *Sanshi Nian He Dong: Quanli Shichang Jingji de Kunjing* [Thirty Years of Reform: The Dilemma of the Power Market Economy]. Wuhan: Wuhan Press.

Yang, Kuisong. 1999. *Mao Zedong Yu Mosike de Enen Yuanyuan* [The Hate and Love Relationship between Mao Zedong and Moscow]. Nanchang: Jianxi People's Press.

Yang, Shengqun and Chen Jin (eds.), 2009. *Qinlizhe de Jiyi: Lishi Zhuanzhe Beijing 1977–1978 [Memoirs of the Witnesses: The Background of the Historic Turn 1978–1979].* Beijing: SDX Joint Press.

Yang, Tianshi. 2008. *Xunzhao Zhenshi de Jiang Jieshi [Looking for the Real Chiang Kai-shek].* Taiyuan: Shanxi People's Press.

Yao, Xinzhong. 2000. *An Introduction to Confucianism.* New York: Cambridge University Press.

Yao, Yang. 2008. "The Disinterested Government: An Interpretation of China's Economic Success in the Reform Era," Paper presented at the 2008 Chicago Conference on China's Market Transformation.

Yu, Guangyuan. 2008. 1978: *Wo Qin Li de Nachi Lishi Da Zhuanzhe* [1978: The Historic Turn that I Witnessed]. Beijing: Central Compilation and Translation Press.

Yu, Nan and Haiguang Wang. 2004. "Lin Biao Jituan and Lin Biao Shijian" [Lin Biao Clique and Lin Biao Incidence], in *The Thematic History of the People's Republic of China,* ed. Dehong Guo, Haiguang Wang, and Gang Han. Vol. 3, pp. 302–324. Chengdu: Sichuan People's Press.

Yu, Ri. 2002. "Lu Yin Shi Nian – Chongxin Renshi Ziben Zhuyi" [Ten Years in England – Recognition of Capitalism]. *Chen Duxiu Yanjiu Dongtai* [Chen Duxiu Research Trends] (Issue 3–4).

Yu, Ying-shih. 2004. *Zhongguo Zhishiren Zhi Shi de KaoCha* [Investigations of the History of Chinese Intellectuals]. Nanning: Guanxi Normal University Press.

Zeng, Douglas Zhihua. 2011. "How Do Special Economic Zones and Industrial Clusters Drive China's Rapid Development?" Policy Research Working Paper 5583, World Bank.

Zhang, Gensheng. 2004. "Hua Guoofeng Tan Fensui Sirenbang" [Hua Guofeng on the Arrest of the Gang of Four], *Yan Huang Chun Qiu* (Issue 7, July).

Zhang, Guangyou and Longjia Ding. 2006. *Wan Li.* Beijing: Zhonggong Dangshi Press.

Zhang, Hua. 2004. "1975 Nian de Quanmian Zhendun" [The Comprehensive Rectification of 1975], in *The Thematic History of the People's Republic of China,* ed. Dehong Guo, Haiguang Wang, and Gang Han. Vol. 3, pp. 491–510. Chengdu: Sichuan People's Press.

Zhang, Shuhua. 2006. *Qi Qian Ren Dahui Shimo* [History of the Seven-Thousand People Cconference]. Beijing: China Youth Press.

Zhang, Jun. 1991. *Xiaodai Chanquan Jingjixue* [Modern Property Rights Economics]. Shanghai: SDX Joint Press.

—— 2010. *Bu Wei Gongzhong SuoZhi de Gaige* [Reform unknown to the Public]. Beijing: China CITIC Press.

Zhang, Weiying. 2008. "Shuan Guizhi he Jiege Gaige" [The System of Dural Track and the Reform of Price Control], in *Zhongguo Jingji Wushi Ren Kan Sanshi Nian* [Thirty Years of the Chinese Economy: From the Eyes of Fifty Economists], ed. Jinglian Wu et al., pp. 581–99. Beijing: China Economic Press.

———. 2010. *Shichang de Luoji* [The Logic of the Market]. Shanghai: Shanghai People's Press.

Zhang, Wenkui and Dongming Yuan. 2008. *Zhongguo Jingji Gaige Sanshi Nian: Guoyou Qiye Juan* [Thirty Years of Chinese Economic Reform: The State-owned enterprises]. Chongqing: Chongqing University Press.

Zhao, Dexin (ed.). 1988–1999. *Zhonghua Renmin Gongheguo Jingjishi* [The Economic History of the People's Republic of China.] 5 Vols.; Vols. 1–4 published 1988; Vol. 4 publihsed 1999. Zhengzhou: Henan People's Press.

Zhao, Dingxin. 2001. *The Power of Tiananmen: State-Society Relations and the 1989 Beijing Student Movement*. Chicago: University of Chicago Press.

——— 2009. "The Mandate of Heaven and Performance Legitimation in Historical and Contemporary China," *American Behavioral Scientist* 53: 416–33.

Zhao, Ziyang. 2009. *Prisoner of the State: The Secret Journal of Premier Zhao Ziyang*. New York: Simon & Schuster.

Zheng, Yougui. 2009. "Noncun Gaige de Xingqi yu Fazhan [The Rise and Development of Rural Reform]," in *The Thematic History of the People's Republic of China*, ed. Dehong Guo, Haiguang Wang, and Gang Han. Vol. 4, pp. 233–249. Chengdu: Sichuan People's Press.

Zhou, Hancheng. 2003. *Zhu Rongji Zouxiang Zhongnanhai Zi Lu* [Zhu Rongji's Road to Zhongnanhai]. Hong Kong: Zhonghua Ernu Press.

Zhou, Qiren. 2008. "The Unfolding of Deng's Drama," Paper presented at the 2008 Chicago Conference on China's Market Transformation.

Zhou, Xiaochuan and Li Zhu. 1987. "China's Banking System: Current Status, Prospect for Reform," *Journal of Comparative Economics* 11: 399–409.

Zhou, Yiliang. 1998. *Bijing Shi Shusheng* [Still a Scholar]. Beijing: October Wenyi Press.

Zhu, Jingwen (ed.). 2007. *Zhongguo falü fazhan baogao (1979–2004)* [China Legal Development Report] (1979–2004). Beijing: People's University Press.

Zhu, Xuefeng (2009). "The Influence of Chinese Think Tanks in the Chinese Policy Process," *Asian Survey* 49: 333–357.

Zhu, Zhen. 1998. *1957 Nian de Xiaji: Cong Baijia Zhengming Dao Liangjia zhengming* [The Summer of 1957: From a Hundred Schools Contending to Two Schools Contending]. Zhengzhou: Henan People's Press.

Zong, Han. 2007. *Guoqi Gaige Sanshi Nian Qinli Ji* [Personal Witness of Thirty Years of Reform of the State-owned enterprises]. Shanghai: Shanghai People's Press.

Zweig, David. 1997. *Freeing China's Farmers: Rural Restructuring in the Reform Era*. Armonk, NY: M. E. Sharpe.

Index